# IRC HACKS™

*Paul Mutton*

# O'REILLY®

Beijing · Cambridge · Farnham · Köln · Sebastopol · Tokyo

# IRC Hacks™

by Paul Mutton

Copyright © 2004 O'Reilly Media, Inc. All rights reserved.
Printed in the United States of America.

Published by O'Reilly Media, Inc., 1005 Gravenstein Highway North,
Sebastopol, CA 95472.

O'Reilly books may be purchased for educational, business, or sales promotional use. Online editions are also available for most titles (*safari.oreilly.com*). For more information, contact our corporate/institutional sales department: (800) 998-9938 or *corporate@oreilly.com*.

| | | | |
|---|---|---|---|
| **Editor:** | Rael Dornfest | **Production Editor:** | Sarah Sherman |
| **Series Editor:** | Rael Dornfest | **Cover Designer:** | Hanna Dyer |
| **Executive Editor:** | Dale Dougherty | **Interior Designer:** | David Futato |

**Printing History:**

| | |
|---|---|
| July 2004: | First Edition. |

ISBN: 978-0-596-00687-7
[LSI]

[2011-12-16]

# Contents

# Foreword

The last 20 years have introduced us to new ways of communicating with other people. One of the most interactive new communication techniques is keyboard-based chatting, in which the text typed on the keyboard of one person is shown straightaway on the screen of another person, or a group of people, located far away, perhaps on the other side of the world.

Internet Relay Chat (IRC) is an open source distributed chat environment used widely around the Internet. There are thousands of chat programs, and there were at least hundreds of chat programs before IRC saw the first light in August 1988. What made IRC different from these other chat programs? It was and still is the possibility to network individual chat programs (IRC servers) to one another, thus forming a worldwide, distributed, and decentralized chat network.

The ability to network, without maintaining a central location of control, has been the key for success for IRC, WWW, USENET News, and many other systems. Similarly, the inability to distribute control has been the reason for failure for many occasions. Giving out control and empowering others with the power to work, learn, and develop software allows for new innovations. Keeping control to yourself is often much easier to do, but it slows down progress by making it difficult, sometimes impossible, to innovate.

IRC started as one summer trainee's programming exercise. A hack grew into a software development project that hundreds of people participated in and became a worldwide environment where tens of thousands of people now spend time with one another. I have found many of my present friends through IRC and learned a significant part of my present software engineering knowledge while using and working with IRC. That would not have been possible without learning from code examples and hacks from others.

I believe this book presents excellent tools and techniques for both IRC new-comers and old-timers. The hacks will help the readers to dig in the inner workings of IRC, learn from that, and enable them to further develop their own ideas into better software and new hacks for themselves and others.

—Jarkko Oikarinen, Helsinki, April 5, 2004
*Head of R&D, Capricode Oy*
*CTO, Numeric Garden Oy*

Jarkko Oikarinen wrote the original IRC program at the University of Oulu, Finland, in 1988. He was granted a Dvorak Award in 1997 for personal achievement as a result of developing IRC.

# Credits

## About the Author

Paul Mutton is a PhD student at the University of Kent in the United Kingdom, frantically trying to finish off his thesis at the same time as writing this book. He previously graduated with first-class honors in Computer Science, winning the IEE Institution Prize for being the best overall student in his department. He uses Internet Relay Chat (IRC) to collaborate with researchers in other countries and to talk to people in his office when they have their headphones on. In his remaining spare time, he uses his Sun Certified Java Programmer skills to develop all sorts of open source software on his personal web site (*http://www.jibble.org*). Some of his research has culminated in the creation of the popular PieSpy application (*http://www.jibble.org/piespy*), which infers and visualizes social networks on IRC and even appeared on slashdot once. He can normally be found jibbling around in *#jibble* and *#irchacks* on the *freenode* IRC network with the nickname *Jibbler*, or *Paul* on smaller networks.

## Contributors

The following people contributed their writing, code, and inspiration to IRC Hacks:

- Alex North is married with children and works 9–5. In the hours outside of work he is immersed in the wonderful world of IRC. He can be found in this world using the nickname *DeadEd* and can usually be found haunting the *QuakeNet* network. He is a Java jibbler and certified game addict and has authored *MatchEd* and *PPF*, and he spends large amounts of time and fun playing with them on *http://www.deaded.com*.

- Chris Smith is an IRC addict who spends most of his time writing bots in strange languages, playing games, or idling on IRC. He can normally be found idling on *QuakeNet* with the nickname *MD87*, attempting to work out why his latest bot has decided to kick random people from his channel.

- David Leadbeater is currently an undergraduate in software engineering at Sheffield Hallam University. He spends much too much time on IRC, mostly on *Blitzed.org* with the nickname *dg*. He is the author of *CGI: IRC*, and he likes Perl.

- Hunter Pine was born in New York and started using a Mac at the age of five, just a month after Wozniak and Jobs unleashed their new computing machine. Hunter now runs *Integrate New York*, a consulting company in Manhattan specializing in small business computing needs, and spends his leisure time as a server operator on *irc.choopa.net*, as well as berating people who are too lazy to use Google in *#windows*. Hunter lives with his lovely wife, Anna, and their two kittens, Andromeda and Cassiopeia. He also despises writing about himself in the third person.

- Jennifer Golbeck is a Computer Science PhD candidate at the University of Maryland, College Park, where she studies complex systems. She likes to avoid any interactions that require leaving her two golden retrievers or changing out of pajamas, ergo can be found conducting all of her business on irc.freenode.net using the nickname *golbeck*. Her other interests include marathon running, surfing, travel, and the Chicago Cubs.

- Jim Hughes develops trading systems so that chaps who still wear red braces can wager vast sums on the seemingly random fluctuations of financial exotica. Jim is also a mobile technology fanatic and spends far too much time tinkering with and writing about mobile phones for *Mobitopia* and *All About Symbian* and not enough time developing for them. He can frequently be found loitering as *JimH* in *#mobitopia* on *freenode*.

- Maurits Dijkstra has been coding since his uncle bought him a QBasic book at the age of 12. If he's not busy studying for his exams, he works on *BitlBee* and tries to write proper Python code.

- Nicholas S. Copeland is a Des Moines Area Community College student transferring to Iowa State University where he will study Computer Engineering. He purchased the *Bersirc* IRC client and shocked the Net by announcing that all future versions will be free (as in freedom and as in free beer). You can find him as *TsTech* in *#bersirc* on *irc.free2code.net*.

- Petr "Pasky" Baudis is a geeky Czech student who wasted his youth in front of a computer, addicted to IRC and the idea of free software. He is an *IRCNet* IRC operator, Linux and *irssi* fanatic, and maintains the *ELinks* text WWW browser. He also likes to read good stuff while listening to some nice music or the BBC World Service.

- Steve Jolly is a particle physicist, mountaineer, photographer, and dilettante bot programmer. Once upon a time he held the *Extreme Ironing World Altitude Record*. When he grows up, he wants to be a fireman or an astronaut. Steve likes pie.

- Thomas Whaples is currently a freshman and prospective Computer Science major at Wake Forest University. He has been involved in Internet community-related projects since 1999 and is currently a sysop on *Wikipedia*. He also works on the *Economic History Services Network* site (*http://eh.net*). He raises parakeets and lovebirds and dabbles in occasional artistic endeavors. He is available via IRC on *freenode* as *Fennec-Foxen* and on *WorldIRC* as *Fennec*. His web site is sometimes available off his laptop at *http://fennec.homedns.org*. His Wikipedia user page is *http://en.wikipedia.org/wiki/User:Fennec*.

- Wilmer van der Gaast (simply known as *wilmer* on most free software–minded IRC networks) became addicted to computer programming soon after he learned to read. Some time ago he also discovered IRC and wrote some bots and *BitlBee*. Meanwhile, he tries to finish his Computer Science study and spends most of the time at music festivals every summer.

## Acknowledgments

First and foremost, I wish to thank all of the contributors for their innovative hack ideas, their time, and their code. Writing this book has been a real experience, and I have learned a lot of interesting things from them along the way.

Thanks must also go to Jarkko Oikarinen for being kind enough to write a great foreword, and of course for inventing IRC in the first place. Millions of people would be lost without him.

May I also thank Rael Dornfest and the rest of the O'Reilly team for letting me write this, which is my first book. I hope you enjoy it.

Thanks also to Morbus for putting the idea into my head several months ago.

Special thanks to Charlotte for being patient while I filled up my spare time by working on this book, and thanks to Monty for always being there.

Finally, not many people can claim to be working while they are using IRC, so thanks to everyone who actually believed me!

# Preface

Internet Relay Chat (IRC) has continued to grow in popularity since its inception way back in 1988. Millions of people all over the world now use IRC to chat with friends, discuss projects, and collaborate on research. With a simple, clearly defined protocol, IRC has become one of the most accessible chat environments, with clients written for a multitude of operating systems.

Users of alternative chat systems will find IRC pretty easy to pick up and may even be surprised to find that it is more powerful, allowing not just chat between pairs of users, but among groups of hundreds, even thousands. It is the scalable nature of IRC that has helped it to succeed and to make it the most mature chat system on this planet.

This book presents an opportunity to learn how IRC works and how to make best use of some of its features. *IRC Hacks* delves deep into the possibilities, featuring contributions from some of the most renowned IRC hackers. Many of the contributors collaborated on IRC, grouping together to form the channel #*irchacks* on the freenode IRC network (irc.freenode.net). We look forward to seeing you there and hearing how you've used this book.

## Why IRC Hacks?

The term *hacking* has a bad reputation in the press. They use it to refer to someone who breaks into systems or wreaks havoc with computers as their weapon. Among people who write code, though, the term *hack* refers to a "quick-and-dirty" solution to a problem, or a clever way to get something done. And the term *hacker* is taken very much as a compliment, referring to someone as being *creative*, having the technical chops to get things done. The Hacks series is an attempt to reclaim the word, document the good ways people are hacking, and pass the hacker ethic of creative participation on to the uninitiated. Seeing how others approach systems and problems is often the quickest way to learn about a new technology.

While IRC is easy to get into, it is evident that there is a demand for better understanding. Many people are happy to use it without being aware of what's happening beneath the scenes, but others hunger for more knowledge, and this book is for them. IRC is more than just a simple chat system—it is a network of intercommunicating servers, allowing thousands of clients to connect from anywhere in the world using the IRC protocol.

Some hacks in this book are designed to demonstrate the IRC protocol and how to exploit it—not in bad ways, but in ways that facilitate better use of IRC. Not only will you be shown how to enhance several of the most popular IRC clients, but you can also experiment with scripting some autonomous IRC clients, or *IRC bots*. It is quite exciting to see your very own IRC bot, crafted by your own fine hands, connecting to a server and joining a channel for the first time. Many of the hacks then show you how to add extra features to create useful or fun IRC bots.

Each hack has been created to save you time and show you how to perform new tricks on IRC without having to look up the information. This collection of hacks should appeal to people who are just about to experience IRC for the first time, as well as those who consider themselves to be more seasoned users. *IRC Hacks* provides hands-on solutions to problems faced, and solved, by people who use IRC on a daily basis.

## How to Use This Book

You can read the book from cover to cover if you like, but you may be better served by picking an interesting item from the table of contents and just diving in.

If you're relatively new to IRC, you should consider starting with a few hacks from each progressive chapter. Chapter 1 starts you off by showing you how to connect to IRC, while Chapter 2 acquaints you with the everyday concepts you'll need to use IRC effectively. Chapter 3 is all about users and channels, and it introduces the first pieces of code. Chapter 4 shows you how to make useful enhancements to IRC clients. Chapter 5 is where you will learn the basics about creating IRC bots, with Chapters 6–12 introducing more complex bots that can be used for logging, servicing communities, searching, announcing, networking, managing channels, or simply having fun. Chapter 13 delves into the IRC protocol in more detail, and Chapter 14 demonstrates some interesting alternative methods for connecting to IRC. Finally, Chapter 15 will move you on to new pastures by showing you how to set up your own IRC server.

# How This Book Is Organized

There are several different areas you need to master to become a true IRC hacker. At the core is the conceptual model of IRC, while layered around that are the protocols and clients used to access the IRC networks. The book is divided into 15 chapters, starting with the basics and progressing to cover interesting hacks involving bots and client enhancements:

Chapter 1, *Connecting to IRC*
> Before embarking on the journey through the rest of the hacks, it's important to make sure you know how to connect to IRC. This chapter shows you how to use a variety of IRC clients, on a variety of operating systems, to connect to an IRC server and join the *#irchacks* channel.

Chapter 2, *Using IRC*
> To use IRC effectively, you need to be aware of how users, channels, servers, and networks fit into the equation. This chapter also introduces you to the common abbreviations and acronyms that you are likely to encounter on a foray through IRC. You will also learn how to protect your channel and nickname using *Services*.

Chapter 3, *Users and Channels*
> One common question asked by IRC newcomers is, "What channels should I join?" This chapter shows you how to find channels that are relevant to you, either by searching on a specific network or through all the networks in the world. You will also be shown how to perform some investigative work to find out where a user is from and to generate amusing statistics for your channel.

Chapter 4, *Enhancing IRC Clients*
> IRC clients have a lot of functionality built in, and this chapter helps to expose those features. Some of these hacks make use of client scripts to perform useful tasks that would otherwise not be possible. As you read through this chapter, you'll soon start to realize that if an IRC client doesn't do what you want it to do, you can easily add the feature yourself.

Chapter 5, *Writing IRC Bots*
> IRC bots are autonomous clients that run without direct human input. This chapter explores what needs to be done to write an autonomous client that can connect to IRC, using Perl, Java, and Python. You will also be introduced to some popular libraries that simplify the process of writing IRC bots.

Chapter 6, *Logging Bots*
> Bots that log IRC activity come in various guises. This chapter demonstrates how to create bots that use logging in different ways to achieve

useful results, such as remembering when people were last active, logging URLs, running blogs, and recapping conversations.

Chapter 7, *Community Bots*

IRC is a chat system that is inherently amenable for use by communities. These communities can be served by IRC bots that perform useful tasks. Some of these applications are fun, such as generating social network diagrams of a community, while others are more useful, such as being able to pass messages on to other users.

Chapter 8, *Search and Query Bots*

IRC bots are often used to provide a gateway or interface to another service. This chapter shows you how to make bots to search Google and look up words on FOLDOC, the Free Online Dictionary of Computing. Web services can be used to make bots that search for books on Amazon, check the weather, translate languages, or convert currencies. On a more local scale, you can also create a bot to find out whether users are connected to an IRC network.

Chapter 9, *Fun Bots*

One reason for getting into IRC is that it is fun to chat. We reinforce this principle by demonstrating some fun bots that create comic strips, calculate mathematical expressions, and even act as a quizmaster. You can even try to fool your friends with the artificial intelligence bot described in this chapter.

Chapter 10, *Announcement Bots*

IRC bots are ideal for making announcements. They don't argue back if you disagree with them. With the growing popularity of RSS, this chapter shows you how to create an IRC bot that reads news into a channel from RSS feeds. Other hacks show you how to announce items posted to newsgroups or even events happening on a game server.

Chapter 11, *Network Bots*

As IRC bots run on machines with Internet access, it seems foolish not to make use of this fact. This chapter shows you how to link bots together to share information and provide remote resources to users of your bots, letting them get remote shells and tail log files over IRC.

Chapter 12, *Channel Management Bots*

As IRC is accessible by anybody, you occasionally find the odd user who is intent on causing trouble. The primary target of such abuse is usually a channel, where messages may be spammed or topics may be changed. This chapter shows you how to take care of such troublemakers by using bots to thwart their evil intentions.

Chapter 13, *The IRC Protocol*

Having already explored the possibilities of bots, this chapter goes into more detail about the IRC protocol, which is essential if you wish to write your own IRC applications. This chapter covers some of the points you will need to consider when writing IRC bots or clients.

Chapter 14, *Other Ways to Connect to IRC*

Chapter 1 covered the "conventional" IRC clients that most people use to connect to IRC. This chapter provides alternatives, such as web-based clients that do not require users to install any software, IRC clients that can run on mobile phones and Pocket PCs, and access to IRC through a proxy.

Chapter 15, *Servers and Services*

IRC servers play an obviously important role in the whole story of IRC, allowing clients to connect to them and chat with one another. This chapter shows you how to run your own IRC server and let people connect to it from the Internet. For greater resilience, you can even network more than one server. You can also find out how to access MSN, ICQ, and AIM from your IRC client.

## Conventions Used in this Book

The following is a list of the typographical conventions used in this book:

*Italic*

Used to indicate new terms, URLs, filenames, file extensions, directories, and program names. For example, a path in the filesystem will appear as */Developer/Applications*.

`Constant width`

Used to show code examples, commands and options, the contents of files, and the output from commands.

**`Constant width bold`**

Used for emphasis and user input in code.

`Constant width italic`

Used in examples and tables to show text that should be replaced with user-supplied values.

*Color*

The second color is used to indicate a cross-reference within the text.

You should pay special attention to notes set apart from the text with the following icons:

This is a tip, suggestion, or general note. It contains useful supplementary information about the topic at hand.

This is a warning or note of caution.

The thermometer icons, found next to each hack, indicate the relative complexity of the hack:

beginner     moderate     expert

## Using Code Examples

This book is here to help you get your job done. In general, you may use the code in this book in your programs and documentation. You do not need to contact us for permission unless you're reproducing a significant portion of the code. For example, writing a program that uses several chunks of code from this book does not require permission. Selling or distributing a CD-ROM of examples from O'Reilly books *does* require permission. Answering a question by citing this book and quoting example code does not require permission. Incorporating a significant amount of example code from this book into your product's documentation *does* require permission.

We appreciate, but do not require, attribution. An attribution usually includes the title, author, publisher, and ISBN. For example: "*IRC Hacks* by Paul Mutton. Copyright 2004 O'Reilly Media, Inc., 0-596-00687-X."

If you feel your use of code examples falls outside fair use or the permission given above, feel free to contact us at *permissions@oreilly.com*.

## How to Contact Us

We have tested and verified the information in this book to the best of our ability, but you may find that features have changed (or even that we have made mistakes!). As a reader of this book, you can help us to improve future editions by sending us your feedback. Please let us know about any errors, inaccuracies, bugs, misleading or confusing statements, and typos that you find anywhere in this book.

Please also let us know what we can do to make this book more useful to you. We take your comments seriously and will try to incorporate reasonable suggestions into future editions. You can write to us at:

O'Reilly Media
1005 Gravenstein Highway North
Sebastopol, CA 95472
(800) 998-9938 (in the U.S. or Canada)
(707) 829-0515 (international/local)
(707) 829-0104 (fax)

To ask technical questions or to comment on the book, send email to:

*bookquestions@oreilly.com*

The web site for *IRC Hacks* lists examples, errata, and plans for future editions. You can find this page at:

*http://www.oreilly.com/catalog/irchks*

For more information about this book and others, see the O'Reilly web site:

*http://www.oreilly.com*

## Got a Hack?

To explore Hacks books online or to contribute a hack for future titles, visit:

*http://hacks.oreilly.com*

# CHAPTER ONE

# Connecting to IRC
## Hacks 1–4

One of the great features about IRC is its accessibility. You can connect to any IRC network using an *IRC client* (read: application). For many users, the IRC client is the friendly face of IRC, allowing you to chat with individuals or groups of users. IRC clients are available for virtually all operating systems. In fact, several different IRC clients are available for Windows, Linux, and Mac OS X, so you are spoiled for choice if you have time to experiment with all available choices.

This chapter will show you how to use some of the most popular IRC clients to connect to IRC. Later hacks will then show you how to go beyond the basics and enhance the functionality of some of these IRC clients by exploiting existing features and writing your own IRC client scripts.

## HACK #1 IRC from Windows

Ask any Windows user what he uses to connect to IRC, and the chances are he will say mIRC.

mIRC is undoubtedly the most popular IRC client for Windows, offering lots of tools, functions, and features. mIRC is shareware, but this fact has not dampened its success over free clients such as Bersirc (*http://bersirc.free2code.net*) and ChatZilla [Hack #4]. This can be partly attributed to its ease of use, but seasoned IRC users will also find that it provides all of the powerful features they want. mIRC provides extensive scripting support, and thousands of mIRC scripts are available on the Web. mIRC is under active development.

You can grab mIRC from *http://www.mirc.com*. Like most Windows software, installation is quite straightforward, and it will offer you the chance to create a desktop icon to run it. The first time you run mIRC, it will pop up the Connect dialog automatically, where you must provide some details (as in Figure 1-1).

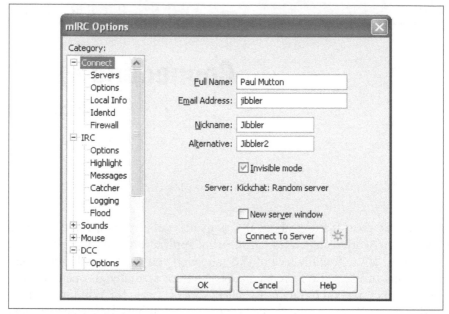

*Figure 1-1. mIRC Options dialog box*

*Full Name*

This is where you can specify your full name (if you want!). Because this is visible to all other IRC users, most people try to protect their anonymity to some extent by entering something funny instead.

*Email Address*

This is obviously useful if you want other IRC users to be able to contact you, but most people tend to enter fake addresses for fear of spam.

*Nickname and Alternative*

Here you can specify your nicknames. Whenever you say something on IRC, it will appear to come from your nickname. Because all nicknames on an IRC server must be unique, the dialog requests an alternative nickname, as somebody else may already be connected and using your preferred nickname.

If you are ultraparanoid about your privacy, then make sure you leave the *Invisible Mode* checkbox ticked. This will make it harder for people to find you, unless they know your nickname or are in the same channels as you.

Click on the OK button, and you will be faced with the main Status window. Messages from the IRC server typically end up here. freenode is an IRC network where many people gather to discuss peer-directed projects, and it is often a good place to ask questions about Java, Perl, PHP, and other programming languages. You can use the freenode IRC network by entering **/server irc.freenode.net** into the Status window. After a moment, you will be connected to one of the servers in this IRC network.

When you join a channel by typing **/join #irchacks**, you will see a new window appear inside mIRC. This will be used to display all messages sent to that channel. It also contains a list of all users in that channel, as shown in Figure 1-2. Typing a message and pressing Enter will cause your message to be sent to the channel and received by all of these users.

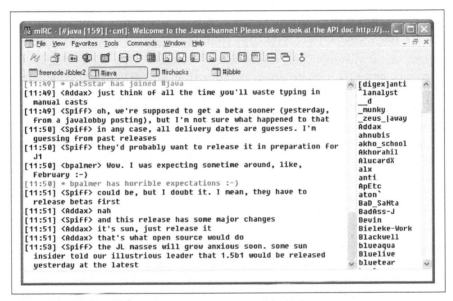

*Figure 1-2. Using mIRC*

You can send a private message directly to another user by double-clicking on her nickname. This brings up a new window in which you can talk directly to that user.

As you become more experienced with mIRC, you will probably feel like exploring the configuration options. With these, you can change colors, fonts, aliases, pop-up menus, and sounds and use advanced scripting features. Some of the hacks later in this book will show you how to get the most out of mIRC.

## IRC from Linux

XChat is a popular IRC client with a graphical user interface. You can download the source code or precompiled binaries for a variety of platforms.

XChat can be downloaded from *http://xchat.org*, either as source code or in the form of precompiled binaries or packages. If you have a packaging system such as *apt* or Gentoo's *emerge*, then you may be able to get away with apt-get xchat or emerge xchat.

### Nicknames, Usernames, and Real Names

When you first run XChat, you will be presented with a Server List dialog box. The first task is to go down to the bottom and select *Edit Mode*. From there, you can see all your server settings. Next examine the top area marked *Global User Info*. The top three boxes are for your *nickname*. Most of the time, you will connect with your first listed nickname; however, if that name is already in use by another user, it will try again with the second and then with the third. You shouldn't make these the same, but they can be close variants, for example:

```
Bob, Bob_, Bobby
Foo, FooBar, Foo_Bar
CoolDude, Cool_Dude, KewldOOd
```

Your *username* is used internally by the server to form your host mask, although some servers will try to use an Ident call **[Hack #80]** to look up your username instead. Your chosen username will be used if the Ident call fails. You can use your nickname, an alternate nickname, or just about anything you want here—although it may be truncated and must not contain any special characters. Your *real name* can also be anything you want, but it can be longer and can include spaces. As an example, your IRC nickname might be "Han" with username "solo" and real name "Harrison Ford." Be as creative as you like.

### Server Configuration

The next step is to configure your servers. XChat comes with a lot of servers listed, and it may already have the one you want; if not, you can click *Add* above the list of servers to create a new one. This will create a *New Network*. To rename this network to something more informative, slowly click it twice (don't double-click, as that will make XChat connect to the server). Once you've done this, you should look at the list of *Servers* on the far right. This is a list of servers; each server is of the form *server/port*. Your network will be set with *newserver/6667* and, unless you've explicitly set one up on your local network, chances are there is no server called "newserver." So instead, click on this, and replace it with the address and port of the server you want. If you leave off the */port* portion, the default port number of 6667 will be used. Most IRC servers will let you connect to this port, and many will even have alternative ports as well. Here are some example servers:

```
irc.freenode.net
irc.worldirc.org/6660
```

Finally, if you know what channels you want to connect to, place them in the *Join Channels* box. Use commas to specify more than one channel, for example:

```
#wikipedia,#java,#gimp,#jibble
```

You are now ready to connect to an IRC server. Click the *Connect* button and wait until you are connected. If you'd like to connect to another server as well, return to the list with Ctrl-S, or use the menu: XChat → Server List. Select the new server from the list, but this time use *Connect in a New Tab* to create a separate tab for this new server. If you forget to do this, you will disconnect from your current server and connect to the new one in the existing tab.

## Advanced Options and Autoconnects

If you use IRC only occasionally, you probably won't mind picking your favorite network from the list every time you start XChat. But if you connect to several IRC servers regularly, you'll probably want to connect to all of them automatically. To do this, select the network from your server list and check *Auto Connect at Startup*. If you do this, you may also want to check the *No Server List at Startup* option.

## Setting Up Autologin

If you're on a standard IRC network, you can usually set yourself up to automatically log in by specifying a *Connect command* in the server details screen. For example:

```
msg nickserv identify password
```

Notice that this command does not begin with a / character. If you'd like to use more than one command here, you need to set up a user command (as described later) with multiple entries and type its name here instead.

## Selecting a Stable Server

Most IRC networks are made up of more than one server; many will list these at the network's web site. In most cases, you will connect to a *round-robin* server, which will automatically pick a server and direct you there. Generally, you won't need to change this, but you may sometimes want to connect to a specific server. If you find a particular server that behaves more stably that any of the others, you can set the server of your choice at the top of the server list for your network. You can then click the *Add* button to add another one in case your preferred one is down. For example:

```
Klagenfurt.AT.EU.WorldIRC.org, Bleisen.DE.EU.WorldIRC.org, irc.worldirc.org
```

## Different Nicknames on Different Networks

If you want to use a different nickname on a certain network, select the network in the server list and uncheck *Use Global User Info*. You can then fill in a nickname, username, and real name for this server.

## Setting Up the User Interface

The XChat interface can be customized in a number of ways. The first few are simple visibility options. Right-click a blank area in the IRC window, and you can select on and off options for the menu bar, topic bar, mode buttons, and user list buttons. Select whatever combination makes you happy. The next set is available from the menu bar or the right-click menu, Settings → Preferences. There are far too many preferences to detail here, so you may like to play around with them and see what you can achieve. Here are some items worth noting:

**Interface/Text Box.** Besides setting the colors and fonts for chatting, the checkboxes also affect the way you see your chat. Try turning on Nick Coloring or Timestamp, for example, or perhaps you prefer to turn off the Indented Nicknames feature?

*Input Box*
   The *Nick Completion Suffix* is used for two things. First, if you type a partial nickname at the start of the line and press the Tab key, XChat will attempt to complete the nickname and add this suffix to it. Second, if you check *Automatic Nick Completion*, whenever you type a partial nickname followed by this suffix, XChat will replace it with the full nickname.

*User List*
   The Lag Meter and Throttle don't take up much room and are informative; it is a good idea to set this to *Both*. Here you can also change the user list sort order or set a double-click command.

*Tabs*
   Tabs are used to store channel and server windows. This lets you adjust the layout of your screen and how you use tabs.

*Colors*
   These settings let you change the colors of your text box and user list.

**Chatting/General.** Here you can set the default messages for when you quit IRC, leave a channel, or go away. You can add words that will trigger the highlight/beep feature. Also, if you don't like the way XChat announces your away messages, you can uncheck that here.

**Logging.** If you wish to log conversations (for reference or for generating IRC statistics), you can check *Enable Logging of Conversations* here. You shouldn't change the other options unless you know what you're doing, especially if you want to use a third-party program to generate statistics.

**Network/Setup.** Most users won't need to make any changes to the settings here, but there are some useful options for file transfers. This lets you change where XChat places incoming files or adjust the speed at which the files are transferred. If you are behind a firewall, you can also restrict the DCC ports used when you send files.

## Hacking XChat

Here are some neat hacks you can do with XChat:

**Tab in a window.** If you want to remove a tab and give it its own window, press Ctrl-I. Press them again to place it back as a tab. You can also right-click on the tab and select *Detach Tab*. If you'd like to change the default behavior of windows and tabs, see the Preferences dialog box under the *Tabs* section.

**Per-channel options.** Right-click on a tab, and choose the Channel Name submenu. You can turn off join/part messages for the busy channels, set the channel to beep on activity for the important but quiet channels, or allow color pasting in the channel.

**All-server commands.** If you'd like to set up a command to go to all your servers or all your channels, type **/allserv** *command* or **/allchan** *command*. For example:

    /allserv away down south in Dixie

This will set your status to Away (and your away message to "down south in Dixie") for all of the servers you are connected to.

**Use colors.** Many people recommend that you don't use colors. They're more often abused than used effectively. Many consider them to be garish and ugly. Furthermore, they're not IRC standards, they're not supported by all clients, and you can't even tell whether another person's IRC client has a white background or a black one. However, if you find you simply must use color codes:

%C##

> Typing this as part of a message will cause it to be interpreted as a color code. The ## must be replaced with a two-digit number (see Settings → Preferences → Colors for the list).

%B

> This will make a message bold.

%U

> This will underline your message.

%O

> This will set your output back to normal, using the default color.

Alternatively, you can right-click the channel tab and select *Insert mIRC Color Code*.

**Display output with /exec.** Under Unix and Linux systems, you can display output from any command that you run. For example:

> `/exec uptime`

This will execute the `uptime` command and show your system's uptime and load averages. This, however, is displayed in the window and not sent to the IRC server. If you want to brag about your system's uptime, though, you can do this:

> `/exec -o uptime`

The output will now be sent to the IRC channel you're currently active in.

You can also call commands that do not immediately exit. For instance:

> `/exec -o tail -f` /var/log/httpd/access_log

This will print the accesses to your web server as they occur, if you really need to. You can even send input to the command with /execwrite, stop it with /execstop, resume with /execcont, and kill it with /execkill.

Be careful what programs you call. /exec -o yes or /exec -o cat /dev/urandom, especially in a DCC chat, will probably crash XChat, and they are generally considered silly things to try. Having heard that, you'll probably want to try it just to see what happens.

**Setting up auto-replace strings.** An auto-replace is a string of text that gets automatically replaced with another. For example, XChat will automatically replace "teh" with "the" as you type it. To review or change this behavior or add new auto-replace options, go to Settings → Lists → Auto-replace. To add a new option, click the *New* button and then edit the *New* and *EDIT ME* regions. For example:

> `billy => Over and Under General War Commander Sergeant Billy Goat-Legs`

Now, whenever you type in **billy** followed by a space or Enter, you'll see his full title appear.

**Setting up user commands.** Setting up a user command in XChat is simple. First, go to Settings → Lists → User Commands. Click *Add New*, and choose a name. Then you can type in your command. You can click the *Help* button for a list of substitution strings. Here's an example:

```
whine => me whines, complains, and makes a nuisance of himself.
```

Now, go to your least-favorite channel and type **/whine**. You'll be making yourself feel unwelcome in no time.

You can also give your commands arguments:

```
greet => me greets %2 in the manner of the Courts of Chaos.
```

You can now stab your friends in the back—erm—*greet* your friends with a flourish, with a simple command, like /greet Corwin or /greet JackBauer.

If you want the rest of your string to be used as an argument instead of just one word per argument, you use the & character:

```
hero => say &2 is my hero!
```

Now, with a simple /hero Linus Torvalds, you can cast your vote in support of free software!

Commands can be multiple action as well. They will be performed in the order listed, for example:

```
rofl => me is on the floor
rofl => me is rolling around...
rofl => me is laughing!!!
```

You can call external commands with the /exec command detailed earlier. For example, to counter those annoying mIRC "sysinfo" scripts, you could try this:

```
sysinfo => exec -o uname -a && uptime &&df -h | egrep "(hda1|hda3|hda5)"
```

If you have other system information scripts, you can call them instead of, or in addition to, the ones found here.

> It is inadvisable to call exec multiple times in a row, because XChat can be running only one process per text box at any time.

**Customize messages/colors and set sounds.** You can change the message format and colors of any event in IRC or assign a custom sound to play. First, go to the Settings → Lists → Events menu. Then find the event you want to change.

For example, to have a sound play whenever the topic changes, you would select *Topic Change* and enter a path to a sound file.

If you want your messages to be surrounded with, say, yellow square brackets ([ ]) instead of purple pointy brackets (<>), select *Your Message* and enter:

```
%C8[%0$1%C8]%0$t$2%0
```

The arguments to each message ($1, $2, etc.) are listed below the message as you select them. $t refers to the tabbed line, if you have *Indented Nicknames* on. %C, %B, and %0 are color codes, as described earlier.

One often-requested format change is to display an @ in front of operators and a + in front of voiced users. To do this, modify the Channel Message format string like so:

```
%C2<%0$3$1%C2>%0$t$2%0
```

$3 will display an @, +, or nothing, as appropriate.

**Add user list buttons and menu commands.** Assuming you have the user list buttons turned on (right-click empty space, then select *User List Buttons*), you can add buttons to this list or to the user list pop up (which appears when you right-click a username in the chat window or the user list). The syntax for such a command is the same as for a user command, except the *name* of the command is used for the label of the button or the menu item, and there are more substitutions available. Use existing entries as guidelines if you want to.

**Add CTCP replies.** Care to set up some useful information for CTCP? Want to mess up people who PING and VERSION you? Using Settings → Lists → CTCP replies, you can set it up to do anything when someone sends you a CTCP message. In general, use the same guidelines as the other lists (and see *Help* for useful substitutions). Note, however, that the proper way to send a reply is:

```
nctcp %s (query) (result)
```

So a sample reply to a TIME request would be:

```
nctcp %s TIME Sat Nov 12 22:04:00 1955
```

This will ensure maximum compatibility with other clients.

*—Thomas Whaples*

## IRC from Mac OS X

**#3**   Several IRC clients are available for Mac OS X. Check them out for your favorite features.

There is no shortage of IRC clients for Macintosh users. ChatZilla **[Hack #4]**, the truly outstanding IRC client integrated into Mozilla, is popular among Mac users and can also be used on other operating systems. Non-Mozilla users have many alternatives, too. Some applications, such as Fire (*http://fire.sourceforge.net*), combine IRC chat with ICQ, AIM, and JabberIM. However, because the features of IRC are different than the set for other chat applications, IRC users may find themselves frustrated with these programs. The server-channel model is not clearly supported, and sending standard IRC commands is difficult when they are not all fully supported. One of the friendliest and three of the more popular, and more powerful, IRC clients available for OS X are presented here: Conversation, X-Chat Aqua, Snak, and IRCle.

### Conversation

Conversation (*http://www.conversation.pwp.blueyonder.co.uk*) is about as close as you'll come to using iChat for IRC. It sports a rather iChat-like look-and-feel (Figure 1-3) with just about everything accessible through an intuitive set of buttons and switches and drag-and-drop support throughout. A Favorites list holds your best buddies and preferred channels so you can just log on and click your way to conversation. A Recent Channels and Users list helps you find that person you were chatting with yesterday or where you had that fabulous conversation last week. Or just set things up so you automatically log in and join your various discussion channels automatically.

While you're best off comparing and contrasting Conversation's feature set with the other clients covered here, it's a good bet you'll find it an intuitive vehicle for your first foray into IRC.

### X-Chat Aqua

X-Chat Aqua is an OS X version of the popular Unix IRC client, XChat. It is freeware that can be downloaded from *http://xchataqua.sourceforge.net*.

When X-Chat launches, you are prompted to enter nicknames and personal information and to choose a server in the Server List window (see Figure 1-4). A list of networks is provided by default, and you have the option to add to the list. Once nicks and server are selected, clicking Connect will connect and open a server window.

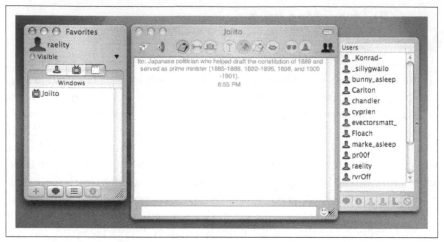

*Figure 1-3. Conversation, an iChat-like IRC client*

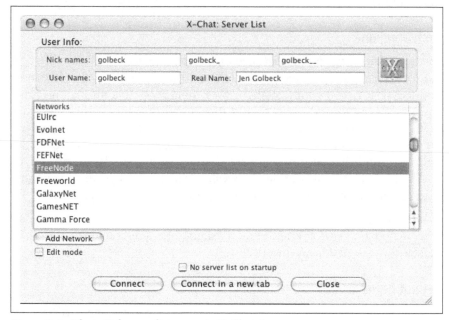

*Figure 1-4. The initial server list popup in X-Chat Aqua*

X-Chat Aqua can use a tab- or window-based view of channels and servers. The default setup puts each channel in a tab at the bottom of the window as it is joined. Channels can be opened in new windows, instead of as tabs, by using File → New Channel Window.

Figure 1-5 shows a connection to the freenode IRC network (shown at the top of the window) and three channels (shown in tabs at the bottom of the window). Channel participants are displayed in the bar on the right. While this window is white on black, colors can be configured to your preferences.

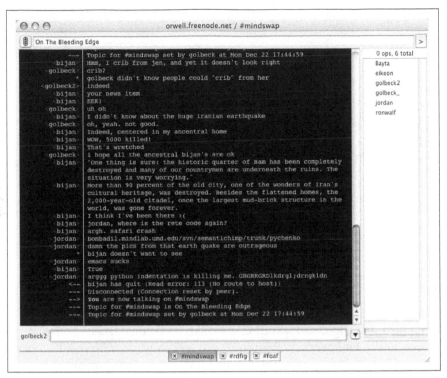

*Figure 1-5. A main window for X-Chat Aqua*

The File menu also has options to connect directly to a new server in either a tab or a new window or to use the Server List to establish a new connection. All commands and messages can be given in the input line at the bottom of each window, and some are also included as selectable options under the User menu.

## Snak

The Snak IRC client is shareware that is free for 30 days. After that time, Snak will automatically quit after 30 minutes until it is registered for $20. Snak can be downloaded from *http://www.snak.com*.

The Server List is the window in the lower-right corner (Figure 1-6). Notice that the #rdfig and #mindswap channels have been grouped into one window, while the server, *irc.freenode.net*, is in a separate window in the upper right.

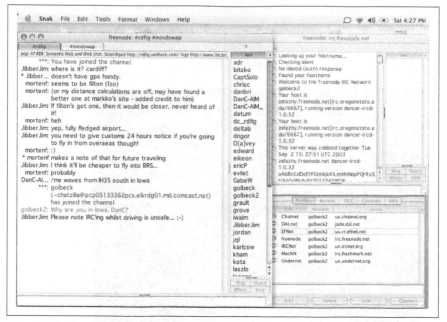

*Figure 1-6. The main Snak window*

The first time Snak is launched, a wizard walks you through the process of creating a nickname and selecting a preferred channel. This information is stored in the Preferences. Connections to any server can be made through the Profile list. This window will come up by default and can also be found in the Windows menu. It lists all of the stored IRC servers with your preferred nick and startup commands. To connect to one of the servers, you can just locate it in the Server List and click *Connect*.

Docking is an interesting feature of Snak. Channels can be open in separate windows. Using the Dock command in the Windows menu, the windows can be changed into tabs in other windows. This allows you to group multiple channels any way you like; they need not necessarily be docked with the server window. Channels can also be customized by appearance. Each channel window can have its own color scheme, set using Edit → Channel Settings.

## IRCle

IRCle is a Macintosh-only IRC client. It is available as shareware from *http://www.ircle.com*. The trial period is 30 days, and all features are enabled during the trial. Registration is $20 and gets rid of the warning messages that will appear when the application is launched.

When IRCle is run for the first time, the Connections list needs to be modified. The Connections window should appear by default (as shown in Figure 1-7) but can also be found in the Windows menu if it doesn't. There will be 10 default connections—the maximum number of server connections that IRCle supports—and they will all be configured to use the nickname "ircleuser." To change this, click on a connection and then click the *Edit...* button at the bottom of the window. This will bring up a dialog box (Figure 1-8) where you can change your nickname, real name, exit message, and other properties.

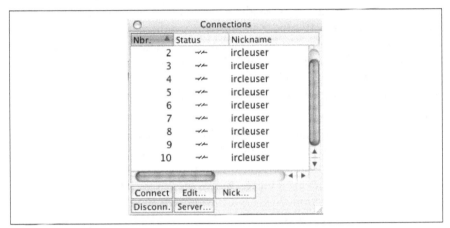

*Figure 1-7. Connections window in IRCle*

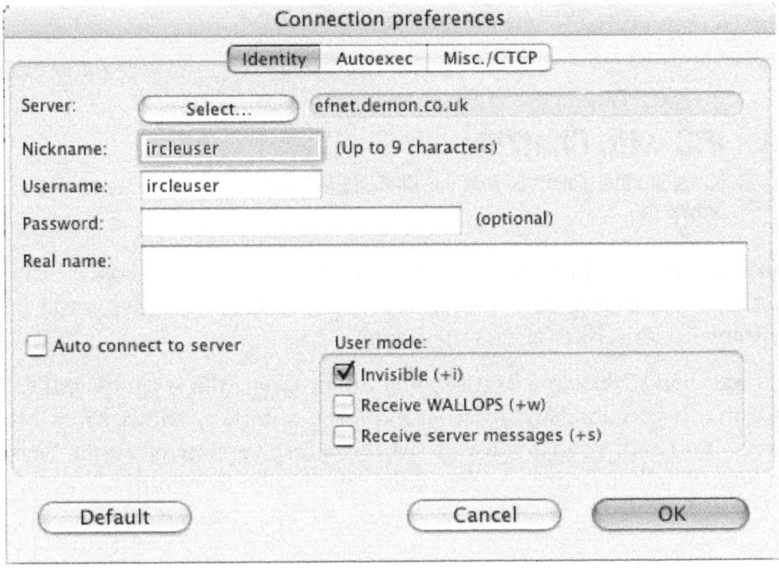

*Figure 1-8. Changing your nickname in IRCle Connection Preferences*

To connect to an IRC server with this new nickname, select the connection in the Connections window, and then click the *Server...* button. A window with a long list of servers will come up. You can choose from that list or click *Add* to add a new server. Once you have found the server you want in the list, click it, and then click *Select*. The connection is now configured to connect to the server. Click the *Connect* button in the Connections window to attach to the server.

The server messages will appear in the Console window. The Inputline window is used to join channels, send commands, and type messages to a channel. Each channel will appear in its own window. Depending on which window is in focus, the Userlist window will change to show the name and participants of the current channel. Private chats established using /query will also get their own window. If someone else sends a private message to you without a separate window, the message will appear in the Console.

The multitude of windows in IRCle, as seen in Figure 1-9, can become overwhelming. A feature called the Channelbar is available to make them a bit more manageable. Found under the Windows menu, the Channelbar puts a bar across the top of the window with buttons for each channel, console, and chat window. Clicking a button brings the corresponding channel to the foreground. Using option-click on a button will hide the selected channel window without disconnecting from it.

Now that you know about lots of Mac OS X IRC clients, it's up to you to decide which one you want to use. Perhaps after you've read this book, you may even be tempted to write your own.

—*Jennifer Golbeck*

### HACK #4    IRC with ChatZilla

Jump around platforms with the ChatZilla IRC client for Mozilla-based web browsers.

ChatZilla is a cross-platform IRC client written for Mozilla-based browsers. If you're like me and work under various operating systems, you'll have a consistent IRC interface across the board.

If you are using Netscape or a Mozilla build, ChatZilla is quick and easy to start using. If you are using Internet Explorer, Safari, or another non-Mozilla browser, you will need to download the latest version of either Netscape from *http://home.netscape.org/downloads* or Mozilla from *http://mozilla.org*.

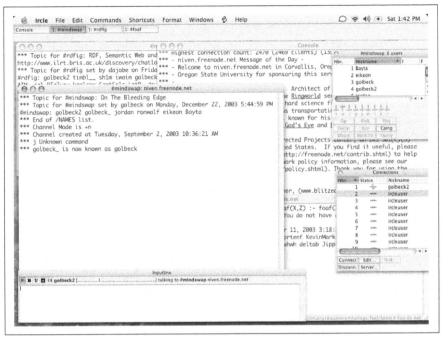

*Figure 1-9. IRCle running full screen*

## Installing ChatZilla

ChatZilla can be installed directly through the web browser at *http://www.hacksrus.com/~ginda/chatzilla*. This page contains news and installers. Toward the bottom of the page, you will find the Download section. Several revisions will be listed in the table. If the version has a yellow star next to it, this means the release is probably stable but may contain some bugs. Releases that are expected to be stable will be marked with a green tick. Every version will contain a list of any reported bugs, so you can decide which one you want to install.

The last column of the table has install links, each pointing to an XPI file. These types of files are installers for Mozilla chrome packages. When you click an install link, you will be prompted to accept the install. When you click OK, the software will automatically download and install itself (see Figure 1-10).

Once the installation is complete, you should close your browser. Some versions of Windows may also require you to restart the operating system. Once all the restarts are complete, ChatZilla is ready to use.

*Figure 1-10. Installing ChatZilla*

## Using ChatZilla

ChatZilla can be launched in three ways. The IRC Chat option will appear in the Window menu in your browser. Selecting this will launch the client. You can also use the irc command in the URL bar. Typing just **irc:** will launch ChatZilla. You can also type a full URL, like **irc://irc.mozilla.org**, and that will take the additional step of connecting to the specified server. These URL methods are currently the only way to launch ChatZilla if you are using the Mozilla Firebird web browser. Finally, if you launch Netscape or Mozilla from the command line, you can use the –chat option to start up ChatZilla instead of the normal browser window.

Once ChatZilla has launched (Figure 1-11), you can use all of the basic IRC commands. Nickname and command completion are both supported. After typing a few characters of the nickname or command, pressing the Tab key will fill in the rest. If there is more than one option for the characters you typed, ChatZilla will complete up until there is a choice to be made.

For example, typing **/q** followed by the Tab key will fill in the command up to **/qu**. It stops there because there are several options for what comes next. A quick double-Tab will display all of the options that can complete the text. In this case, ChatZilla shows the following line:

```
4 matches for "/qu": [/query, /quit, /quit-mozilla, /quote]
```

Mousing over a message will show the timestamp in the status bar at the bottom of the window. It also gives the nickname and IP address/hostname of the sender. Each sender's nickname appears as a link next to the message. Clicking that link will open a private chat session with the person. Private messages and chats can also be started with commands. Typing **/msg** *nickname message* will send a private message to the nickname you provide. If someone sends a private message to you using the /msg command, it will automatically open a new tab to show your conversation. Using the **/query** *nickname* command will open this private tab as well, but without sending a message. The tab will be labeled with your chat partner's nickname. Messages typed in these new tabbed windows are, obviously, private.

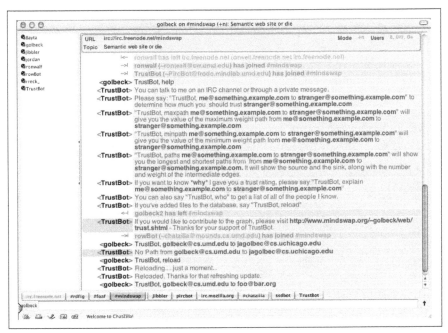

Figure 1-11. *ChatZilla in use*

When sending messages, the default input field lets you type one line of text. For pasting multiline text, such as snippets of programming code where lines really matter, it can be tedious to cut and paste each individual line. In ChatZilla, there is an up arrow next to the input field (see Figure 1-12). Clicking that arrow expands the text box into a text field.

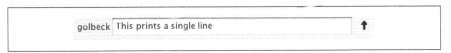

Figure 1-12. *Default input field*

Multiple lines can be typed or pasted into the larger box (see Figure 1-13) and will appear in much the same way in the actual chat. Clicking the new, bent arrow next to the text area will send the message. To return to single-line input, click the down arrow.

If you are using multiline text entry, as shown in Figure 1-13, you will see this appear identically in your client, as shown in Figure 1-14.

ChatZilla has great support for changing the appearance of the chat windows with motifs. A few default options come installed. Several more motifs are available at *http://www.hacksrus.com*. However, motifs are just CSS files. That means that you can easily use a CSS from another web site or create your own

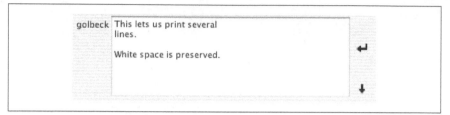

Figure 1-13. Sending text with multiple lines

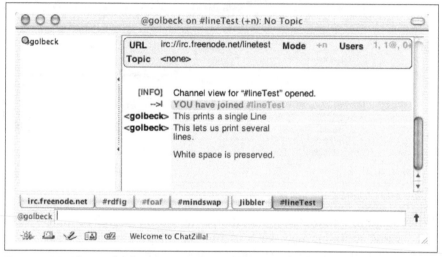

Figure 1-14. The result of sending a multiline message

motif especially for chat. To set a motif, choose a default one from the View →
Color Scheme menu or set your own. To use your own CSS file, either drag a
link to the *.css* file into the message window, or use the /motif command.

    **/motif** *http://example.com/myMotif.css*

Any CSS file accessible over the Web can be used in this way.

## See Also

- FAQs, links, source code, bug reports, and a wealth of other information are available at the Mozilla project's homepage for ChatZilla (*http://
  www.mozilla.org/projects/rt-messaging/chatzilla*).

- The ChatZilla page on hacksrus (*http://www.hacksrus.com/~ginda/
  chatzilla*) has installs, motifs, and more technical information.

- The ChatZilla newsgroup is netscape.public.mozilla.rt-messaging and
  can be found on the public news server news.mozilla.org. There is, of
  course, an IRC channel for ChatZilla: *irc://irc.mozilla.org/#chatzilla*.

—*Jennifer Golbeck*

# CHAPTER TWO

# Using IRC

## Hacks 5–11

Now that you know how to connect to IRC, it's time to get familiar with the way it works. It is essential to understand the IRC model of networks, servers, channels, and users to chat with individuals and groups alike. IRC is quite often a free-for-all, where unique nicknames are allocated to the first people to ask for them. If you are lucky enough to get the nickname you want, this chapter will show you how to protect this valuable asset and ensure that you can always use it when you reconnect to that particular IRC network.

As with all mature Internet-based technologies, a variety of acronyms and abbreviations are commonly used on IRC. This chapter will familiarize you with the essential lingo, so you won't get confused when people start asking WTH you don't RTFM.

IRC gives you the freedom of creating your own channels—groups of users that share a common interest or theme. This chapter also provides your first glimpse into channel management, showing you how to use ChanServ and CHANFIX to protect your own channel from abuse and to keep out unwelcome visitors.

## The IRC Model

### #5

If you are totally new to IRC, you may be wondering where to begin. Understand the conceptual model of Internet Relay Chat for a good start.

Internet Relay Chat was originally implemented so that users of bulletin board systems could chat with one another in real time. It has grown considerably since then, and thousands of networks of servers are now available for public use. The IRC protocol is text based, so programs that connect to IRC servers are easy to write.

## Network of Servers

Each IRC network consists of at least one server. If there is more than one server, they are linked together to form a spanning tree. A spanning tree is a structure that allows each server in the network to communicate with all the other servers in the network, even if there is no direct connection between them. Because the servers in an IRC network are connected like this, two users can talk to each other even if they are using different servers on the same IRC network.

## Clients

Anything that connects to an IRC server that is not another server is called a client. This includes the set of programs that most people use to chat with each other on IRC. An IRC client can connect directly to one of the servers on the IRC network and allow the user to chat with other users on the network. When a private message is sent to another client, it is sent via the IRC network, so there is no need for a separate connection to be made.

Each client that connects to an IRC network must have a unique nickname. Some servers still enforce a limit of nine characters for this nickname, but most servers these days allow much longer nicknames. Nicknames cannot contain spaces or certain punctuation characters.

## Channels

Communication on IRC is not limited to just sending messages between pairs of users. IRC is very strongly oriented toward the concept of channels. A channel is something rather analogous to a room, where a group of clients can stay and chat as a whole. When a message is sent to a channel, all clients in that channel will receive it. The process of entering a channel is called *joining*, and leaving a channel is known as *parting* or *leaving*.

> To be strict, *parting* is the most correct term for leaving a channel. This is because IRC clients send a PART message to the server when they want to leave a channel. However, most IRC clients provide a more natural command alias that lets you *leave* a channel.

All channel names are unique and typically prefixed with a # character. These channels can be joined by anybody on the entire IRC network. Other prefixes exist, such as &, which is used for channels belonging only to a particular local server. In any case, channel names cannot contain spaces or commas.

For example, to join the channel #irchacks, you would type:

*/join #irchacks*

When you are in the #irchacks channel, you can leave it by typing **/part** or **/leave**.

A channel does not actually exist until the first client joins it. The channel no longer exists after the last client has left. If the channel is configured to allow external messages, a client can send messages to the channel without needing to join it. Most channels disallow this, as it inevitably leads to abuse and confusion.

An individual client can join more than one channel, but for performance reasons, most servers impose a limit. When there is a limit, it is usually set to the recommended value of 10. If within the limit, a client can usually join any channel, but a couple of exceptions are worth noting. A channel can be configured to ban clients that have a nickname or host mask matching a particular pattern, thus preventing such clients from joining the channel. Channels can also be set to be "invite only," which means you must be invited by a user in the channel before you can join it.

## Operators

An operator is a client that has special access to the IRC network. Operators can carry out maintenance tasks on the network, such as connecting and disconnecting other servers in the network. In extreme cases, operators may exercise their ability to forcibly remove users from the IRC network. Not only can they disconnect any client, but they can also prevent that client from reconnecting to the network.

## Channel Operators

If you are the first client to join a channel, you will probably be made a channel operator for that channel. This allows you to kick other clients out of the channel and to set the topic if it is protected. If the channel is marked as "invite only," you can issue invitations to other clients on the network. A channel operator can also change the *mode* of the channel. This lets you do a variety of tasks including banning certain users from the channel or making other clients in the channel become channel operators like you. You can tell if a user is a channel operator, as he will have an @ character in front of his nickname. Most users refer to channel operators incorrectly as "operators," or more informally as "ops."

# Common Terms, Abbreviations, and Phrases

**HACK #6**

Once you get into IRC, you need to understand the barrage of abbreviations and phrases that are commonly used.

People will do anything to be lazy—especially where typing is concerned. Anyone who uses IRC will come across abbreviations and certain jargon that will stump them initially. Do not look like a fool by asking unless you absolutely must!

## Noun-Verb Duality

One peculiarity you may notice is that IRC commands are often treated as both verbs and nouns. You can refer to your IRC client documentation for additional commands, but here are some examples:

op

> *n.* A person in a channel who has the +o flag in a channel. Usually has the @ prefix in the username.
>
> *v.* The act of setting mode +o. Used with omitted subject "me" as a request.
>
> ```
> <lamer> op
> /mode #channel +o lamer
> * idiot sets mode +o lamer
> ```

oper

> *n.* A person who has been granted special privileges on the IRC server.
>
> ```
> <w8> TsTech is an oper, right?
> ```
>
> *v.* To identify to an IRC server with an administrator login and password, for example.
>
> ```
> /oper User Password
> ```

msg (*short for* privmsg)

> *n.* A private message to a user.
>
> ```
> [lamer(idiot@some-host.com)] you're cool
> ```
>
> *v.* To send someone a private message.
>
> ```
> /msg lamer I know am.
> ```

## Leet Speak

```
1E3+ $Pe@K IS EVErywh3rE, 4nd iT'$ nO+ COn51$t3nt.
l33t $pEAK 15 3V3rYWH3RE, @nd 1+'5 noT cOn515TeNt.
Le3T $P3aK 15 EVERYwh3RE, 4Nd iT'5 No+ cON$15+EnT.
l3eT 5p34K i5 Ev3rYWH3R3, 4nD 1T's nO+ COns15+3N+.
L33T $P3@k 15 EVerYWH3R3, @ND 1+'5 NO+ cONS15+3N+.
```

"Leet" (from "*elite*") speak is novelty English commonly used on IRC, instant messaging, and gaming. The use of leet speak is considered childish; however, it may also be used with sarcasm, so don't expect to be taken too seriously if you choose to use it.

With practice, you'll be able to read the preceding examples almost as quickly as normal text. Leet speak is quite often derived by replacing letters with numbers that look similar; for example, *o* could be replaced by *0* and *e* could be replaced by *3*, which looks like a reversed *E*. Leet speak is not consistent, so you may even see an *o* being replaced by parentheses or an *m* being replaced by |\/|.

## Correction Syntax

After a user finds an error that she made on the previous line, she may try to correct the mistake. Many methods exist for delimiting corrections. The most common is the asterisk method, which is used like so:

```
<ScOOter> I want a glass of lemonaid.
<ScOOter> *lemonade.
```

It doesn't matter if the asterisk is placed at the beginning or the end of the correction. "*lemonade" and "lemonade*" are both commonly used asterisk correction statements.

Another popular way of correcting a mistake is the "s-slash" method. Addicts of the Perl programming language commonly use this. It works like this:

```
<Marcel> My bolonie sandwich fell on the floor :(
<Marcel> s/bolonie/bologna
```

s/*mistake*/*correction* is how it's done. This is derived from the search-and-replace regular expression syntax found in Perl code. Its meaning is mostly esoteric, but people can figure out "mistake" slash "correction" easily enough for it to work.

## Phonetics and Keyboard Layouts

Many mistakes and typos can be interpreted. Spelling "ever" as "evar" is an obvious mishap, but "gppf" ("food") isn't so easy to detect. If you are chatting with an English speaker, keep in mind the standard QWERTY keyboard layout when encountering a typo. It is better to think than to ask for clarification. In most cases, people answer their own question by the time they press Return to send the question, for example:

```
<BeetleJuice> I just saw that AYBABTU animation for the 167th time!
<Jquest> ?
<Jquest> Oh! I get it.
<Jquest> All your base are belong to us.
```

```
...
<Hungary> AFK! wife brought gppf
* Hungary is away
<Turkey> gppf?
<Boliver> Turkey: He means "food"
```

*—Nicholas Copeland*

## HACK #7    Common Acronyms and Initialisms

Master the obscure acronyms people use on IRC to save keystrokes.

IRC attracts a curious breed of user—people who seem happy to sit around chatting all day, yet are too lazy to type full words at times. Understanding the acronyms they use will make it easier to fit in, but you are advised not to join in with their acronym overload.

Here is a list of the most commonly used abbreviations and acronyms on IRC. Some of them may already be familiar to users of Usenet groups or web boards:

*AFAIK*
As far as I know.

*AFK*
Away from keyboard. People often type this if they are in the middle of a conversation and want other people to realize they are not around. It is sometimes added to the end of a user's nickname to indicate the same fact; for example, Jibbler may change his nickname to Jibbler|afk.

*ASL*
Age/Sex/Location. This is something asked of all newcomers in prepubescent channels.

*ATM*
At the moment.

*BBIAB*
Be back in a bit.

*BBIAF*
Be back in a few.

*BBL*
Be back later.

*BBS*
Be back soon.

*BRB*

Be right back. Often said when someone is in the middle of a conversation but has to dash off to do something, with the intention of returning to the conversation.

*BTW*

By the way.

*CYA*

C (see) you.

*DCC*

Direct Client Connection. The name given to the connection used to transfer files or chat directly to another user without going via the server.

*DL*

Download.

*DW*

Don't worry.

*FFS*

For f*#&'s sake.

*FIIK*

F*#&ed if I know.

*FUBAR*

F*#&ed up beyond all repair/recognition.

*FY (FU)*

F*#& you.

*FYI*

For your information.

*GN*

Good night.

*IANAL*

I am not a lawyer.

*IIRC*

If I recall correctly.

*IM(H)O*

In my (humble) opinion.

*IRL*

In real life.

*JK (J/K)*

Just kidding.

**LART**

Loser/luser/lamer attitude readjustment tool. Channel operators may ready the LART to deal with users who don't seem to have a clue.

**LMAO**

Laughing my ass off.

**LO**

Short for hello.

**LOL**

Laughing out loud. This is a common response from people after you've said something funny.

**LTNS**

Long time no see.

**MOTD**

Message of the day. This is normally announced when you connect to an IRC server.

**MYOB**

Mind your own business.

**NM**

Not much or never mind.

**NP**

No problem.

**OIC**

Oh, I C (see).

**OMG(D)**

Oh my God (darn).

**PLS,PLZ**

Please.

**RE**

Re-hello. People may welcome you with this if you part a channel and rejoin it a while later.

**RO(T)FL**

Rolling on (the) floor laughing.

**RTFM**

Read the f*#&ing manual. A common response to users who join a channel and ask a question that is already answered in some documentation.

**TTYL**

Talk to you later.

*TY*
> Thank you.

*URL*
> Uniform Resource Locator (Internet address).

*W/*
> With.

*WB*
> Welcome back.

*WE (W/E)*
> Whatever.

*W/O*
> Without.

*WTF*
> What/who/why/where the f*#&.

*WTG*
> Way to go.

*WTH*
> What/who/why/where the heck/hell.

—*Nicholas Copeland*

## Register with NickServ

**#8**

All nicknames on an IRC network must be unique, so if someone steals your nickname, you won't be able to use it. Protect your nickname and get it back with NickServ.

It may have happened to you already—someone trying to impersonate you or just "stealing" your nickname for the fun of it. NickServ will solve this problem for you.

Impersonating someone on IRC is quite easy. When logging in, you can specify your nickname, and the server will never check whether you really are who you pretend to be. This could be considered a weakness. Fortunately, NickServ tries to fix this weakness.

NickServ is one of the Services available on a large number of IRC networks. It sits on the IRC network and sees all the connecting and disconnecting users and nick changes. Of course, just that isn't enough. When you register your nickname with NickServ, you can ask NickServ to *kill* someone if they are already logged in with your nickname. This can be useful when someone's impersonating you, but it's probably even more useful if your Internet connection fails and you have to log back in—your old session will probably still be active on the server, so you won't be able to use your regular nickname. But if you ask NickServ to kill your old connection, you can take your nickname back.

A more important advantage of registering your nickname with NickServ is that it allows you to register new channels with ChanServ and/or be in channel access lists. This means, among other things, that you can get channel operator status from ChanServ [Hack #9].

## Registering Yourself with NickServ

The first step is to register your nickname. This is quite easy on most IRC networks, as all you have to do is send a register message to NickServ. To do this on the freenode IRC network, open a query with NickServ and send the register message like this:

```
<Wilmer> register password
<NickServ> Your nickname is now registered under the hostmask [*~blabla@*.
ipv6.gaast.net].
<NickServ> Your password is [password].  Please remember this for later use.
<NickServ> Freenode is a service of Peer-Directed Projects Center, an
<NickServ> IRS 501(c)(3) (tax-exempt) charitable and educational
organization.
<NickServ> For frequently-asked questions about the network, please see the
<NickServ> FAQ page (http://freenode.net/faq.shtml).
```

If someone else has already registered this nickname, you'll receive an error message and you'll just have to pick a different nickname. Sadly, nicknames on IRC are very much a first-come first-served affair. After you have registered, you can check to see if everything worked by reconnecting to the IRC server. You should receive the following message:

```
<NickServ> This nickname is owned by someone else
<NickServ> If this is your nickname, type /msg NickServ IDENTIFY <password>
```

You should then do what NickServ told you to do, so type:

```
/msg NickServ IDENTIFY password
```

If everything goes correctly, NickServ will recognize you and mark you as registered. You can check whether you (or someone else) are indeed identified correctly using the info command. This is also sent as a private message to NickServ, for example:

```
<Wilmer> info Wilmer
<NickServ>            Nickname: wilmer << ONLINE >>
<NickServ>          Registered: 1 year 50 weeks 3 days (23h 21m 18s) ago
<NickServ>  Last Seen Quit Msg: ballard.freenode.net irc.freenode.net
<NickServ>       Email Address: wilmer@gaast.net
<NickServ>                 UIN: 267762
<NickServ>     Nickname Options: Secure, AllowMemos, MemoNotify, MemoSignon
```

If you don't see the << ONLINE >> text behind your nickname or any other sign of you being identified, you can be sure something went wrong. Nick-Servs on other IRC networks may behave slightly differently, so be prepared to accept some different formatting of the output. In particular, some Nick-Servs require you to specify your email address as a second argument when you register.

If you still have problems, it's probably a good idea to read the help information. Most (if not all) NickServs will give you more information about how they work when you send them a help command in a private message:

```
/msg NickServ help
```

Usually, you can get more information about a specific command by adding it as an argument to the help command:

```
/msg NickServ help register
```

One command you might find interesting is the set command. This is used to change your settings. You can use it to set a new password, enable stronger security, and automatically authenticate using your hostname. You can use it to set your contact information, such as your email address, which people will get when they use the info command shown earlier.

> Automatic authentication based on hostnames may sound convenient, but it's sometimes a bad idea. If you're running your IRC client on a Unix machine that is also used by other people, it makes it very easy for others to fool NickServ. If you think having to send a password every time you log in is annoying, there are scripts that can do this for you.

## Fixing Nick Collisions

Now that you're registered with NickServ, you're ready to use some of the useful NickServ features. For example, let's say you accidentally unplugged your computer's power cable. When you start your IRC client again, the IRC server will probably complain that your nickname is already in use. This happens because your old session is still alive and using your nickname. The IRC server doesn't know about your mistake, so you'll receive a message like this:

```
-!- Your nick is owned by Wilmer van der Gaast [~blabla@tosca.ipv6.gaast.
net]
```

If your IRC client is clever, it will have chosen an alternative nickname or appended an underscore to your nickname to enable it to connect successfully using a unique nickname. This will let you open a query with NickServ again so you can remove your "ghost" from the server:

```
<Wilmer_> ghost Wilmer password
```

```
-!- Wilmer [~blabla@tosca.ipv6.gaast.net] has quit [Nick collision from
services.]
<NickServ> [Wilmer] has been killed
```

Because the "ghost" has been removed from the server, you can take back
your own nickname.

## Changing Nicknames

If you change your nickname frequently, a feature called *nick linking* allows
you to link multiple nicknames together. When two nicknames are linked,
you can change from one nick to the other without having to identify yourself again. Also, the channel privileges are shared.

To link your nickname with another one, open a query with NickServ and
enter the `link` command. The `link` command requires two arguments: the
nickname you want to link to and the password for that nickname. This is
required because you shouldn't be allowed to link to any other person and
gain his channel privileges.

```
<lintux> link wilmer password
23:56:28 -NickServ(NickServ@services.)- Your nickname is now linked to
[wilmer]
```

One thing you should be careful with when linking nicks is to try to avoid
losing some privileges. On freenode, the nick under which you run the link
command will lose all its own privileges and get the privileges assigned to
the nick you're linking to. So it might be a bad idea to link two of your nicks
if both have special privileges assigned in some channels already. If you want
to know how your IRC network handles this, read the help information
about the link command:

```
/msg NickServ help link
```

Now that you have mastered NickServ, you can be assured that your nickname is safe.

—*Wilmer van der Gaast*

HACK
#9

## Register Your Channel with ChanServ

Are you having problems with unruly users causing mayhem in your channel?
Protect your channel with the ChanServ service.

So you've just created your own channel. If you were the first person to join
the channel, then it is likely that the IRC server will have made you into a
channel operator. Other users are free to wander into your channel, but you
have ultimate control over what goes on. Having operator status means that
you can kick and ban unruly users or even moderate the channel, which
means people can speak only if you allow them to. Several users have

already gathered in your channel, but a software installation requires you to reboot your computer. When you return to your channel, you discover that you are no longer a channel operator! More importantly, nobody else in the channel is a channel operator. The only way to restore your operator status is to ask everybody to leave the channel and be the first to rejoin. Practically speaking, this isn't going to happen.

One solution to this problem would have been to use your operator status to grant the same status to other users in your channel. The problem with this approach is that you need to be able to trust those other users to *op* you when you rejoin the channel. Another problem is that *netsplits* (where servers in an IRC network become disconnected) and server maintenance can easily wipe out entire sets of channel operators.

## Introducing ChanServ

The best solution to this problem is *ChanServ*. Many IRC networks run *Services* such as ChanServ, which allow users to manage their channels. Not all ChanServs behave identically, but on the whole they are pretty similar. This hack makes use of the ChanServ on the freenode IRC network. ChanServ can be treated just like any other IRC user, and you can interact with it by sending private messages. To get help on any of the features of ChanServ, simply send the help command via a private message:

```
/msg ChanServ help
```

## Registering a Channel

To use ChanServ, you may first need to register your nickname with Nick-Serv [Hack #8]. Many IRC networks use both ChanServ and NickServ Services. In most cases, ChanServ won't recognize you until you have identified yourself with NickServ. Also, you will need operator status in the channel you want to register. Remember that anyone with operator status can register the channel, so it's a good idea not to give away operator status to anyone else until the channel has been registered.

To register a channel, you must send some private messages to ChanServ. You can do this by opening a query window and using the register command:

```
<Wilmer> register #futurama password
<ChanServ> The channel [#futurama] is now registered under your nickname.
<ChanServ> Your channel password is [password].  Please remember it for
later use.
<ChanServ> Channel guidelines can be found on the freenode website
<ChanServ> (http://freenode.net/channel_guidelines.shtml).
<ChanServ> Freenode is a service of Peer-Directed Projects Center, an IRS
501(c)(3)
<ChanServ> (tax-exempt) charitable and educational organization.
```

If you have not already done so, this would be a good time to read the channel guidelines for the IRC network you are using. Some networks have strict policies against off-topic or illegal channels, and finding out that a server operator has closed your channel is not a pleasant surprise.

## Restoring Channel Operators

Each time you connect to the IRC network, you can register with NickServ so that it knows who you are. Because ChanServ and NickServ work together, ChanServ will now be aware that you are the owner of your channel. If you join your channel and find that other people are already there, the network will not grant you operator status by default. Even if there are no other operators in the channel, you can send an op request to ChanServ to restore your operator status. Because you may be in more than one channel, this command must take the channel name as a parameter:

> /msg ChanServ op #futurama

Note that some IRC networks also require you to specify your nickname as well:

> /msg ChanServ op #futurama Wilmer

## Access Lists

An access list lets you assign other rights to the users in your channel. For example, you can allow another user in your channel to use ChanServ to obtain operator status. To get the current access list from ChanServ, you can send another private message:

> /msg ChanServ access #futurama list

ChanServ will reply with a list that shows everyone who has special ChanServ privileges for your channel. Initially, this will be just you:

```
<ChanServ> -- Access List for [#futurama] --
<ChanServ> Num Level Hostmask                          Time since last use
<ChanServ> --- ----- --------                          -------------------
<ChanServ> 1   30    Wilmer                             5m 58s
<ChanServ> -- End of list -
```

Something worth noting here is the *access level*. Each user can have a different access level. You probably don't want everyone to have the same rights as you have. Some people should be able to let ChanServ grant them operator status, but they shouldn't all be able to change channel settings or add other people to the access list. Being able to set the access level for each user gives you some control over this.

By default, people with an access level of 10 or more can use ChanServ to grant themselves operator status. People with an access level of 15 and higher can add people to the AKICK list, which automatically kicks and bans them. People with an access level of 30 and higher can add people to the access list. For a complete list of access levels, you can use the level command:

> /msg ChanServ level #futurama list

You can, of course, change these values if you want to. For example, you may want some people to be granted operator status automatically when they join the channel. Read the help information about the level command for more information about this.

## Adding Users to the Access List

In some cases, it is useful to add someone to the access list. For example, one of the users in your channel may have written a bot that requires channel operator status to do some of its jobs. If you are unsure whether to trust the author of this bot, you can use access levels to make things a bit safer. You don't want to give the bot more rights than it needs, so you can give the bot an access level of 10:

```
<Wilmer> access #futurama add Bender 10
<ChanServ> [Bender] has been added to the access list for #futurama with
level [10]
<Wilmer> access #futurama list
<ChanServ> -- Access List for [#futurama] --
<ChanServ> Num Level Hostmask                         Time since last use
<ChanServ> --- ----- --------                         -------------------
<ChanServ> 1   10    Bender
<ChanServ> 2   30    Wilmer                            51m 24s
<ChanServ> -- End of list -
```

The bot called Bender can now also get operator status in #futurama through ChanServ.

Don't forget that if someone wants to be in the access list, she must have registered her nickname with NickServ first. If this has not been done, ChanServ will not know whether that person really is who she claims to be.

## Other ChanServ Features

Of course, there is more to ChanServ than you have seen so far. ChanServ can unban you from your channel when someone has banned you and you are unable to join and fix it. Suppose there was a bug in Bender that caused him to kick me from #futurama. To unban myself, all I have to do is this:

> /msg ChanServ unban #futurama

ChanServ can also be used to send a welcome message when someone joins the channel. This is not like a greeting from a bot. The user will get this welcome message in a NOTICE directly from ChanServ. People who are in the channel already won't see the message.

>    /msg ChanServ set #*futurama* entrymsg *Welcome to the world of tomorrow!*

Another useful ChanServ feature is MLOCK, so that you can force some channel modes. If a channel mode has been forced, none of the users in that channel will be able to set or unset it. You can force a channel to be moderated (+m) like so:

>    /msg ChanServ set #*futurama* mlock +m

If you are using an IRC network with a slightly different ChanServ that does not accept these commands, remember that you can usually work out what the correct command syntax should be by using the help command.

Some IRC networks choose not to have ChanServ or NickServ Services. *IRCnet* is one of these networks. If you lose operator status in your channel on IRCnet, the only way to get it back is to rejoin the channel after everybody else has left. This is not the easiest thing to do, so your channel is likely to become a free-for-all after a while. This is how IRCnet works. Some people prefer this kind of unruliness, while others may prefer the stricter model of using ChanServ. This is just one of the factors in choosing which IRC network you wish to use most often.

*—Wilmer van der Gaast*

## The QuakeNet L Channel Bot

**#10**    ChanServ and NickServ aren't always available. When on QuakeNet, use the L bot to manage your channels.

QuakeNet provides some service bots for you to use so that you can maintain a channel on their servers. The two channel management bots are called Q and L. The Q service provides a few more features than the lighter L bot, but requires a little more effort to request it to join your channel. If you just want a channel for a few friends to chat in or for a small gaming clan, then L is the bot for you. The L bot will allow you to auto-op, voice friends or clan members, and keep your channel open and protected.

You can connect to QuakeNet by typing /server irc.quakenet.org in your favorite IRC client.

This is a quick guide to getting and configuring an L bot. Detailed information and help about these bots can be found at *http://www.quakenet.org*.

## Create an Account

First you need to create an account with Q. All L account information is dealt with through Q, so you need to be *authed* with Q whenever you want to do anything with an L bot.

Imagine your nickname is ChatterBox and you want to register your nickname. You can do so by sending a private message to Q, like so:

```
/msg Q HELLO chatterbox@wanttochat.com chatterbox@wanttochat.com
```

Q will respond with the following:

```
-Q- Hello, ChatterBox. A new user account has been created for you, with
nick ChatterBox.
-Q- OK, Your login information has been sent to "chatterbox@wanttochat.com".
    please check your email for further instructions.
```

When you receive the email, you should change the password as instructed in the email.

Let's say that your password is "password". Now you can auth with Q:

```
/msg Q@CServe.quakenet.org AUTH ChatterBox password
```

If you used the correct password, Q will respond with:

```
-Q- AUTH'd successfully.
```

Now that you are authenticated with Q, you can set up your L bot.

## Getting L

To get an L bot to join your channel, you must meet the requirements set by QuakeNet. These requirements may change occasionally as they improve the service, so check the *L FAQ* on *http://www.quakenet.org* for the current details.

To prevent unnecessary requests, you need to join the channel that you want and make sure you have at least three friends in there. You will then need to wait for about two hours. Then you must log in to the QuakeNet web site with your Q auth details and request L for your channel from the *Services* link. If the request was successful, you will be informed, and L will join your channel shortly afterward.

## Setting Up L for Your Channel

You will probably want to allow friends or clan members to receive channel operator status when they join the channel, providing they are authed with Q. You can make your authenticated friend ChitterBox automatically receive operator status when he joins your new channel (#mynewchan) by sending this private message to L:

> /msg L chanlev #mynewchan ChitterBox **+ao**

If all went well, L will respond with:

> -L- Done.

At the end of the private message, you can specify a number of flags:

+n

> Owner of the channel

+m

> Master of the bot

+o

> Operator

+v

> Voice

+g

> Voice even if opped

+a

> Automatically apply the given flags

In the previous case, the flag +ao means to apply operator status when the user joins the channel.

You can check the users for your channel and what access rights they have by typing:

> /msg L chanlev *#mynewchan*

L will respond with something similar to this:

```
-L- Users for channel #mynewchan
-L- Authname          Access flags
-L- ----------------------------
-L- ChatterBox              amno
-L- ChitterBox                ao
-L- End of chanlev for #mynewchan
```

You can see the access flags you just added for the user ChitterBox.

You can add a welcome message for your channel by sending a private message to L:

> /msg L welcome *#mynewchan Hi! This is my new channel :)*

Again, if this worked, L will respond with:

> -L- Done.

When people join your channel, they will now receive a notice from L:

```
-L- [#mynewclan] Hi! This is my new channel :)
```

That's all there is to it, really. Now your channel has a service bot in it, and the channel is reserved for you so you can be found easily by staying in that channel. You can tell your friends about the channel or advertise on your web page for people to join.

*—Alex North*

## Fix Channel Problems with CHANFIX

EFnet is the oldest IRC network in the world and does not use IRC Services. But it's CHANFIX to the rescue if problems occur in your channel.

Many IRC users are familiar with Services. NickServ and ChanServ keep order on IRC and make problems like "nick juping" (someone preventing your reconnecting by using your nickname) and "channel takeover" a rare event on many IRC networks. However, *IRC Services* as we know it today was first written in 1995 by Brian "Morpher" Smith and was implemented on the DALnet IRC network, which started up in 1994.

The EFnet IRC network was created in 1988 and is the oldest and one of the largest networks in the world. By 1995, EFnet had achieved 15,000 concurrent users, which was quite a lot back then. To implement Services at that point would undermine the sometimes years of work that had gone into maintaining a channel. It could cause unjust channel takeovers if one user managed to register a channel before the real founder. People who regularly use the same nickname could lose out by being offline when NickServ was implemented and find that someone else had registered their nickname.

For those reasons, EFnet has chosen to go without Services and will continue to do so for the foreseeable future. In its place, Chris "comstud" Behrens has coded a service known as CHANFIX, which monitors channels on the network, tracks who has ops and how often, and can restore channels to their original state in the event of a takeover or complete loss of ops due to splits or attacks against the channel operators.

### Channel Monitoring

CHANFIX is linked to EFnet via a custom Services module, giving it an omniscient presence, capable of seeing all channels and users on any server of the network. No registration is required; CHANFIX indexes all channels on EFnet.

Every five minutes, CHANFIX does an index of every channel it sees on EFnet and keeps track of who has ops. Every time CHANFIX runs an index pass, it awards the user@host a single point and keeps a score for the past two weeks. Thus, the maximum score any user can have for a channel is 4032.

There are, of course, some caveats to this procedure. First, CHANFIX does not index any channel with fewer than four users, and CHANFIX ignores all users without a working Ident (matched by the host mask *!~*@*), as well as all users with hosts that appear to be dynamic (*!*@*dialup* and *!*@*ppp* for example). The reasons why will be made clear later.

In addition, CHANFIX will index only if 75% or more of the network is linked. CHANFIX will not run any indexes when it's on the short side of a major split.

The following is an example of a CHANFIX score list for a channel:

```
<CHANFIX> Top 10 scores for channel "#windows" in the database:
<CHANFIX> 3740, 3714, 3682, 3497, 3478, 3448, 3402, 3304, 3196, 3155
<CHANFIX> Top 10 scores for current ops in channel "#windows":
<CHANFIX> 3740, 3714, 3682, 3497, 3478, 3448, 3402, 3196, 3155, 3074
<CHANFIX> Top 10 scores for current non-ops in channel "#windows":
<CHANFIX> 3714, 2843, 2310, 2122, 1429, 1038, 203, 192, 58
```

Here's an example of a score for a specific user@host:

```
<CHANFIX> User "windows@pound.windows.bot"'s score in channel "#windows":
3714
```

## Automatic CHANFIX

Upon a channel becoming "opless," either from the last remaining channel operator losing the link to her server or from an op accidentally performing a de-op of all ops, CHANFIX immediately begins the process for an automatic fix of the channel.

CHANFIX first checks its database for the channel and breaks the scores down from highest to lowest, to create a one-hour "cycle down" period split into five-minute blocks. This causes the highest-scored ops to be re-opped first and the lowest-scored ops to be re-opped last.

CHANFIX then joins the channel and removes +i, +l, or +b modes that could be preventing scored ops from joining the channel. If one or more of the current ops in the channel have scores in the top 8.3% of all of the scores in the database, they are opped immediately. If none of the current ops are in the top 8.3% or CHANFIX can't op five ops, CHANFIX waits five minutes until the next pass or until the channel has five ops again.

+i means that a channel is invite-only, so you cannot join it until you are invited in by a channel operator. +l is used to set the maximum number of users that can join the channel at any one moment. +b is used to ban users from joining a channel.

When CHANFIX checks the channel again 5 minutes later, it tries to op the top 16.6% scored ops in the database (a high-scoring op could have joined in the past 5 minutes, so it includes all previous scores). This continues for 60 minutes or until there are 5 ops in the channel again. After 60 minutes, CHANFIX will op anyone with a score as soon as he enters the channel.

This means that it's possible for someone who had ops for 30 seconds (perhaps when you were having fun in your channel) to become the guy who gets ops after a catastrophic channel event, so be careful who you op, always!

The following is an example of an automatic CHANFIX:

```
* BBS sets mode: -o BBS
<BBS> Oops, I messed up!
* CHANFIX (services@services.int) has joined #windows
* services.int sets mode: +o CHANFIX
* CHANFIX sets mode: -bbbb *!*@152.3.* *!*@thefoundry.co.uk *!*@*.no *!*@*.
duke.edu
* CHANFIX sets mode: -b *!*@pool-141-153-*.mad.east.verizon.net
* CHANFIX sets mode: +o BBS
<CHANFIX> 1 client should have been opped.
* CHANFIX (services@services.int) has left #windows
*** 5 minutes later ***
* CHANFIX (services@services.int) has joined #windows
* services.int sets mode: +o CHANFIX
* CHANFIX sets mode: +ooo Zorlak WinSpy WinInfo
<CHANFIX> 3 clients should have been opped.
* CHANFIX (services@services.int) has left #windows
```

## Manual CHANFIX

Due to the nature of EFnet, channel takeovers do happen from time to time. Sometimes a client gets hacked or an op may accidentally op the wrong person. When this happens, CHANFIX can be called manually by a CHANFIX administrator and instructed to fix a channel and restore ops to the regular ops.

In addition, CHANFIX is used to fix channel *desyncs*. While increasingly rare, it is possible for a channel to be seen as slightly different from server to server. Fixing channel desyncs is a side effect of how CHANFIX fixes channels when called manually.

The following is an example of a channel that's been taken over:

```
[14:52] <CHANFIX> Top 10 scores for channel "#windows" in the database:
[14:52] <CHANFIX> 3740, 3714, 3682, 3497, 3478, 3448, 3402, 3304, 3196, 3155
[14:52] <CHANFIX> Top 10 scores for current ops in channel "#windows":
[14:52] <CHANFIX> 3, 1, 1, 1, 1, 1, 1, 1, 1
[14:52] <CHANFIX> Top 10 scores for current non-ops in channel "#windows":
[14:52] <CHANFIX> 3714, 2843, 2310, 2122, 1429, 1038, 203, 192, 58
```

You can clearly see that the channel has been taken over. Someone got ops about 15 minutes ago, then waited about 10 minutes before performing a mass de-op, then a mass op of their friends or some IRC bots.

When you trigger a manual fix, CHANFIX first inspects the channel's timestamp. If it's 2 or greater, CHANFIX SJOINs the channel with a TS-1 **[Hack #84]**. This causes all servers on the network to yield to CHANFIX as the older channel, and each server de-ops all ops in the channel.

The SJOIN also clears +l, +b, and +i channel modes, allowing the original ops to join the channel if they were banned. From this point on, CHANFIX treats the channel like any normally opless channel and performs the preceding automatic steps. If the channel were simply desynced, the reset of the TS and clearing of modes on all servers would likewise fix that problem, and the automatic CHANFIX process would take over.

In the unlikely event that a channel already has a TS of 1 or 0, CHANFIX joins with the same TS and sends SA (Services Administrator) modes to de-op and reset modes. Letting the individual servers change modes is simply a cleaner solution.

The following is an example of using CHANFIX to fix a channel takeover. Notice the TS change and the removal of +b and +l modes:

```
<TO-Leader> Haha, we took over your channel!
<BBS> Not for long!
-> [msg(chanfix)] chanfix #windows
* irc.choopa.net sets mode: -oooo TO-One TO-Two TO-Three TO-Four
* irc.choopa.net sets mode: -oooo TO-Five TO-Six TO-Seven TO-Eight
* irc.choopa.net sets mode: -oo TO-Nine TO-Leader
* irc.choopa.net sets mode: -v WinInfo
-irc.choopa.net:#windows- *** Notice -- TS for #windows changed from
1078875452 to 1078875451
* services.int sets mode: -l
* CHANFIX (services@services.int) has joined #windows
* services.int sets mode: +o CHANFIX
* CHANFIX sets mode: -bbbb *!*@152.3.* *!*@thefoundry.co.uk *!*@*.no *!*@*.
duke.edu
* CHANFIX sets mode: -b *!*@pool-141-153-*.mad.east.verizon.net
* CHANFIX sets mode: +o BBS
<CHANFIX> 10 clients should have been deopped.
<CHANFIX> 1 client should have been opped.
```

```
* CHANFIX (services@services.int) has left #windows
*** 5 minutes later ***
* CHANFIX (services@services.int) has joined #windows
* services.int sets mode: +o CHANFIX
* CHANFIX sets mode: +ooo Zorlak WinSpy WinInfo
<CHANFIX> 3 clients should have been opped.
* CHANFIX (services@services.int) has left #windows
```

## Interesting CHANFIX Facts

EFnet server operators cannot manually op or de-op anyone unless they are channel operators themselves. EFnet operators also can't join +i channels or bypass bans as on some other networks. This is what makes CHANFIX such a valuable resource.

CHANFIX administrators cannot see into +i channels to find out who currently has ops. All they can see are the scores. This ensures users' privacy on the network, while still allowing the operators to do their jobs.

CHANFIX does not display the nicks of scored ops to the network operators. CHANFIX was designed to provide protection to large, stable channels on EFnet while maintaining the privacy of the users.

CHANFIX is not a replacement for good channel management skills. It is possible to set a ban on CHANFIX, so it will stop indexing and fixing channels that abuse the service. Running a channel on EFnet requires trusted friends and, in most cases, a good set of IRC bots to handle ops and small attacks.

## See Also

For more information on CHANFIX on EFnet, see *http://www.efnet.org/chanfix*. If you are an EFnet user and need a manual CHANFIX, please join the channel #chanfix, but be sure to read the aforementioned URL first.

While CHANFIX itself is closed source, Thomas "Beige" Mannfred Carlsson and Joost "Garion" Vunderink have reverse-engineered CHANFIX's processes and written an open source (*http://opensource.org*) version of CHANFIX. It's currently being used on EFnet in a monitor-only capacity. You can learn more about it at *http://www.garion.org/ocf*.

*—Hunter Pine*

# CHAPTER THREE

# Users and Channels
## Hacks 12–16

Users and channels are the main components in the conceptual model of IRC. Users are the people you talk to, and you can also talk to channels, which contain groups of users. Channels are often built around a particular topic or theme, and one of the problems for any IRC user is finding the right channel to join. This chapter shows you how to find suitable channels by filtering entire channel lists from a network or how to search on a more global scale and find all relevant channels on any public server in the world. To satisfy the curious, there are also hacks to show you how to find users in channels and to try to guess where in the world a particular user is located.

One of the fun hacks in this chapter shows you how to generate interesting statistics. This lets you bring life to the community in your channel by displaying their photos, along with amusing information such as who talks most, who is least popular, and what time of day the channel is busiest.

### Find Relevant Channels and Servers
**#12** If you're new to IRC, one of the biggest problems is working out which network to use. Find a perfect match with one of the search engines for IRC channels.

If you haven't got a clue which IRC network to use, picking a random one is not always the best idea. You may find that the one you choose doesn't cater to your interests. A surefire method of picking the right network is to use an IRC search engine.

One popular IRC search engine can be found at *http://irc.netsplit.de/ channels*. This is maintained by Andreas Gelhausen and uses a collection of IRC bots to connect to hundreds of IRC networks and collect data.

## Finding Help on IRC

Let's assume that you are new to IRC and need some help, so you enter "irc for beginners" into the search box and click on the *Search* button. This will search through all of the IRC networks it knows about, looking for channels with topics that match your search terms. The results are shown in Figure 3-1.

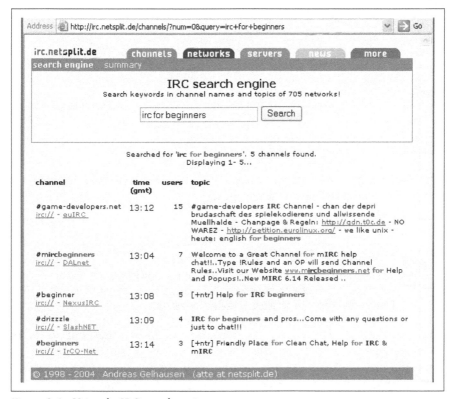

*Figure 3-1. Using the IRC search engine*

The search results are presented as a list of all channels that have topics containing the words you searched for. Each row shows the name of the channel, the name of the network, the time the data was collected, the number of users in the channel, and the topic of the channel. From these results, you can decide which channel you want to join.

If you have an IRC client installed, you can click on the "irc://" link beneath the channel name to automatically connect to that server and join that channel.

## Other Interesting Statistics

You can also use the IRC search engine at *http://irc.netsplit.de/channels* to view statistics about networks and servers. Figure 3-2 shows the growth of the freenode IRC network over the past five years.

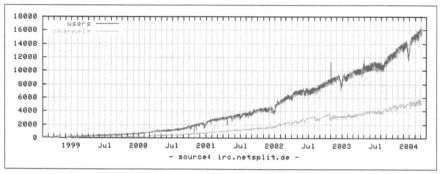

*Figure 3-2. Plotting the growth of the freenode IRC network*

This graph shows the number of users and channels over time. Why not see how your favorite IRC network has grown?

*—Alex North*

## HACK #13    Guess the Time Zone of a User

You're almost off to bed while other users on the channel seem to just get out of bed. That's what happens when IRC is available all over the world, but how can you find out if someone is likely to be awake?

There are several ways to guess the local time of an IRC user, but not all of them are guaranteed to be accurate. The most obvious is to simply ask them what the time is. But what if they aren't around to answer your question? How do you know if they're asleep, not there, or simply ignoring you?

First, you can try to get the user's hostname. You can get it using the /who or /whois command, which reveals information about a user **[Hack #15]**, or maybe you have the hostname already. Most IRC clients will offer you the option of displaying it when a person joins or parts the channel.

In most cases, you'll see a hostname ending with a two-character country code. Take cc123-a.hnglo1.ov.home.nl as an example. As you may know, NL is the abbreviation for the Netherlands. Now you can look up the current time there. One way to do it is using the Time Zone Converter (*http://www.timezoneconverter.com*). You can see it in action in Figure 3-3. If you don't know the capital of the country, open the *Lookup Time Zone by Country* link on the left.

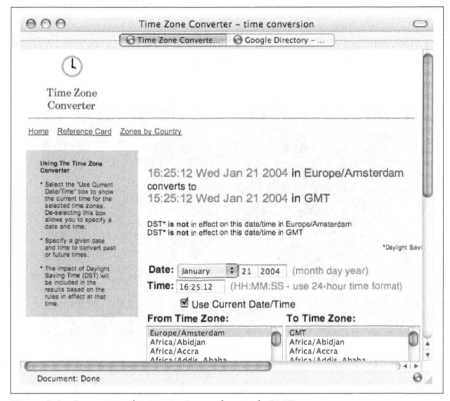

*Figure 3-3. Comparing the time in Amsterdam with GMT*

There is an obvious problem when you deal with countries that have more than one time zone. Also, with domain extensions like .com or .net, you can't be sure about the user's location. Usually, they point at hosts in the United States, but there are six U.S. time zones in the winter and seven in the summer. Also, there is no guarantee that a .com or .net address even points to somewhere in the United States. Fortunately, there's still a way of finding out where these hostnames belong. For example, you can use the Whois service to check out where the owner of the domain name lives. If that doesn't give any useful information, your last chance is to fetch the Whois information for the IP address the user's hostname points at. To get the Whois information, you can use the whois command available on most Unix machines, or you can look for an Internet Whois service, such as *http://www.register.com/whois_lookup.cgi*.

The whois command can be supplied with an IP address or hostname. For example:

```
% whois t-dialin.net
```

will show you something like Figure 3-4. Usually the whois output is very long, so you'll have to read most of it before you find what you're looking for. This screenshot reports on a t-dialin.net IP address. From this, you can tell that a *.t-dialin.net address is usually located in Germany.

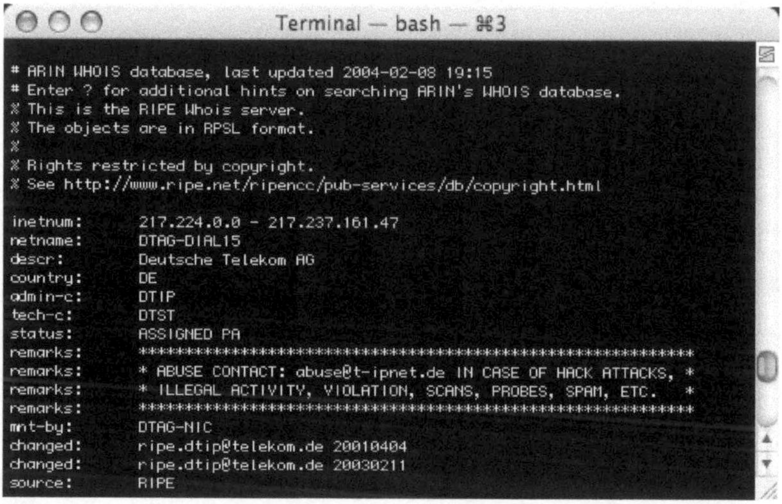

```
        Terminal — bash — ⌘3

# ARIN WHOIS database, last updated 2004-02-08 19:15
# Enter ? for additional hints on searching ARIN's WHOIS database.
% This is the RIPE Whois server.
% The objects are in RPSL format.
%
% Rights restricted by copyright.
% See http://www.ripe.net/ripencc/pub-services/db/copyright.html

inetnum:       217.224.0.0 - 217.237.161.47
netname:       DTAG-DIAL15
descr:         Deutsche Telekom AG
country:       DE
admin-c:       DTIP
tech-c:        DTST
status:        ASSIGNED PA
remarks:       *****************************************************************
remarks:       * ABUSE CONTACT: abuse@t-ipnet.de IN CASE OF HACK ATTACKS, *
remarks:       * ILLEGAL ACTIVITY, VIOLATION, SCANS, PROBES, SPAM, ETC.   *
remarks:       *****************************************************************
mnt-by:        DTAG-NIC
changed:       ripe.dtip@telekom.de 20010404
changed:       ripe.dtip@telekom.de 20030211
source:        RIPE
```

Figure 3-4. Whois results for a t-dialin.net IP address

By now, you should have some idea of where the user could live, but there could still be more you need to know—for example, some countries have more than one time zone. There's still one last way to find out the user's time zone.

Most IRC clients respond to the CTCP TIME request. They send back the local time for the machine they're running on (assuming the clock is set correctly). For example:

```
17:25:41 [ctcp(jibbler)] TIME
17:25:42 CTCP TIME reply from Jibbler: Wed Jan 21 16:25:42 2004
```

As you can see, Jibbler's machine is one hour behind the time zone I'm in. So now that you know what time zone he could be in, I'll leave the calculations (converting the time into a time zone) up to you.

There is one caveat to this approach. Some people log in from a remote box. This box might be somewhere completely different from where they live. There is only one way to be completely sure about a person's time zone, and that is to ask her (and hope she is telling the truth!).

Since some people don't like to receive CTCP messages (or sometimes they make their IRC client ignore them), it's a good idea to try the methods described earlier first, before falling back to the CTCP TIME approach.

*—Wilmer van der Gaast*

## HACK #14 Study Channel Statistics with pisg

Most IRC clients will give you the option of saving messages to a log file. Generate entertaining statistics from these log files.

*pisg* is the Perl IRC Statistics Generator. It's available from the web site *http://pisg.sourceforge.net* and is one of the most popular IRC statistics generators in use today. This hack will show you how to use it to create amusing statistics for your channels and display them to everybody on the Web.

### Running pisg

The most important thing you need in order to run *pisg* is a log file. This log file should contain timestamps so *pisg* can tell when each message was sent. *pisg* supports several log file formats, including those used by mIRC, XChat, Eggdrop, *irssi*, *infobot*, and PircBot. You will also need Perl in order to run *pisg*.

**Editing pisg.cfg.** Editing *pisg.cfg* should be your first step. Set up a channel item that corresponds to the options you would like for your channel. This lets you specify the name of the channel, the log file to read from, the format of the log file, the maintainer of the log file, and the name of the output file, for example:

```
<channel="#irchacks">
Logfile = "#irchacks.freenode.log"
Format = "mIRC"
Maintainer = "Bob"
OutputFile = "irchacks.html"
</channel>
```

Once everything is set up, it's just a simple case of executing the *pisg* script:

```
% ./pisg
```

*pisg* will then tear away at your log files and churn out its statistics. In a matter of seconds to minutes (depending on your computer's speed and the size of the log), you will have a file called *irchacks.html* (or whatever else you called it) containing all of the statistics.

## Publishing pisg Statistics

Copy the output HTML file to somewhere that can display web pages. Any old web server will do the job, as it is just a static HTML page with no server-side content.

If you run your own web host, you could set the *OutputFile* to be a full path in a directory where the document would be visible on the Web. On a Unix/Linux box, you could even set up a *symlink* to the file. Wherever you decide to place the HTML file, you must also ensure that the files from the *gfx* directory are in the same place. These are used to create the colored bar charts in the *pisg* output.

**Setting up statistics options.** *pisg* has more configuration options than you can shake a stick at. They are generally well documented. One common option to change is to use ShowWords and SortByWords instead of sorting by number of lines (which is more vulnerable to users attempting to pad their stats).

**Nickname tracking.** *pisg* has automatic nickname tracking. When it is enabled, this feature watches for people who change their IRC nickname and will merge the statistics for two nicknames if it thinks it is appropriate. Unfortunately, many channels have periods of silliness in which people may temporarily play a game of "musical nicks," or various people may switch to the same nick temporarily. This can seriously mess up the statistics. If this is an issue, you can use *user lines* instead.

**User lines.** User lines are little lines in the configuration file that contain information about a user. They support several options:

```
<user nick="Fennec" alias="Fennec* Foo* Jacob* Jake|PDA" sex="m"
    link="http://fennec.homedns.org">
```

The user's nick is the name of the user, as it will appear on the stat page. The aliases are all other nicknames that should be considered to be the same user. Wildcards are allowed with the * character, but they have a tendency to slow down statistics generation. The sex can be set to m or f and will cause the name to display as blue or pink and will also set several pronouns to use, for example, "he" or "she" instead of "he/she."

Either nickname tracking or user lines is necessary for a meaningful *Users With Most Nicknames* section.

Other useful options available for user lines include the ignore="y" option, which can be added to ignore a user. This is often applied to bots; however, some channels also include their bots in statistics, and it can be particularly amusing if the bots talk as much as some regular users.

**Photos and photo galleries.** If you can cajole a channel's user base into sending pictures of themselves (or if you manage to track them down, stalk them, and take pictures yourself), you can use *pisg* as a sort of impromptu photo gallery. First, set your `ImagePath` to where the images will be accessible. Then you can add `pic="nickname.png"` to each user line.

With `PicHeight` and `PicWidth`, you can set a default picture height and width for your page. Dimensions of approximately 66×48 pixels allow for a compact but effective gallery.

Setting a user's `bigPic` option will cause the user's picture to link to the specified file. Including a wildcard as a user's picture will cause one of the pictures that match the wildcard for that user to be randomly selected. Setting the `UserPics` option will allow more than one picture per row. The `DefaultPic` option will allow you to set up a default user picture.

**Headers and footers.** A custom header (or footer) with some spiffy and topical images or a quote is a nice way of adding a personalized touch to your statistics. This should be in HTML (ideally, XHTML). For example, here are the contents of a generalized header file:

```
<table border="1"><tr><td>
 <table border="0">
  <tr><td><img src="image.png" alt="caption" /></td>
      <td align="center"><div align="center">
       Spiffy amusing headline here!
        <hr />
        <font size="-4"><span style="color: #AAAAAA; font-size: 9px;">
         Informational byline here.
        </span></font>
       </div></td>
       <td><img src="picture.png" alt="Caption" /></td>
   </tr>
  </table>
</td></tr></table>
```

Change *image.png*, *picture.png*, the captions, and the headline/byline as you see fit. This header works well with images approximately 48 pixels high.

## The Results

If you've set everything up correctly, you'll end up with something like Figure 3-5, with a colorful bar chart showing which times of the day are most active, along with pictures of each user. This bar chart is interesting in that it shows activity starting at 8 a.m. and steadily growing before falling back down at lunchtime. Even IRC users have to stop for lunch.

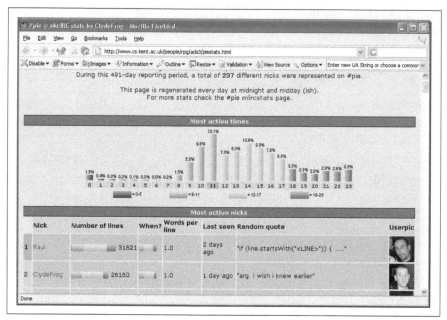

Figure 3-5. Output from pisg, showing activity periods and user info

pisg also generates several other pieces of information that are not readily obvious, such as the *Big Numbers* section, shown in Figure 3-6. This shows who asked the most questions, who shouted the most, who was most aggressive, who was most disliked, and who was the happiest.

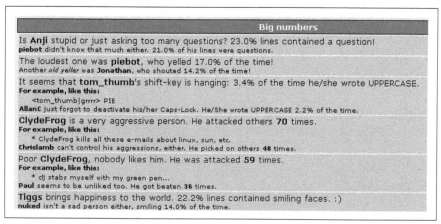

Figure 3-6. Some of the other statistics obtained from pisg

The *pisg* web site (*http://pisg.sourceforge.net*) contains links to hundreds of real examples of *pisg* in action.

—*Thomas Whaples*

# Find Users in Channels

### #15

Finding someone on IRC is not always that easy, particularly if you don't know his exact nickname. Write some scripts and discover who's in a channel.

Sooner or later, you will probably want to write an IRC gadget that finds specific people in a channel (and possibly sends them a message or does something else to them). In a usual scenario, you can get the list of people dwelling in the channel quite easily, with varying efficiency depending on what approach you take.

Let's take a look at the problem from several different perspectives and see how to solve it in various programming environments.

## Nick Seeking

You could have different criteria for your search. Perhaps you just want to examine whether a user with a given nick is around on the channel. For example, you could be writing a simple !seen robot, which records the time of the last visit of a given person (usually identified by her nick), and you want to check whether the queried nick is actually present on the channel.

If you are interested only in the nick, you could use the NAMES #channel command. This is the command that is automatically executed whenever you join a channel. The command returns a few lines of 353 numeric, ending with the 366 numeric [Hack #78]. One sample line could look like this:

```
:x.fn.net 353 nickseek @ #irchacks :DeadEd MD87 Monty dg @Jibbler +elvum
+pasky
```

As you can see, the command reveals not only the nicknames of all users in that channel, but also their status. Channel operators will have nicknames that start with @, half-opped users will start with %, and voiced users will start with +. However, there's a danger here: if the user is both opped and voiced, only the op status will be shown in the NAMES list. When the user loses his op status, he will still be voiced, but you will not know about it. Even some popular IRC clients suffer from this problem, unfortunately.

## Advanced Search

If you want anything more than just a nickname, NAMES will not be very helpful. You could get more information by sending a WHOIS for each individual nickname, but that would be tedious, especially on larger channels. You will need to use something more elaborate, and the WHO #channel command is a perfect fit. It returns each user on a separate line (as a set of 352 numerics and terminated by a 315 numeric) with a rich set of additional information, for example:

```
:x.fn.net 352 nickseek #irchacks ~pasky pasky.or.cz irc.fn.net pasky H+ :0
IRC Name
```

The first bit of useful information you get to see is the host mask. This shows where the user is coming from—~pasky@pasky.or.cz in this case. It is followed by the name of the server that the user is connected to. Some IRC networks (freenode for example) have hidden internal topology to prevent targeted DDoS attacks—in that case, this item will always be irc.freenode. net and is mostly meaningless.

Next is the user's nickname (pasky) and a flag indicating whether the user is Here or Gone. A user can change this flag by using the AWAY command, which is typically invoked by typing **/away reason** in an IRC client. The user status (op, half-op, voice) is also appended to this flag, if appropriate. A * will be appended to the flag for IRC operators. After the colon is a number that represents the distance between your server and the other user's server (see the earlier remark about hidden network topology). Everything after that represents the user's IRC name.

## A Strategy for Finding Users

You already know how to extract the necessary information from an IRC channel, so now the question is when to extract it. This largely depends on the purpose of your project, but there are two feasible approaches. One is to just execute the WHO command every time you need to check the channel list. This is a very simple approach that certainly works; however, it is terribly inefficient and becomes a bottleneck when you need to check the list very often.

The alternative approach is to capture the WHO output once and then watch the JOIN, PART, KICK, QUIT, and MODE commands, updating the in-memory list on your own. This list tracking is more complicated, but if you need to get the list more frequently, it is the only sensible way to do it. Of course, you won't be able to monitor the status of the AWAY flag using this approach, but that is not too much of a loss.

## The Code

The first piece of code for this hack is based on the ultimate shell IRC client [Hack #41]. You can implement a user lookup in this script. You will need to add the lookup function to the script:

```
function lookup () {
    chan=$1;
```

```
    host=$2;
    echo "WHO $chan"
    while read input; do
        input=`echo "$input" | tr -d '\r\n'`

        # WHO item
        num=`echo "$input" | cut -d " " -f 2`
        if [ "$num" -eq "352" ]; then
            thishost=`echo "$input" | cut -d " " -f 6`
            if [ "$host" = "$thishost" ]; then
                return 0;
            fi
        fi

        # Stop WHO
        if [ "$num" -eq "315" ]; then
            break;
        fi
    done
    return 1;
}
```

This function checks whether there is anyone on a channel from a given host. This way, it should be trivial to alter the code to match for different criteria. Note that, ideally, the numeric checking should be part of the main input loop instead of having another one in the function, since the server could send us anything between the WHO request and the delivery of the first 352 numeric.

**Finding users with Net::IRC.** Shell scripts aren't everyone's favorite cup of tea, so now you can implement the same function for Net::IRC **[Hack #33]**, by adding a few extra features along the way. Instead of looking for something specific in the WHO output, you can just insert the entire output into a hash:

```
# Indexed by nick, contains list of people.
use vars qw (%userlist);

# Working copy, it is copied to %userlist when complete.
my %who;

sub on_whoreply {
  my ($self, $event) = @_;

  # Split the WHO reply message into its separate arguments.
  my ($me, $chan,  $ident, $host, $server, $nick, $flags, $data)
      = $event->args ();
  my (@z) = $event->args ();

  # Process the flags.
  my ($gone, $serverop, $op, $halfop, $voice) = (0, 0, 0, 0, 0);
  foreach my $flag (split (//, $flags)) {
```

```
      if ($flag eq 'G') { $gone = 1; next; }
      if ($flag eq '*') { $serverop = 1; next; }
      if ($flag eq '@') { $op = 1; next; }
      if ($flag eq '%') { $halfop = 1; next; }
      if ($flag eq '+') { $voice = 1; next; }
    }

    # Process the ircname and hopcount.
    my ($hops, $realname) = split (/ /, $data, 2);

    # Insert the newly extracted record to a working user list.
    $who{$nick} = {
      host => $ident . '@' . $host, server => $server,
      gone => $gone, serverop => $serverop,
      op => $op, halfop => $halfop, voice => $voice,
      hops => $hops, realname => $realname
    };
}

$conn->add_handler ('whoreply', \&on_whoreply);

sub on_endofwho {
  my ($self, $event) = @_;

  # The working user list (%who) is ready, so switch over the main one.
  %userlist = %who;
}

$conn->add_handler ('endofwho', \&on_endofwho);

# This triggers the update.
sub update_userlist {
  my ($conn, $channel) = @_;

  # Clean up the working user list.
  %who = ();
  $conn->who($channel);
}
```

When you want to fill the %userlist hash, you simply have to call update_
userlist($conn, '#channel'). It may take a few seconds to actually get the
results you're after, so you can put a hook to on_endofwho() in order to get
notified once the operation is complete. The obvious issue with the preceding code is that it does not work if you want to work on more than one
channel at once. Fixing this is left as an exercise for the reader, but it should
be trivial—just extend %userlist and %who to be indexed by a channel name
first.

**irssi.** If you are making scripts for the irssi IRC client **[Hack #24]**, you will
surely be delighted to read that the client keeps track of the user list for you.

First, you need to get the channel object—*irssi* passes it to your event hook, or you can get it by doing this:

```
$server = Irssi::server_find_tag('ServerTag')
$server->channel_find('#channel')
```

Then you can get a list of all the associated nick objects through `$chan->nicks()` or a specific nick by `$chan->nick_find('nick')`. You can even find nicknames by searching for a matching host mask, for example:

```
$chan->nick_find_mask('nick!ident@*.example.com')
```

The nick object features the same properties as the hash element of our previous Net::IRC code, except that it does not provide the server element.

**PircBot.** PircBot **[Hack #35]** also maintains an internal user list for each channel it is in, so you don't have to worry about maintaining it manually. If your PircBot is already in the channel #irchacks, you can get an array of user objects for that channel by calling the getUsers method, for example:

```
User[] users = getUsers("#irchacks");
```

Each User object contains a getNick method that returns the user's nickname, so to print out all the nicknames in #irchacks, you can loop through each element of the array:

```
for (int i = 0; i < users.length; i++) {
    User user = users[i];
    String nick = user.getNick();
    System.out.println(nick);
}
```

Now that you know how to find other users on IRC, you can spend more time enjoying chatting.

—*Petr Baudis*

## Filter Channel Lists

**#16**

Even if you've already found a satisfactory IRC network, you may have missed some interesting channels. Discover them in the output from the LIST command.

One way of finding a relevant channel on a particular IRC network is to ask the network for the list of channels currently in use. Apart from guessing the names of these channels or finding them by word of mouth, you can apply appropriate filters to the list of all the available channels. To acquire such a list, you can use the LIST command, which returns the list of all public channels, together with their topic and number of users.

## The Code

You can use the skeleton code from the RSS to IRC hack [Hack #66], again using the Net::IRC Perl module [Hack #33]. For improved performance, you should precompile the regular expressions that get passed from the command line, as you will be matching them over and over many times. Eventually, you can use *printf* to pretty-print the matching channels with the columns nicely aligned.

Save the following as *filterlist.pl*:

```perl
#!/usr/bin/perl -w
# filterlist.pl - Filter a list of channels based on given criteria.
# MIT licence, (c) Petr Baudis <pasky@ucw.cz>.

use strict;

### Configuration section.
use vars qw ($nick $server $port);
$nick = 'filtelst';
$server = 'irc.freenode.net';
$port = 6667;

### Preamble.
use Net::IRC;

### Arguments munching and data structures setup.
# Arguments.
use vars qw ($chanre $topicre $userlimit);
($chanre, $topicre, $userlimit) = @ARGV;
$chanre ||= ''; $topicre ||= ''; $userlimit ||= 0;

# Precompile the patterns.
$chanre = qr/$chanre/i;
$topicre = qr/$topicre/i;

# List of matched channels, and maximal length of each field for pretty-
printing.
use vars qw (@channels $chanlen $userlen);

# This will eventually print out the channels list when it gets called.
sub list_channels {
  my (@channels) = @_;
  foreach my $chan (@channels) {
    my ($channel, $topic, $usercount) = @$chan;
    printf ("\%-${chanlen}s \%${userlen}d \%s\n", $channel, $usercount,
$topic);
  }
}

### Connection initialization.
use vars qw ($irc $conn);
```

```
$irc = new Net::IRC;
$conn = $irc->newconn (Nick => $nick, Server => $server, Port => $port,
                       Ircname => 'Channels List Filter');

### The event handlers.
# Connect handler - we immediately try to get the channels list.
sub on_connect {
  my ($self, $event) = @_;
  $self->list ();
}
$conn->add_handler ('welcome', \&on_connect);

# Received one channel item.
sub on_list {
  my ($self, $event) = @_;
  my (undef, $channel, $usercount, $topic) = $event->args;

  # Filter.
  return unless ($channel =~ $chanre);
  return unless ($topic =~ $topicre);
  return unless ($userlimit == 0
                 or ($userlimit < 0 ? $usercount <= -$userlimit
                                    : $usercount >= $userlimit));

  # Enqueue for listing.
  push (@channels, [ $channel, $topic, $usercount ]);

  # Update the pretty-printing skids.
  $^W = 0; # Undefined $chanlen.
  $chanlen = length ($channel) if (length ($channel) > $chanlen);
  $userlen = length ($usercount) if (length ($usercount) > $userlen);
  $^W = 1;
}
$conn->add_handler ('list', \&on_list);

# Received the whole channels list.
sub on_listend {
  my ($self, $event) = @_;
  list_channels (@channels);
  exit;
}
$conn->add_handler ('listend', \&on_listend);

# Fire up the IRC loop.
$irc->start;
```

## Running the Hack

The script takes three arguments. The first one is a regular expression that
will be used to filter the name of each listed channel (including the channel
prefix, such as # or +). This regular expression can be left empty to find all

channels. The second argument is another regular expression, which is used to filter the channel topics. The third and final argument is a population limit. If it is a positive number, at least that many users must be in the channel. If this argument is negative, there must be at most that many users in the channel. If the last argument is zero or missing, no user-count checking is performed.

The script returns a list of matching channels, together with a user count and topic for each one, all slickly formatted. Here's an example where you want to find all channels with names that end in a "nonword" character followed by two "word" characters, such as "-cs" or ".cz", common notation for national channels. The channels' topics must also contain "linux" and contain at least three users:

```
% ./filterlist.pl '\W\w\w$' 'linux' 3
#linux.cz 134 ??? linux | toto neni hotline. this is not a hotline.
#linux.hu  15 nullinux
#linux-kr   4 Linux @ Korea
#linux.pl 208 potrzebuje kogo¶ co programuje w borlandzie /msg linuxer
```

Don't forget to adjust the configuration section of the script before executing it. Prepare some good activity to perform while the script is running, as it can take quite some time to complete. Also, read the next section if you are running this on a large IRC network and it gets disconnected before it has finished running.

## Hacking the Hack

The problem with the LIST command is that it can generate a massive amount of output for large IRC networks. The number of channels in the most popular IRC networks ranges from 50,000 to 200,000, and dealing with messages to and from those channels already takes up a fair amount of bandwidth. It then takes quite some time and a lot of bandwidth to fetch and process the list—quite often, a server may disconnect you if you exceed the size of the output buffer (known as a send queue, or *SendQ*). Although this problem is not solved by the IRC protocol itself, some IRC server daemons have addressed the problem by not letting anyone execute the LIST command if the resulting list would be too big, or they may trim it as appropriate.

One way of fixing this problem is to resort to *ircd*-specific features. There are a large number of forks of the original *ircd* as well as various rewrites. The original *ircd* is not used very widely, except on the IRCnet IRC network, as its feature set is rather traditional. EFnet mostly uses *ircd*-hybrid, which is a fork of the original *ircd* codebase (up to Version 6; Version 7 was a large-scale rewrite), and *ircd-ratbox*, which is an *ircd*-hybrid v7 fork. Another original *ircd* fork is *ircu* (Universal *ircd*), which is used on Undernet and Quakenet. If you're not lost yet, another original *ircd* fork is freenode's dancer-*ircd* IRC daemon.

If you are using an *ircu*-based network (such as Quakenet or Undernet), the LIST command comes with an extended syntax. You can chain several comma-separated criteria in its argument. <N and >N will match only channels with fewer than N users or more than N users, respectively. C<N and C>N filters the channels based on the channel age in minutes, while T<N and T>N perform a similar selection based upon topic age. So, to list all channels with three people and a topic set, you would have to send the command:

```
LIST <4,>2,T>0
```

IRCnet chose another approach by providing an original *ircd*-style service called ALIS (Advanced List Service). ALIS provides quite rich means for searching through the channel list—you can search by name (including wildcards), population, mode, and topic. With IRCnet services, you talk through a special SQUERY name_of_service command (SQUERY service HELP usually gathers some useful usage information).

The ALIS command for searching all Linux-related national channels, with a population of at least three, would then look like:

```
SQUERY ALIS :LIST #*.?? -min 3 -t linux
```

Hopefully this hack will have given you a good insight into the variety of methods that enable you to find channels of interest. You may never know what you're missing out on until you look.

*—Petr Baudis*

# Enhancing IRC Clients
## Hacks 17–30

Most IRC clients provide the same basic subset of functionality, but you can really improve your IRC experience by exploiting the features provided by your particular IRC client. Almost all IRC clients offer various shortcuts to prevent your having to type more than necessary. Nickname completion is seemingly universally supported and means you don't have to type the full nickname of another user when you address her. This is particularly useful when you encounter channels that contain users with strange nicknames.

Some of the enhancements introduced by this chapter are simple yet useful, such as adding timestamps to your messages and highlighting keywords from other users. You will also be introduced to IRC scripting, which enables you to customize the functionality of your IRC client. Practical examples include filtering banned words, managing huge debate channels, getting your IRC client to talk out loud, and controlling captions on webcams.

IRC is primarily a text-based chat system, but that doesn't mean you are limited to using just plain text. This chapter shows you how to add colors and other formatting to your messages, making them stand out among the rest.

While older IRC clients could connect to only one server at a time, modern IRC clients allow you to connect to any number of servers. Even the most paranoid user can feel safe using IRC, as this chapter also shows you how to secure your IRC connection or tunnel it through other machines.

 **H A C K**
**#17**

## Automatic Completion of Nicknames
Your client does the typing so that you don't have to.

Often when chatting on IRC you spend much of your time just typing in people's nicknames. This can get tedious, so many clients have some kind of automatic completion facility that works out whose nick you're trying to type and finishes the job for you. This hack will explain the nick-completion functionality provided in several popular IRC clients.

## mIRC

mIRC provides basic tab-completion functionality that will be familiar to anyone who's used a modern command-line interface. Type the first letter or so of a nickname and press the Tab key. mIRC will then complete the rest of the nickname for you, as shown in Figure 4-1. If more than one nick starts with the part that you typed, mIRC will allow you to cycle through the available options by repeatedly pressing the Tab key.

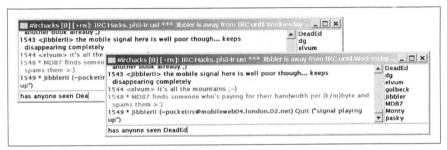

*Figure 4-1. Tab completion in mIRC: before (left) and after (right) pressing Tab*

## irssi

*irssi* provides tab-completion features similar to those found in mIRC. If the nick you tab-complete is the first word in a message, *irssi* assumes that you're addressing someone, and automatically adds a colon to the end of the nick. In addition, the concept of tab completion has been extended to the rest of the *irssi* interface. You can see a list of all user completions by entering **/completion**.

## XChat

XChat offers some more advanced nick-completion features, which are configured in the Interface → Input Box page of the Preferences dialog. As with *irssi*, if the nick you are trying to complete is the first word of a line, XChat will assume that you are addressing the person in question and add an optional suffix to the nick. By default, this suffix is a comma, as shown in Figure 4-2. Unlike mIRC and *irssi*, XChat does not cycle through options if more than one nick starts with the character(s) you entered; instead, it displays all the options and expects you to enter enough extra characters to eliminate the ambiguity.

XChat also has automatic nick completion, a feature that people either love or hate: when it is turned on, any characters at the start of a message that are followed by the nick-completion suffix will be magically expanded when you press the Enter key. The characters will expand into the first matching

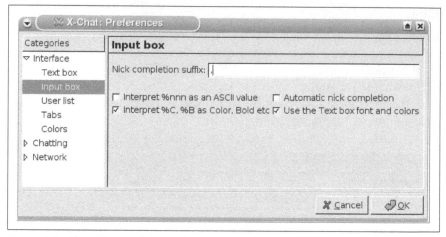

*Figure 4-2. The XChat preferences for nick completion*

nick, alphabetically. An example of how this works and the problems it can cause are shown in Figure 4-3. Autocompletion can be enabled and disabled in the XChat preferences.

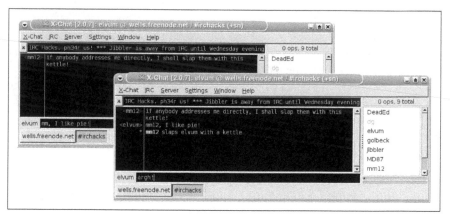

*Figure 4-3. An example of XChat's nick autocomplete feature: before (left) and after (right) pressing Enter*

## ChatZilla

ChatZilla provides tab-completion facilities that are similar to those found in *irssi*. It does not cycle through nicks if there is ambiguity, but completes the nick as far as it can and displays the available options if you press Tab twice quickly. If the nick is the first word of a line, ChatZilla suffixes it with a comma.

## BitchX

BitchX provides tab-completion facilities equivalent to those found in mIRC, but does not cycle through the available options when asked to complete an ambiguous nick. Instead, like XChat, it displays the available options.

*—Steve Jolly*

## HACK #18 Add Timestamps to mIRC Messages

If you leave your IRC client running all the time, learn when each message was sent.

Many people leave their IRC client running 24 hours a day in order to receive private messages even during their absence. It also allows them to scroll up to see what conversations they have missed in all of their channels.

When you listen to a message on your voice mail, you are typically told when it was sent so you know how fresh the message is. If you've just come back from vacation, this can be useful so you know whether it's worth acting on each message. Similarly, it's useful to know when IRC messages were sent during your absence.

mIRC, the most popular Windows IRC client, doesn't display timestamps by default. Figure 4-4 shows mIRC running without displaying any timestamps. From this, it is impossible to know when Monty said, "hello," or when JimH quit from the network—maybe they happened in rapid succession; maybe they didn't. Fortunately, turning on and customizing mIRC timestamps is a piece of cake.

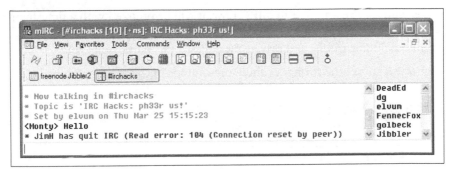

*Figure 4-4. mIRC without timestamps*

## Adding Simple Timestamps

To turn on timestamps, open up the mIRC Options dialog, as shown in Figure 4-5, by choosing Tools → Options from the menu bar. Navigate to the IRC → Messages category and check the checkbox titled *Timestamp Events*. Now click on *OK* to close the dialog.

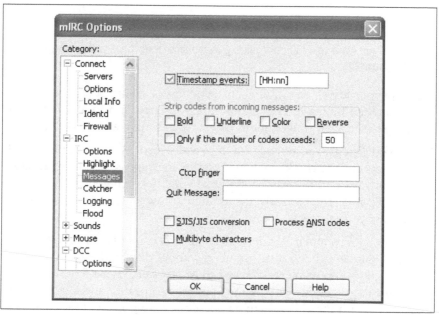

*Figure 4-5. Enabling timestamping of events in mIRC*

When you receive an event in mIRC now, it will be prefixed with a timestamp so you can see when the event occurred. Timestamps will be prefixed to all events, including public and private messages, joins, parts, quits, and so on.

Figure 4-6 shows the format of these timestamps in the main window.

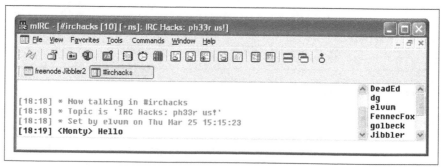

*Figure 4-6. mIRC displaying the default format for timestamps*

## Hacking the Timestamp

Sometimes you might want a greater resolution on your timestamps. After all, the difference between one second and one minute is quite significant when it comes to real-time chat. Conversely, you may like to use the timestamp to show what day it is. This can be useful if you are away from your IRC client for more than a day or if you simply keep forgetting what day it is.

To the right of the *Timestamp Events* checkbox in Figure 4-5, you can specify your own timestamp format using standard time and date identifiers. The default is [HH:nn], which displays the time in hours and minutes with leading zeros, for example [18:01].

Timestamps are best kept as short as possible, so it is probably not a great idea to include the full day name in them. Instead, you can use the short version (ddd), which also has the advantage of being the same length whatever day it is. Seconds (with a leading zero) can be added to the end of the timestamp using ss. So, to use this new and improved timestamp, you just have to enter the following:

    [ddd HH:nn:ss]

This results in the style of timestamp shown in Figure 4-7.

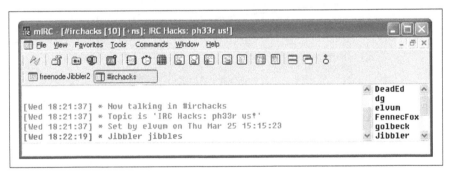

*Figure 4-7. mIRC timestamps now showing the day and seconds*

Investigate the mIRC help file if you want to find out what other time and date modifiers are available. Some useful examples are h to display the hours on a 12-hour clock and tt to display am or pm.

## Highlight Lines in mIRC

Some channels are just too busy for you to keep track of everything that's happening. Highlight lines that contain certain keywords to easily see what's relevant to you.

IRC can be a fun way to kill some time, although it's all too easy to get carried away and find it taking up more time than you'd like. After using IRC for a while, you tend to join more channels that interest you and get to know more people you never knew before. Following the conversation in several active channels is difficult, if not impossible.

## Highlight Your Own Messages

The first useful feature you can add to a client is to make your own messages stand out. This may sound trivial, but it's actually quite useful to be able to scroll back and see when you spoke, as most replies to your messages are likely to be close beneath. This way, you can use your own messages as visual markers to show when you were active in a channel.

To change the color of your own text, open up the mIRC Colors dialog by selecting View → Colors... from the menu bar. In the *Appearance* field, click on the *Own Text* label, as shown in Figure 4-8, and select what color you would like your messages to be.

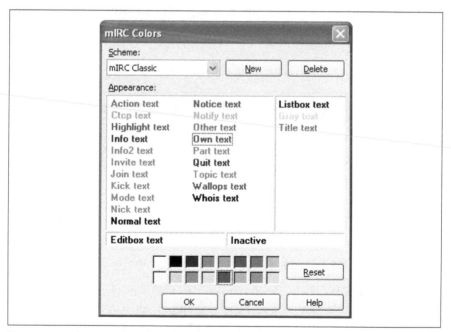

*Figure 4-8. Changing the color of your own text in mIRC*

Click on *OK*, and all of your messages will now be a different color so you can find them more easily.

## Highlight Messages from Other People

Highlighting messages from your friends or bots is also straightforward. If you choose a different color for each user, IRC will become much more intuitive to use. To enable highlighting, open up the mIRC Options dialog by selecting Tools → Options..., and select the IRC → Highlight category, as shown in Figure 4-9. Check the *Enable Highlighting* box, and you will now be able to add some entries to the Highlight List.

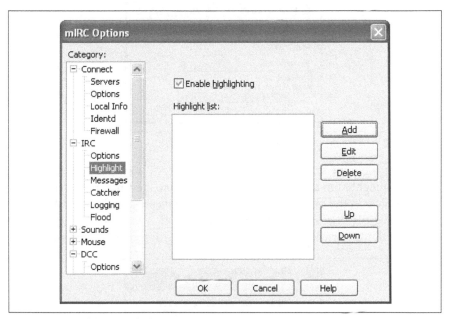

*Figure 4-9. Enabling highlighting in mIRC*

To add a new entry to the highlight list, click the *Add* button. Figure 4-10 shows how to highlight a line that has been sent by a bot called Monty. Monty's nickname is entered in the first text box, and a color is chosen from the *Color* drop-down list (in this case, the chosen color is orange). Select *Nickname Only* from the *Match On* drop-down list. All messages sent by Monty will now be colored orange.

## Highlight Messages Containing Keywords

The most useful reason for highlighting a line is so you can tell if people are talking about you or trying to attract your attention. Add a list of your nicknames or aliases, separated by commas, as shown in Figure 4-11. Pick a color and select the highlight rule to match on the message only.

*Figure 4-10. Highlighting messages sent from Monty*

Whenever someone sends a message that contains "jibbler" or "paul," the line will be highlighted in the color you chose. To make it even harder to miss this, you can click on the button underneath *Play Sound* so it reads Beep. As well as highlighting the line, mIRC will now also beep at you so you can even leave mIRC minimized without worrying about missing anything important.

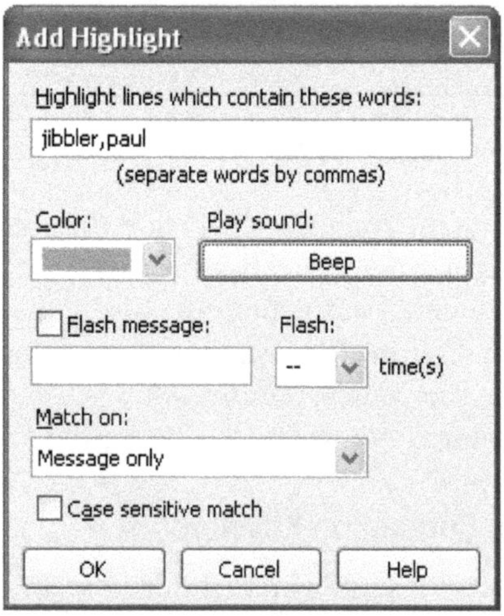

*Figure 4-11. Highlighting messages that contain your name or nickname*

Now you can concentrate on your work and leave your IRC client to do the arduous task of working out when you need to look at it.

**Automate mIRC with Scripting**

mIRC is already a friendly and easy-to-use IRC client. Master its scripting
capabilities to automate lots of useful tasks.

mIRC is one of the most popular IRC clients available for Windows, and it
comes complete with a robust scripting engine. Thousands of ready-to-run
scripts are available from sites like *http://www.mircscripts.org*, although it is
often hard to find a script that does *exactly* what you want, which is why
many people decide to write their own scripts, or alter existing ones.

### Opening the Scripts Editor

mIRC comes with its own integrated scripts editor (Figure 4-12), which can
be accessed by pressing Alt-R while the client is active.

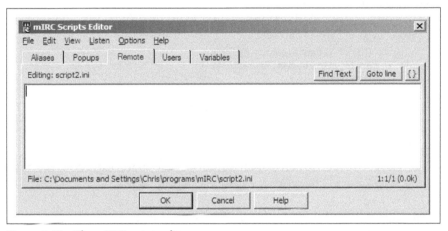

*Figure 4-12. The mIRC scripts editor*

The five tabs in the scripts editor are Aliases, Popups, Remote, Users, and
Variables. Almost all scripts fall into the Remote section. Remote means that
the script can respond to remote events, such as people joining a channel or
your connecting to an IRC server.

### Making a Bad Word Banner

One of the most common types of script is the bad word banner, which bans or
kicks users who say a bad word. To do this, the script must be supplied with a
list of bad words, and it must "listen" for these words in channel messages.

To make the script nice and flexible, you can use a text file to store the list of
bad words. First, you need to make the file, so create a file called *badwords.
txt* in your mIRC directory (for example, *c:\Program Files\mIRC\*) and place

some bad words in it, one per line. If you want, you can also match phrases that contain spaces, as shown in Figure 4-13.

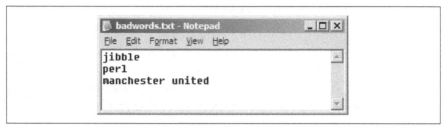

*Figure 4-13. The list of bad words*

Save the bad words list and return to mIRC. Now open up the script editor (using Alt-R again) and make sure that the Remote tab is selected. Add the following code:

```
alias matchbad {
  set %i 1
  while (%i <= $lines(badwords.txt)) {
    if ($read(badwords.txt,%i) isin $1-) {
      return $true
    }
    inc %i
  }
  return $false
}
```

This script will return $true if the given phrase matches a bad word, or $false if it doesn't. The script is explained step-by-step:

**alias.** This tells mIRC that you are creating an alias for a group of commands—instead of the main part of the script doing these commands over and over again itself, you can group them into an alias, which lets us repeat the code contained within it easily. The alias you have made is called matchbad. The word immediately following the alias command is the name given to the alias, which executes all the code contained in the outermost curly braces ({ ... }). If you are used to other programming languages, you can think of an alias as a method or function.

**set.** The set command allows us to set a variable so it contains a value. Variables begin with the % character in mIRC scripts. The set command here sets the %i variable to 1.

**while.** As with other languages, the while loop executes a group of commands while a condition is true. The condition in this case is %i <=

$lines(badwords.txt), which roughly translates into English as, "while %i is less than or equal to the number of lines in badwords.txt". $lines is a predefined alias to count the number of lines in a given file.

The code that gets executed while this condition is true is once again included in curly braces and is typically indented for clarity.

**if.** The if statement causes a block of code to be executed only if the condition is true. The read alias used in this condition reads the given line from the specified file, line %i from badwords.txt. The isin operator checks to see if one string is a substring of another. So in this script, it is essentially checking to see if the text in the line read from badwords.txt is in $1-.

$1- is a special variable that returns all the arguments passed to the alias, so if a script calls $matchbad(This is,a test), $1- will be set to "This is a test". There are numerous other variables that reference arguments: $1 and $2 get the first and second arguments, respectively, while suffixing one of these with a - (for example, $1-, $2-, etc.) gives you that argument and everything after it.

**return.** The return function makes the alias return a given value to the caller. In our example, the value $true is returned if the arguments contain a phrase in badwords.txt and $false if it doesn't.

**inc.** The inc command increases a variable by 1 or by an optional specified amount, for example, inc %foo 200.

## Putting It All Together

When you put all of this together, you get an alias that scans through a text file and checks to see if any of the phrases within it are contained in the arguments passed. If they are, it returns $true; otherwise it returns $false.

The next part of the script listens to channel messages and bans users who say a phrase that is banned. To do this, use the on TEXT event, which is triggered whenever mIRC receives a private or channel message.

Add the following text to the script using mIRC's editor. Again, let's examine the code bit-by-bit:

```
on *:TEXT:*:#:{
  if ($matchbad($1-) == $true) {
    mode $chan +b $address($nick,3)
    kick $chan $nick Bad phrase detected!
  }
}
```

**on TEXT.** This event, as mentioned earlier, is triggered on all private or channel messages. The * before the TEXT means that there are no conditions attached relating to you or the user. You can specify user levels here if you want—see the built-in help system by typing **/help user list**. The * after it is a wildcard that matches all text. You could use *e* to match only text with an *e* in it, for example. The # means that only messages sent to a channel will be caught.

**if.** The if statement should be familiar from the alias created earlier. This particular if statement calls the $matchbad alias with the text as a parameter and checks to see if the result equals $true. $1- is the first word of the message and everything after that.

**mode.** This is exactly the same as the /mode command you may have used in mIRC or other IRC clients. The $chan variable contains the name of the channel the message was sent to. The $address alias returns part of a given nickname's address (see /help $address), and the $nick variable contains the user's nickname. The line mode $chan +b $address($nick,3) will place a ban on the user's host.

**kick.** The kick command kicks a given user from the specified channel (with an optional Kick message). This example kicks the user from the channel, with the reason, "Bad phrase detected!" If you want, you can change this to something more fitting.

## Running the Hack

Put both the alias and the on TEXT event into your Remote section using the mIRC script editor, and create a *badwords.txt* file with a few banned phrases in. Now try it out! Note that the on TEXT event will not trigger when you say something, so you will need to use another client or get a friend to help you test the script. Anybody caught saying words on the bad word list will be kick-banned from the channel.

Further information about scripting can be found in the mIRC help system. This is extremely detailed. Simply type **/help** from mIRC (or press F1) to view it.

*—Chris Smith*

**Format Text**

HACK #21 IRC does not limit you to using plain text. Add extra formatting, such as underlining and italics, to your messages.

Even though most IRC clients support color, simpler formatting can sometimes be more effective. Too much use of color tends to annoy people. In such circumstance, channel operators have at their disposal the option of banning the use of color. If this happens, it will still be possible to send messages with simpler formatting. To highlight a particular word in a message, you could underline it. To catch somebody's attention, you could make your message bold. To emphasize something, you could make it italic. All of these options are possible, regardless of channel restrictions.

## Formatting Text in mIRC

mIRC lets you view and send formatted text. Many other IRC clients behave in similar ways. Three main types of text formatting are available from mIRC. All of these can be accessed by keyboard shortcuts. These styles are complementary, so you can make text both bold and underlined, for example.

**Bold.** When composing a line or message, the text can be formatted as bold by pressing Ctrl-B. You will see a control character appear in your message. Anything you type after this will appear in bold. You will not see the result of this until you actually send your message to the server.

**Underline.** You can underline part of your message by pressing Ctrl-U. This will cause a control character to be inserted into your message. Everything after this character will be underlined.

**Italic or reversed.** Italic text can also be used. However, because some clients are incapable of rendering italic text, you will find that most clients (including those that *can* render italic text) display this as normal text with the background and foreground colors swapped. For this reason, it is also known as reversed text formatting and can be achieved in mIRC by pressing Ctrl-R.

**Normal.** To return text to its unformatted state, press Ctrl-O. This removes all formatting, even if more than one style has been applied.

Combinations of these options are illustrated in Figure 4-14.

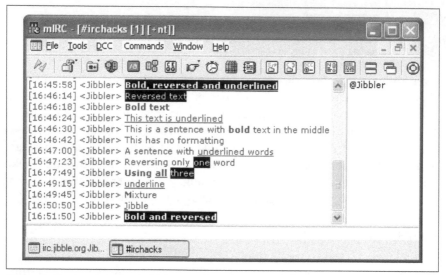

*Figure 4-14. Combinations of formatting rendered by mIRC*

## Formatting Text with a Bot

Formatting text with the aforementioned attributes is simpler than applying colors, as only one control character is required for each style. There are no parameters to add after each style character.

**Bold.** Bold text can be achieved by prefixing the text with ASCII character 0x02, which can be represented in Unicode as \u0002. The following Java code creates a bold IRC message:

```
String bold = "\u0002This is bold";
```

**Underline.** Text can be underlined with ASCII character 0x1F, which can be represented in Unicode as \u001F.

```
String underlined = "\u001FThis is underlined";
```

**Italic or reversed.** Italic or reversed text is formatted with ASCII character 0x16, or Unicode character \u0016.

```
String reversed = "\u0016This is reversed";
```

**Normal.** To remove all formatting from a message, use ASCII character 0x0F, or Unicode character \u000F. Any text after this point in the message will return to its normal state, unless other formatting characters are applied again.

```
String mixture = "\u0002Bold\u000F and gone";
```

## Formatting Text with PircBot

The Colors class in the PircBot Java IRC API **[Hack #35]** contains useful constants, not only for coloring, but also for formatting text with these styles. Using these is probably easier than remembering the Unicode characters.

```
String bold = Colors.BOLD + "This is bold";
String underlined = Colors.UNDERLINE + "This is underlined";
String reversed = Colors.REVERSE + "This is reversed";
String mixture = Colors.BOLD + "Bold" + Colors.NORMAL + " and gone";
```

 Just because you can use formatting doesn't mean you have to. Remember to use it sparingly and only when necessary, otherwise you'll start to annoy people and they may start ignoring you!

Some of the bots covered later in this book use bold formatting to make parts of messages stand out more clearly.

 ## Colorize Text

HACK #22

Not only can you add formatting to text, but you can also add colors. Use them to make your messages stand out.

Color can be useful. With it, one can add extra emphasis to typed words, and make them look prettier and more eye-catching. Color can also be annoying. It is important to steer clear of color combinations that are unnecessary or hard to read. Color is most effective when used sparingly.

Most IRC clients support color, both in terms of displaying colors correctly and allowing you to type messages that contain colors. Colors are achieved by placing special control codes within messages. IRC clients that do not support colors are likely to remove these special codes. At worst, they may actually display the characters used to make up the control codes. This can look rather peculiar, as they are not visible ASCII characters.

For the majority of IRC clients that *do* support color, there are 16 basic colors to choose from. The appearance of these colors is entirely dependant on your IRC client, but fortunately there is agreement on what these colors are. They are listed in Table 4-1.

*Table 4-1. IRC color codes*

| 0 | White | 8 | Yellow |
|---|-------|---|--------|
| 1 | Black | 9 | Green |
| 2 | Dark blue | 10 | Teal |
| 3 | Dark green | 11 | Cyan |
| 4 | Red | 12 | Blue |
| 5 | Brown | 13 | Magenta |
| 6 | Purple | 14 | Dark gray |
| 7 | Olive | 15 | Light gray |

## Using Colors in mIRC

mIRC fully supports the set of 16 basic colors. When you are writing a message, you can change the color by pressing Ctrl-K. This inserts a special control character into the message and pops up a small window with a list of all 16 colors, as shown in Figure 4-15. If you click on one of these colors, it will insert the number for that color. Anything you type after this will be displayed in your chosen color.

*Figure 4-15. Sending colored messages from mIRC*

When composing a message, you will notice that color does not show until you have sent it to the server. You will, however, be shown the color codes that will be used. You can use more than one color in the same message. Unlike HTML, you do not need to end these color code "tags"—if you want to start using a new color, just enter a new color code and mIRC will forget about the old color, as shown in Figure 4-16.

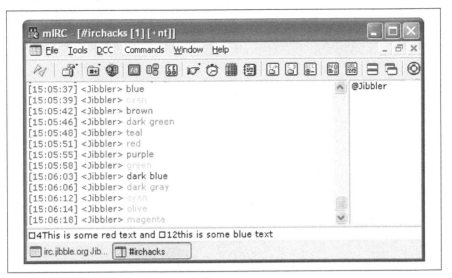

*Figure 4-16. Using red and blue text in the same message*

## Backgrounds

mIRC uses a pure white color for its default background, so it may not make sense to send white text. Unfortunately, not all IRC clients use the same background color, so this is another thing you will need to take into account when formatting text. Some clients, particularly those with Unix origins, use black backgrounds, so it may not even make sense to use black text!

Fortunately, you can specify the background color as well as the foreground color. This is done by adding another color code after the foreground color. A single comma is used to separate the two codes, as shown in Figure 4-17.

## Problems with Coloring Numbers

If you wanted to color the number 123 in black, then you may fall foul of a slight problem with the color chooser in mIRC. The color code will be set as 1 (black), but because the next character in the message is also a number, it will result in 23 being colored in cyan (color code 11), rather than 123 being colored in black (color code 1). The solution to this problem is to ensure that all of your color codes contain two digits. That way, any subsequent digits will be interpreted as being part of the message text instead of a color code. If your desired color code consists of one digit, simply bulk it up by adding a leading zero.

*Figure 4-17. Specifying foreground and background colors*

## Sending Colors from Bots

If you are sending colored messages from an IRC bot, you can insert the special characters into the string that you are going to send. The special character used to signify the start of a color code is ASCII character 0x03, which can be represented by the Unicode character \u0003.

Here are some examples of color codes being placed into Java Strings:

```
String plain = "A plain message";
String red1 = "\u000304A red message";
String red2 = "\u0003" + "04" + "A red message";
String whiteOnBlack = "\u000300,01" + "White text on black background";
```

## Sending Colors from PircBot

The PircBot Java IRC API **[Hack #35]** includes a class called Colors, which can be used to add color to messages. It contains some useful constants so you don't have to keep remembering all the special color codes.

Creating a colored string with PircBot is more intuitive:

```
String red = Colors.RED + "A red message";
```

> Some IRC channels can be configured to reject any messages that contain colors. Older IRC clients may not render these colors correctly or at all. Channel mode +c indicates that colors are not allowed.

Some of the bot hacks later in this book use colored messages to make the text stand out more.

## Play Sounds

### HACK #23

IRC doesn't have to be solely text based. Add excitement by getting your IRC client to play sounds and share those sounds with other users.

One of mIRC's most underused features is the ability to play sounds and to send and receive sound requests. This allows multiple users or whole channels to listen to the same sound at the same time, which is excellent for getting people's attention while they are busy doing something else.

### Enabling Sound Requests

The first thing to do is allow mIRC to handle sound requests. To do this, open the Options dialog (Tools → Options) and browse to the Sounds → Requests category, shown in Figure 4-18.

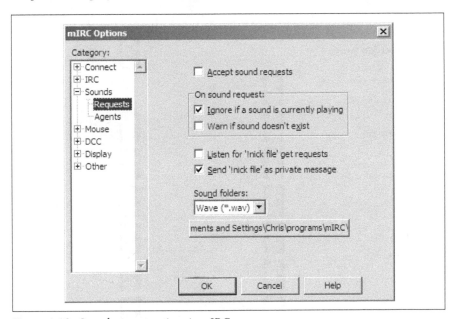

*Figure 4-18. Sound request options in mIRC*

Make sure that the topmost option (*Accept Sound Requests*) is checked, and also check the Listen for '!Nick File' Get Requests option. Both of these will be unchecked by default. These two options allow mIRC to listen for sound requests sent by other users—that is, it will play sounds when others request them and also allow other users to request sounds from you if they don't have them.

## Adding Sounds to mIRC

Now that sound requests are enabled, you will need to put some sound files where mIRC can find them. Going back to the sound requests settings category, look at the button near the bottom—this is the folder where mIRC will look for default sounds. You can change this location by clicking on it and selecting a new folder.

If you do not have any sounds, many web sites offer sound "packs" especially for mIRC. One good site is *http://www.scumperson.eu.org/mircsounds*, but you can find lot more by searching on Google for "mirc sounds download" and similar terms. When you have found some suitable sound files, place them in the directory located earlier. To help you organize your sounds better, you can also place sounds in subdirectories, as shown in Figure 4-19.

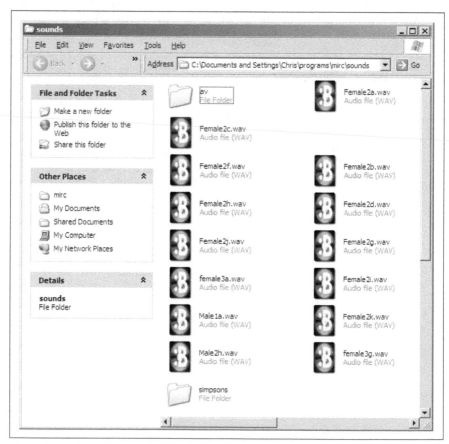

*Figure 4-19. Organizing sound files in the mIRC sounds directory*

Placing files in subdirectories has no effect on mIRC's ability to play them, but it will certainly make it easier for you to manage all of your sounds.

## Sending Sound Requests

To cause someone else to start playing a sound file, you can use the /sound command. Switch to the channel you wish to trigger the sound in, and type:

```
/sound some_file.wav
```

Obviously, you will need to replace *some_file.wav* with the name of one of your sound files. This will cause the sound to be played on the other users' clients. If they don't have that particular file on their computers, they may try to request the sound from you.

## Requesting Sounds

If someone else in your channel plays a sound that you do not have, you can request the file from his IRC client (assuming he has this feature enabled in his options). To request the file *dontpanic.wav* from the user MD87, you would type:

```
!MD87 dontpanic
```

MD87 will then send you the requested file via DCC **[Hack #72]**, as shown in Figure 4-20.

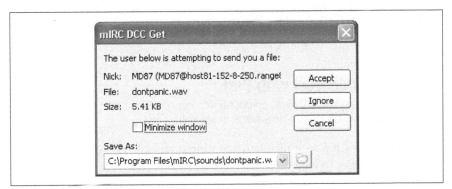

*Figure 4-20. Receiving the requested sound file from the user MD87*

Other users can now instruct your IRC client to play this sound.

## Agents

Another sound-related feature that mIRC boasts is the ability to integrate with Microsoft Agents. These little characters can read private messages or channel text out loud, so you can listen to chat rather than reading it. To enable agent support, open the Options dialog again and select the *Agents* tab from under the *Sounds* menu. If no agents are listed in the drop-down box, you will need to download one. Find full instructions on how to do this (and on how to use almost all of the agent-related features) at *http://www.mirc.co.uk/agents.html*. When you have selected an agent, tick the boxes for events you want the agent to read out loud. For example, ticking just *Private Events* will make the agent read out private messages only. When you receive a private message, an agent will pop up on top of mIRC and read the text, as shown in Figure 4-21.

*Figure 4-21. Using Microsoft Agent from mIRC*

mIRC's sound-related features are quite elaborate and when combined with a script can produce amazing results. The documentation on the sound system is also quite elaborate—be sure to read the details at /help agents and /help sounds.

—*Chris Smith*

### H A C K   Enhance irssi with Perl
### #24
irssi is a popular IRC client. Enhance it with Perl scripts you write yourself or select from the large range available on the Web.

*irssi* is a client with a very nice Perl scripting interface. You don't have to be a Perl programmer to enjoy this fact, as many scripts are already available. In fact, it's hard to find original ideas for new scripts, because everything seems to exist already!

Here we'll demonstrate some interesting scripts that let you see what films people are watching, find out what their real names are, obfuscate text, and so on. All of these scripts (and more) are available for download at *http://www.irssi.org/scripts*. Before you start downloading lots of scripts, now would be a good time to explain how to use them.

## Using an irssi Script

There are two ways to do this. First, of course, you have to download a script. Save it anywhere you want. To try the script, use the /script load command. Then do whatever you want to see how the script works for you. If it doesn't seem to work, don't forget to read the documentation that accompanies the script to see if you have to change any settings to make it work.

If you like the script, just copy it to the *.irssi/scripts/autorun* directory in your home directory. Next time you start *irssi*, the script will be loaded. Of course, if you don't like the script, you can unload it using the /script unload command. Remember that the unload command doesn't accept complete paths to files. Just the filename is enough.

For example, if you have downloaded the *imdb.pl* script and saved it in your home directory, this is how you would load and unload it:

```
> /script load /home/wilmer/imdb.pl
-!- Irssi: Loaded script imdb
> /script unload imdb
-!- Irssi: Unloaded script imdb
```

If the /script command doesn't seem to work, you may need to recompile *irssi* with Perl scripting support, or you may need to manually load the Perl module using the **/load perl** command. If you still can't get it working, please read the *irssi*-building documentation for more information.

Now you can take a look at some scripts of interest and some useful hints.

## See What Film Everyone's Watching

You may have heard of the Internet Movie DataBase at *http://www.imdb.com*. While using IRC, you may also have noticed people with seven-digit numbers after their nickname. Usually, this number corresponds to a film on IMDB. Of course, you can look up the film on IMDB when the user puts it in her nick—but why do that if a script can do it for you?

The script is called *imdb.pl* and can be found at *http://www.irssi.org/scripts/scripts/imdb.pl*. When you load it and someone changes his nick to something with an IMDB number in it, it looks up the name of the film and tells you what it is. Here's an example of it in use:

```
<pengu> i'm going to watch a movie
-!- pengu is now known as tux|0208092
-!- pengu is watching Snatch. (2000)
```

Certainly more informative than just a number.

## Who's Behind That Nick?

Another script you may like is *autorealname.pl* (*http://www.irssi.org/scripts/ scripts/autorealname.pl*). When someone joins a channel, it gets the person's "real name" from the server and puts it in the join message. It looks like this:

```
-!- AxE (Alex Bylund) [~AxE@nextgentel.com] has joined #bitlbee
```

## Strange Dialects

You may have seen some people talk like this on IRC:

```
<Pink> PpfPpmMfm, fmpmfpmppffm pmpmffpmfpmfmppmpm pmpmppppppppffm!
```

There are a lot of strange people on IRC, so it's quite easy to dismiss such a message. It may seem unlikely to you, but this really means something! To find out what it means, you can load the *kenny.pl* plug-in (*http://www.irssi.org/ scripts/scripts/kenny.pl*). It decodes these lines automatically, and it even allows you to write like this, using the /kenny command. When you have the kenny script loaded, the previous line will be rendered like this:

```
[kenny] <Pink> OMG, they killed kenny!
```

This is certainly not the most useful script ever, but still it's fun to play with for a while. Some other encodings you can try are *morse.pl*, *binary.pl*, *dau.pl*, *figlet.pl*, and *foo.pl*, all available directly from *http://www.irssi.org/scripts*.

## Automatically Get Ops When the Channel Is Empty

There is a script called *autocycle.pl* (*http://www.irssi.org/scripts/scripts/ autocycle.pl*), which is useful for regaining operator status if you have lost it. When you're in an unregistered channel and don't have operator status, this script automatically parts and immediately rejoins the channel after the last person has left. This usually makes you the new channel owner and gives you operator status for that channel.

## Keep Everyone Amused When You're Away

Another amusing script is *eliza.pl* (*http://www.irssi.org/scripts/scripts/eliza.pl*). When you're away and people send you a private message, this script generates a reply and sends it back. Although it's not hard for people to find out that they're talking to a bot, it's still good for some very funny conversations.

You can find some very nice Eliza conversations here: *http://www.xs4all.nl/ ~hanb/documents/eliza*.

## What Was That Query About Again?

Sometimes you close a query window because you don't expect a reaction any more, only to find that the person sends a reply a few seconds later. Being a busy person, you don't have the slightest idea what it was about any more. The *queryresume.pl* script (*http://www.irssi.org/scripts/scripts/queryresume.pl*) provides a useful solution. If you have logging enabled, it puts the last lines from the log file in the query window when it opens—usually enough to understand what the person is talking about.

For example, without QueryResume, you might not have any idea what this "wheeee" was referring to:

```
22:16:35 ,--[QueryResume]
22:16:35 | 21:35     pengu| yeah :)
22:16:35 | 21:36     pengu| so now i'm a groupie?
22:16:35 | 21:36     pengu| ;p
22:16:35 | 21:36    wilmer| *grin*
22:16:35 | 21:36    wilmer| yes, you're the first
22:16:35 `--<~/.irssi/irclogs/FLUT/pengu.log>->
22:16:35    -!-    Irssi: Starting query in FLUT with pengu
22:16:35     pengu| wheeee
```

By default, QueryResume gives you the last 10 lines from the logs. If you want more (or fewer) lines, you can change the number using the queryresume_lines setting. For example, to get just five lines, type **/set queryresume_lines 5**.

## Other Interesting Scripts

Many more scripts are available—enough to write another book about. If you haven't found what you're looking for yet, just look at the list on the *irssi* web site at *http://www.irssi.org/scripts*. Likely, someone has already written what you're looking for. If not, maybe it's time to write a script yourself. Unfortunately, there is little documentation about writing *irssi* scripts, so you'll just have to look at other examples to see how things are done.

## The Code

Following is a small example script. It makes a person believe she is in your ignore list, which can help to kill some boring discussions from time to time:

```perl
#!/usr/bin/perl -w

use strict;
use vars qw($VERSION %IRSSI);

# This file is partially based on rainbow.pl
$VERSION = "1";
%IRSSI = (
```

```
            authors     => 'Wilmer van der Gaast',
            contact     => 'lintux@lintux.cx',
            name        => 'Fake-Ignore',
            license     => 'GNU GPLv2 or later',
    );

    use Irssi;
    use Irssi::Irc;

    sub fignore {
            my ($text, $server, $dest) = @_;

            if (!$server || !$server->{connected}) {
                    Irssi::print("Not connected to server");
                    return;
            }

            return unless $dest;
            if ($dest->{type} eq "CHANNEL" || $dest->{type} eq "QUERY") {
                    $text = `date +%H:%M:%S` . ' Ignoring ALL from ' . $text;
                    $text =~ s/[\n\r ]+/ /gs;
                    $dest->command("/msg " . $dest->{name} . " " . $text );
            }
    }

    Irssi::command_bind( "fignore", "fignore" );
```

The %IRSSI hash is used to define some information about the module. This is usually the best place to put the information about your module, such as who wrote it and how he can be contacted. The module defines a couple of subs and, in the end, those subs are linked to either *irssi* commands or events. This example script is tied to a client command, so if you were to type **/fignore** *nickname*, the target user would see a message suggesting that she is being ignored by your client. If you want to know more about event-based scripts, you can take one of the many other scripts as an example. Here is the result from running this script:

```
/fignore brannigan
23:51:29 Ignoring ALL from brannigan
```

*—Wilmer van der Gaast*

HACK
#25

# Connect to Multiple Servers

Use more than one IRC network at a time from a single IRC client.

With an ever-increasing number of IRC servers and networks, the chances are that you're going to want to connect to more than one at a time at some point. Most IRC clients these days have the ability to handle connections to multiple servers at the same time. This hack explains how to do it in some of the more popular clients.

## mIRC

To connect to an additional server in mIRC, bring up the server-selection dialog by clicking File → Select Server. Choose the new server you want to connect to from the *IRC Network* and *IRC Server* drop-down boxes. Ensure that the *New Server Window* checkbox is checked, and then click *Connect to Server*, as shown in Figure 4-22.

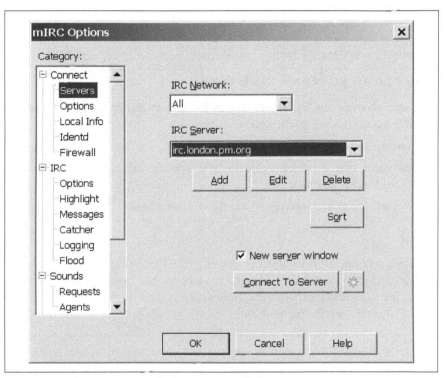

*Figure 4-22. Connecting to multiple servers in mIRC*

A new status window will be opened for the new server, into which you can type /join commands and so on as necessary. Figure 4-23 shows mIRC connected to two IRC servers: freenode and MAGnet. The client has joined the #irchacks channel on the freenode server.

Type **/server -m** *new_server* for a quicker method of adding a new server in mIRC. The -m flag tells mIRC to create a new connection rather than to nuke the existing one. So to create another connection to the freenode IRC network, you would type:

```
/server -m irc.freenode.net
```

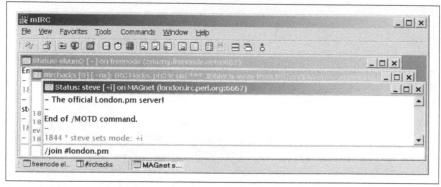

*Figure 4-23. A mIRC client connected to multiple servers*

You can also use the `-j` flag to get mIRC to automatically join a channel when it has connected to the server:

```
/server -m irc.freenode.net -j #irchacks
```

To join more than one channel, you must specify their names as a comma-separated list, for example:

```
/server -m irc.freenode.net -j #irchacks,#java,#jibble
```

## XChat

To open a connection to another server in XChat, bring up the *Server List* dialog by clicking X-Chat → Server List. Choose the new server or network you want to connect to from the *Networks* list, and then click *Connect in a New Tab*, as shown in Figure 4-24.

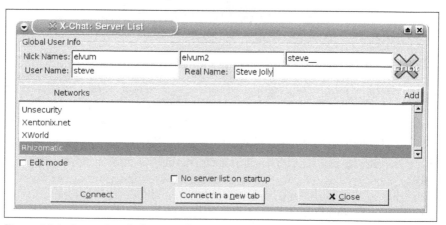

*Figure 4-24. Server List dialog in XChat*

A new tab will be opened for the new server, into which you can type all the necessary /join commands again, as shown in Figure 4-25.

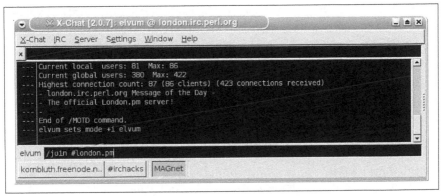

Figure 4-25. XChat connected to two servers

### irssi

To connect to a new server in *irssi*, simply enter the command **/server** **servername**, where *servername* is the domain name of the new server.

*—Steve Jolly*

## HACK    Secure Your IRC Connection with SSL
## #26    Hide your conversations on IRC from prying eyes on the Internet.

Let's face it—IRC was not designed for the paranoid. Messages, commands, passwords, *everything* gets sent to the server unencrypted, which frankly just makes life easy for eavesdroppers. The Internet has demanded a solution to this problem, and the Internet has provided one: SSL, the Swiss Army knife of network encryption solutions. If your IRC server of choice supports SSL, you can open an encrypted connection between your computer and the IRC server and *tunnel* your IRC connection through it, hiding your precious conversations from all eavesdroppers with fewer resources than a national government.

Securing IRC with SSL has a number of advantages over SSH tunneling. Most importantly, no user account is required on the machine at the remote end of the tunnel. Secondly, the information usually remains encrypted at every point between the client and the server, rather than just between the start and end of the tunnel. Finally, the tunnel can be automatically established and destroyed when the IRC client connects and disconnects, relieving the user of the job of starting and stopping a separate SSH session.

> # Security Limitations of SSL Tunneling
>
> While tunneling your connection via SSL can increase the security of your IRC sessions considerably, you should always be aware of the limitations of the method. Most obviously, even if your link to the IRC server is encrypted, there's no guarantee that the links of all the other people on your channel are also encrypted; nor do many networks encrypt data as it is passed between the servers in a network. In addition, SSL tunneling cannot prevent your communications from being monitored by the owner of the IRC server(s) you are connected to nor by key-logging software installed covertly on your computer or the computers of the people with whom you chat. Fortunately for most people, all these possibilities are exceedingly unlikely.
>
> SSL is not the only way to encrypt your IRC connections. "Tunnel Your IRC Connection with SSH" **[Hack #27]** also encrypts your data, at least between the two endpoints of the SSH tunnel. Chapter 13 presents a novel solution in which the data in your message is sent encrypted **[Hack #83]** at the individual message level, maintaining security from client to client.

However, SSL tunneling cannot be used to bypass firewalls in the same manner as SSH.

Many modern IRC clients and servers have SSL support built in. This hack will explain how to establish secure connections with mIRC, XChat, and *irssi*. The use of an external SSL package such as *stunnel* to create the encrypted link will also be explained. To make a secure connection to your IRC server or network, it must support SSL connections at the server end—contact your server administrator or read your network's FAQ to find out if this is the case.

## Securing Your IRC Connection with mIRC

mIRC Versions 6.14 and later support SSL-encrypted IRC connections, but at the time of writing, mIRC does not include the required SSL libraries for legal reasons. Fortunately, all you have to do to install the libraries is download and run the latest self-installing OpenSSL package from *http://www.shininglightpro.com/products/Win32OpenSSL.html*. mIRC's SSL support will then be enabled automatically.

To configure mIRC to connect to a server using SSL, open the FileSelect Server dialog, select your IRC server from the *IRC Server* list, and click the *Edit* button. In the *Edit Server* dialog that appears, change the port number to the port on which the server listens for SSL connections and prefix it with a + to tell mIRC to use SSL when connecting, as shown in Figure 4-26.

Finally, click *OK* and then *Connect to Server* to connect securely to the server.

---

## Self-Signed Certificates

When you connect to a server with SSL, the server presents the client with a *certificate*. This is an electronic document identifying the server and is signed cryptographically to prove that the server is really the computer it claims to be. The certificate is only as trustworthy as the person or company that signed it, and so a number of commercial Certificate Authorities that will sign your server's certificate for a price have come into being.

Rather than pay that price, many IRC servers use *self-signed* certificates that are signed only by their administrators. An SSL connection to a server presenting such a certificate is encrypted just as securely, but there is *no guarantee* that the server you are connecting to is the one you think it is. It is possible (but extremely unlikely) that a sufficiently powerful and motivated eavesdropper could forge a certificate containing the same identifying information and use it to trick you into connecting to a server under their control instead.

---

If your server presents a self-signed certificate, mIRC will display the dialog shown in Figure 4-26. To accept the certificate and complete the IRC connection, click *Accept*.

### Securing Your IRC Connection with XChat

To open a secure IRC connection with XChat, first bring up the *Server List* window by selecting X-Chat → Server List from the main menu. Select your network from the *Networks* list and check the *Edit Mode* checkbox. The *Servers* window should now look like Figure 4-27. Check the *Use Secure SSL* checkbox. To connect to a server that presents a self-signed certificate, you must also check the *Accept Invalid Cert.* checkbox. Most IRC servers listen for SSL connections on a nonstandard port number—if this is the case, you will have to edit the *Servers* list appropriately. Finally, click the *Connect* button to connect securely to the server.

### Securing Your IRC Connection with irssi

Specifying in *irssi* that a connection should be encrypted using SSL is as easy as adding an −ssl parameter to the /connect command. If your server were *irc.example.com* and it listened for SSL connections on port 6668, you would simply launch *irssi* and type:

```
/connect -ssl irc.example.com 6668
```

*Figure 4-26.  mIRC warning that a certificate has been self-signed*

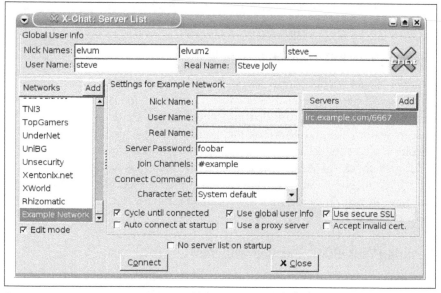

*Figure 4-27.  Setting up an SSL-secured connection in XChat*

*irssi* supports a number of other SSL-related commands, including ones that attempt to verify the authenticity of server certificates before connecting. By default, *irssi* will accept all valid certificates, even self-signed ones. See the *irssi* documentation for further details.

## Securing Your IRC Connection with stunnel

If your IRC client doesn't support SSL natively, you can create a secure connection to the IRC server with a separate package, and then tunnel your IRC connection through it. One such free package is *stunnel*, available for both Windows and Linux/Unix operating systems from *http://www.stunnel.org*. For installation instructions, see the *stunnel* installation FAQ at *http://www.stunnel.org/faq/install.html*. This hack is based on *stunnel* Version 4.0 or later.

To set up *stunnel* to secure your IRC connections, you need to create a configuration file, *stunnel.conf*. On Linux/Unix, this file should go in your home directory. On Windows, it should go in the same directory as the *stunnel* executable. If your server were *irc.example.com* and it listened for SSL connections on port 6668, then for simple IRC session encryption, the contents of the file should be as follows:

```
client = yes
verify = 0
delay = yes
#
[irc]
accept = 6667
connect = irc.example.com:6668
```

Now run *stunnel*. On Linux/Unix, run *stunnel ~/stunnel.conf*. On Windows, just launch *stunnel.exe* from wherever you installed it. Finally, to set up the secure link and tunnel your IRC connection through it, simply tell your IRC client to connect to port 6667 on localhost. The preceding sample configuration file does not prevent *stunnel* from connecting to servers with self-signed certificates: details of how to do so are in the *stunnel* documentation.

The SSL connection will not be made until your IRC client tries to connect, so it is safe and convenient to start *stunnel* automatically by adding it to your Start menu's Startup folder, or by adding the previous command to your *.profile*.

—*Steve Jolly*

## Tunnel Your IRC Connection with SSH

Encrypt your conversation and access IRC servers through firewalls using SSH.

Firewalls are a fact of life these days, and if you want to connect to a private IRC server via the Internet, chances are you're going to have to deal with one. Many firewalls block IRC but allow SSH connections. This hack explains how to take advantage of this fact to *tunnel* your IRC connection via SSH and bypass the firewall.

Unsurprisingly, you will need an SSH client to use SSH. If you run Linux/Unix, then you almost certainly already have an SSH client installed or can easily obtain it from the provider of your operating system. If you use Windows, a number of SSH clients are available. The most popular seems to be PuTTY, which is free and can be downloaded from *http://www.chiark.greenend.org.uk/~sgtatham/putty*. This hack contains instructions for both PuTTY and OpenSSH. You will also need an account on an SSH-accessible machine on the same side of the firewall as the IRC server (perhaps the IRC server itself).

The concept of tunneling is quite simple. The SSH client listens on a port of your choosing on the client machine and forwards everything via the encrypted link to the SSH server. This then passes everything on to a remote machine and port also of your choosing. An additional advantage of tunneling your connection with SSH is that your IRC session is encrypted and thus concealed from prying eyes between the two end-points of the SSH tunnel.

### Setting Up an SSH Tunnel with OpenSSH

Once you can log into the SSH server, creating the tunnel is as simple as adding an extra command-line parameter to *ssh*. For example, let's say that your IRC server is called *irc.example.com* and runs IRC on port 6667, and your SSH server is *ssh.example.com*. The command to connect to the SSH server and set up the tunnel will be:

```
% ssh -L 6030:irc.example.com:6667 username@ssh.example.com
```

This example uses 6030 as the port at the local end of the tunnel, but it could be any port you like. If you use a *privileged* port number between 0 and 1023, you will have to run *ssh* as root. It is usually easier (and safer) to simply choose any unused port from 1024 to 65534.

To connect to the IRC server via the tunnel, tell your IRC client that its server is localhost, port 6030. The IRC client will then connect to the local end of the IRC tunnel, which will forward the data to the other end.

To avoid having to type in the whole command every time, you can add a section to your SSH configuration file that will establish the tunnel every time you connect to the SSH server. Open (or create) the file ~/.ssh/config and add the following lines to the end:

```
Host irc
HostName ssh.example.com
LocalForward 6030 irc.example.com:6667
User username
```

Now you need only run *ssh irc* to connect to the SSH server and establish the tunnel.

Note that the domain name you should use for the IRC server is its internal name. In many cases, this may just be the unqualified name of the server, which in the case of *irc.example.com* would be *irc*.

## Setting Up an SSH Tunnel with PuTTY

PuTTY works in terms of *sessions*, which contain all the configuration details for a connection to a particular SSH server. To add tunneling of IRC connections to an existing PuTTY session, launch PuTTY and load the saved session. Select the Connection → SSH → Tunnels page, shown in Figure 4-28. In the *Add New Forwarded Port* section of the page, enter into the *Source Port* box the port on the local machine that you wish to use as the entrance to the tunnel (for example, 6030). In the *Destination* box, enter the hostname of the IRC server and the port it listens on, separated by a colon (for example, **irc.example.com:6667**). Return to the *Session* page and save the changes that you have just made before connecting to the SSH server. The tunnel will be established, and you can connect to the IRC server by instructing your client to connect to your chosen source port on **localhost**.

## Allowing Third Parties to Bypass the Firewall

Most SSH clients that support port forwarding also allow the user to permit IRC clients running on *any* machine to use the tunnel and bypass the firewall. In OpenSSH, you can do this by adding the -g command-line option. This can be useful in some situations (for example, allowing all staff in a small branch office to access a server at the company headquarters), but you should be aware that if the SSH client machine is not behind a firewall, then *anyone on the Internet* can connect to the hitherto private IRC server. You should always check with your network administrator before enabling third-party access.

—*Steve Jolly*

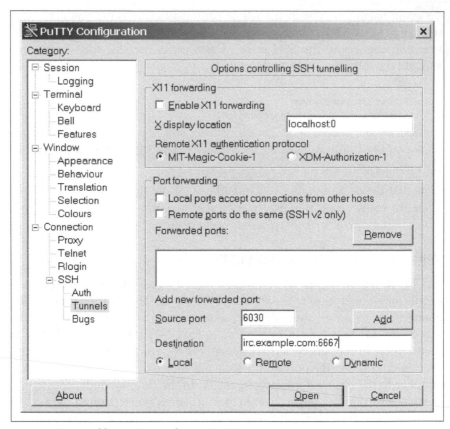

*Figure 4-28. Enabling IRC tunneling in PuTTY*

### HACK #28   Automate Voice Management

Large channels are inevitable targets for abuse. Help prevent problems by creating a client script that is responsible for handing out voice status to deserving users.

Let's say you're the one in charge of managing a huge channel that is dedicated to some important event that's going on. Hundreds of people are joining and leaving and, like any large channel, it will inevitably attract some abusers as well, wanting to flood, swear, and spew out vile colorful text.

Your ban list is already full and a new horde of savages has just entered the channel. What do you do? A simple step would be to *voice* everyone as soon as they join the channel, make the channel moderated, and just *devoice* the user if he becomes abusive. The simple flaw here is that the evildoer can part and rejoin the channel and get voiced.

If you are a channel operator, you can voice another user by entering **/mode #channel +v User**. To moderate the channel, you must enter **/mode #channel +m**. While a channel is moderated, only channel operators and users with voice will be able to talk. Everyone else will still be able to see what's being said, but won't be able to join in with the conversation.

This hack comes in form of an *irssi* script and is implemented in Perl. It does not require any other modules and needs no special configuration, so you simply have to place it into your scripts directory (*~/.irssi/scripts*) and perform /script load autovoice in order to get it running.

The script automatically voices every newcomer on the channel, so make sure you have operator status on the channel or it won't work. However, if anyone gets devoiced, the script will remember this and save the host mask of the offender. If the offender rejoins the channel, she will not get autovoiced again. If anyone manually voices an offender, he will be removed from the blacklist and will be autovoiced if he joins the channel at a later moment. You can inspect the blacklist contents at any time by using the /AUTOVOICE command.

## The Code

This is a fairly simple *irssi* Perl hack, so the comments in the code should explain what is going on. Every *irssi* script should have an %IRSSI hash that contains some basic information and $VERSION that shows the current version number of the script. Other scripts can then extract and use these pieces of information automatically. A good example of this is *scriptassist.pl*, which helps you manage your scripts repository and interfaces the *http://scripts.irssi.org* central *irssi* scripts repository. All good *irssi* scripts should announce themselves when they are loaded, just as ours politely does.

```perl
use strict;
use vars qw($VERSION %IRSSI);
use Irssi;

$VERSION = "0.0.1";
%IRSSI = (
  name        => 'autovoice',
  authors     => 'Petr Baudis',
  contact     => 'pasky@ucw.cz',
  description => 'Smart voice management on a channel',
  license     => 'BSD',
);

# In this blacklist we keep all the offending hostmasks
```

```perl
# Keys: channels, Values: pointers to arrays of strings
my %dmasks;

# This command lists the blacklist's content
sub cmd_autovoice {
  my ($data) = @_;
  foreach my $chan (keys %dmasks) {
    next unless ($dmasks{$chan});
    my $str = "[$chan] ";
    foreach my $mask (@{$dmasks{$chan}}) {
      $str .= $mask . ", ";
    }
    $str =~ s/, $//;
    Irssi::print($str);
  }
}

# Triggered when someone joins a channel
sub event_massjoin {
  my ($channel, $nicks_list) = @_;
  my @nicks = @{$nicks_list};

  return unless ($channel->{chanop});

  # Each nick in a batch...
  foreach my $nickrec (@nicks) {
    my $in_blacklist = 0;
    # Do we keep a blacklist for this channel?
    if (defined $dmasks{$channel->{name}}) {
      foreach my $mask (@{$dmasks{$channel->{name}}}) {
        # Is this user blacklisted?
        if ($channel->{server}->mask_match_address($mask, $nickrec->{nick},
                         $nickrec->{host})) {
          $in_blacklist = 1; last;
        }
      }
    }
    $channel->command("/voice ".$nickrec->{nick}) unless $in_blacklist;
  }
}

# Triggered when someone changes channel mode (including voice/devoice)
sub event_mode {
  my ($server, $data, $nick, $addr) = @_;
  my ($channel, @mmode) = split(/ /, $data);
  my ($mode, @args) = @mmode;
  my $operation;
  my $chanptr = $server->channel_find($channel);

  return if ($nick eq $server->{nick});
  foreach my $mchar (split //, $mode) {
    if ($mchar =~ /[+-]/) { $operation = $mchar; next; }
    if ($mchar =~ /[eIbolk]/) { shift @args; }
```

```
    if ($mchar ne 'v') { next; }

    # This is a voice/devoice
    my $victim = $args[0];
    my $victptr = $chanptr->nick_find($victim);
    if ($operation eq '+') {
      if (defined $dmasks{$channel}) {
        my @masks = @{$dmasks{$channel}};
        for (my $i = 0; $i < @masks; $i++) {
          if ($server->mask_match_address($masks[$i], $victim,
            $victptr->{host})) {
            splice(@masks, $i, 1);
            $i--;
          }
        }
        $dmasks{$channel} = \@masks;
      }
    } else {
      my $in_blacklist = 1;
      foreach my $mask (@{$dmasks{$channel}}) {
        if ($server->mask_match_address($mask,
          $victim, $victptr->{host})) {
          $in_blacklist = 0; last;
        }
      }
      push(@{$dmasks{$channel}}, $chanptr->ban_get_mask($victim, 0))
        unless $in_blacklist;
    }
  }
}

Irssi::command_bind('autovoice', 'cmd_autovoice');
Irssi::signal_add_last('massjoin', 'event_massjoin');
Irssi::signal_add_last('event mode', 'event_mode');

Irssi::print "AutoVoice.PL $VERSION (c) Petr Baudis <pasky\@ucw.cz> loaded.";
```

## Running the Hack

The script will be active as soon as it is loaded. You can load the script by typing:

```
/script load autovoice
```

You can then enjoy a sensible debate channel, without having to worry about people ruining the karma.

## Hacking the Hack

The main problem with the preceding script is that its state is not persistent. This means that if you restart *irssi*, the whole blacklist will be lost and you are left starting from scratch. This is easy to fix—just use the Data::Dumper module and print Dumper(\%dmasks) to a file each time you modify the hash. If the file already exists at startup, you can load its content into %dmasks.

This hack was originally written for a single *irssi* instance that is connected via a fast link and acts only as a given channel's gatekeeper. If you run it on multiple channels, the IRC session will start to get much more vulnerable to lag, as voicing/devoicing on so many channels will slow it down due to the rate limiting imposed by the IRC server. If your *irssi* client is in multiple channels and you would like to play gatekeeper on only one of them, you will need to hack some settings to control that behavior into the previous code. Also, if you are connected to multiple networks at the same time and would like your script to work properly, you will need to add support for multiple connections (for example, you could keep the blacklist as a hash of hashes, indexed by the server tag first).

It would also be good to have some way of manually editing the blacklist, allowing you to add some more general host masks to it or remove a good host mask. The script already provides a very simple interface for displaying the blacklist contents, but improving this is one thing you can experiment with.

*—Petr Baudis*

## HACK #29 Make IRC Talk

Even when you can't keep your IRC client in view, keep track of IRC by making your IRC client talk to you.

Ever wondered if you could touch the future just a little? What about getting your computer to read out what's happening on a channel or at least just your private messages? You would be able to do something else while listening to the cheery activity of IRC, perhaps even establish a bot that tells you fairy tales while you drift off to sleep. The possibilities are endless—if only your IRC client could speak!

It is not impossible, but because this is still very much a cutting edge and not a mass technology, it will not be easy to set up either. You will be hacking in Perl, this time to create a script for the popular *irssi* IRC client. At the backend, you can employ the Festival speech engine.

The first step is to install a speech synthesizer, and then you have to find a Perl interface for it. Neither of these tasks is particularly easy.

For the speech synthesizer, we will be using Festival. Its main advantage is that it is a universal engine, so you can teach it to speak virtually any language (from English to Spanish to Czech). It is perhaps not as effective as a native speech synthesizer would be, but it will be enough for our purposes.

You can get Festival from *http://www.cstr.ed.ac.uk/projects/festival/download. html*. However, if you are not sure which tarballs to grab, you can try reading *http://www.cstr.ed.ac.uk/cgi-bin/lists.cgi?config=festival_faq&entry=installing_ festival/what_do_i_need.html*. It comes with support for English, but chances are someone has implemented rulesets for other languages as well. After you have set up Festival, start up the *festival-server*, as you are going to use it to process requests from your script.

Now you need to grab the Perl Festival interface, Speech::Festival. You can download it through the popular CPAN interface, but make test will fail. You will need to run make install manually, although you may notice the modules will install to the wrong location. To fix this, you must move to the directory where the modules were installed (for example, */usr/lib/perl/site_perl/5.6.1/ Speech*), move the *Audio* subdirectory to its parent directory, and move the contents of the *Speech* subdirectory to the current directory. Next, you will probably want to remove *print "connected\n";* from *Speech/Festival/Synthesiser. pm* and *print "disconnected\n";* from *Speech/Festival.pm*.

By now, you should hopefully have an idea how important it is to do some basic quality assurance before releasing a module to the world. Of course, the Speech::Festival maintainer might already spare you of this valuable lesson by the time you read this hack.

## The Code

So you don't block *irssi* while pushing data to the Festival server, you must spawn a helper in a child process to take care of things. You can give it everything through a pipe and close it if the child dies (you probably want to restart it in case the settings change).

```
# Talking irssi gadget (c) Petr Baudis <pasky@ucw.cz>, BSD licence.

use strict;

use vars qw($forked $wh $type $lang);

use Irssi;
use Irssi::Irc;
use Speech::Synthesiser;

# Spawn a helper which will feed our Festival backend, so that we do not
# block the main irssi process while pushing data all around.
sub fork_me {
  my ($rh, $pid);
  pipe($rh, $wh);
  $forked = 1;
  $pid = fork();
  if ($pid > 0) {
```

```
        # The main irssi process
        close $rh;
        # This makes sure we do not get a zombie
        Irssi::pidwait_add($pid);
        return;
    } else {
        # The helper child
        close($wh);
        my $synth = new Speech::Synthesiser(-type => $type);
        start $synth;
        if ($lang) { voice $synth $lang; }
        while (my $in = <$rh>) {
          chomp $in;
          speak $synth $in;
        }
        stop $synth;
        close($rh);
        POSIX::_exit(0);
    }
}

# The incoming message event handler.
sub event_privmsg {
  my ($server, $data, $nick, $address) = @_;
  my ($msgtarget, $text) = split(/ :/, $data, 2);
  my (@channels) = split(/\s+/, Irssi::settings_get_str('speech_channels'));

  # The ~ substitution
  return unless (grep {s/^~$/$server->{nick}/x; $_ eq $msgtarget}
@channels);

  # Restart the backend if something changed.
  my ($otype, $olang) = ($type, $lang);
  $type = Irssi::settings_get_str('speech_backend');
  $lang = Irssi::settings_get_str('speech_language');
  if ($forked and ($type ne $otype or $lang ne $olang)) {
    print $wh "\n";
    close($wh);
    $forked = 0;
  }
  if (!$forked) {
    fork_me();
  }

  # Some emoticon replacements (e.g. ":-)"->"hehe!"
  # add your own if you need more!
  $text =~ s/:.?\)/hehe!/g;
  $text =~ s/:.?\(/sniff/g;

  # The exclamation point helps to get the right intonation.
  print $wh "$nick! $text\n";
}

# Our command interface.
```

```
sub cmd_speech {
  my ($cmd) = @_;
  if ($cmd =~ /^languages/i) {
    my $synth = new Speech::Synthesiser(
                       -type => Irssi::settings_get_str('speech_backend'));
    start $synth;
    my @voices = voice_list $synth;
    Irssi::print("These languages are supported: @voices");
    stop $synth;
  }
}

Irssi::command_bind('speech', \&cmd_speech);
Irssi::signal_add("event privmsg", "event_privmsg");
Irssi::settings_add_str('speech', 'speech_backend', 'Festival');
Irssi::settings_add_str('speech', 'speech_language', '');
Irssi::settings_add_str('speech', 'speech_channels', '~ #irchacks');
```

## Running the Hack

Now you can venture to add *speak.pl* to your *~/.irssi/scripts* directory and
type:

> /script load speak

Now you need to adjust your settings: speech_language should be set to one
of those listed when you type:

> /speech languages

speech_channels controls which channels (separated by spaces) should trigger a speech output (~ stands for private messages).

## Hacking the Hack

The preceding code is no more than a skeleton script, which could of course
be extended and polished in so many ways. A good *irssi* script should follow some basic conventions, which can also help it to make it into the *http://
scripts.irssi.org* repository—the script should ideally provide an %IRSSI hash
containing some basic information about itself (author, version, description, license, required modules).

While you're adding those features, you should extend the /SPEECH command interface so that it provides some status information and perhaps
could even send some commands to the Festival server. I also recommend
that the script print a short announcement when it is loaded.

Another area of improvement would be the relevant text transformations.
The script substitutes only the most frequent *smileys* now (:), :-), :o), etc.),
but all of this should be configurable so that people can expand this list and
adjust it to their language preference.

Speaking of languages, another interesting direction of expansion could be to make the language settings channel-specific. Non-English people frequently idle in both English and foreign channels, therefore *irssi* should speak in a different language in each channel.

Yes, Festival is great and cool, but for most languages, the reality is that better speech synthesizers exist, being optimized specifically for the given language. Therefore, a larger project would involve hacking Perl interfaces for other synthesizers as well, perhaps also fixing some of the problems in the Festival interface as described earlier.

—*Petr Baudis*

## HACK #30  Add Your IRC Nickname to Your Webcam

Webcams are a great way of showing people what you're doing. With a little IRC scripting, show people your current nickname, too.

Webcams are the best way to let people know exactly what you're doing—after all, a picture is worth a thousand words, or so they say. Adding extra text to your webcam image can reveal a lot more, particularly if you are not there to be seen. This hack shows you how to display your current IRC nickname on your webcam image.

The Windows webcam software used in this hack is *Dorgem*. This unusual name doesn't actually mean anything; it is a combination of letters that *could* sound like a word and didn't return any results on search engines at the time of its creation. So the chances are that if you Google this, you'll be able to find it easily. If not, you can download it from *http://dorgem.sourceforge.net*.

One useful feature of Dorgem is that it allows you to overlay captions on your webcam image. These captions can be either bitmap images or plain text. If you go for the plain text option, you can choose to overlay a string that you type in, or tell it to read the contents of a file. The latter choice allows you to include whatever text is in the file, so you can easily create a script for your IRC client that updates the file with your current nickname.

### Writing Your Nickname to a File

As this hack is to run on a Windows machine, it will use mIRC as the IRC client. To update the contents of the file every time you change your nickname, it's going to be necessary to trap that event. The easiest way of doing this is to override mIRC's /nick command so that it saves the new nickname in a file.

Open up the mIRC Scripts Editor (Tools → Scripts Editor...) and select the Aliases tab. Now create the alias for the /nick command shown in Figure 4-29.

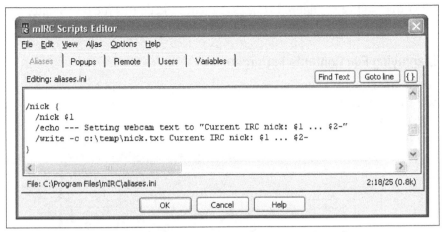

*Figure 4-29. Modifying the behavior of mIRC's /nick command*

This overrides the /nick command and causes a sequence of three other commands to be executed instead. The first of these passes the $1 variable to the /nick command. $1 is the first argument that is supplied to your alias, so this has the effect of changing your nickname as usual.

The second line echoes a string to your active window so you can receive a confirmation of what your webcam message will say. $2- is a variable that refers to the second argument, including everything after it. This means you can add some more details after your nickname, and they will also be included in this message.

The third line writes the same message to a file. The -c means that the file will be cleared before it is written to. In this example, the message will be written to *c:\temp\nick.txt*.

The alias lets you add extra parameters to the /nick command in case you want to add more detail to your webcam message. For example, if *Paul* wants to change his nickname to *Paul|desk-less*, he can do so in the usual way by entering:

```
/nick Paul|desk-less
```

This would cause *nick.txt* to contain:

```
Current IRC nick: Paul|desk-less ...
```

If he wanted to include some more information about his nickname, he could simply add some more details after the /nick command:

```
/nick Paul|desk-less they came and stole my desk :(
```

This would cause *nick.txt* to contain:

```
Current IRC nick: Paul|desk-less ... they came and stole my desk :(
```

Now that you've configured your IRC client to keep this file up-to-date, you just have to set up Dorgem to display its contents on your webcam image.

## Displaying File Contents in Dorgem

Assuming Dorgem is up and running properly, you can add a caption to the webcam image by clicking on the *Caption Settings* button, as shown in Figure 4-30.

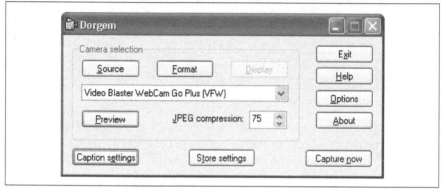

*Figure 4-30. The main Dorgem window*

In the *Caption Settings* dialog (Figure 4-31), click on *Add* to add a new caption overlay. When prompted, select a *Text* caption and click on *OK*.

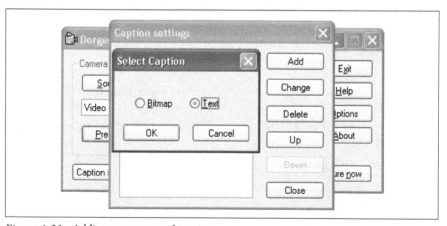

*Figure 4-31. Adding a new type of caption*

In the *Text Caption Settings* dialog, shown in Figure 4-32, give the caption a meaningful name, such as "IRC nick." This will not appear on the webcam image, but it will help you work out what this caption is used for if you end up adding any others.

Make sure the *Enable* checkbox is checked and that the length is set to 0 (unlimited). Enter the filename in the *File* box. For best results, you should make the text transparent, otherwise it will be printed on an opaque rectangle. If you want to make it stand out better, you could add a full shadow and use a contrasting color for background and foreground.

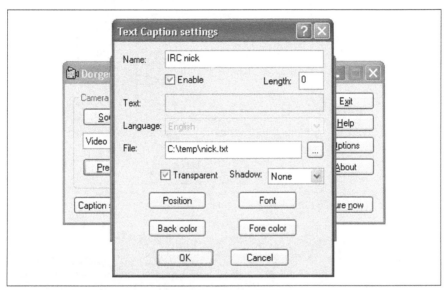

*Figure 4-32. Setting up the caption to read from a file*

Clicking on the *Position* button reveals the *Caption Position* dialog, as shown in Figure 4-33. This example places the caption at the bottom right of the webcam image. If you know the dimensions of your webcam image, you can even experiment with absolute positioning.

## The Results

Figure 4-34 shows the final results: a webcam image with the user's current IRC nickname and personalized message in the bottom right.

When people look at your webcam now, they will no longer be left guessing what you're up to when you're not there.

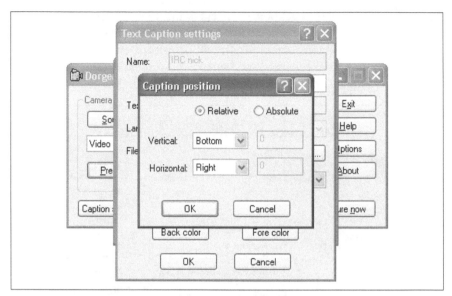

Figure 4-33. Setting the position of the caption

Figure 4-34. The webcam image with IRC nickname and message

# Writing IRC Bots
## Hacks 31–39

IRC bots are programs that connect to IRC. They differ from the classic IRC client in that they are usually autonomous—they think for themselves and do not require direct human input to work.

Programming IRC bots is fun and allows you to be very creative, as you are responsible for everything they say and do. Later chapters will show you how to create all sorts of IRC bots to log channels, create comic strips, pass on messages, share files, and so on. The limit is your imagination.

The first step in creating your own IRC bot is to understand the basic handshake that goes on when you connect to an IRC server. An example is given, showing you how to connect to an IRC server using no more than a basic Telnet application. Once connected, you can use Telnet to join channels and send messages to people. This illustrates the simplicity of the text-based IRC protocol, and the chapter continues by showing you how to write simple Perl, Java, and Python programs to connect to IRC.

This chapter also introduces some libraries for connecting to IRC. This lets you forget about the intricacies of the IRC protocol and concentrate on the functionality of your IRC bot. This covers the Net::IRC module for Perl, the PircBot package for Java, and the IRCLib module for Python.

Of course, one can perform many tasks with IRC bots, and not all of them are good. The chapter is rounded off with a brief discussion of the ethics of running IRC bots.

# IRC Over Telnet

Make a raw connection to an IRC server and spend a little time trying out the IRC protocol commands you'll be using in your program directly.

Jarkko Oikarinen first introduced IRC to the world in 1988. Five years later, he clearly defined the IRC protocol in RFC 1459, which made the whole protocol much more accessible. Armed with this information, you can get a better understanding of this simple text-based protocol and learn how to connect to IRC servers without using a special client. Once you have mastered this, you should find it a trivial task to write programs that connect to IRC.

You can find all of the Internet RFC (Request for Comments) documents on *http://www.faqs.org/rfcs*. You can search the archives by word or document number. RFC 1459 can be found at *http://www.faqs.org/rfcs/rfc1459.html*.

Fortunately, you do not need to know about the full specification to connect to an IRC server. Connecting to an IRC server requires only a few commands be sent. A good way of understanding how these commands work is to connect directly to an IRC server with Telnet and type these commands in directly. Telnet allows you to establish a TCP connection to a port on a remote machine and simply start typing in commands for the service listening on that port.

Most IRC servers run on port 6667, although you may find a few that operate on different port numbers to assist users who are stuck behind corporate firewalls. For this example, you can try connecting to the freenode IRC network by running Telnet from a command prompt with the following command-line parameters:

```
% telnet irc.freenode.net 6667
```

If the connection was successful, you will see the server respond with something similar to this:

```
NOTICE AUTH :*** Looking up your hostname...
NOTICE AUTH :*** Found your hostname, welcome back
NOTICE AUTH :*** Checking ident
NOTICE AUTH :*** No identd (auth) response
```

Although the socket is physically connected to the IRC server, you still need to do a couple of things. The IRC server will need to know your login, your real name, and the nickname you want to use.

The NICK command is used to set your nickname. This is pretty straightforward, so if I wanted my nickname to be "Paul," I would type the following into the Telnet window and press Enter:

```
NICK Paul
```

If the nickname you choose is already in use on the server, you will be told so and you will have to keep sending the same command with a different nickname each time, until you find one that is available. This is the kind of message you will see if the nickname is already in use:

```
:kornbluth.freenode.net 433 * Paul :Nickname is already in use.
```

The USER command is used to set the login, user modes, and real name. If I wanted to have a login of "paul," I would type the following, followed by Enter:

```
USER paul 8 * :Paul Mutton
```

Most servers these days respect commands from the updated IRC RFC 2812. This USER command makes use of some features specified in this updated document. In particular, the 8 is a numeric mode parameter that is used to automatically set user modes when registering with the server. This parameter is a bit mask, with bit 2 representing user mode w and bit 3 representing user mode i, so using a value of 8 means that you are asking the server to set you to be invisible. Currently, only these two bits have any significance. Also note that the text after the : is where you would enter your real name.

After successfully sending the NICK and USER commands, the server will send several lines of text to you. If nothing seems to be happening for a while, don't worry—the server may impose an artificial delay of up to a minute if it did not find an Ident server running on your machine. At first, the lines sent from the server may look rather confusing, but you may recognize some of them as being part of the message of the day. You are now connected to the IRC server!

Ident (Identification Protocol) is documented in RFC 1413. See *http://www.faqs.org/rfcs/rfc1413.html* for more details.

Now that you are connected, you are able to perform anything a fully functional IRC client would be capable of doing.

## Staying Alive

Sometimes it is difficult for IRC servers to keep track of who is still connected. One trick they employ is to send PING commands to clients that have not exhibited any recent activity. The client is expected to respond with a PONG message to effectively say, "Hey, I'm still here!" If the client does not respond in a timely fashion, the server will close the connection. As a general rule, the PONG reply must include the arguments that were sent as part of the PING command from the server. So if you were to receive the following message:

PING :*kornbluth.freenode.net*

You would reply with the following PONG command:

PONG :*kornbluth.freenode.net*

## Joining Channels and Sending Messages

The usual IRC client commands like /join and /msg won't work here, as you are dealing with the raw protocol. You can think of your Telnet connection as a form of primitive IRC client—you can still do anything an IRC client can do, but it just looks a little ugly and the commands are different. Despite this, it is still pretty easy to join a channel and send messages to other users. To join the channel #irchacks, you just have to enter:

JOIN *#irchacks*

If all went well, you should see the IRC server replying with a few lines of text. IRC clients use these lines to determine who is in the channel so they can update their user lists. For now though, you needn't worry about how to parse that information.

Sending messages is slightly less intuitive and is achieved with the PRIVMSG command. As you might expect from the name, this command can be used to send private messages to other users; however, it is also the command used to send messages to entire channels. To send a message to the channel #irchacks, you could try the following:

PRIVMSG *#irchacks :Hello everybody!*

Sending private messages is just as easy—simply use the recipient's nickname in place of the channel name. If you want to send a private message to the user with the nickname "Dave," you would enter:

PRIVMSG *Dave :Hi Dave.*

When you get bored with showing off your newfound protocol skills, you can quit from the server with the QUIT command. Using this command will cause the server to close your connection.

QUIT

The QUIT command can also take an optional parameter. The parameter must be immediately preceded by a : character. Whatever you supply here will be displayed to other users as your reason for quitting from the server:

QUIT :*Telnet sucks!*

Whichever method you use to quit from the server, before it disconnects you, it will respond with something along the lines of:

```
ERROR :Closing Link: Paul (Client Quit)
```

It is also possible for you to close the connection by closing Telnet, but this does not allow you to specify a reason for quitting.

While all commands should be capitalized, you may find that most servers are quite relaxed about this policy. Now that you know what to type to connect to IRC, the rest of the hacks in this chapter will show you how to create programs that connect to an IRC server.

## A Simple Perl IRC Client

Build a simple IRC robot that connects to an IRC server and joins a channel of your choosing.

If you have managed to connect directly to an IRC server with Telnet, you are probably ready to use this knowledge and start writing your own programs that connect to IRC automatically. In this example, you will build a simple IRC bot that connects to an IRC server and joins a channel. The term "*bot*" is commonly used to describe an automated IRC client and is a contraction of "*robot*." You will get the bot to output information as it receives it from the server.

Many people find that Perl is a very suitable language for making simple IRC bots, as it is easy to use regular expressions to parse the data from the server. A single TCP socket is used to send and receive the text-based data, so you will need to use IO::Socket.

This will be quite a simple bot. All it has to do is connect to the server and join a channel. For this implementation, you must be aware that the IRC RFC states that each command or message must end with a return and new line (i.e., \r\n). To avoid getting disconnected by the server, you will also need to make sure that it responds appropriately to PING messages.

### The Code

Enter the following code into your favorite plain text editor and save it as *irc.pl* or the like:

```
#!/usr/local/bin/perl -w
# irc.pl
# A simple IRC robot.
# Usage: perl irc.pl

use strict;
```

```perl
# We will use a raw socket to connect to the IRC server.
use IO::Socket;

# The server to connect to and our details.
my $server = "irc.freenode.net";
my $nick = "simple_bot";
my $login = "simple_bot";

# The channel which the bot will join.
my $channel = "#irchacks";

# Connect to the IRC server.
my $sock = new IO::Socket::INET(PeerAddr => $server,
                                PeerPort => 6667,
                                Proto => 'tcp') or
                                    die "Can't connect\n";

# Log on to the server.
print $sock "NICK $nick\r\n";
print $sock "USER $login 8 * :Perl IRC Hacks Robot\r\n";

# Read lines from the server until it tells us we have connected.
while (my $input = <$sock>) {
    # Check the numerical responses from the server.
    if ($input =~ /004/) {
        # We are now logged in.
        last;
    }
    elsif ($input =~ /433/) {
        die "Nickname is already in use.";
    }
}

# Join the channel.
print $sock "JOIN $channel\r\n";

# Keep reading lines from the server.
while (my $input = <$sock>) {
    chop $input;
    if ($input =~ /^PING(.*)$/i) {
        # We must respond to PINGs to avoid being disconnected.
        print $sock "PONG $1\r\n";
    }
    else {
        # Print the raw line received by the bot.
        print "$input\n";
    }
}
```

## Running the Hack

Simply invoke the script on the command line with no arguments at all, like so:

```
% perl irc.pl
```

## The Results

After the script has connected successfully, you will see it outputting all of the lines it receives from the IRC server, for example:

```
1 :simple_bot!identd@82-69-0-0.dsl.in-addr.zen.co.uk JOIN :#irchacks
2 :calvino.freenode.net 332 simple_bot #irchacks :IRC Hacks channel.
3 :calvino.freenode.net 333 simple_bot #irchacks Jibbler 1075562584
4 :calvino.freenode.net 353 simple_bot @ #irchacks :simple_bot DeadEd golbeck
      Jibbler dg Monty Wilmer
5 :calvino.freenode.net 366 simple_bot #irchacks :End of /NAMES list.
6 :Jibbler!~pjm2@torax.ukc.ac.uk PRIVMSG #irchacks :Hi simple_bot
7 :Monty!~monty@myrtle.ukc.ac.uk PRIVMSG #irchacks :It's simple_bot!
```

This may look quite confusing at first, but you can look at the lines one by one and work out what it means. The first line announces that the script has joined the channel #irchacks. Lines 2–5 contain information about this channel, such as what the channel topic is, who set it and when it was set, and who is in the channel. Lines 6 and 7 show messages being sent by other users in the channel.

You may like to use Perl's regular expression features to process the output into a neater format, as you may not want to display all of this information. Taking a closer look at line 6 again:

```
:Jibbler!~pjm2@torax.ukc.ac.uk PRIVMSG #irchacks :Hi simple_bot
```

You can see that the message came from a user named Jibbler, with the login pjm2 and connecting from torax.ukc.ac.uk. The PRIVMSG indicates that this is a normal message being sent to the channel #irchacks. The contents of the message are "Hi simple_bot".

## HACK #33 IRC with Perl and Net::IRC

The IRC protocol looks a bit weird and can be hard to understand. Fortunately, you don't have to know it to make a bot.

Net::IRC is a Perl module that lets you make IRC clients. It allows you to think about what your bot actually does, instead of having to think about all those little noninteresting protocol details **[Hack #32]**. This hack will explain how to write a simple Perl IRC bot using Net::IRC.

## Preparations

You can download the Net::IRC module from CPAN at *http://search.cpan.org/ dist/Net-IRC*. If you're lucky, you may be able to get it straight from your operating system's package manager. It is worth noting that Net::IRC is known to work on Unix systems only. It may work on Windows; it's just not very well supported.

To demonstrate how Net::IRC works, we're going to write a little infobot. The bot will do one simple task: remember facts and repeat them when asked. This will end up covering enough detail for you to make your own bots with Net::IRC.

## The Code

Create a file called *infobot.pl* and write the following:

```perl
#!/usr/bin/perl

use Net::IRC;

# Set up the connection to the IRC server.
$irc = new Net::IRC;
$conn = $irc->newconn( Server => 'irc.freenode.net',
                       Nick => 'InfoBot_pl',
                       Ircname => 'InfoBot.pl' );

# Open the database.
dbmopen( %info, 'infobot', 0644 );

# Connect the handlers to the events.
$conn->add_handler( 376, \&join_channel );
$conn->add_handler( 422, \&join_channel );
$conn->add_handler( 'public', \&message );

# Start the Net::IRC event loop.
$irc->start;

sub join_channel
{
    my( $conn, $event ) = @_;

    print( 'We\'re connected!' . "\n" );
    $conn->join( '#irchacks' );
}

sub message
{
    my( $conn, $event ) = @_;
    my( $msg ) = $event->args;
```

```
if( $msg =~ /^(.*)\?$/ )
{
    # Someone requested information. Let's see if we know it.
    if( $info{lc($1)} ne '' )
    {
        $conn->privmsg( $event->to, $event->nick . ': ' .
                        $1 . ' == ' . $info{lc($1)} );
    }
}
elsif( $msg =~ /^(.+?) *=+ *(.+?)$/ )
{
    # Someone gave us information. Save it.
    $info{lc($1)} = $2;
    $conn->privmsg( $event->to, $event->nick . ': OK' );
}
}
```

As you may have noticed, Net::IRC is another event-driven IRC bot framework. So as soon as a certain event happens, a handler is called to handle this event. The preceding code illustrates two event handlers: one to join the necessary channels as soon as the connection to the server is successfully made, and one to process incoming messages.

To handle an event, one should first write the handler. A handler is a subroutine that accepts two arguments. The first argument is a connection object, which allows the handler to get some information or perform some operations on the connection where the event happened. The second argument is the event object, which describes the event itself. For example, a channel message or someone joining a channel might trigger an event, which will be described by the event object. Information can be retrieved from these objects by calling methods. You may notice a few of the available methods in the previous source code. Others can be found in more complete example programs (one comes with the Net::IRC module source).

After writing the handler, you have to tell Net::IRC to use it. And, of course, *when* to use it. To get a list of all possible events, see the documentation (perldoc Net::IRC::Event). As you can see in the code, you also may specify a numeric event. This number is an IRC status reply code. A list of valid reply codes can be found in the IRC RFC (RFC 2813, *http://www.faqs.org/rfcs/rfc2813.html*). The numbers used here are the "No MOTD here" and "End of MOTD" codes. Most (if not all) IRC servers try to send the MOTD (message of the day) as soon as the user is connected, so it's a good idea to send the JOIN commands as soon as the MOTD is sent.

In case you were wondering, dbmopen( ) ties a Perl hash to a database file. This means that everything you store in the %info hash will be saved in that file. And of course, if a database already exists, all the information in there will suddenly appear in the %info hash. This means you can restart the bot without it forgetting the things it just learned. Regular expressions are used in the message handler to work out whether someone is asking a question or if they are saying a new fact that the bot can learn. If you are interested in extending this bot, you can get more information about Perl regular expressions by typing **perldoc perlre** on the command line.

## Running the Hack

You can run the bot by entering:

```
% perl infobot.pl
```

## The Results

When the bot connects to your server and joins your channel, you can begin feeding it with facts. Unless you change the preceding source code, the bot will be called InfoBot_pl:

```
-!- InfoBot_pl [~wilmer@jona.ipv6.gaast.net] has joined #irc_hacks
<lintux> Perl?
<InfoBot_pl> lintux: Perl == Cool
<lintux> Perl = Cool, but sometimes hard to read
<InfoBot_pl> lintux: OK
<lintux> Perl?
<InfoBot_pl> lintux: Perl == Cool, but sometimes hard to read
<lintux> IRC Hacks?
<InfoBot_pl> lintux: IRC Hacks == A very cool book from O'Reilly
<lintux> Is there anything else you can tell me?
```

As you see, the bot didn't answer the last question, because it didn't have an answer. You might wonder why it doesn't say, "Hey, I don't know that." The reason for this is quite simple—you don't want your bot to start talking every time someone asks a question. Good bots talk only when they're asked something. It's often a good idea to remember this when you're writing your own bots, otherwise you may kick off some nasty debates. As a matter of fact, the bot shown here might also be regarded as a bit too trigger-happy. But since it's just a proof of concept, let's not worry about that.

This should be enough to get you started. If you want to learn more, you can look at some other (more complete) examples. There's a nice sample bot inside the Net::IRC tarball. If you want more, try to find more examples by searching for "Net::IRC bot" on Google. I also recommend you to take a look at Pink, at *http://www.lintux.cx/~lintux/pink.html*, which is quite a versatile bot, written using the Net::IRC module. Unfortunately, some parts of the source may be hard to understand for people who don't read Dutch.

—*Wilmer van der Gaast*

# A Simple Java IRC Client

If you want to make an IRC client that can run on a variety of platforms, Java provides one possible solution.

To illustrate how easy it is to connect to IRC with other languages, you can apply the protocol information learned from the earlier Telnet experiments [Hack #31] and port the Perl example to Java. Using a Java program to connect to IRC is perhaps the most flexible solution, as it can run on any machine that has a Java Virtual Machine installed and can also run inside a web browser as an Applet.

## The Code

Save the following code to a file called *HackBot.java*:

```java
import java.io.*;
import java.net.*;

public class HackBot {

    public static void main(String[] args) throws Exception {

        // The server to connect to and our details.
        String server = "irc.freenode.net";
        String nick = "simple_bot";
        String login = "simple_bot";

        // The channel which the bot will join.
        String channel = "#irchacks";

        // Connect directly to the IRC server.
        Socket socket = new Socket(server, 6667);
        BufferedWriter writer = new BufferedWriter(
                new OutputStreamWriter(socket.getOutputStream( )));
        BufferedReader reader = new BufferedReader(
                new InputStreamReader(socket.getInputStream( )));

        // Log on to the server.
        writer.write("NICK " + nick + "\r\n");
        writer.write("USER " + login + " 8 * : Java IRC Hacks Bot\r\n");
        writer.flush( );

        // Read lines from the server until it tells us we have connected.
        String line = null;
        while ((line = reader.readLine( )) != null) {
            if (line.indexOf("004") >= 0) {
                // We are now logged in.
                break;
            }
            else if (line.indexOf("433") >= 0) {
```

```
                    System.out.println("Nickname is already in use.");
                    return;
                }
            }

            // Join the channel.
            writer.write("JOIN " + channel + "\r\n");
            writer.flush( );

            // Keep reading lines from the server.
            while ((line = reader.readLine( )) != null) {
                if (line.toLowerCase( ).startsWith("PING ")) {
                    // We must respond to PINGs to avoid being disconnected.
                    writer.write("PONG " + line.substring(5) + "\r\n");
                    writer.write("PRIVMSG " + channel + " :I got pinged!\r\n");
                    writer.flush( );
                }
                else {
                    // Print the raw line received by the bot.
                    System.out.println(line);
                }
            }
        }
    }

}
```

## Running the Hack

You must first compile the hack with the `javac` command. If you have the Java SDK installed and set up correctly, you can do this from the command prompt:

```
% javac HackBot.java
```

This will compile the source code into platform-independent bytecode and create the file *HackBot.class*. You can now run the HackBot from the same command prompt:

```
% java HackBot
```

The HackBot will now leap into life.

## Results

When you run the Java HackBot, it should connect to the IRC server you specified. Any exceptions will be allowed to propagate from the main method, so if something goes wrong, you will find out what it was. When it comes to adding a few more features to this IRC bot, you may like to consider dealing with these exceptions more neatly. As with the simple Perl bot, the HackBot should display the raw lines it receives from the server after it has connected successfully.

Each time this bot receives a PING from the server, it will respond with a PONG and use the PRIVMSG command to tell the channel that it got pinged. The format of this message will be something like this:

```
PRIVMSG #irchacks :I got pinged!
```

The PRIVMSG command is to send messages to individual users as well as channels. All you have to do is write your nickname instead of the channel name:

```
PRIVMSG YourNick :I got pinged!
```

This hack forms the basis of a bot that is able to connect to an IRC server and stay connected. With a little experimentation with the IRC protocol [Hack #78], you can add extra features to this bot and make it do something useful.

## HACK #35    IRC with Java and PircBot

Use the PircBot Java IRC API to make bots that connect to IRC.

PircBot is a Java framework for writing IRC bots quickly and easily. It allows you to abstract yourself away from the underlying protocols and concentrate on making bots that do something useful. Using this framework is much easier than implementing all of the grunt work by yourself. Connecting to a server, for example, takes just one line of code.

You can get PircBot from *http://www.jibble.org/pircbot.php*. To make your own bot that uses this framework, you will need to open the PircBot ZIP file and place the *pircbot.jar* file in a new directory. This directory will also be used to store the source code for the bot.

The file *pircbot.jar* contains all of the classes and source code that make up the PircBot package. Curious users will also note that the ZIP file contains full documentation for the package, which is essential for exploring the more advanced capabilities of PircBot. The package contains an abstract class named PircBot, which you can extend and inherit from. Creating an IRC bot is a simple case of extending this class, although you may like to change the nickname of the bot from its default of "PircBot."

Writing a bot becomes much simpler, as illustrated in this second Java version of a simple IRC bot. Save the following code as *HackBot2.java*:

```java
import org.jibble.pircbot.*;

public class HackBot2 extends PircBot {

    public HackBot2() {
        this.setName("HackBot2");
    }

}
```

Believe it or not, that's all you have to do to create a bot. Creating an instance of the HackBot2 class gives you an object that inherits all of the methods from the PircBot class, thereby allowing you to tell it to connect to a server, join a channel, and so on.

Create another class in a new source file, *Main.java*, which contains a simple main method to create an instance of the bot. The main method also tells it to connect to a server and join a channel. A separate class called Main is used to store the main method so it is easier to work out how to run the bot—when a newcomer stumbles across your project, it is obvious where the main method is without having to look at any source code.

```java
import org.jibble.pircbot.*;

public class Main {

    public static void main(String[] args) throws Exception {

        // Start the bot up.
        HackBot2 bot = new HackBot2( );

        // Enable debugging output.
        bot.setVerbose(true);

        // Connect to an IRC server.
        bot.connect("irc.freenode.net");

        // Join the #irchacks channel.
        bot.joinChannel("#irchacks");

    }

}
```

The bot.setVerbose(true) method call is used to turn on verbose mode. This means that your bot will print out all of the raw commands it receives from the server, as well as printing out the commands the bot itself sends to the server. This is handy for diagnostic purposes if you can't get your bot to work.

## Event-Driven Framework

So far, HackBot2 will connect to the IRC server and respond to pings from the server, much like the previous Java HackBot. You can easily add a few more features because PircBot is an event-driven framework. This means you can easily make your bot respond to events as they happen, for example, saying what time it is whenever it is asked. Getting a PircBot to respond to such messages is a simple case of overriding the onMessage method.

Add this method to the *HackBot2.java* source code:

```
public void onMessage(String channel, String sender,
                      String login, String hostname, String message) {
    if (message.equalsIgnoreCase("time")) {
        String time = new java.util.Date().toString( );
        sendMessage(channel, sender + ": The time is now " + time);
    }
}
```

If your bot is in a channel, the preceding method will be called whenever anybody says something. If anybody says, "time," your bot will respond by telling her what the current time is.

```
<Jibbler> time
<HackBot2> Jibbler: The time is now Sun Dec 14 13:49:36 GMT 2003
```

As IRC is accessible by people from all over the world, it is a good idea to use this style of presentation, as it also states what time zone the bot is running in.

## Running the Hack

Open up a command prompt and change to the directory that contains *pircbot.jar*, *HackBot2.java*, and *Main.java*. If you are running Windows and have the Java SDK installed and set up correctly, you can compile your bot with the javac command. It is necessary to tell it to look in *pircbot.jar* to find the required PircBot classes.

```
C:\java\HackBot2> javac -classpath .;pircbot.jar *.java
```

If you are using Linux or Unix, the command-line parameters will differ slightly, as the : character is used to separate paths in the classpath list. You will need to run the following command:

```
% javac -classpath pircbot.jar:. *.java
```

If your bot compiled successfully, without any errors, it should now be ready to run. Your directory will now contain the files *HackBot2.class* and *Main.class*. Again, you must tell the Java runtime where to find the required PircBot classes. Windows users can run the bot with the following command:

```
C:\java\HackBot2> java -classpath pircbot.jar;. Main
```

Once again, Linux and Unix users can run the bot by replacing the ; with a :. The bot should then spring into life and join the specified channel, ready to tell people what time it is.

## Hacking the Hack

The documentation contained in the downloaded PircBot ZIP file is an abundant source of information, with full descriptions of all methods contained in the package. Reading this documentation is a good way to get ideas for features to add to your bot. Because PircBot is suitable for use in Java Applets, you could even use this as a starting point to create a basic IRC client that you can embed into a web page.

You may find inspiration for ideas on the PircBot Implementations page at *http://www.jibble.org/pircbot-implementations.php*. This page lists some of the existing bots and clients based on the PircBot framework. Some of my favorites are:

*ChoonBot (http://www.jstott.me.uk/choonbot)*
> This provides an IRC interface to Winamp, so everyone in our office can select what music we all listen to.

*PieSpy (http://www.jibble.org/piespy)*
> This sits in an IRC channel and infers and visualizes social networks **[Hack #44]**.

*Azureus (http://azureus.sourceforge.net)*
> This is a BitTorrent file-sharing client that uses PircBot to run an integrated IRC client, letting file-sharers chat with one another.

*mobibot (http://www.thauvin.net/mobitopia/mobibot)*
> This bot was designed to capture URLs posted in a channel, and you can find it in #mobitopia on the freenode IRC network.

*TellyBot (http://www.jstott.me.uk/tellybot)*
> This is an IRC bot that provides an interface to TV listings information. It allows you to search for programs and can remind you when they are about to start.

## A Simple Python IRC Client

Python doesn't include an IRC module as standard, but connecting is nonetheless easy. Make a simple client that connects to an IRC server.

Python is becoming a popular language for writing IRC bots. This can be attributed to the way you can achieve quite a lot with just a little bit of code. Python does not include an IRC module as standard, but there are a few Python IRC modules written by other people.

In some cases, you're better off writing your own IRC client from scratch instead of using something like IRCLib **[Hack #37]**. Fortunately, Python is a powerful language, and you can write a client with as few as 30 lines of code. The following example connects to IRC and responds to PINGs.

## The Code

Save this as *simplebot.py*:

```python
import sys
import socket
import string

HOST="irc.freenode.net"
PORT=6667
NICK="MauBot"
IDENT="maubot"
REALNAME="MauritsBot"
readbuffer=""

s=socket.socket()
s.connect((HOST, PORT))
s.send("NICK %s\r\n" % NICK)
s.send("USER %s %s bla :%s\r\n" % (IDENT, HOST, REALNAME))

while 1:
    readbuffer=readbuffer+s.recv(1024)
    temp=string.split(readbuffer, "\n")
    readbuffer=temp.pop()

    for line in temp:
        line=string.rstrip(line)
        line=string.split(line)

        if(line[0]=="PING"):
            s.send("PONG %s\r\n" % line[1])
```

Lots of this code should be self-explanatory by now. It starts by importing all the modules you're going to need. The second block of code is a bunch of variables that you can change. These determine which server we connect to, the nickname we use, and so forth.

The block of code after that is the first one that actually does anything. It creates a socket and connects to the server of choice. This example will connect to the freenode IRC network (irc.freenode.net). It also registers the client by sending NICK and USER commands to the server.

The bot then enters an infinite loop (to shut it down, press Ctrl-C). The first block of code inside the loop reads a maximum of 1024 bytes from the server and appends it to the readbuffer. You need a readbuffer because you might not always be able to read complete IRC commands from the server (due to a saturated Internet connection, operating system limits, etc). So whatever you read, you need to append it to the read buffer. The read buffer is then split into a list of strings, using \n as a separator. The last line in this list is possibly a half-received line, so it is stored back into the read buffer.

Before we're able to process the lines from the read buffer in a normal manner, there's one thing left to do. You need to remove the trailing \r character from the end of the lines. The string.rstrip( ) function does exactly this.

I can hear you thinking, "IRC uses \r\n as a message separator. Why don't you just split the lines using that as a separator, instead of just \n? You won't end up with an \r in the first place, then." This would be a better solution, if it weren't for some stubborn IRC networks that choose to ignore the RFC and use \n instead. So although the RFC says each message is supposed to be separated by an \r\n, you need to treat \r as optional.

Now that you have "clean" lines to process, you need to look for PING commands sent to the client. If the server sends it PING :randomstring, you need to reply with PONG :randomstring. The last three lines of code do this. The line is split into a list of strings, using a space as a separator. The if statement checks to see if the line started with a PING and sends back a PONG in response.

That's all there is to it. Of course, this bot doesn't *do* anything yet, but I'm sure you're able to figure out how to go on from here. One last thing—you may have noticed that I'm not using a send buffer. If you send something over an Internet socket, it's not guaranteed that all data is actually sent. So if you wanted to make this example completely resilient, you'd need to implement a send buffer to store any data you might not be able to send. This simple bot does not include this feature, as it isn't often required and would make the example more complex. If this is a concern, you can use IRCLib [Hack #37], which implements the send buffer for you.

### Running the Hack

Run the bot on from the command-line by typing:

```
% python simplebot.py
```

—*Maurits Dijkstra*

## #37   IRC with Python and IRCLib
Rather than reinventing the wheel each time you want to make a Python IRC bot, use an IRC library such as the IRCLib module.

While IRCLib is relatively new and doesn't have support for the entire IRC protocol yet, it offers a powerful API. It also has support for extensions so a programmer can add his own events and functions to the library. The latest IRCLib can be downloaded from *http://irclib.bitlbee.org*.

We'll assume you already know how to install Python modules, since explaining that is beyond the scope of this book. To find out how to install modules, take a look at the excellent documentation available at *http://www.python.org/ topics/learn.*

## The Code

Writing clients with IRCLib is really easy. Take a look at the following example:

```
import irc

MyIRC=irc.IRC_Object()
MyConn=MyIRC.new_connection()

MyConn.nick="MauBot"
MyConn.ident="maubot"
MyConn.server=("irc.freenode.net", 6667)
MyConn.realname="Maurits his bot"

while 1:
    MyIRC.main_loop()
```

The first line of this example imports the irc module. You need this line to be able to use any of IRCLib's functions and classes.

The script starts by creating an instance of the IRC_Object class. This class could be seen as the main object of IRCLib—it creates and destroys connections and lets them know when there's data to read and write. The next line creates an instance of the IRC_Connection class. This class represents a single connection to an IRC server (a single client). You can create as many connections as you like.

The next block of code sets the client information for the connection you just created. nick is the nickname to use on IRC, ident is the Ident part of your host mask (nick!ident@host), server is the server to connect to, and realname is the name you want to show when somebody performs a /whois on you.

The rest of the program just sets the IRC client in action, connecting to the server you specified and doing whatever you told it to do (in this case, nothing).

## Event Handlers

Having an IRC bot is fantastic, but what's the point if it doesn't do anything? To allow a client to respond to things that happen on IRC, IRCLib uses an event model. Again, it's probably best to demonstrate this by adding some functionality to our previous example:

```
import irc

# Define event listeners.
def handle_state(newstate):
    if newstate==4:
        MyConn.send_string("JOIN #irchacks")

def handle_raw(line):
    print line

def handle_parsed(prefix, command, params):
    if command=="PRIVMSG":
        if(params[0]=="#irchacks" and params[1]=="hi"):
            MyConn.send_string("PRIVMSG #irchacks :Hello World!")

# Connect as usual.
MyIRC=irc.IRC_Object()
MyConn=MyIRC.new_connection()

MyConn.nick="MauBot"
MyConn.ident="maubot"
MyConn.server=("irc.freenode.net", 6667)
MyConn.realname="Hoi"

# Before starting the main loop, add the event listeners.
MyConn.events['state'].add_listener(handle_state)
MyConn.events['raw'].add_listener(handle_raw)
MyConn.events['parsed'].add_listener(handle_parsed)

while 1:
    MyIRC.main_loop()
```

The program now starts by defining the event handlers. Event handlers are functions that are called each time an event of a specific type occurs. This bot will listen for three different events:

*State*

This handler lets you check the bot's current *connection state*. This is used to see when the client is connected (state 4).

*Raw*

This one is used to print whatever the client is reading from the server. This is useful for debugging purposes.

*Parsed*

This one is used to receive parsed *irc* commands, sent to the client by the server. This is probably the most useful event. In this case, the bot is waiting to receive a message saying "hi" in the channel #irchacks. Whenever this message is received, the bot will send the message "Hello World" back to the channel.

Before the bot enters its main loop, you must connect the event handlers to their specified events. With these three lines, you're telling IRCLib to call the correct event handler whenever an event of the specified type occurs.

### Learning More About IRCLib

So, that's all the code that is needed to write a simple IRC bot. For a complete overview of all the things IRCLib can do, see the documentation at *http://irclib.bitlbee.org*. If you want to learn about writing an extension for IRCLib, this is detailed in the following hack.

—*Maurits Dijkstra*

## HACK Extend the Python IRCLib
## #38 Not every program needs the same features from an IRC library. Extend
IRCLib for your specific purposes.

This hack shows you how to write an extension for IRCLib **[Hack #37]**. Extensions are simply Python scripts that add events and/or methods to the IRCLib classes. This allows you to have a modular, incremental approach to creating bots, adding one feature at a time.

Let's take a look at an example.

### The Code

Save this as *helloworld.py* anywhere in your Python path:

```
import irc

dependencies=[]
IRC_Object=None

def send_hi(self, channel):
    self.send_string("PRIVMSG %s :Hello World!" % channel)

def handle_parsed(prefix, command, params):
    if command=="PRIVMSG":
        if params[1]=='hi':
            IRC_Instance.active.events['hi'].call_listeners(params[0])

def initialize():
    irc.IRC_Connection.send_hi=send_hi

def initialize_connection(connection):
    connection.add_event("hi")
    connection.events['parsed'].add_listener(handle_parsed)
```

The first line is the import irc needed to get access to the IRCLib classes.

The first variable defined in this extension script is dependencies. If your extension depends on other extensions to work, you can put the names of the extensions in this list. IRCLib will then load these extensions first before loading yours. IRC_Instance is a reference to the IRC_Object instance in the program that is loading your extension.

The script then continues to define four functions:

send_hi
> This function will get added to the IRC_Connection class. It sends the string "Hello World!" to the channel specified by channel.

handle_parsed
> This is an event handler for the 'parsed' event. It's used to get the parsed lines from IRCLib. If the line matches with "hi," all listeners for the 'hi' event are called. The destination of the message (was it said in a channel or private message?) is given to the event handlers as the first argument. Note that it's using IRC_Instance.active to get the connection that triggered the event. This variable exists so you don't have to pass IRC_Connection references to each event handler.

initialize
> This function is called immediately after the script is loaded. This sets the send_hi function as a method for the class IRC_Connection.

initialize_connection
> This function is called each time a new connection is created, with the IRC_Connection instance as its only argument. The first line of the function adds a 'hi' event to each connection. The second line connects 'handle_parsed' to the 'parsed' event for each connection.

## Loading Your Extensions

Now that you have an extension, let's use it in an IRCLib program:

```
import irc

def handle_hi(destination):
    MyConn.send_hi(destination)

MyIRC=irc.IRC_Object( )
MyIRC.load_extension("helloworld")
MyConn=MyIRC.new_connection( )

MyConn.nick="MauBot"
MyConn.ident="maubot"
MyConn.server=("irc.oftc.net", 6667)
MyConn.realname="Hoi"
```

```
MyConn.events['hi'].add_listener(handle_hi)

while 1:
    MyIRC.main_loop( )
```

This example doesn't contain much new code, except for the `MyIRC.load_extension("helloworld")` line. As you've probably guessed, this call loads the `'helloworld'` extension. Later on in the script, you add an event handler for the type `'hi'` (added by the extension script). This causes the `'handle_hi'` method to be called whenever the `'hi'` event happens. This event handler uses the `'send_hi'` method (also added by the extension) to send back a response.

## Built-in Extensions

IRCLib comes with a number of built-in extensions. To see a complete list of the extensions you can load, consult the IRCLib web site at *http://irclib.bitlbee.org*. There are also a number of advanced features, such as event handler priorities and the blocking of events.

—*Maurits Dijkstra*

## The Ethics of IRC Bots

**HACK**
**#39**

You put your shiny new bot in a channel and suddenly a channel operator comes along and kicks it out. Why did they do that?

Most IRC networks have policies against certain kinds of bots. You may wonder why—after all, what's the difference between a bot and regular chatter? They're totally identical as far as the server is concerned, and even human users may find it difficult to see the difference immediately.

Most IRC networks will clearly specify their rules in their message of the day (MOTD), which is announced when you connect to a server. For example, see this little snippet from the IRCnet's MOTD:

```
- Keep in mind: IRC is a privilege, not a right
-
- Basic rules:
-
- - Only 2 connections per person allowed. Please note that this is not
-   per host, but per person. This limit is for global connections, so
-   not only for this server, but for the entire network.
-
- - No bots! They will be removed from this server without hesitation.
-
- - No abuse. This is a rule which describes many actions. Always try to
-   use your common sense.
```

You may notice some other servers also ban the use of bots completely, as shown by this snippet of an MOTD from a server on the EFnet network:

```
- ...      o No "Bots" are allowed on this server.              ...
- ...      o No mass inviting, messaging or flooding.           ...
- ...      o No idling or faking usernames.                     ...
- ...      o No Link Looking.                                   ...
- ...      o Clients *MUST* respond to CTCP requests.           ...
```

In the last example, most of these rules seem designed to prevent the use of bots or automated scripts. For example, some "spam bots" trawl through a server and invite many people to a spam-advertisement channel. This works because many users have the "auto-join-on-invite" feature of their IRC clients turned on. "Idling" is the term given to connecting to a server and not doing anything other than joining a few channels. Idling on IRC is not that uncommon, but other users don't seem to like "log bots" that do nothing but listen and log everything that's said. Link looking is actually forbidden on many other networks, as it reveals the structure of links between each server on the IRC network. A good reason for this ban is that "war bots" can use it to get a list of the other servers, which they can use to make flood attacks even worse, evade K-lines, or circumvent server connection limits. Simple implementations of IRC bots usually ignore CTCP requests or do not respond to them correctly, so that could be the reason for the last rule.

So why do some networks have this strict antibot policy? The most likely reason is that the server operators don't feel like having war bots on their networks—usually because they are designed to waste bandwidth and serve no useful purpose. In many people's minds, a war bot is essentially a small program that makes many connections to a server, joins the same channel, tries to create some mess and in the end allows the channel to be taken over. A different type of war bot is one that guards channels and tries to prevent these kinds of attack. Obviously, this is one of the least-useful uses for a bot, especially on networks that provide decent services that make attacks more difficult.

So, you can imagine why most operators don't want to allow bots on their networks. Fortunately, most networks have decent services these days, so there isn't much use in having a "defensive" war bot in your channel anymore. Taking over a channel is not very useful when the channel owner can undo the action with a single ChanServ command.

On the other hand, many networks let you use bots. Most bots these days serve a more useful purpose, with functionality that includes greeting people, responding to commands in the channel, saying what's on television, warning about new Slashdot articles, and so on. The features are certainly more useful than the average war bot and usually not that much of a bandwidth waster. You could even argue that such bots are less "floody" than some of the real people in the channel. Log bots are not really a problem either, but it's usually nice to warn everyone if your bot logs everything and puts it on the Web. Some people assume they can say what they want and that the people in the channel are the only ones who will ever read it—so it can be a bit annoying to find out that your words are logged, put online, and even end up being indexed by Google.

So, although a few servers still disallow bots, it's probably not that much of a problem to put a nice bot in your channel. However, if the channel does not belong to you, it's probably a good idea to ask the channel owner first. Most people don't like it when there are more bots than real people in a channel—after all, IRC is there for people to talk to people, not to talk to bots. Also, there is no point in having four bots in the channel to respond to **!google** requests—one answer is usually enough!

*—Wilmer van der Gaast*

# Logging Bots
## Hacks 40–43

Logging is a natural function for bots and clients alike. Many IRC clients offer the ability to append messages to log files, and it is trivial to add such features to a bot. The secret of effective logging is to work out what you want to log and how people can access the information. This provides some quite creative ideas that go beyond the simple task of merely logging every message to a file.

A bot that monitors all messages sent to a channel is effectively monitoring the activity of all users in that channel. By providing an interface that lets people talk to the bot, you can let them find out when a particular user was last seen and what that user said in the channel. This chapter shows you how to implement such a bot using the PircBot package covered in Chapter 5.

It is perhaps surprising to learn that bots can even be written in shell scripts. This chapter shows you how to write a basic bot that uses *bash* to connect to IRC and log all URLs that it sees. Another bot written in Java can tell you what people were talking about before you joined a channel, so you will never feel as if you've blindly wandered into the middle of a conversation.

A more complicated example uses a Java bot to run a group blog, logging URLs to a MySQL database. A web-based frontend then lets people view the logged URLs.

 **HACK** **Keep Tabs on People**

**#40**  Keep track of when visitors to a channel last spoke and what they said.

People aren't always online and, even if they are, they aren't necessarily sitting in front of their computers. Getting a hold of your friends on IRC is difficult if you don't know if they are present and paying attention. Many people leave their IRC clients online all the time and do not set their Away status when they are absent, either on purpose or because they forget. In these cases, a good indicator of whether a user is likely to be present or not is to know when she was last active and what she last said.

If a user has recently said something, there is a good chance that he is still around, possibly reading your messages. If a user hasn't spoken for several hours, it is likely that he has popped out to the shops, gone to bed, or otherwise wandered away. Sometimes the last message written by the user confirms the suspicion.

## !seen

Remembering when a user last spoke and what she said is a fairly trivial task. Some users include this kind of functionality in their IRC clients by means of third-party scripts or plug-ins.

A common way to invoke these scripts is to type **!seen** *nickname*. A typical response includes what the user last said and when he said it. However, for such functionality to be useful, it is important that the client is permanently connected to the IRC server. For this reason, it can be worth creating a standalone IRC bot that implements "!seen" functionality.

## The Code

This bot will maintain a collection of nicknames that it has seen, along with what they last said and when they said it. Users will be allowed to query this information with the !seen command.

In Java, the HashMap class makes it easy to remember details pertaining to each nickname. The keys of the HashMap can be nicknames, and the values can contain the last message sent by each nickname and the time it was sent. So each time the bot sees anybody say something, it must put a new entry into the HashMap, overwriting any previous entry if necessary. When a user says **!seen** *nickname*, the bot can look up the nickname in the HashMap and quickly respond with the last message sent by that user. If there is no corresponding entry in the HashMap, this means the bot has not seen that user say anything.

This has been implemented in *SeenBot.java*:

```java
import org.jibble.pircbot.*;
import java.util.*;

public class SeenBot extends PircBot {

    // This maps nicknames to when they were last seen and what they said.
    private HashMap lastSeen = new HashMap();

    public SeenBot(String name) {
```

```
            setName(name);
        }

    public void onMessage(String channel, String sender,
            String login, String hostname, String message) {

        // Add this nickname and message to the lastSeen map.
        lastSeen.put(sender.toLowerCase(), getDate() + ", saying " +
message);

        message = message.trim().toLowerCase();

        // Check for people calling the !seen command.
        if (message.startsWith("!seen ")) {
            String nick = message.substring(6).trim();
            String seen = (String) lastSeen.get(nick.toLowerCase());
            if (seen != null) {
                // Tell the channel when this nickname was last seen.
                sendMessage(channel, nick + " was last seen on " + seen);
            }
            else {
                sendMessage(channel, "I haven't seen " + nick + " on this
server.");
            }
        }
    }

    private String getDate() {
        // Return the current date as a String.
        return new Date().toString();
    }

}
```

Notice that the nicknames are converted to lowercase before being placed into the HashMap. This is because string comparisons are case sensitive when looking for keys in the HashMap.

This bot is capable of joining more than one channel. When a user issues a !seen command, it will respond with the most recent activity, regardless of which channel it was in.

Create a class in *SeenBotMain.java* to tell the bot to connect to a server and join some channels:

```
public class SeenBotMain {

    public static void main(String[] args) throws Exception {
        SeenBot bot = new SeenBot("SeenBot");
        bot.setVerbose(true);
        bot.connect("irc.freenode.net");

        // Join multiple channels.
```

```
                   bot.joinChannel("#irchacks");
                   bot.joinChannel("#test");
            }

      }
```

## Running the Hack

Compile the bot:

```
C:\java\SeenBot> javac -classpath pircbot.jar;. *.java
```

Run it:

```
C:\java\SeenBot> java -classpath pircbot.jar;. SeenBotMain
```

Figure 6-1 shows the SeenBot in action, responding to !seen commands in a channel.

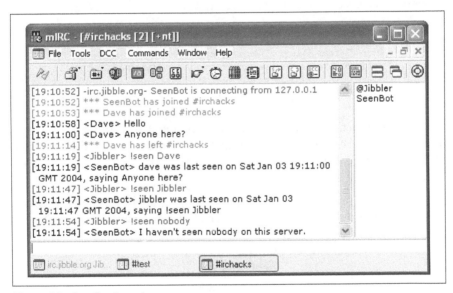

*Figure 6-1. SeenBot in action*

## Hacking the Hack

This bot will suffice for general use, but it does have some limitations at the moment. As stated earlier, such a bot is useful only if it is permanently connected to the IRC server. But let's face it, machines can crash and connections can sometimes drop. So some kind of persistence is required to be sure that the bot never misses a message.

One way of achieving persistence is to save the contents of the HashMap each time it changes. Writing the contents to a file means that they will still be accessible after a system crash or similar problem. Iterating through the HashMap and saving each entry in a plain text file is probably the best method, as it is easy to read. However, because String and HashMap both implement the Serializable interface, the easiest way is to use the ObjectOutputStream class from the java.io package.

Add this save method to *SeenBot.java*:

```
public void save() throws IOException {
    // Write the HashMap contents to the file brain.dat.
    FileOutputStream fileOut = new FileOutputStream("brain.dat");
    ObjectOutputStream out = new ObjectOutputStream(fileOut);
    out.writeObject(lastSeen);
    out.flush();
    fileOut.close();
}
```

Restoring the object is equally simple. Add this load method to *SeenBot.java*:

```
public void load() throws IOException, ClassNotFoundException {
    // Read the HashMap contents from the file brain.dat.
    FileInputStream fileIn = new FileInputStream("brain.dat");
    ObjectInputStream in = new ObjectInputStream(fileIn);
    lastSeen = (HashMap) in.readObject();
    fileIn.close();
}
```

Both of these methods will throw an IOException if something goes wrong. It would probably be a good idea to call the load method each time you start the bot and to call the save method every time the lastSeen HashMap is modified.

Another way of improving the bot is to make it aware of other IRC events— not all interactions are made using normal channel messages. Making the bot remember action, notice, join, and quit events will make the bot more useful. Here is an example of making the bot remember quit events:

```
public void onQuit(String sourceNick, String sourceLogin,
        String sourceHostname, String reason) {

    lastSeen.put(sourceNick.toLowerCase(), getDate() +
            ", quitting from the server with the reason " + reason);
}
```

If you take care to observe the various ways a user can exhibit activity on an IRC network, you'll end up with a bot that can tell you where and when a user was last active—perhaps with even more accuracy than a human observer!

# Log URLs People Mention

Logging URLs on IRC is useful in case you need to refer to them later on. Learn an unusual and interesting way to do it with a shell script on Linux/Unix.

Often, useful URLs are mentioned on a channel, and you cannot visit them straightaway but would like to check them out later. Perhaps you remember someone mentioning the URL of a really cool page containing various useful IRC hacks, but you just cannot remember it. Or maybe you just hate the constant cutting and pasting of URLs that your friends keep posting.

In this hack, you will look at a simple IRC client that will be absolutely passive—it will just sit in your channel, silently noting down the URLs passing by. Because such a task would be too simple in a language like Perl, let's show at the same time that you can make useful IRC hacks in a pure shell script!

## The Code

The trivial solution would be to have an input block, emitting just a few commands required to negotiate the connection and join the channel. This block would be piped to *netcat*, with *netcat*'s output then redirected to another block, munching the server's lines and selecting the PRIVMSG messages that contain a URL.

But the world is never this simple. This architecture has a fatal problem that means you cannot send any commands to the server later. The basic flaw is the inability to reply to PINGs from the server, which means that the server will decide the connection is dead and close it unexpectedly. You could, of course, cheat it by showing some periodic activity. However, what if you want to make some more elaborate interface available, like being able to join more channels on request? Or handle various errors properly?

You should ideally remove this limitation and somehow connect the input and output blocks. But how can one do that? Try thinking about it and see if your ideas work as you expected.

The bash shell can do wonderful things with redirections. You can, for example, redirect to or from a special file that triggers some magic inside of bash. One of these files is */dev/tcp/hostname/port*, which establishes a TCP connection. You can say, "Whatever, I have my *netcat* and love it!", but first realize that this way the socket behaves like a file for redirection purposes and that considerably expands our possibilities.

What about the other redirection trick? You need to direct both your input and output to the socket. The answer is using the <> redirection operator, which will open the given (magic) file for both input and output. But it acts upon stdin, so you also need to redirect stdout to stdin with >&0.

In case something goes wrong and you cannot connect, or if the server dies, you should try again. That is easy—the read in the main input while loop fails and it bails out, therefore you must add yet another while loop around the whole block. You should not forget to sleep for some reasonable time between the iterations in case the connection failure is repetitive.

Save the following as *urlgrab.sh*:

```sh
#!/bin/sh
# IRC URL grabber: records all URLs mentioned to a log file.
# This script is public domain.

# Configuration section.
SERVER="irc.freenode.net"
PORT="6667"
NICK="urlspy"
IDENT="urlspy"
IRCNAME="URL Grabber"
CHANNEL="#irchacks" # We can specify multiple channels separated by a comma.
LOGFILE="url.log"

# Try to reconnect in case the connection fails.
while true; do

# Standard input/output of this block is redirected to an IRC connection.
{

# We prepare few raw IRC commands and send them out in advance.  We do not do
# any error checking, therefore if one of the commands fails, the game is over.
echo "USER $IDENT x x :$IRCNAME"
echo "NICK $NICK"
echo "JOIN $CHANNEL"

while read input; do

    # Strip the CRLF at the end of each line.
    input=`echo "$input" | tr -d '\r\n'`

    # If this is a PING, then send a PONG back.
    ping=`echo "$input" | cut -d " " -f 1`
    if [ "$ping" = "PING" ]; then
        data=`echo "$input" | cut -d " " -f 2-`
        echo "PONG $data"
        continue
    fi

    # One PRIVMSG line looks like:
    # :pasky!pasky@pasky.or.cz PRIVMSG #elinks :(IRC hack ;)
    # --------source---------- --cmd-- -dest-- ---text-----
    cmd=`echo "$input" | cut -d " " -f 2`
```

```
    if [ "$cmd" != "PRIVMSG" ]; then
        continue
    fi


    # Extract the other fields from the message.
    # We must not forget to strip the leading colons from $source and $text.
    source=`echo "$input" | cut -d " " -f 1`
    source=`echo "$source" | sed 's/^://'`

    target=`echo "$input" | cut -d " " -f 3`

    text=`echo "$input" | cut -d " " -f 4-`
    text=`echo "$text" | sed 's/^://'`

    # Our URL-matching regular expression is of course far from perfect.
    # Some more complex ones can be found
    # (e.g., at http://www.regexp.org/486).

    # Sed won't print the lines out on its own because of -n and the 'p'
    # command will utter the line only if the preceding address (a regexp
    # in our case) is found.  This hack requires GNU sed.

    # Note that the continuation lines of the sed expression MUST start at
    # the beginning of the lines!

    url=`echo "$text" | sed -n 's/^.*\(\(http\|ftp\)s\{0,1\}:\/\/'\
'[\-\.\,\/\%\~\=\@\_\8\:\?\#a-zA-Z0-9]*'\
'[\/\=\#a-zA-Z0-9]\).*$/\1/gp'`

    if [ "$url" ]; then
        # One line in the log shall look like:
        # ----date---- :: ---source--- -> ---dest--- :: ---url---
        echo `date` ":: $source -> $target :: $url" >>$LOGFILE
    fi
done

} <>/dev/tcp/$SERVER/$PORT >&0

sleep 30

done
```

## Running the Hack

First, you need to change the settings at the start of the file and tweak the
configuration to suit your needs. Then just execute the script and watch
your log file slowly grow.

To make the script executable, you can use the chmod command:

```
% chmod u+x urlgrab.sh
```

Then you can run the script from the command line:

```
% ./urlgrab.sh
```

Whenever a URL is detected within a message, it will append a line like this to the log file:

```
Mar 20 19:39:23 2004 :: pasky!pasky@pasky.or.cz -> #ch :: http://hacks.
oreilly.com/
```

You can use this log file in any way you want, whether it's for your own personal use or to display the most popular links on a web page.

## Hacking the Hack

The basic flaw here is obviously the lack of portability of our redirection tricks. This one is, however, easily fixed. There are alternative solutions, perhaps less elegant, but still very usable.

The simplest approach would involve having an "input" file that you tail -f to *netcat*. Then you can turn the rest of the script into an output block, where you just append all the commands to the input file, for example:

```
# ... configuration ...

# If you don't have mktemp installed (http://www.mktemp.org/mktemp/) you can
# use `/tmp/urlgrab.$$` instead, at the risk of a security problem.
TMPFILE=`mktemp`

tail -f $TMPFILE | nc $SERVER $PORT | {

# ... the original block's body ...

} >>$TMPFILE

rm $TMPFILE
```

Alternatively, you could use mkfifo to pass the data through a named pipe, which is less portable, but takes virtually no disk space and might be more effective. In that case, you could use a simple cat instead of tail -f.

Of course, there are a lot of other possible enhancements. You should ideally handle any errors correctly. That means some code inflation, as you can't just dump the startup commands blindly, but you would have to wait for some numerics from the server to indicate that you have succeeded in connecting before you send the JOIN command.

Another issue is cycling between multiple IRC servers, which is a must for a reliable IRC bot. It is easy to do using cut and a cycling counter.

Maybe you would like to log the whole line containing the URL instead of just the URL itself? This is useful if you are interested in the context or if

---

there is a description placed near the URL. All you will need to do is modify the sed script from s/regexp/\1/gp to /regexp/p.

A significantly more challenging problem is handling the possibility of multiple URLs in the same message. When you use just a simple search instead of the substitution, as outlined earlier, this is not an issue, but otherwise you would need to weed out the non-URL parts. Even though this problem would probably be solvable in sed, at this level of complexity it is wiser to switch to something more convenient, such as Perl. This would result in replacing the sed statement with something like this:

```
perl -nle 'print join (" ",
    m$((?:http|ftp)s?://[-\.,/%~=\@_\&:\?#a-zA-Z0-9]*[\/=#a-zA-Z0-9])$g);'
```

The -e flag will make Perl execute the given statement, -n will run the statement for each line of input, and -l will make it add a newline at the end of each line. m$regexp$g will match the input as many times as necessary and output a list of matched URLs, which is then joined by spaces and printed out.

This hack doesn't even consider all the possibilities regarding various uses of the logged URLs, from automatic opening in a web browser to storing them in an SQL database **[Hack #42]**. This part is definitely up to your imagination.

—*Petr Baudis*

## HACK #42 Blog from IRC

Your IRC channel is essentially a community of people. Publish the thoughts of this community by using an IRC bot to place them on a group web log.

Blogging has taken the Internet by storm in recent years, and why should your IRC channel be left out? Most channels see people regularly paste URLs for the entertainment and information of those present, so why not collect them and stick them on a web site for future reference? Here's a flexible and easily extensible way to do it using a bot. The bot stores any incoming message that contains a URL in a MySQL database. A separate PHP script is used to display all blog entries made in the last seven days.

You will need:

- A MySQL database (*http://www.mysql.com*)
- Java SDK 1.4+ (*http://java.sun.com/j2se*)
- MySQL Connector/J (*http://www.mysql.com/products/connector/j*)
- PircBot (*http://www.jibble.org/pircbot.php*)
- A suitable web server—e.g., Apache and PHP 4 with MySQL support compiled in (*http://www.apache.org* and *http://www.php.net*)

For the sake of simplicity, it will be assumed here that everything's running on the same computer.

First, set up your database according to the following scheme:

```
CREATE TABLE weblog (
    commenter TINYTEXT NOT NULL,
    comment MEDIUMTEXT NOT NULL,
    timestamp TIMESTAMP NOT NULL,
    PRIMARY KEY (timestamp)
);
```

Next, create a user with permissions to access that table:

```
GRANT SELECT, INSERT ON database.weblog TO weblogbot@localhost
        IDENTIFIED BY 'password';
```

Replace *database* with the name of your MySQL database and *password* with a password of your choice.

## The Code

Now let's write the code for the bot. The Weblog class inherits functionality from the PircBot class to allow it to connect to IRC, so you will also need to ensure that you have *pircbot.jar* at hand.

Create a file called *Weblog.java*:

```java
import org.jibble.pircbot.*;
import java.text.*;
import java.sql.*;
import java.util.regex.*;

public class Weblog extends PircBot {

    private String dbHost = "localhost";
    private String dbName = "database";
    private String dbUserName = "weblogbot";
    private String dbPassword = "password";
    private Pattern urlRegEx;
    private Matcher urlMatcher;

    public Weblog (String botName) {
        this.setName(botName);
        this.setLogin(botName);

        // Precompile the URL-matching regular expression.
        urlRegEx = Pattern.compile("^.*(((http|https|ftp)://|www.)" +
            "[a-z.0-9/A-Z~_+\\-&?=,:;#@%!]*).*$");
    }

    public void onMessage (String channel, String sender,
            String login, String hostname, String message) {
```

```
        urlMatcher = urlRegEx.matcher(message);
        if (urlMatcher.matches( )) {
            try {
                // Connect to the MySQL database.
                Class.forName("com.mysql.jdbc.Driver").newInstance( );
                Connection conn = DriverManager.getConnection(
                    "jdbc:mysql://" + dbHost + "/" + dbName +
                    "?user=" + dbUserName +
                    "&password=" + dbPassword);

                // Prepare and execute the database query.
                PreparedStatement pstmt = conn.prepareStatement(
                    "INSERT INTO weblog (comment, commenter) VALUES(?, ?);");
                pstmt.setString(1, message);
                pstmt.setString(2, sender);
                pstmt.executeUpdate( );
            }
            catch (Exception e) {
                // Something went wrong...
            }
        }
    }
}
```

Finally, we'll need some code to create the blog from the database. The following bit of PHP—saved on the web server as *weblog.php*—does the trick. It executes an SQL query to get all the entries out of the database that are less than seven days old. These are then displayed in a table.

```
<html>

<head>
    <title>IRC Hacks weblog example</title>
</head>

<body>
  <table>
    <tr>
      <td>when</td><td>who</td><td>what</td>
    </tr>

<?php
  // Set up the SQL query.
  $earliest = mktime(0, 0, 0, date("m"), (date("d") - 7), date("Y"));
  $querytext = "SELECT UNIX_TIMESTAMP(timestamp), commenter, comment " .
               "FROM weblog WHERE UNIX_TIMESTAMP(timestamp) > $earliest " .
               "ORDER BY timestamp DESC LIMIT 200";
  // Connect to the database.
  $link = @mysql_connect("localhost", "weblogbot", "password")
          or die("Could not connect to database server");
  mysql_select_db("database")
          or die("Could not select the database");
```

```
// Execute the SQL query.
$result = mysql_query($querytext)
        or die("database query failed");

// Format the blog entries.
while ($row = mysql_fetch_array($result, MYSQL_ASSOC)){
  $comment = strip_tags($row[comment]);
  // Turn URLs into hyperlinks.
  $comment = preg_replace("(((((http|https|ftp)://|www.)" .
            "[a-z.0-9/A-Z~_+\\-&?=,:;#@%!]*))",
            "<a href=\"\\1\">\\1</a> ", $comment);
  $time = date("r", $row["UNIX_TIMESTAMP(timestamp)"]);
  print "<tr><td>" . $time . "</td><td>" . $row[commenter] .
        "</td><td>" . $comment . "</td></tr>\n";
}
?>
  </table>
</body>
</html>
```

Finally, you just need a main method to tell the bot which server to connect to and which channels to join. Save the following as *WeblogMain.java*:

```
public class WeblogMain {

    public static void main(String[] args) throws Exception {
        Weblog bot = new Weblog("blogger");
        bot.setVerbose(true);
        bot.connect("irc.freenode.net");
        bot.joinChannel("#irchacks");
    }

}
```

## Running the Hack

When you first visit weblog.php with your web browser, the page will obviously be empty. To populate the database, you must make the IRC bot join a channel and send it some URLs.

Compile the bot like so:

```
C:\java\Weblog> javac -classpath .;pircbot.jar;mysql-connector.jar *.java
```

Then run the bot:

```
C:\java\Weblog> java -classpath .;pircbot.jar;mysql-connector.jar WeblogMain
```

Once the bot is running, it will add all messages containing URLs to the database, ready to appear on the web page.

## The Results

As you can see from the rather plain output in Figure 6-2, you could easily spice up the appearance with a few images and other HTML hacks. Other possibilities are to allow searching of the database for entries that are older than seven days or to provide alternative output formats such as RSS.

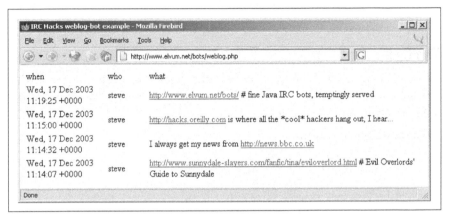

*Figure 6-2. Output from the simple Weblog bot*

A more advanced implementation of a blog bot called *scot* is available from Steve Jolly's web site at *http://www.elvum.net/scot*.

—*Steve Jolly*

### A Continuity Bot

#43

What was everyone talking about just before you joined the middle of their conversation?

Joining an IRC channel in the middle of a conversation can be a frustrating experience for all concerned, so wouldn't it be nice if there were someone there to tell you what people were talking about? Wouldn't you like to know if the awkward silence following your appearance was because everyone was busy insulting you before you joined? Now, with the miracle of the Continuity Bot Hack, you can ease seamlessly into the conversation and find out what your friends really think of you in the bargain.

This hack takes the form of *cont*, a simple bot based on the PircBot framework. When someone joins the channel it sits on, the bot sends her the last 10 events that occurred there via private message. Many people set up their clients to join multiple channels on startup. As the history is sent via private message, you may want to modify the message format to include the channel name in this case.

Do not run multiple versions of this bot on the same server—when your client autojoins multiple channels on startup, the messages from the multiple bots will get all jumbled up.

For the sake of simplicity, this bot will keep track of only what is said in a channel. This requires only normal messages and actions to be monitored.

## The Code

The file *Cont.java* will contain the code that is used to keep an eye on what people are saying in the channel. The Cont class inherits from the PircBot class to make this rather straightforward.

Save the following as *Cont.java*:

```java
import org.jibble.pircbot.*;
import java.util.*;

public class Cont extends PircBot {

    // Remember up to 10 things that happened in the channel.
    private ContextList contextList = new ContextList(10);
    private CurrentTime now = new CurrentTime();

    // Constructor used to set the name of the bot.
    public Cont() {
        this.setName("cont");
        this.setLogin("cont");
    }

    // Handle on-channel messages.
    public void onMessage(String channel, String sender,
            String login, String hostname, String message) {
        contextList.add(now + " <" + sender + "> " + message);
    }

    // Handle actions.
    public void onAction(String sender, String login,
            String hostname, String target, String action) {
        contextList.add(now + " * " + sender + " " + action);
    }

    // Handle people joining the channel.
    public void onJoin(String channel, String sender,
            String login, String hostname) {
        if (!sender.equals(getName())) {
            // Send out the history of messages to the new channel user.
            Iterator messageIt = contextList.iterator();
            while (messageIt.hasNext()) {
```

```
                sendMessage(sender, messageIt.next().toString());
            }
        }
    }

}
```

As you may have noticed, the Cont class makes use of two classes that
haven't been made yet! The first of these is ContextList, which has the
responsibility of remembering the last 10 events seen by the bot. The second is CurrentTime, which performs the trivial task of creating a simple timestamp, similar to that used by most IRC clients.

ContextList is what you might call a *ring buffer*. It is an ordered list, but its
size is limited to 10 items in this case. If the list is full and a new item is
added, the oldest item in the list is simply removed. The bot uses this class
to store the last 10 (or fewer) events that occurred on-channel, ready to be
sent to each user who joins the channel.

Now create the file *ContextList.java*:

```
import java.util.*;

public class ContextList extends Vector {

    private int maxListSize;

    public ContextList(int maxListSize) {
        this.maxListSize = maxListSize;
    }

    public boolean add(Object o) {
        if (this.size() >= maxListSize) {
            // Remove the first item if the list is full.
            this.remove(0);
        }
        // Add the new item to the end of the list.
        return super.add(o);
    }

}
```

To give the user a greater feel of temporal location, it is useful to apply timestamps to the messages. It often helps if you can tell if a message was sent 30
seconds ago or 30 minutes ago. The quickest way of getting the current time
is to call the toString() method on a new instance of the java.util.Date
class. This method may return slightly different things depending on your
locale, but it will look something like this:

```
Sat Feb 14 14:45:13 GMT 2004
```

This is rather long for messages that appear in an IRC window, and most of it is unnecessary. Not many channels are idle for more than a year, and if they are, it's unlikely that you'll want to keep your bot running in there. The CurrentTime class will generate a timestamp like 14:45.

Save this as *CurrentTime.java*:

```java
import java.io.*;
import java.util.*;
import java.text.*;

public class CurrentTime {

    private SimpleDateFormat shortDateFormat = new SimpleDateFormat("H:mm");
    private FieldPosition fp = new FieldPosition(0);

    public String toString() {
        Date now = new Date();
        StringBuffer output = new StringBuffer();
        try {
            shortDateFormat.format(now, output, fp);
        }
        catch (NullPointerException e) {
            // Date cannot be null. Ignore this.
        }
        return output.toString();
    }

}
```

All you need to do now is create a main method to run the bot from, and you're done. Save the following as *ContMain.java*:

```java
public class ContMain {

    public static void main(String[] args) throws Exception {

        Cont bot = new Cont();

        // Connect to a server and join a channel.
        bot.connect("irc.freenode.net");
        bot.joinChannel("#irchacks");
    }

}
```

## Running the Hack

Compile the classes with the javac command:

```
C:\java\ContBot> javac -classpath .;pircbot.jar *.java
```

Start the continuity bot by running the main method in the ContMain class:

```
C:\java\ContBot> java -classpath .;pircbot.jar ContMain
```

If all goes well, the bot should spring into life.

When a user joins the channel, the bot will send private messages containing the last 10 lines of text sent to the channel, as shown in Figure 6-3.

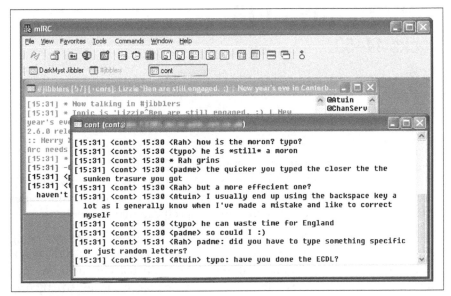

*Figure 6-3. Receiving private messages from the bot*

Using a bot like this is a great way of making sure nobody feels lost when he enters the middle of a conversation.

—*Steve Jolly*

# CHAPTER SEVEN

# Community Bots
## Hacks 44–50

IRC is strongly oriented around communities. Each channel is essentially a community in which everybody knows one another and everybody shares a common interest in the channel's topic or theme. Lots of IRC communities run a bot so they can access useful features specific to that channel.

One fun application is to use a bot like *PieSpy* to monitor messages being sent within a channel. This can be used to infer a social network in the channel and draw pretty diagrams that show the main players and how they interact with other users. While you could argue that this is not strictly useful, it is certainly entertaining, and most people find this kind of use interesting. A more practical use of social networks is employed by *TrustBot*, which can be used to determine how much you should trust a stranger on IRC.

*Infobots* are a useful way of storing factoids, which can be accessed later by asking the bot about a particular factoid. Not only is this useful for forgetful people, but you can introduce channel newcomers to factoids stored in the bot without having to do all the typing yourself.

The final hack in this chapter shows you how to pass notes to other users—an answering machine for IRC, if you prefer. This will allow messages to flow promptly and smoothly around your community, even if the recipient isn't online when the message is sent.

### HACK #44 Infer Social Networks from IRC

Most IRC channels are like small communities, and communities make patterns. Use this hack to produce pretty drawings of the social structure in your channel.

If you see a group of people talking to one another in real life, it is reasonable to assume there is some kind of relationship or friendship between them. The same principles can be applied to IRC channels. By drawing lines between users, you can produce some interesting visualizations of the social networks present.

PieSpy (*http://www.jibble.org/piespy*) is a tool that can be used to generate these diagrams automatically. It is an IRC bot that monitors a set of channels and attempts to estimate what the social network structure should look like. It does this by guessing who is talking to whom. The name of the bot originates from a channel called #pie, where it was first used to "spy" on the channel inhabitants and produce social network diagrams.

## Installing PieSpy

You can download PieSpy from *http://www.jibble.org/piespy*. It is precompiled, but the source code is also available if you feel like hacking it yourself. Unzip the archive into a new directory.

If you have Java installed, the bot is ready to run by executing the *run.bat* file on Windows or *run.sh* on Linux/Unix.

The *README.txt* file briefly describes the bot and the commands that it accepts.

## Configuring PieSpy

All configuration settings are specified in *config.ini*. Open this file in your favorite text editor.

You will need to change the server settings so you can tell the bot which server to connect to, which channel to join and so on:

```
# Server Settings:

Nick = HackSpy
Server = irc.freenode.net
ServerPassword =
Port = 6667
ChannelSet = #irchacks
```

The Nick field sets the nickname of the bot. The bot will connect to the specified Port on the Server, using the ServerPassword if required (some IRC servers are password protected). When the bot connects to the server, it will join all channels listed in the ChannelSet.

PieSpy is capable of running in multiple channels. If you want to add extra channels to the ChannelSet, simply separate them with commas, for example:

```
ChannelSet = #irchacks,#jibble
```

You need to change just one other setting, the administrator password:

```
# Administrator settings:

Password = password
```

The default value is "password," so you may wish to change it. This is the password that is used to remotely control the bot over IRC.

## Running PieSpy

Windows users can run PieSpy by double-clicking on the *run.bat* file. On Linux/Unix, you can run PieSpy by executing the *run.sh* script, like so:

```
% chmod u+x run.sh
% ./run.sh
```

The bot will then connect to the server and join the appropriate channels.

> If you are running the bot in a Linux/Unix terminal window without access to an X server, you may need to edit *run.sh* so that it has -Djava.awt.headless=true as a parameter to the java command. If you do not do this, the bot will be unable to draw anything!

## Getting Output from PieSpy

PieSpy will generate output in PNG (Portable Network Graphics) format. All modern web browsers can view these types of files. The default output directory is *./images/*, and the bot will create new directories inside this one for each channel it's in.

Each time the bot detects a change in the structure of the social network for a channel, it will write a new image. If your bot is in #irchacks, the most recent image for that channel will always be called *irchacks-current.png*. An archive is also kept, allowing you to piece together frames to create animations. Archive images are saved as *irchacks-00000000.png*, *irchacks-00000001.png*, and so on.

The bot will also save a file called *irchacks-restore.dat*. This contains information about the data used to create the images and allows the bot to save its state between invocations. If your machine crashes for some reason, you can restart the bot, and it will continue from where it left off without having to rebuild the social network from scratch.

If your output directory is visible to a web server, you can tell people to look at *irchacks-current.png*, and they will always see the latest state of the social network for #irchacks.

## Controlling PieSpy

PieSpy can be controlled remotely if you know the administrator password. If you have left it as the default of "password," other people may be able to take control of your bot.

Each command you send to the bot must be sent as a private message. For example, you can get information about the graphs being made by the bot by sending the stats command. Each command must be prefixed by the password, like so:

```
/msg HackSpy password stats
```

The bot will respond by saying how much data it has collected for each channel:

```
<HackSpy> #irchacks: Graph: 11 nodes and 0 edges.
<HackSpy> #jibble: Graph: 17 nodes and 6 edges.
```

If there are not yet any edges in the graph, the bot will not be able to generate any output. You will have to wait until people start chatting in that channel.

If you want to remove the bot from a channel, send the part command:

```
/msg HackSpy password part #irchacks
* HackSpy has left #irchacks
```

To make the bot go back to that channel, send the join command:

```
/msg HackSpy password join #irchacks
* HackSpy has joined #irchacks
```

If someone is being silly on the channel and you want the bot to ignore her, you can add her nickname to the ignore list in *config.ini*. You can also add nicknames to the bot's ignore list while it is running, by using the ignore command. It is sometimes useful to add so-called *welcome bots* to the ignore list; otherwise, they end up looking rather popular with everybody:

```
/msg HackSpy password ignore WelcomeBot
```

WelcomeBot will now be ignored whenever it says anything, so it won't be included in the social network. If WelcomeBot already existed in the graph, it would have been removed when you used the ignore command.

If you do not have direct access to the file store on which the bot is running, you can tell it to send you the current image via DCC:

```
/msg HackSpy password draw #jibble
<HackSpy> Trying to send "jibble-00000014.png"... If you have difficulty in
    receiving this file via DCC, there may be a firewall between us.
```

The bot will then send the file to you via DCC. Note the warning about firewalls—if you are unable to connect directly to the bot, you will not be able to receive the image.

Using the raw command, you can tell the bot to send a raw line to the IRC server. If you know enough about the IRC protocol, you will be able to get the bot to do practically anything you want with this command. For example, to get the bot to send a message to the channel, you could do this:

```
/msg HackSpy password raw PRIVMSG #irchacks :Hello, I'm a PieSpy bot!
```

## The Results

When you look at the output from the PieSpy bot, you will see a collection of nodes scattered about. Some of these nodes will have lines connecting them to show that there is some kind of relationship present.

The diagram shown in Figure 7-1 was taken a couple of days after the O'Reilly Emerging Technology Conference in 2004. A large number of attendees used the channel to chat with one another. The graph shows only the active users at that time. In particular, note how popular the user "jibot" seems—jibot is an IRC bot that introduces people when they join the channel, so PieSpy infers relationships between them.

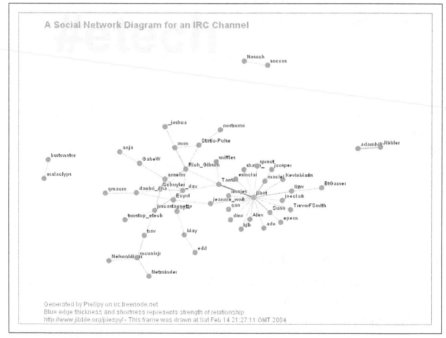

*Figure 7-1. PieSpy running in #etech after the O'Reilly Emerging Technology Conference in 2004*

Strong relationships are represented with thicker, shorter lines with more opacity. PieSpy uses temporal decay to ensure that each relationship slowly fades away over time, resulting in much more exciting animations. If you are feeling adventurous, you can try changing the temporal decay settings in the *config.ini* file.

## Run an Infobot

#45 Set up an infobot to sit in your channel, learning facts and reeling off useful information.

Infobots are handy. You can use them for any number of things: to leave notes for other users, inquire when someone was last seen around the channel, do quick math problems, or simulate dice rolls. But the most important feature of the infobot is undoubtedly its *factoid* support. These are simply a combination of a key phrase and a response. For example, if you have an infobot called Fiona, you can feed it a factoid like this:

```
<Fennec> Fiona, the official site is http://www.reuben.org/holbrook/index.
htm
```

Every time someone comes into your channel and asks:

```
<RandomGuy> Where is the official site?
```

He'll get a fast and effective reply from the infobot, saving you the effort of typing the answer:

```
<Fiona> The official site is http://www.reuben.org/holbrook/index.htm
```

The infobot source also allows for some variation, to better serve the clueless. For example, it would also respond to the following questions:

```
<RandomGuy> so where is the official site?
<RandomGuy> the official site?
<RandomGuy> but what is the official site?
```

### Getting Infobot

Your first step is to obtain the infobot source code. You can get this from *http://www.infobot.org*. You will also need to have Pcrl installed, as infobot is implemented in this language.

**Configuration.** All the configuration files are in the *conf* directory. Your first stop should be to edit *infobot.config*. Open this in your favorite text editor and review all of the options, but note especially the values that you will probably want to change for your bot:

ident

> The name of the infobot, for internal purposes. The bot will respond to this identity and use its value for certain pronouns. This is perhaps the most important setting for your bot. You should try to make it appropriate for the channel's general theme.

wantNick

> The nickname of the infobot, for the IRC server. The bot will attempt to connect under this nickname.

dbName

> The prefix for the infobot's database filenames. You may wish to change it to match the name of the bot.

logfile

> The name of the bot's log file.

server

> The IRC server to connect to.

port

> The port to use for the IRC server. You will need to specify this if you use something other than port 6667.

join_channels

> The channels your infobot should automatically join.

allowed_channels

> The channels the bot should generally be allowed to join.

friendlyBots

> If you know of other bots whose knowledge you can trust, place their nicknames here, and the bot will ask them questions that it is unsure about.

The parameters *addressing* and *no-require-question* should also be considered, along with the needs of your channel.

## Set Up Users

Now you should edit *infobot.users*. This file holds all the user information and permissions data for your infobot. After the opening comment, which describes the meaning of all flags this file should have by default:

```
UserEntry default {
    flags    +trmcs;
    }
```

Consider what kind of permissions you want your infobot to have. +tmrc means that anyone can teach the bot or remove or change a factoid. If you trust people with your bot, this is the best option, but it leaves you prone to vandalism. Alternatively, you could leave it as:

```
flags;
```

and give out accounts under the infobot to whomever you trust.

The first infobot account should be your own. Change the following to suit yourself:

```
UserEntry FooBarBaz {
      name    "Jacob Riis";
      title   "Bot owner";
      flags   +frtmcsSope;
      mask    *!*@*.wfu.edu;
      mask    *!*@152.17.*.*;
      mask    *!*@*.mis.prserv.net;
      mask    *!*@eh.net
}
```

The portion after `UserEntry` (in this case, `FooBarBaz`) is the name of the account. This name is used when querying the infobot about who has been setting factoids. The name and title fields are primarily for your benefit as the infobot maintainer, so you can remember who the user is. The flags are simply a list of all the powers you wish to grant to the user—in this case, all powers.

## Using the Infobot

Once the infobot is up and running with your chosen setting, you are ready to use it. In the following examples, the infobot is called Fiona. The following dialogs show off most of the factoid features.

As a general rule, the infobot will respond when you address it with a new factoid, in this case a quote from a film:

```
<Foo> Fiona, today is a good day to die!
<Fiona> Okay, Foo.
```

The infobot will then learn that "today" is "a good day to die!"

You can then ask the infobot about this factoid in several different ways:

```
<Foo> Fiona, today?
<Fiona> today is a good day to die!
<Foo> today?
<Fiona> today is a good day to die!
<Foo> today?
<Foo> what is toDay?
<Fiona> toDay is a good day to die!
<Foo> who is today?
<Fiona> today is a good day to die!
```

If you try to teach the infobot a factoid that it has already learned, it will refuse to add it, and it will tell you what the existing meaning is:

```
<Foo> Fiona: today is the day after yesterday.
<Fiona> ... but today is a good day to die! ...
```

To add an extra meaning, you can add the "also" token:

```
<Foo> Fiona, today is also the day after yesterday.
<Fiona> Okay, Foo.
```

So when you ask what "today" is, the infobot will now respond with both factoids:

```
<Foo> today?
<Fiona> today is a good day to die! or the day after yesterday
```

You can also tell an infobot to forget a factoid:

```
<Foo> Fiona, forget today.
<Fiona> Okay, Foo.
```

If you tell the infobot to forget a factoid that doesn't exist, it will let you know:

```
<Foo> Fiona, forget tomorrow.
<Fiona> I didn't have anything matching "tomorrow", Foo.
```

You can also customize the way in which the infobot responds to questions. By adding <reply> to the start of your fact, you can get the infobot to reply with exactly what you want:

```
<Foo> Fiona, tomorrow is <reply> ./~ Tomorrow, tomorrow, I love you,
tomorrow, you're always a day away! ./~
<Fiona> Okay, Foo.
<Foo> Tomorrow?
<Fiona> ./~ Tomorrow, tomorrow, I love you, tomorrow, you're always a day
away! ./~
```

To tell an infobot to forget about an existing factoid and replace it with a new one, you can use the "no" token, like so:

```
<Foo> no, Fiona, tomorrow is another day.
<Fiona> Okay, Foo.
```

To start introducing some random replies, you can use the | character to specify alternatives. This next example adds "Christmas!" to the list of possible replies:

```
<Foo> Fiona, tomorrow is also | Christmas!
<Fiona> Okay, Foo.
```

So when you ask the infobot what "tomorrow" is, it will randomly give one of two replies:

```
<Foo> Tomorrow?
<Fiona> Tomorrow is Christmas!
<Foo> Tomorrow?
<Fiona> Tomorrow is Christmas!
<Foo> Tomorrow?
<Fiona> Tomorrow is another day.
```

```
<Foo> Tomorrow?
<Fiona> Tomorrow is Christmas!
```

You can also define alternative replies in a single line. The next example tells the infobot to respond with one of three actions. The $who variable gets replaced by the nickname of the user who talks to the infobot:

```
<Foo> Fiona, Coke is <action> serves $who a glass of ice cold coke. |
<action> cannot serve $who more coke, too much caffeine for you. | <action>
happily serves
$who a can of cold Coca Cola (tm)
<Fiona> Okay, Foo.
<Foo> Coke?
* Fiona serves Foo a glass of ice cold coke.
```

You can then see the literal definition for "coke":

```
<Foo> literal coke?
<Fiona> Foo: coke =is=  <action> serves $who a glass of ice cold coke. |
<action>
cannot serve $who more coke, too much caffeine for you. | <action> happily
serves
$who a can of cold Coca Cola (tm)
```

You can even find out who set the factoid:

```
<Foo> Fiona, who set coke?
<Fiona> coke was set by Foo
```

The infobot can also pass messages on to other users:

```
<Foo> Fiona, note to Foo: Silly user.
<Fiona> Okay, I will tell that to Foo.
<Foo> Fiona: note to Fennec Fun stuff, man!
<Fiona> Sorry, I don't know who Fennec is; perhaps you mistyped it?
(private message) <Fiona> Foo left you a note: Silly user.
```

## Reprogramming the Infobot

The infobot was programmed in Perl. Reprogramming the infobot's internals to change its behavior often results in a mess, so you're on your own here. But if you'd just like to add a new capability, it should be pretty simple. Just edit *extras/myRoutines.pl*. That file should already contain fairly detailed instructions on what is expected. Here's a sample that implements dice rolls for the Freeform Universal Do-It-Yourself Gaming Engine (FUDGE). Somewhere in sub myRoutines, enter:

```
    if($addressed && $message =~ /(roll|fudge|fudgeroll|fudge roll)? (\
d+)?dF/i) {
        return fudgeroll($2);
    }
```

Later on in the file, insert the subroutine that will perform the dice rolling:

```
sub fudgeroll { # Freeform Universal DIY Gaming Engine
    (my $dicecount) = @_;
    my $rollstring = "$who, the FUDGE dice read: (";
    my $rolltotal = 0;
    if($dicecount == 0){ $dicecount = 4; } # standard FUDGE roll has 4 dice
    if($dicecount > 20){ return "Too many dice, $who!"; }
    if($dicecount < 1){ return "Too few dice, $who!"; }
    for($x = 0; $x < $dicecount; $x++){
        $a = int(rand(3)) - 1;
        $rolltotal += $a;
        $rollstring .= $a;
    }
    $_ = $rollstring . "): ";
    s/-1/&/g; # make pretty +/- marks
    s/1/\+/g;
    s/&/\-/g;
    return $_ . $rolltotal;
}
```

You will now be able to use the roll (or fudge, fudgeroll, fudge roll) command to get the infobot to roll some dice for you. (For example: Fiona, roll
10dF.)

—*Thomas Whaples*

## HACK #46  Use PPF for Gaming Clans

Many online gamers hang out together on IRC. Extend the IRC bot PPF with
plug-ins to support these communities and provide various game-related
tools.

PPF is a great tool for gamers using IRC, especially for clans. It has plug-ins
for querying some online game systems, game servers, searching, and even
for customizing your own triggers. This hack shows you how to go about
configuring and using PPF from a clan's perspective. PPF stands for PircBot
Plug-in Framework—it is an IRC bot based on the PircBot framework and
uses plug-ins to facilitate easy addition of features.

### Get PPF

PPF can be downloaded from *http://www.deaded.com*. It is available in two
versions:

- A version containing just the bot, which is recommended if you already
  have Java installed.
- A version containing the bot and the Java Runtime Environment. This
  allows you to use a single installer to set up Java and PPF.

After PPF is installed, the directory will look similar to Figure 7-2.

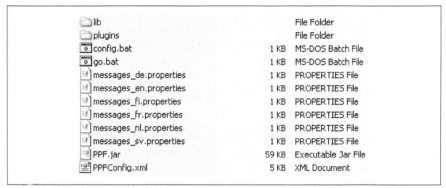

*Figure 7-2. A complete installation of PPF*

Within the PPF directory are the startup files and the main bot configuration files. The *plugins* directory contains subdirectories relevant to each plug-in that is installed. The default plug-ins are shown in Figure 7-3.

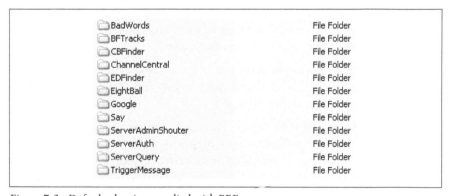

*Figure 7-3. Default plug-ins supplied with PPF*

If the plug-in has a configuration file, it will be found within the relevant subdirectory and be named <plugin_name>Config.xml–e.g., the *Say* plug-in will have a config file called *SayConfig.xml*.

## PPF Core

The core is where the main IRC configuration, bot info, and plug-ins are managed. The bot alone is pretty useless—adding the plug-ins creates the functionality of the bot. Plug-ins can be loaded, configured and reloaded, or unloaded even while PPF is running.

The main config file is *PPFConfig.xml* and is stored in the root of the PPF installation. Let's quickly go over some of the settings to get you started.

Auth levels are used to control access to the bot's commands. There are currently three levels: bot owner, bot master, and trusted. The owner can do things like manage the plug-ins, move the bot to other channels, change its name, or even kill the bot. Each plug-in allows the use of certain commands, and each plug-in gets to control which auth level is needed for these. The password for each auth level is set in `adminPassword`, `masterPassword`, and `trustedPassword`.

The `servers`, `nicks`, and `channels` sections are for telling the bot which server you want it to connect to, what nickname it should have, and what channels to join when it starts up.

One setting to take care with is the `messageDelay` setting. This defines how fast the bot will send messages to the IRC server. If it sends messages too rapidly, it will get kicked for flooding. Different networks have different tolerances, so you may have to play with that a little.

`onJoinMessage` is what the bot sends as a notice to anyone who joins the channel. By default, it will send a message telling people what the help command is. As a clan, you may want to give some useful clan information first and then say what the rest of the help is afterward.

Some of the core commands can be configured; for example, many other bots have **!help** as their help command, so you can change the PPF help command to something else if you want.

Finally, there is the `plugins` section. This is where the plug-ins that will be available to the bot are configured. The plug-ins can be configured here, and you can decide if you want them loaded at startup or not. Later on, if a new plug-in is made available, this is where the configuration is added, and then you will be able to load it.

## Running PPF

PPF is written in Java, so it can be run on any system that has a Java Runtime available.

Once you have configured your bot, you are ready to run it:

```
C:\java\PPF> set CLASSPATH=%CLASSPATH%;.;PPF.jar;lib\pircbot.jar;lib\jaxen-\
core.jar;lib\jaxen-jdom.jar;lib\jdom.jar;lib\saxpath.jar;lib\xerces.jar

C:\java\PPF> java net.sourceforge.ppf.PPF
```

Alternatively, Windows users can run the supplied *run.bat* file.

As soon as the bot is up and running, you can auth with it through your IRC client (assuming the bot is called PPF):

```
/msg PPF auth adminPassword
```

## ChannelCentral

This plug-in gives some control or information about the channels that the bot is in. The configuration is stored in the file *ChannelCentralConfig.xml*.

Basic channel commands such as voice and op are available to someone with the correct auth level. This plug-in also allows topic showing and setting, channel stats, and the possibility to auto voice or op people based upon their auth level with the bot.

This plug-in also tracks statistics in a *LiveStats.xml* file, which contains current information about the channel. You could then do some simple XML parsing to create a web page that shows live information about the channel.

## TriggerMessage

This plug-in lets the bot respond to things that are said in a channel. You can change settings for this plug-in in *TriggerMessageConfig.xml*.

Perhaps you would like people to know about the homepage, servers, or members in your clan? A trigger for the homepage could be !www. When this is typed in the channel, you could get the bot to respond with something like this:

```
<PPF> Homepage for Clan KsR is http://www.clan-ksr.com
```

To manage the triggers, you must auth with the bot as a trusted (or more powerful) user and type into the channel:

```
<Paul> !at "!www" "Homepage for Clan KsR is http://www.clan-ksr.com"
```

You may also want to tell everyone the IP address and port numbers of your servers. This is one way of doing it:

```
<Paul> !at "!server" "KsR BF server: 213.253.57.28:14567:23000
    :: Type !qf for status"
<Paul> !at "!ip" "KsR BF server: 213.253.57.28:14567:23000
    :: Type !qf for status"
```

As you can see, you can have triggers for whatever you like and even make different triggers for showing the same info to make it easier to use. Users can get the IP address by saying either **!server** or **!ip**. The !qf command will be covered in the ServerQuery plug-in section later in this hack.

You can set up a trigger to announce the members of the clan:

```
<Paul> !at "!members" "Plexor, Mad_Bear, Saint, Deady, Buscape, Deadly
    Style, TaN, Mark Gor, Qball, Blackhawk, Lostworld, Godfather, Sicillian,
    Aggressor, Sisu, DeadEd, Heavens Gate, Sgt.Mac, Goateh, Sidewinder, Seeker"
```

Now that there are some triggers, the list can be seen by sending a private message to the bot:

```
/msg PPF !st
```

The bot will request a DCC chat session with you and then send the list of the triggers and the responses. Each trigger can then be removed using the !rt command in the channel:

```
<Paul> !rt !server
```

This will result in the !server trigger being removed. The bot will no longer respond to that command.

Finally, a new trigger can be made to tell users how to get info about your clan:

```
<Paul> !at "!claninfo" "Commands are: !www - !ip - !members - !help"
```

The onJoinMessage in the main configuration file (*PPFConfig.xml*) could now be changed to "Welcome to Clan KsR". Type !**claninfo** for help. Users entering the channel will then receive the message telling them what commands are available to get further information.

## ServerQuery

With this plug-in, you can currently query Half-Life and Battlefield 1942–based servers for basic server and player information. You can also manage a list of shortcuts so that you don't need to remember IP addresses and port numbers. The commands and output styles can be configured by editing *ServerQueryConfig.xml*.

Add the IP address of your clan server as a defaultServers in the configuration file. Default servers can be queried by just typing !**qf**, which returns the server details and scores ("frags"). By adding the Battlefield 1942 server 213.253.57.28 (with default query port of 23000), typing !**qf** would show something like this:

```
<Paul> !qf
<PPF> -=Kingsize Rizla=- [KsR] :: IP: 213.253.57.28:14567 :: BF1942 :: Map:
    stalingrad :: Players: 3/32 [LK]Fubar [12,10,6], [KsR]DeadEd [10/2/3],
    Jibbler [2/2/2]
```

To query a different server, you can specify the IP address and port number after the !qf command. To see only "frag" information, you can type !**f**. To just query the server details, you can use the !q command:

```
<Paul> !q 194.29.194.31:27015
<PPF> The Gory Grave of -GG- :: IP: 194.29.194.31:27015 :: Counter-Strike ::
    Map:de_inferno :: Players: 1/15
```

This can be made easier by adding a shortcut (shortcut management requires trusted or higher auth level):

```
!sc gg 194.29.194.31 27015
```

This now means that you can use gg when querying:

```
<Paul> !q gg
<PPF> The Gory Grave of -GG- :: IP: 194.29.194.31:27015 :: Counter-Strike ::
Map:de_inferno :: Players: 1/15
```

A list of the shortcuts can be seen by sending a private message to the bot:

```
/msg PPF !ssc
```

The bot will then request a DCC chat session with you and send the list of shortcuts, with the IP address and port number for each one. The shortcuts can then be removed with the !rsc command:

```
<Paul> !rsc gg
```

## ServerAdminShouter

With this plug-in, you can monitor game servers for certain names or for large negative scores and receive alerts via private messages on IRC. It can be configured by editing the file *ServerAdminShouterConfig.xml*. You can currently monitor Half-Life and Battlefield 1942 servers with this plug-in.

You can become one of the people who gets notified in two ways. One is to have your nickname listed in the admins section of the configuration file. The other is to auth and then give the "on duty" command. The default for this is !onDuty.

Add the servers that you want to monitor to the servers section in the configuration file. Set the checkTimer to the interval, in seconds, that you want the bot to check for the names or score that you set in the triggers section. If there is a problem on a game server and there isn't an administrator around to fix it at the time, players will often change their name to something that indicates the need for an administrator, in the hope that someone will see it in the log file or game browser. Names such as adminneeded could be added as triggers, and then a server message or message of the day (MOTD) can be added to the server, telling people how to grab the attention of an administrator.

Now, when someone in the server changes her name to adminneeded or a score goes below the allowed limit, administrators will receive a private message telling them which server help is needed on.

## CBFinder

This plug-in lets you find out information about a clan from the ClanBase system (*http://www.clanbase.com*). This can be configured by editing *CBFinderConfig.xml*.

Querying the ClanBase system can reveal details such as a clan's ladder rank-ing, what ladders they are in, the last five wars they played, whom the wars were against, on which map they played, and what the scores were. To search ClanBase for the Battlefield 1942 clan KsR, you would type the following:

```
<Paul> !cb BF KsR
```

If the bot can find the requested information, it will generate a quite lengthy reply:

```
<PPF> Clan Information:
<PPF>    Name: Kingsize Rizla *
<PPF>    Tag: [KsR]
<PPF>    CB Home: http://www.clanbase.com/claninfo.php?cid=75433
<PPF> Ladder Information:
<PPF>    Name: Battlefield1942 Conquest  (Europe)
<PPF>    Rank: 28 :: Points: 1,206
<PPF>    Match Information (last 5 played):
<PPF>      Date, Opponent, Maps, Clan score, Opponent score
<PPF>      19 Feb, reborn, stalinggrad/wake island, 126, 407
<PPF>      11 Feb, DW, stalinggrad/berlin, 288, 40
<PPF>      4 Jan, BFD, stalinggrad/el alamein, 258, 254
<PPF>      14 Dec \ 03, DerQ, stalinggrad/el alamein, 130, 262
<PPF>      7 Dec \ 03, FTA, stalinggrad/wake island, 349, 218
<PPF>
<PPF>      Name: Battlefield1942 Battlefield 1942 Conquest Cup
<PPF>    Rank: N/A :: Points: N/A
<PPF>    Match Information (last 0 played):
<PPF>    No match information available
<PPF>
<PPF>    Name: Battlefield1942 Battlefield 1942 Conquest Cup
<PPF>    Rank: N/A :: Points: N/A
<PPF>    Match Information (last 5 played):
<PPF>      Date, Opponent, Maps, Clan score, Opponent score
<PPF>      26 Nov \ 03, PIRATAS, stalingrad/operation battl, 403, 472
<PPF>      17 Nov \ 03, IP, el alamein/kursk, 940, 222
<PPF>      29 Oct \ 03, wb, operation marke/, 662, 74
<PPF>      26 Oct \ 03, SSS, operation aberd/, 539, 0
<PPF>      15 Oct \ 03, BuD, iwo jima/, 433, 501
```

It can take some time for the bot to output everything due to the flood pro-tection features, so there is also a DCC chat version available. This allows you to create a connection directly to the bot, letting it send the data as fast as it can:

```
!cbdcc BF KsR
```

Your own clan details can be added to the default settings so that you only need to type !cb.

## BFTracks

This plug-in lets you find information about players who are being tracked with the BFTracks system (*http://www.bftracks.net*). You can get static information about players, or even live information showing where they are playing. The commands, output of the commands, and number of lines returned can be configured by editing *BFTracksConfig.xml*.

To request information about a player (with the results being sent to the channel), you can use the !bf command, followed by the name:

```
<Paul> !bf deaded
<PPF> [KsR]DeadEd :: [4535](620 points) ::
     http://bftracks.net/appl/bft/Player/view/742845
```

Information about a clan yields a longer set of results, so these are sent to you via private messages:

```
<Paul> !bfclanlist [KsR]
<PPF> [KsR]Heavens :: [767](837 points) ::
     http://bftracks.net/appl/bft/Player/view/943822
<PPF> [KsR]Sidewinder :: [-](799 points) ::
     http://bftracks.net/appl/bft/Player/view/1694267
<PPF> [KsR]Mark Gor :: [1289](776 points) ::
     http://bftracks.net/appl/bft/Player/view/104324
<PPF> [KsR]**Sgt.Mac** :: [2626](687 points) ::
     http://bftracks.net/appl/bft/Player/view/1497664
<PPF> [KsR]Qball :: [3514](653 points) ::
     http://bftracks.net/appl/bft/Player/view/103982
     ...
<PPF> [KsR]Seeker :: [-](378 points) ::
     http://bftracks.net/appl/bft/Player/view/1698625
<PPF> [KsR]Buscape[AWOL] :: [-](294 points) ::
     http://bftracks.net/appl/bft/Player/view/1764651
```

You can get live information about players with the !bflive command:

```
<Paul> !bflive [KsR]
<PPF> [KsR]Heavens[7/5/4] :: Server: EAUK 04 - Western Front IP:
     159.153.178.75:14567:: Map: bocage
<PPF> [KsR]TaN[5/5/2] :: Server: EAUK 04 - Western Front IP:
     159.153.178.75:14567:: Map: bocage
```

## EDFinder

This plug-in lets you find out information about a clan from the Enemy Down system (*http://www.enemydown.co.uk*).

This !ed command gives you some basic information about a clan and a link into the system:

```
<Paul> !ed roffs
<PPF> Clan Information:
```

```
<PPF>    Name: -=ROFFS=-
<PPF>    Tag: ROFFS
<PPF>    ED Home: http://www.enemydown.co.uk/clan.php?id=137
<PPF>    Website: www.roffs.co.uk
<PPF>    IRC Channel: #roffs
<PPF>    Server IP: 195.20.108.172:27015
```

Once again, it can take some time to output everything due to the flood protection, so a DCC chat version—!eddcc—is also available.

## Google

Everyone loves Google. Just type **!google** and some search phrase and the top result will be given as a link to the channel:

```
<Paul> !google PPF bot framework
<PPF> [PPF bot framework] http://www.deaded.com/ (DeadEd.com - PPF (Pircbot
    Plugin Framework) and MatchEd IRC Bot ...)
```

## Other Plug-ins

Several other plug-ins are available for PPF. New and existing plug-ins are being constantly developed. Some of the other plug-ins are: Advertiser, BadWords, EightBall, MySQLQuery, Say, Seen, ServerAuth, and Translate1337.

*—Alex North*

## HACK
## #47     Write a Plug-in for PPF

Now that you know how to use the PircBot Plug-in Framework and configure its various plug-ins, let your creative juices flow by making your own plug-in.

PPF (PircBot Plug-in Framework) is an open source (*http://opensource.org*) plug-in framework built on top of the PircBot IRC API. It provides some basic functionality, such as connecting to IRC, joining channels, and some auth levels for access control. The PPF core itself doesn't really do very much at all, as the functionality comes from each of the plug-ins you use. Full details about the project, latest releases, plug-ins, documentation, and source code (via CVS) can be found at *http://www.sourceforge.net/projects/*ppf.

The plug-ins can be built quite easily by extending an abstract class called PPFPlugin. By inheriting the functionality of this class, a plug-in can include features such as XML configuration, and it can store persistent data, be internationalizable, and also provide dynamic online help.

This hack will show you how to create a simple plug-in and demonstrate some of the features that make it easy to do frequently performed tasks.

## The Code

The simple plug-in will be called Simple, so create a new directory called *Simple* under the *plugins* directory. Then create the directory path for the source code under that (*src/net/sourceforge/ppf/plugin/simpleplugin*). You should end up with something like Figure 7-4.

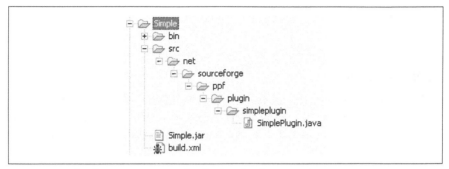

*Figure 7-4. The directory structure for the Simple plug-in*

Now create a file called *SimplePlugin.java* in the *simpleplugin* directory:

```
package net.sourceforge.ppf.plugin.simpleplugin;

import net.sourceforge.ppf.PPF;
import net.sourceforge.ppf.PPFPlugin;
import net.sourceforge.ppf.util.PPFHelp;

public class SimplePlugin extends PPFPlugin {

    static final String PLUGIN_VERSION = "1.0";
    // The commands the plug-in will respond to.
    static final String COMMAND_TIME = "!time";
    static final String COMMAND_HELLO = "!hello";

    public SimplePlugin( ) {
        // Set the plug-in version information.
        setVersion(PLUGIN_VERSION);

        // Set the help responses for this plug-in.
        setHelp(COMMAND_TIME, new PPFHelp(COMMAND_TIME,
                "Show the time of the server that the bot is running on",
                PPF.AUTH_NONE));
        setHelp(COMMAND_HELLO, new PPFHelp(COMMAND_HELLO,
                "The bot says hello back to you", PPF.AUTH_NONE));
    }

    // Respond to channel messages.
    public void onMessage(String channel, String sender, String login,
            String hostname, String message) {
```

```
        if(message.equalsIgnoreCase(COMMAND_TIME)) {
            String time = new java.util.Date().toString();
            getBot().sendMessage(channel, sender +
                    ": The time where I am is currently: "+ time);
        } else if(message.equalsIgnoreCase(COMMAND_HELLO)) {
            getBot().sendMessage(channel, "Hi there " + sender + "!");
        }


    }

}
```

## Running the Hack

PPF uses ANT (*http://ant.apache.org*) as its build system. The main build file has the necessary targets ready to call, so you just need to make a simple build file for the plug-in that sets the name and location of the plug-in and calls the main build file.

Make a file called *build.xml* in the new plug-in directory. An easy way of doing this is to copy an existing one from another plug-in and change the contents so it looks like this:

```
<?xml version="1.0"?>

<project basedir="." default="deploy">

    <property name = "plugin.project" value = "Simple"/>
    <property name = "plugin.name"    value = "Simple"/>

    <path id="plugin.classpath">
      <fileset dir=".">
        <include name="*.jar"/>
      </fileset>
    </path>

    <!-- Call the PPF build script to perform the build.
    You can set the plugin-specific details here and keep
    the PPF classpath in one place -->
    <target name="compile">
        <ant antfile="../../build.xml" target="compile.plugin"
inheritRefs="true"/>
    </target>

    <target name="deploy" depends="compile">
        <jar jarfile="./${plugin.name}.jar" basedir="bin"/>
    </target>
</project>
```

Run the deploy target from the project build file and the source code will be compiled. The compiled bytecode will be placed into a JAR file in the plug-in directory named *Simple.jar*.

PPF now needs to be configured to load this plug-in. In *PPFConfig.xml*, you need to add:

```
<plugin load="yes">
  <name>Simple</name>
  <classname>net.sourceforge.ppf.plugin.simpleplugin.SimplePlugin</
classname>
</plugin>
```

If PPF is not yet running, just start it and the Simple plug-in will be loaded.

If PPF is already running, you can *auth* as admin by entering:

```
/msg BotName auth adminPassword
```

The plug-in can then be loaded dynamically by entering:

```
/msg BotName loadplugin Simple
```

The plug-in is now ready to be used and will respond to !time and !hello:

```
<DeadEd> !time
<PPF> DeadEd: The time where I am is currently: Thu Mar 18 13:48:32 EET 2004
<DeadEd> !hello
<PPF> Hi there DeadEd!
```

### Creating Advanced Plug-ins

This is an example of some of the things that can be achieved with the plug-in framework. All onXxx methods available from the PircBot API are passed to the plugin class. Methods are also available to assist in reading in XML configuration files, making some information persistent, viewing that information, internationalization, and dynamic help.

*—Alex North*

## HACK #48 Getting Friendly with FOAFBot

Come to grips with the Semantic Web by using FOAFBot to find out information about your friends and strangers alike.

The Semantic Web is the next generation of the Web. Instead of being made up of just web pages, the Semantic Web uses languages that store information in a way that computers can understand it. Using standard languages like RDF (*http://www.w3.org/TR/rdf-syntax-grammar*), RDFS, and OWL (*http://www.w3.org/TR/owl-features*), users can create files called *ontologies* that have classes of things and the properties that apply to them. People can then make instances of classes that anyone has defined on the Semantic Web.

FOAF, the Friend-Of-A-Friend ontology (*http://www.foaf-project.org*), is one of the more popular ontologies and Semantic Web applications. The ontology defines a class called Person, and the related properties, such as name, email address, web page address, photographic depictions, and, most importantly, whom the person knows. When people create FOAF data about themselves and their friends, they can point to the FOAF files of their friends. Those files will, in turn, give information about the friends and point to the FOAF files of people the friend knows. This branches out to form a large social network. Some common properties of people in FOAF are listed in Table 7-1.

*Table 7-1. FOAF properties*

| | |
|---|---|
| accountName | mbox |
| accountServiceHomepage | mbox_sha1sum |
| aimChatID | msnChatID |
| based_near | myersBriggs |
| currentProject | name |
| depiction | nick |
| dnaChecksum | page |
| family_name | pastProject |
| firstName | phone |
| fundedBy | plan |
| geekcode | Publications |
| gender | schoolHomepage |
| givenname | surname |
| holdsAccount | title |
| homepage | topic |
| icqChatID | topic_interest |
| img | weblog |
| interest | workInfoHomepage |
| jabberID | workplaceHomepage |
| knows | yahooChatID |

Many web applications show FOAF data and the resulting networks. Foaf-naut (*http://www.foafnaut.org*) is an SVG-based visualization of the FOAF networks. Foaf-a-matic is a web-based form that automatically creates a FOAF file without requiring the user to learn the Semantic Web languages. Several other applications are linked from the FOAF Project web site (*http://foaf-project.org*).

Edd Dumbill created the first FOAFBot, which could be queried for personal information about any person in the network, including who they know. More information, including his original Python source code, is available at *http://usefulinc.com/foaf/foafbot*. This hack will present the steps required to create your own FOAF-aware IRC agent.

## Parsing a FOAF File

FOAF files are written in OWL, the Web Ontology Language. Writing a good OWL parser would take a long time, but luckily, many are available for free on the Web. One of the most popular is Jena, developed at HP Labs (*http://www.hpl.hp.com/semweb/jena.htm*). It is a Java-based parser, available in a single JAR file. The online documentation is excellent, and the API is relatively intuitive. In this section, you will be taken through the stcps of loading a FOAF file with Jena, retrieving the relevant information, and storing it in a data structure.

Before you start, there are some Semantic Web basics that are worth knowing. Everything on the Semantic Web—files, classes, properties, and instances—are all identified by their URIs. A URI (Uniform Resource Indicator) is a web address for the concept. URIs generally take the form of the web address of the file, followed by a "#" and the ID of a concept. For example, the URI of a FOAF file may be *http://example.com/myFoaf.rdf*. If, within that file, you defined an instance of the Person class with the ID "BobSmith," the URI for Bob would be *http://example.com/myFoaf.rdf#BobSmith*.

A statement on the Semantic Web takes a form called a triple. As you might expect, a triple has three parts: subject, predicate, and object. The subject is the thing being described. The predicate is the property of the subject that is being described, and the object is the value of the property. For example, say there was a property "age." Table 7-2 shows an example of a triple representing Bob Smith, age 21.

*Table 7-2. Example of a triple*

| Subject | Predicate | Object |
|---------|-----------|--------|
| BobSmith | age | 21 |

Since everything on the Semantic Web is identified by a URI, every property, class, and instance in the triple is actually identified by its URI. The full triple for the example in the table would be:

```
Subject:   http://example.com/myFoaf.rdf#BobSmith
Predicate: http://example.com/another.rdf#age
Object:    21
```

Here, the object "21" is just a literal value, so it does not get a URI. If you wanted to connect two *objects*—say Bob Smith and Joe Schmoe—in a triple, there would be three URIs:

```
Subject:   http://example.com/myFoaf.rdf#BobSmith
Predicate: http://example.com/another.rdf#knows
Object:    http://example.com/myFoaf.rdf#JoeSchmoe
```

A general familiarity with this triple and URI structure will make the Jena output easier to understand and work with.

To begin coding, you will need a class to store all of the FOAF information about a person. The class should have all the properties available in FOAF. The value for each property value will be a string; however, a person can have multiple values for any of these fields (e.g., a person can have multiple email addresses). Thus, the class will maintain a Vector of Strings to store the values for each property:

```java
import java.util.*;
import com.hp.hpl.jena.rdf.model.*;

public class Person {

    // Store the info in a hash of Vectors.
    public Hashtable foafData = new Hashtable();

    public Person() {
        // For now, we will leave this blank...
    }
}
```

With the class in hand, you need to parse the FOAF file and add the correct values to an instance of the Person class. To parse a file in Jena, you first create a model and then read the FOAF file into the model. The FOAF filename should be given by its address on the Web:

```java
import java.util.*;
import java.awt.*;
import com.hp.hpl.jena.rdf.model.*;
import java.io.*;

public class Foaf {

    private static Hashtable foafHash = new Hashtable();
    private static String inputFile = "http://www.cs.umd.edu/~golbeck/foaf.rdf";

    public static void main (String argv[]) {
        Model model = ModelFactory.createDefaultModel();
        model.read(inputFile);
    }

}
```

Once the model has parsed the file, you have to retrieve the triples. The Jena web docs are useful in this respect. To make the process easier, the code for iterating through the statements is:

```java
// Get a list of the subjects.
ResIterator it = model.listSubjects();
```

```
while (it.hasNext( )) {
    Resource subject = it.nextResource( );

    // Get all the properties of the current subject.
    StmtIterator statements = subject.listProperties( );

    while (statements.hasNext( )){
        // This statement is a triple (subject, predicate, and object)
        Statement s = statements.nextStatement( );
    }
}
```

Now that you have access to the triples in the file, storing the FOAF data comes down to a basic series of if statements. Each time a new *subject* is encountered, you create an instance of the Person class. For each of the properties of the subject, you will check the URI of the predicate and, if it is a FOAF property, add the value to the proper Vector in the Person's Hashtable.

```
while (it.hasNext( )) {
    Resource subject = it.nextResource( );

    // Create the person that this subject may represent.
    Person p = new Person( );
    boolean isPerson = false;

    // Get all of the properties of the current subject.
    StmtIterator statements = subject.listProperties( );

    while (statements.hasNext( )){
        // This statement is a triple: subject, predicate, and object.
        Statement s = statements.nextStatement( );

        // Check to see if this subject is actually a FOAF Person.
        if(s.getPredicate().toString().equals(
            "http://www.w3.org/1999/02/22-rdf-syntax-ns#type") &&
            s.getObject().toString().equals("http://xmlns.com/foaf/0.1/
Person")) {

            isPerson = true;
        }

        // Now check for each foaf property and add it.
        String base = "http://xmlns.com/foaf/0.1/";
        String key = s.getPredicate().toString();
        if (key.startsWith(base)) {
            Vector v = (Vector) p.foafData.get(key.substring(base.length(
)));
            if (v == null) {
                v = new Vector( );
                p.foafData.put(key.substring(base.length()), v);
            }
```

```
        v.add(s.getObject().toString());
    }
} // End statement loop.
```

In the preceding example, the String base is placed within the loop for clarity. Since it is always the same, that line can easily be moved somewhere else in the code to prevent the step of redeclaring the variable on each iteration.

There are two issues to address before adding this Person object, p, to the Hashtable. First, on the Semantic Web, much data can be included in a file. There is no requirement that a FOAF file must contain *only* FOAF data. A file may contain information about *anything*. As the file is parsed, it is necessary to confirm that the object you are parsing is actually a FOAF Person. If it turns out that the object is, in fact, a FOAF Person, you must add it to a Hashtable that will store all of the instances of your Person class. If it is *not* a FOAF Person, you should just throw away the Person object that you created. The following code makes use of the foafHash declared previously:

```
if (isPerson) {

  if (p.foafData.get("mbox")!=null)
    for (int i = 0; i < ((Vector)p.foafData.get("mbox")).size(); i++) {
      String mail = (String) ((Vector)p.foafData.get("mbox")).
elementAt(i);
      if (foafHash.get(mail) != null && foafHash.get(mail) != p) {
        merge(p, mail);
      }
      // Sometimes, people preface their mail address with mailto:
      // We'll take it off to make the interface nicer.
      if (mail.startsWith("mailto:"))
        mail = mail.substring(7);
      foafHash.put(mail, p);
    }
  if (p.foafData.get("mbox_sha1sum")!=null)
    for (int i = 0; i < ((Vector)p.foafData.get("mbox_sha1sum")).size();
i++) {
      String mail = (String)
            ((Vector)p.foafData.get("mbox_sha1sum")).elementAt(i);
      if (foafHash.get(mail) != null && foafHash.get(mail) != p) {
        merge(p, mail);
      }
      foafHash.put(mail, p);
    }
}
```

Notice that in both loops, before the instance of the Person class is added to the Hashtable, the following logic is required:

```
if (foafHash.get(key) != null && foafHash.get(key) != p) {
    merge(p, key);
}
```

Because you may have already parsed information about this Person some-where else in the file and added an instance of the Person class to the Hash-table, there may already be another instance of the class with different information already stored. In this case, you need to merge the data from the two Person objects. The `if` statement checks to make sure that the stored Person object is different from the current Person object to prevent unneces-sarily merging identical objects. The merge function will copy all of the information into one object and then set the two objects equal to each other.

```
private static void merge(Person p, String mail) {
    Person q = (Person) foafHash.get(mail);

    for (Enumeration e = p.foafData.keys() ; e.hasMoreElements() ;) {
        String curKey = (String)e.nextElement();
        // Go through each element in the names Vector.
        for (int i = 0 ; i < ((Vector)q.foafData.get(curKey)).size();
i++) {

            String curVal = (String)
                    ((Vector)q.foafData.get(curKey)).elementAt(i);
            // Don't add a name to p if it's already there.
            Vector psData = (Vector)p.foafData.get(curKey);
            if (psData == null)
                psData = new Vector();
            if (!psData.contains(curVal)){
                // Add the value from q to p.
                psData.add(curVal);
            }
        }
    }

    q = p;
}
```

This code completes the parsing of a single FOAF file. It may seem compli-cated, but that is the bulk of everything that has to be done to build this IRC bot. The next two steps take advantage of all of this parsing with only a few more lines of code.

## Crawling FOAF Files

FOAF is interesting because it creates a social network—many people are interconnected through linked files. The previous code will parse a single file into the Hashtable, but to collect FOAF data, it is necessary to crawl over files that are linked together. This requires only a few additions. First, you can use a Vector to store the URIs of files to parse:

```
Vector uris = new Vector();
```

```
        uris.add(inputFile);

    while (uris.size( ) > 0) {
        // Remove the first element in the Vector.
        inputFile = (String) uris.remove(0);

        /*
         * Here, we insert the previous code that parses the file and builds
         * our model. It is omitted from this example for brevity.
         */
    }
```

You will parse each URL as outlined earlier. As you parse, one more if statement will be required to check for "see also" links. These links point to
other files. When encountered, these links will be added to the Vector of
URIs. The following should be added to the list of if statements that checks
for all of the other FOAF properties:

```
    if (s.getPredicate().toString( ).equals(
            "http://www.w3.org/2000/01/rdf-schema#seeAlso")) {

        uris.add(s.getObject().toString( ));
    }
```

With these two small changes, the code will now crawl along the semantic
links in each file to parse every FOAF file connected to the network!

> The FOAF network is *huge,* and it will take *days* to crawl
> through the whole lot. To get your bot up and running
> quickly, consider skipping the crawl by eliminating this last
> section of code and instead listing a handful of FOAF files
> you want included in your bot's database.

## Writing the IRC Interface

Finally, once the previous code has been executed, the Hashtable foafHash
will contain all of our Person objects with the correct information. That will
take place as an initialization step. The last step to complete FOAFBot is to
create the IRC bot interface. Since this is Java-based code, it will use the
PircBot API **[Hack #35]**. You can assume that the *onMessage* method is overridden to accept input from users in a channel. The rest of this step will just
show how to handle requests from users in this context.

Our Person class has all of the information from FOAF, but you can decide
which properties you want to be queriable through the IRC bot. All of the
people our bot knows about are indexed by email address or email
*sha1sum*—the result of applying the SHA1 mathematical function to a
mailto: identifier. For this reason, you will require users to ask for informa-

tion about a person via an email address. The original FOAFBot also maintains a hash keyed by IRC nickname, since that is easier to find on an IRC channel. To support that, you would simply add another Hashtable to the preceding code, and add Person objects to it by looping over the nick Vector, just as with the email addresses. In the email-indexed bot, a sample query might look like this:

foafbot, name of *golbeck@cs.umd.edu*

Upon receiving this command, the bot looks up the address in the hash to retrieve the associated Person object and then put together a response with the information stored in the object:

```
StringTokenizer t = new StringTokenizer(message);
if (t.nextToken().toLowerCase().equals(
        this.getName().toUpperCase().toLowerCase() + ",")) {
    try {
        String query = t.nextToken();
        if (query.equals("name")) {
            t.nextToken();  // Eliminate the "of".
            String email = t.nextToken();
            Person p = (Person) foafHash.get(email);
            String response = "";

        Vector data = (Vector)p.foafData.get("name");
        if (data!= null && data.size() > 0) {
            response = email + " is named ";
            for (int i = 0; i < data.size(); i++) {
                response += data.elementAt(i);

                // This formats the response nicely with commas.
                if (i + 1 < data.size()) {
                    response += ", ";
                }
            }
        }
        else {
            response = "I don't know the name of ";
            response += email;
        }
        sendMessage(channel, response);
    }
    ...
```

This is just one example of creating a response from the Person object. You can decide which features of FOAF to support and how to support them. With that, the FOAFBot is complete. This is not only an interesting hack by itself, but it also lays the groundwork for any other Semantic Web–based hacks. One of those, TrustBot [Hack #49], is next.

## Running the Hack

In this hack, the *Foaf.java* file contains a main method. Since the bot is based on PircBot, you need to change that. By simply renaming the *Foaf.java* main method to an `init` method and calling that `init` method as one of the first steps in the main method of your PircBot-based bot, the FOAF data crawl will be initialized and stored before the bot joins a channel.

With this change, the only step is to compile and run the bot as usual (see "IRC with Java and PircBot" **[Hack #35]**). When the bot joins a channel, it will process any requests that you wrote code to handle.

A FOAFBot interface is demonstrated in Figure 7-5.

*Figure 7-5. Using FOAFBot to find out about a user*

Now you can use FOAFBot to find out about all the users in your channel.

—*Jennifer Golbeck*

**Interrogate Trust Networks with TrustBot**

Use the network of trust ratings available on the Web to recommend how much to trust an unknown individual and send your recommendations over IRC.

Trust networks are appearing all over the Web, from web sites like Advogato and Epinions to the social networks of the Semantic Web. You were just shown how to create a bot that would load data from a FOAF network **[Hack #48]** and provide that information via IRC. This hack will introduce some simple extensions to FOAF that will parse information about trust relationships and use it to make recommendations about how much a person should trust a stranger.

> The Advogato project (*http://www.advogato.org*) is a community site for free software developers. It uses group trust metrics for peer certification to limit access to certain sections of the site.
>
> Epinions (*http://epinions.com*) uses consumer reviews to rate products and sellers. Users build a web of trusted people, and that data is used to make recommendations across the network.
>
> The Trust Project (*http://trust.mindswap.org*) is a web site dedicated to building a distributed, open trust network. The data and results in this hack use this network.

The premise for trust networks appears frequently in everyday life. If a person meets a new colleague at work, it is common to ask around about this person. The assumption is that people *you* trust will give you good information about whether or not to trust the new person. Unlike FOAF, which connects people only by whether or not they know one another, trust networks add ratings to those relationships. Because trust ratings can be represented numerically, it is simple to compose relationships over paths.

What kind of trust ratings to give and how to make recommendations based on that is an active area of social networks research. In this example, people rate each other's trustworthiness on a scale from 1 to 10, where 1 is very low trust and 10 is very high trust. This network is stored on the Semantic Web as an extension of FOAF. To learn more about the network or add yourself, visit The Trust Project at *http://trust.mindswap.org*. Recommendations about how much to trust a person will be made using a recursive system. The Trust Project will make these calculations, and you can use the calculation they provide instead of writing your own code.

## Getting Trust Data

In FOAFBot, there is code to parse RDF and OWL files and build objects in the Person class. The TrustBot can be built in the same way. You could modify the FOAFBot code so it would process trust files, store the proper information in the Person class (with modifications), and then write a series of functions to make trust inferences. Instead of writing all of that, you can use the server at trust.mindswap.org. It has a database of information from spidered and parsed trust files. You can connect to that server and make queries about how much two people should trust each other.

As with FOAF, people are identified by email address in the trust network. Passing the email address of the person for whom the inference is being made (the *source*) and the person about whom it is being made (the *sink*) will return the recommendation about how much the source should trust the sink.

The result will be retrieved from a URL in this form:

*http://trust.mindswap.org/cgi-bin/botquery.cgi?from=source@example.com&to=sink@example.com*

The email address *source@example.com* should be replaced with the email address of the source, and *sink@example.com* should be replaced with the email address of the sink. The result will return a full sentence that the bot can print out. When this URL is accessed, it prints out a single line of text that has the recommended trust level from the source to the sink. The following getTrust( ) method creates the correct URL and then loads its result:

```
private String getTrust(String sourceEmail, String sinkEmail) {

    URLConnection conn = null;
    DataInputStream data = null;
    String line;
    StringBuffer buf = new StringBuffer( );

    try {

        URL u = new URL ("http://trust.mindswap.org/cgi-bin/botquery." +
            "cgi?from=" + sourceEmail + "&to=" + sinkEmail);
        conn = u.openConnection( );
        conn.connect( );

        data = new DataInputStream(new BufferedInputStream(
            conn.getInputStream( )));

        while ((line = data.readLine( )) != null) {
            buf.append(line + "\n");
        }
        data.close( );
```

```
        return buf.toString();
    }
    catch (Exception e) {
        return "Error. Unable to process this request";
    }
}
```

With this method, the only remaining step is to parse a request from the user, extract the email addresses, and show the result of the method in the IRC interface.

## Modifying the IRC Interface

Using the same code from FOAFBot, the only change you need to make is to add a handler for a command that will process a trust value. The format of that command will mimic the FOAF-based commands. This will allow users to type message like this:

&lt;golbeck&gt; **Trustbot, trust _golbeck@cs.umd.edu_ to _bob@example.com_**

The following code should be added into the onMessage method in the PircBot subclass (after line 54 of the *MyBot.java* file in the FOAFBot code):

```
if (query.equals("trust")) {

    String response = "";
    // Get the first email address.
    String email = t.nextToken();
    // Eliminate the "to".
    t.nextToken();
    // Get the second email address.
    String inQuestionEmail = t.nextToken();

    response = getTrust(email, inQuestionEmail);
    sendMessage(channel, response);
}
```

With this addition, the bot is now ready to handle trust questions and show the user the result that it retrieves from the Web.

## The Results

In Figure 7-6, see the TrustBot being queried for trust recommendations.

Now you can use the bot to find out how much you should trust other people, even if you don't know them already.

—*Jennifer Golbeck*

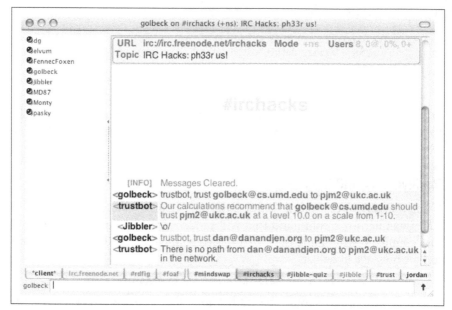

*Figure 7-6. Using TrustBot to give guidance on trust*

## Pass Notes to Other Users

Not everybody can afford to be permanently connected to IRC, but it is still often a preferred medium for communication. Pass messages on to other users when they next join the channel with this simple IRC bot.

For many people, IRC is more than just a place to chat. Social groups form quite easily in channels; after all, you all share the same interest, right? IRC therefore becomes the natural place to talk to this social group. You may not even know the email addresses of the people you talk to, simply because you don't need to. IRC lets you chat in real time, which is often more convenient than waiting for a response to an email. IRC also lets you transfer files directly from one client to another.

Such dependence on IRC sometimes makes people forget that there are alternative communication mediums. Indeed, some people even become frustrated when they have to resort to alternatives! If the person you want to talk to has left the server for a while (perhaps has gone to bed or to the shops) and you don't know his email address, you could use an IRC bot to pass on your message when he comes back.

A bot that passes on messages doesn't have to be too complicated. All it has to do is allow users to give it new messages, store them, and then pass them on when appropriate:

```
<Jibbler> tell DeadEd to look at http://www.jibble.org/comicbot/
<TellBot> Okay, Jibbler
```

The next time DeadEd joins the channel, the bot should pass the message to DeadEd:

```
* DeadEd has joined #irchacks
<TellBot> DeadEd, Jibbler asked me to tell you to look at
    http://www.jibble.org/comicbot/
```

## The Code

We can use a HashMap to store a list of messages to pass on, allowing more than one message to be sent to any one user. The HashMap will be indexed by nickname, and each entry will point to an ArrayList that contains messages for that user.

Create a file called *TellBot.java*:

```java
import org.jibble.pircbot.*;
import java.util.*;

public class TellBot extends PircBot {

    // A map of String (nickname) to ArrayList (message Strings).
    private HashMap messages = new HashMap();

    public TellBot(String name) {
        setName(name);
    }

    public void onMessage(String channel, String sender, String login,
            String hostname, String message) {

        String[] tokens = message.split("\\s+");

        // Check for the "tell" command.
        if (tokens.length > 2 && tokens[0].equalsIgnoreCase("tell")) {
            String nick = tokens[1];
            message = message.substring(message.indexOf(nick) + nick.length(
) + 1);

            // Convert the nickname to lowercase for use in the HashMap.
            String key = nick.toLowerCase();
            ArrayList list = (ArrayList) messages.get(key);
            if (list == null) {
                // Create a new ArrayList if the HashMap entry is empty.
                list = new ArrayList();
                messages.put(key, list);
            }

            // Add the message to the list for the target nickname.
            list.add(sender + " asked me to tell you " + message);
            sendMessage(channel, "Okay, " + sender);
        }
```

```
        }

    public void onJoin(String channel, String sender,
            String login, String hostname) {

        // Convert the nickname to lowercase to get the HashMap key.
        String key = sender.toLowerCase();
        ArrayList list = (ArrayList) messages.get(key);
        if (list != null) {
            // Send all messages to the user.
            for (int i = 0; i < list.size(); i++) {
                String message = (String) list.get(i);
                sendMessage(channel, sender + ", " + message);
            }
            // Now erase all messages for this user.
            messages.put(key, null);
        }
    }

}
```

Notice that the HashMap keys must be converted to lowercase. This effectively makes the nicknames case insensitive, so a message that is left for "Paul" can also be received by "paul."

The onMessage method is invoked whenever someone sends a message to the channel. This method checks to see if a user has entered the "tell" command—if so, it adds the message to the HashMap.

When a user joins the channel, the onJoin method is invoked. If there are any messages for this user, they are sent to the channel and then removed from the HashMap.

To instantiate the bot, you will need a main method. Create this in *TellBotMain.java*:

```
public class TellBotMain {

    public static void main(String[] args) throws Exception {
        TellBot bot = new TellBot("TellBot");
        bot.setVerbose(true);
        bot.connect("irc.freenode.net");
        bot.joinChannel("#irchacks");
    }

}
```

You can also tell the bot to join more than one channel—simply modify the joinChannel method call so it contains a comma-separated list, for example:

```
        bot.joinChannel("#irchacks,#jibble,#pircbot");
```

Messages will be accepted from all channels and delivered to the first one the recipient joins.

## Running the Hack

Compile the bot like so:

```
javac -classpath .;pircbot.jar *.java
```

Run the bot with:

```
java -classpath .;pircbot.jar TellBotMain
```

## The Results

Figure 7-7 shows the bot in action. As soon as DeadEd joins the channel, TellBot passes my message on to him.

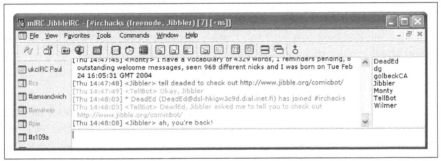

*Figure 7-7. TellBot passing on a message from Jibbler to DeadEd*

This type of bot is very popular among communities. You'll find yourself sending fewer emails once you start using this.

# CHAPTER EIGHT

# Search and Query Bots
## Hacks 51–57

Search and query bots are very common on IRC. You may find that lots of IRC users will use a bot in preference to a web-based search tool, simply because it is less effort than starting up a web browser and typing in a URL.

The first hack shows you how to create a bot that performs Google searches using the Google and PircBot APIs. Conveniently, most IRC clients will highlight the resulting URLs and let you click on them to load the page in your default web browser.

Web Services provide powerful and easy ways to access information over the Internet and present the results in your application. This chapter shows you how to make some Java bots that employ Web Services to see what the weather is like, translate languages, convert currencies, and search for books on Amazon.

Not all searches have to be performed over the Internet. A more local type of search can be used to determine if a certain user is connected to your IRC network, even if she is not in any of your channels. This is useful if you are trying to get a hold of somebody who doesn't use IRC that much and connects only infrequently.

**HACK #51 Search the Web with Google**

Performing Google searches from IRC is not only convenient, but also efficient. See how fast you can Google for something on IRC and click on the URL highlighted by your IRC client.

When someone pops into your IRC channel with a question, you can bet your life that 9 times out of 10, he could have easily found the answer on Google. If you think this is the case, you could tell him that—or you could do it slightly more subtly by suggesting a Google search term to an IRC bot, which will then go and look for a result.

Most IRC clients are capable of highlighting URLs in channels. Clicking on a highlighted URL will open your default web browser and load the page. For some people, this is a lot quicker than finding the icon to start your web browser and then typing or pasting the URL. More obviously, a single Google search will present its result to everybody in the channel.

## Google Web APIs

Searching Google from within your own application is very easy, thanks to the Google Web APIs. The developer's kit (*http://www.google.com/apis*) contains a Java library that provides a wrapper around the Google Web API's SOAP interface. This essentially means that you can use it to perform Google searches from a Java IRC bot.

You will also need to create a Google account and obtain a license key. As I write this, the free license key entitles you to 1000 automated queries per day. This is more than enough for a single IRC channel.

 You'll find oodles of Google goodness and more Google Web API hacking in *Google Hacks* by Tara Calishain and Rael Dornfest (O'Reilly).

The *googleapi.jar* file contains the classes that will be used by the bot when it performs Google searches, so you will need to make sure this is in your classpath when you compile and run the bot.

The goal is to have an IRC bot called GoogleBot that responds to the !google command. It will respond by showing the title and URL of the first Google search result. If the size of the page is known, that will also be displayed.

Your license key will be a simple String, so you can store that in the Google-Bot class as googleKey.

## The Code

Create a file called *GoogleBot.java*:

```
import org.jibble.pircbot.*;
import com.google.soap.search.*;

public class GoogleBot extends PircBot {

    // Change this so it uses your license key!
    private static final String googleKey =
"000000000000000000000000000000";

    public GoogleBot(String name) {
```

```
                    setName(name);
            }

        public void onMessage(String channel, String sender, String login,
                String hostname, String message) {

            message = message.toLowerCase().trim();
            if (message.startsWith("!google ")) {
                String searchTerms = message.substring(8);

                String result = null;
                try {
                    GoogleSearch search = new GoogleSearch();
                    search.setKey(googleKey);
                    search.setQueryString(searchTerms);
                    search.setMaxResults(1);
                    GoogleSearchResult searchResult = search.doSearch();
                    GoogleSearchResultElement[] elements =
                            searchResult.getResultElements();
                    if (elements.length == 1) {
                        GoogleSearchResultElement element = elements[0];
                        // Remove all HTML tags from the title.
                        String title = element.getTitle().replaceAll("<.*?>",
"");

                        result = element.getURL() + " (" + title + ")";
                        if (!element.getCachedSize().equals("0")) {
                            result = result + " - " + element.getCachedSize();
                        }
                    }
                }
                catch (GoogleSearchFault e) {
                    // Something went wrong. Say why.
                    result = "Unable to perform your search: " + e;
                }

                if (result == null) {
                    // No results were found for the search terms.
                    result = "I could not find anything on Google.";
                }

                // Send the result to the channel.
                sendMessage(channel, sender + ": " + result);
            }
        }

    }
```

You now need a main method to tell the bot which channels to join. If you
want, you can tell the bot to join more than one channel, but remember you
are limited in the number of Google searches you can do per day.

Create the file *GoogleBotMain.java*:

```
public class GoogleBotMain {

    public static void main(String[] args) throws Exception {
        GoogleBot bot = new GoogleBot("GoogleBot");
        bot.setVerbose(true);
        bot.connect("irc.freenode.net");
        bot.joinChannel("#irchacks");
    }

}
```

## Running the Hack

When you compile the bot, remember to include both *pircbot.jar* and *googleapi.jar* in the classpath:

```
C:\java\GoogleBot> javac -classpath .;pircbot.jar;googleapi.jar *.java
```

You can then run the bot like so:

```
C:\java\GoogleBot> java -classpath .;pircbot.jar;googleapi.jar GoogleBotMain
```

The bot will then start up and connect to the IRC server.

## The Results

Figure 8-1 shows GoogleBot running in an IRC channel and responding with the URL, title, and size of each of the results of a Google search.

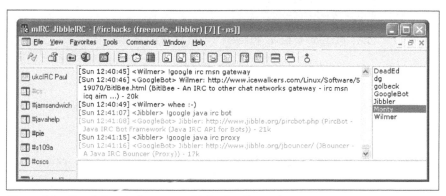

*Figure 8-1. GoogleBot performing an IRC-related search*

Performing a Google search is a very popular task for bots to do. Take this into account if you run your bot in a busy channel, as there may be a bot there that already lets users search Google.

## Use the Dictionary

**#52**    Create a bot to look up the meaning of a word for you or to show the meaning of a word to other people in your channel.

People very often use short acronyms or other jargon on IRC. Sometimes it can be helpful to have a clue what they are saying. One solution is to look these words up in the Jargon file (*http://www.catb.org/~esr/jargon*) or the Free On-Line Dictionary of Computing (FOLDOC—*http://wombat.doc.ic.ac.uk/foldoc*). Another way is to get an IRC bot to do the searches for you.

A convenient way to access both the Jargon file and FOLDOC is via the Dictionary Server Protocol (*ftp://ftp.isi.edu/in-notes/rfc2229.txt*) through dict.org (*http://www.dict.org/bin/Dict*).

### The Code

The bot in this hack will respond to the commands !jargon and !foldoc and give the results of the search to the channel. The PircBot IRC framework will be used to connect to the IRC server and respond to simple IRC commands. The majority of the code will be used to connect to the dictionary server and parse the responses.

Create a file called *DictBot.java*:

```java
import java.io.*;
import java.net.*;
import java.util.regex.*;
import org.jibble.pircbot.*;

public class DictBot extends PircBot {

    private static final String DICT_SERVER = "dict.org";
    private static final int DICT_PORT = 2628;

    public DictBot() {
        this.setName("DictBot");
    }

    public void onMessage(String channel, String sender, String login,
            String hostname, String message) {

        if(message.toLowerCase().startsWith("!jargon ")) {
            String searchString = message.substring(8).trim();
            sendMessage(channel, lookupWord(DICT_SERVER, DICT_PORT,
                    "jargon", searchString));
        }
        else if(message.toLowerCase().startsWith("!foldoc ")) {
            String searchString = message.substring(8).trim();
            sendMessage(channel, lookupWord(DICT_SERVER, DICT_PORT,
```

```
                    "foldoc", searchString));
        }
    }

}
```

When the bot receives a !jargon or !foldoc command, it will pass the para-meters to the lookupWord method. This method will connect to the DICT server and try and return the definition of the word. You should now add this method to the DictBot class:

```
public String lookupWord(String dictServer, int port, String book, String
word) {
    try {
        Socket socket = new Socket(dictServer, port);
        BufferedReader reader = new BufferedReader(
                new InputStreamReader(socket.getInputStream( )));
        BufferedWriter writer = new BufferedWriter(
                new OutputStreamWriter(socket.getOutputStream( )));
        reader.readLine( );
        // Set the book used for search (and double quote the search string).
        writer.write("DEFINE " + book + " \"" + word + "\"\r\n");
        writer.flush( );
        String definition = "";
        String line = null;
        while((line = reader.readLine( )) != null) {
            // 552 No match.
            if(line.startsWith("552")) {
                // Switch to Levenshtein algorithm to try to get *some* result.
                writer.write("MATCH " + book + " lev \"" + word + "\"\r\n");
                writer.flush( );
                line = reader.readLine( );
                // 552 No match
                if(line.startsWith("552")) {
                    socket.close( );
                    // If it's still not found, stop.
                    return "I can't find any words that look like that...";
                // 152 n matches found - text follows.
                } else if(line.startsWith("152")) {
                    String[] parts = line.split(" ");
                    int numMatches = Integer.valueOf(parts[1]).intValue( );
                    // Some similar words were found ...
                    String reply = "";
                    int count = 0;
                    while((line = reader.readLine( )) != null) {
                        if(count > numMatches || line.startsWith(".")) {
                            break;
                        }
                        reply += " " + line.substring(line.indexOf("\""),
                                line.lastIndexOf("\"") + 1);
                        count++;
                    }
                    socket.close( );
```

```
                            return "The only similar words I could find were: " +
        reply;

                    } else {
                        // Something went wrong. Let the user know.
                        return "Something unexpected happened: " + line;
                    }

                }
                // 151 word database name - text follows.
                if(line.startsWith("151")) {
                    if (book.equals("foldoc")) {
                        // Skip first 2 lines returned (header and blank line).
                        reader.readLine();
                        reader.readLine();
                    }

                    definition = "";
                    while((line = reader.readLine()) != null) {

                        if(line.trim().equals("") || line.startsWith("2")) {
                            break;
                        } else {
                            definition += line;
                        }
                    }
                    break;
                }
                if(line.startsWith("2")) {
                    break;
                }
            }
            socket.close();
            // Return the definition.
            Pattern pattern = Pattern.compile("[\\s\\r\\n\\t\\f]+");
            Matcher m = pattern.matcher(definition);
            definition = m.replaceAll(" ");
            return definition;
        }
        catch (Exception e) {
            // Do nothing.
        }

        return "Something went wrong :oP";
    }
```

Now you just need a main method to construct the bot and tell it to connect to a server and join a channel. The bot will be happy to join more than
one channel if you want. Create the following in *DictBotMain.java*:

```
public class DictBotMain {

    public static void main(String[] args) throws Exception {
        DictBot fBot = new DictBot();
```

```
            fBot.setVerbose(true);
            fBot.connect("irc.freenode.net");
            fBot.joinChannel("#irchacks");
    }

}
```

## Running the Hack

Compile the bot with:

```
C:\java\DictBot> javac -classpath pircbot.jar;. *.java
```

Run the bot with:

```
C:\java\DictBot> java -classpath pircbot.jar;. DictBotMain
```

The bot will connect to the server and be ready to look up words as soon as it joins your channel.

## The Results

Here are some examples of the bot being used to look up words in the Free On-Line Dictionary of Computing (FOLDOC):

```
<DeadEd> !foldoc irc
<DictBot> {Internet Relay Chat}

<DeadEd> !foldoc internet relay chat
<DictBot> <chat, messaging> (IRC) /I-R-C/, occasionally /*rk/ A {client-
server} {chat} system of large (often worldwide) networks. IRC is structured
as networks of {Internet} {servers}, each accepting connections from
{client} programs, one per user.

<DeadEd> !foldoc html
<DictBot> {Hypertext Markup Language}

<DeadEd> !foldoc Hypertext Markup Language
<DictBot> <hypertext, World-Wide Web, standard> (HTML) A {hypertext}
document format used on the {World-Wide Web}. HTML is built on top of
{SGML}. "Tags" are embedded in the text. A tag consists of a "<", a
"directive" (case insensitive), zero or more parameters and a ">". Matched
pairs of directives, like "<TITLE>" and "</TITLE>" are used to delimit text
which is to appear in a special place or style.
```

## Hacking the Hack

Many other dictionaries are available at dict.org. All of these can be accessed using the same Dictionary Server Protocol. The communication is basically the same, but some additional parsing may be needed to get a nicer output from some of the dictionaries.

For example, you could easily add a new command !dict that would perform a lookup through all of the dictionaries available on dict.org by adding
the following code to the end of the onMessage method:

```
else if(message.toLowerCase( ).startsWith("!dict ")) {
    String searchString = message.substring(6).trim( );
    sendMessage(channel, lookupWord(DICT_SERVER, DICT_PORT, "*",
searchString));
}
```

You could then ask the bot to look up a word in all of the available dictionaries by typing **!dict** *word*.

—*Alex North*

### HACK #53    Check the Weather

Check the up-to-the-minute weather with an IRC bot that capitalizes on Web
Services—a powerful way of getting current information.

The exchange of information on the Web primarily takes place through the
loading of web pages. Databases and applications can be used to provide
dynamic information, but the result has typically been available only embedded in an HTML document. Web Services were created to better facilitate
the exchange of information by providing more direct access to applications
and their functions over the Web. Web Services have URLs, and by sending
a message to the URL of a service, a user or application can directly call a
function offered by the application providing the service. One example
shown in this hack is to use a U.S. zip code to get the current temperature at
that location. To do this using a Web Service, a message is sent to the service to tell it which zip code to look up. The service processes the request
and sends back the current temperature at that location.

When writing IRC bots, a lot of time is often spent developing the services a
bot will offer. It is not uncommon for the author to have to write a lot of
code to look up the weather, parse a web page to extract the actual data,
and then format that into an IRC message. Using a Web Service to retrieve
the same information requires only a few lines of code. The XMethods web
site at *http://www.xmethods.net* lists many publicly available Web Services
and describes how they are used. In this example, you will use the *weather-
temperature* service listed in the *XMethods Demo Services* section of the
homepage. This service is passed a U.S. zip code and returns the current
temperature at that zip code.

To write code that uses a Web Service, you need several pieces of information about the service. The first is the URL of the *WSDL* description of the
service. WSDL (Web Service Description Language) is an XML standard

used for describing services, the arguments they take, the format of those arguments, and what value is returned. Services listed on XMethods show the WSDL URL on each page. Figure 8-2 has the URL boxed to show where it is found. The XMethods weather-temperature WSDL description is at *http://www.xmethods.net/sd/2001/TemperatureService.wsdl.*

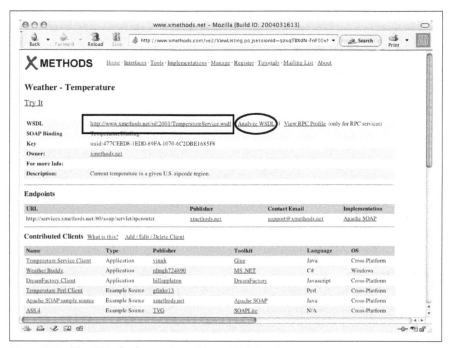

*Figure 8-2. The XMethods page describing a Web Service*

To use the service, you will also need the name of the operation and the arguments for it. An operation is very much like a function call. To get the operation information, the WSDL for the service needs to be analyzed. You can do this by hand, but XMethods can automatically perform the analysis. The link to analyze the WSDL is shown circled in Figure 8-2.

Figure 8-3 shows the WSDL analysis for the weather-temperature service. It shows that one operation is available for the service. By clicking the link to the operation, shown in the box in Figure 8-3, a full description of the operation is returned.

On the operation description page, shown in Figure 8-4, the name of the operation is provided in the boxed area. This operation name is necessary to run the service. The operation name for the weather-temperature service is getTemp.

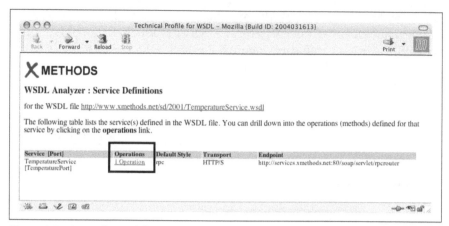

Figure 8-3. An analysis of the WSDL for the weather-temperature service

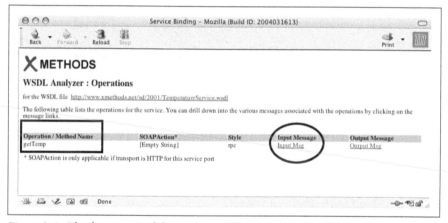

Figure 8-4. The description of the single operation that is part of the weather-temperature service

Finally, to use the operation, an input message that contains the arguments needs to be passed. To see the number and type of arguments, click the *InputMsg* link for the operation, shown in the circled area in Figure 8-4.

Figure 8-5 shows the description of the input message that will contain the arguments for the operation. These are listed as *Parts* and, as shown in Figure 8-5, there is one part to the weather-temperature service. The name of this part is *zipcode*, and it is passed in as a string.

In this example, the *zipcode* is the only part of the input message. Other services will have several parts. For example, a currency conversion service (also provided by XMethods), will require the name of the country whose currency you want to convert and the name of the country that you want to convert to. When there are multiple parts to an input message, they must be kept in order.

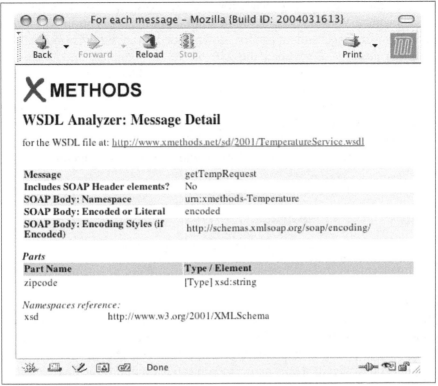

*Figure 8-5. The Input Message format information, provided by the XMethods site*

Returning to the screen shown in Figure 8-4, you will also see information about the output message. Following that link, you will see that the output has one part named *return*. The name of this part will also be needed later on.

After reviewing the pages on XMethods, you will now have the following information about the weather-temperature service:

*WSDL URL*
   *http://www.xmethods.net/sd/2001/TemperatureService.wsdl*

*Operation*
   getTemp

*Input message parts*
   zipcode (a string)

*Output message name*
   return

To use the getTemp operation and get a result back, you need to invoke the service. Instead of writing lots of networking and parsing code by hand, you can use the Apache Axis package for Web Services. Axis is a Java base for implementing Web Services. A full description of the application is at *http://ws.apache.org/axis*, and it can be downloaded from *http://ws.apache.org/axis/download.cgi*. Download the ZIP file of the binaries, and unzip the archive. The *lib* directory will contain several JAR files that you should add to your classpath. In the *samples/client* directory, the DynamicInvoker provides a simple framework for invoking Web Services. You should import samples.client.DynamicInvoker into your Java file. The Java class you will write will contain one static function (getTemperature) that will take a zip code as an argument, and return a String with the current temperature.

```
import java.util.*;
import samples.client.DynamicInvoker;

public class WeatherService {

    public static String getTemperature(String zipcode) {
        // To do...
    }

}
```

Now, you need to take the information about the service and create variables to store them in. In addition to the WSDL location and the operation name, the DynamicInvoker requires a port name. This service does not require you to specify a port name, so you can use a null value there.

```
static String wsdlLocation =
        "http://www.xmethods.net/sd/2001/TemperatureService.wsdl";
static String operationName= "getTemp";
static String outputName = "return";
static String portName = null;
```

The final step before invoking the service is to create an argument list. Arguments are passed to the DynamicInvoker in a String array. The first value is the WSDL location, the second value is the operation name, and the subsequent values are the parts of the input message, listed in order. In our case, the only part of the input message is the zip code value, so it will be the third value in the String array, for example:

```
String[] args = new String[] {wsdlLocation, operationName, "20742"};
```

With this information set up, invoking the function to get the result from the service requires only a few lines of code. The invoker is constructed, the method is invoked, and the result is retrieved.

## The Code

The final version of *WeatherService.java* looks like this:

```
import java.util.*;
import samples.client.DynamicInvoker;

public class WeatherService {

    String wsdlLocation = "http://www.xmethods.net/sd/2001/
TemperatureService.wsdl";
    String operationName= "getTemp";
    String outputName = "return";
    String portName = null;

    public static String getTemperature(String zipcode) {
        String[] args = new String[] {wsdlLocation, operationName, zipcode};
        try {
            DynamicInvoker invoker=new DynamicInvoker(wsdlLocation);
            HashMap map = invoker.invokeMethod(operationName, portName,
args);
            return map.get(outputName).toString( );
        }catch (Exception e){return null;}
    }
}
```

You now have a working piece of code to invoke a weather service. You can write a main method to call the getTemperature method and test it. The next step is to create a bot that will call this method with some user input.

Since this is Java-based code, it will use the PircBot API **[Hack #35]**. You can assume that the onMessage method is overridden to accept input from users in a channel—we recommend that you add this to one of your existing PircBot-based bots, such as that presented in "IRC with Java and PircBot" **[Hack #35]**. The rest of this step will just show how to handle requests from users in this context. The bot will allow user input that comes in the following format:

```
WSBot, temperature 90210
```

You can use a StringTokenizer to parse the input. The getTemperature method will get called, and then the result will be sent to the channel. The following bit of code is placed inside the onMessage method:

```
if (t.nextToken().toLowerCase().equals(getName().toLowerCase( ) + ",")) {
    try {
        String query = t.nextToken( );
        if (query.equals("weather")) {
            String response = "";
            String zip = t.nextToken( );
            if (!zip.equals("")){
```

```
                        sendMessage(channel, "Just a moment while I look that up...
");
                        String result = WeatherService.getTemperature(zip);
                        response = "The temperature at " + zip + " is " + result +
".";
                } else {
                        response = "Please enter a valid zip code.";
                }
                sendMessage(channel, response);
        }
        ...
```

## Running the Hack

Compiling the bot is a bit more complicated than usual, as you will need to ensure that you have all of the Axis components in your classpath:

```
% javac -classpath .:pircbot.jar:
axis-1_1/lib/axis.jar:axis-1_1/lib/axis-ant.jar:
axis-1_1/lib/commons-discovery.jar:axis-1_1/lib/commons-logging.jar:
axis-1_1/lib/jaxrpc.jar:axis-1_1/lib/log4j-1.2.8.jar:axis-1_1/lib/saaj.jar:
axis-1_1/lib/wsdl4j.jar *.java
```

We recommended that you integrate this hack into one of your existing PircBot implementations. Depending on the name of your main class, you can then run the bot like so:

```
% java -classpath .:pircbot.jar:axis-1_1/lib/axis.jar:
axis-1_1/lib/axis-ant.jar:
axis-1_1/lib/commons-discovery.jar:axis-1_1/lib/commons-logging.jar:
axis-1_1/lib/jaxrpc.jar:axis-1_1/lib/log4j-1.2.8.jar:axis-1_1/lib/saaj.jar:
axis-1_1/lib/wsdl4j.jar Main
```

Replace *Main* with the correct name for your main class if it is different. Figure 8-6 shows the bot responding to weather queries on an IRC channel.

## Hacking the Hack

With this framework in place, you can easily add new features to any bot that uses Web Services. Essentially, only the WSDL location, operation name, and input message parts need to be changed. The code for invoking a service and calling the method from the bot interface remains almost identical. Take a gander at the translation Web service used in a similar manner in the next hack.

*—Jennifer Golbeck*

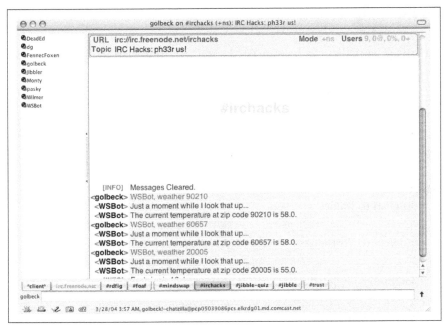

*Figure 8-6. The Web Service bot answering weather queries*

# Don't Get Lost in Translation

Since IRC is accessible from anywhere in the world, cross the language barriers with a translator bot.

Writing a bot to translate phrases between different languages doesn't require a mastery of translation nor the ability to parse output from web-based translators. This bot uses a Web Service to get its data. The translator Web Service is not listed on XMethods but is provided by RestlessDelusions. net. Here is the information about the service that you need:

*WSDL URL*
> http://www.restlessdelusions.com/projects/services/translate/translate.
> asmx?WSDL

*Operation*
> TranslateLanguage

*Input message parts*
> *Language list*
>> This has the original language and the language to translate to. Each language is given a two-letter code and is separated by a | character. To translate from English to French, the argument would be en|fr.

*Output message name*
    TranslateLanguageResult

Language pairs that can be translated and their abbreviations are as follows:

en|de
    English to German

en|es
    English to Spanish

en|fr
    English to French

en|it
    English to Italian

en|pt
    English to Portuguese

de|en
    German to English

de|fr
    German to French

es|en
    Spanish to English

fr|en
    French to English

fr|de
    French to German

it|en
    Italian to English

pt|en
    Portuguese to English

## The Code

Now, to use this Web Service, you need to change only a few parts from the WeatherService class **[Hack #53]**. The changes are simple—replace the values of key variables with the correct values from this service and adjust the method to use two arguments. The lines you need to change are bold in the following example:

```
import java.util.*;
import samples.client.DynamicInvoker;
```

```
public class TranslatorService {

    static String wsdlLocation = "http://www.restlessdelusions.com/projects/
    services/translate/translate.asmx?WSDL";
    static String operationName= "TranslateLanguage";
    static String outputName = "TranslateLanguageResult";
    static String portName = null;


    public static String translatePhrase(String languages, String phrase) {
        String[] args =
            new String[] {wsdlLocation, operationName, languages, phrase};
        try {
            DynamicInvoker invoker=new DynamicInvoker(wsdlLocation);
            HashMap map = invoker.invokeMethod(operationName, portName,
args);
            return map.get(outputName).toString( );
        }catch (Exception e){return null;}
    }
}
```

You now have a working method for using the Web Service to translate text
and need to write the code for the bot to use the service. It is convenient to
add the code here into the onMessage method from the previous Web Services hack. You can assume that the user input will come in the following
format:

```
WSBot, translate en to fr Hello world!
```

This line assumes that users know the codes for each language. You may
want to provide a help message that lists each language and its code.

To process this request, you can begin as with the previous example, using a
StringTokenizer to parse the input.

```
String query = t.nextToken( );
if (query.equals("translate")) {
    String response = "";
```

Then the next step will be to pull out the two languages:

```
String sourceLanguage = t.nextToken( );
t.nextToken( );    // Get rid of the "to".
String targetLanguage = t.nextToken( );
```

Now, the rest of the tokens store the message to be translated. Unfortunately, StringTokenizer does not have a method to nicely return the rest of
the tokens, so you must use a loop to aggregate them into a string:

```
String messageToTranslate = "";
while (t.hasMoreTokens( ))
    messageToTranslate = messageToTranslate + " " + t.nextToken(
);
```

Now, with a little error checking, you can make the call to your translatePhrase method:

```
if (!sourceLanguage.equals("") &&
    !targetLanguage.equals("") &&
    !messageToTranslate.equals("")){

    String lang = sourceLanguage + "|" + targetLanguage;
    String result = TranslatorService.translatePhrase(
            lang, messageToTranslate);
    response = result;
} else {
    response = "I could not understand your input.";
}
sendMessage(channel, response);
}
...
```

## Running the Hack

As with the previous Web Services hack, you will need to ensure that you have all of the Axis components in your classpath when you compile the bot:

```
% javac -classpath .:pircbot.jar:axis-1_1/lib/axis.jar: \
  axis-1_1/lib/axis-ant.jar: \
  axis-1_1/lib/commons-discovery.jar:axis-1_1/lib/commons-logging.jar: \
  axis-1_1/lib/jaxrpc.jar:axis-1_1/lib/log4j-1.2.8.jar: \
  axis-1_1/lib/saaj.jar: \
  axis-1_1/lib/wsdl4j.jar *.java
```

Depending on the name of your main class, you can then run the bot like so:

```
% java -classpath .:pircbot.jar:axis-1_1/lib/axis.jar: \
  axis-1_1/lib/axis-ant.jar: \
  axis-1_1/lib/commons-discovery.jar: \
  axis-1_1/lib/commons-logging.jar: \
  axis-1_1/lib/jaxrpc.jar:axis-1_1/lib/log4j-1.2.8.jar: \
  axis-1_1/lib/saaj.jar: \
  axis-1_1/lib/wsdl4j.jar Main
```

Replace *Main* with the correct name for your main class if it is different.

As soon as the bot connects to the server, it is ready to offer its translation service to all of the channels you dispatch it to:

```
<Jibbler> WSBot, translate en to de I love IRC
<WSBot> Ich liebe IRC
```

This hack is a good demonstration of the power of Web Services. Anybody who's tried to achieve a similar task by parsing raw HTML from a web page will certainly appreciate the simplicity.

—*Jennifer Golbeck*

## Convert Currency

**#55** Most people refer to a newspaper or web site to do currency conversions. Let an IRC bot using an appropriate Web Service do all the hard work for you.

Using Web Services again, you can create an easy hack that will convert currencies. Users can enter the names of two countries and see the exchange rate or convert a specified amount from one currency to another. This hack uses another service provided by XMethods. As with the other two previous Web Services examples, you need four pieces of information:

*WSDL URL*
   *http://www.xmethods.net/sd/2001/CurrencyExchangeService.wsdl*

*Operation*
   getRate

*Input message parts*
   Country1 (a string), country 2 (a string)

*Output message name*
   Result

A list of countries that can be used as inputs is provided near the end of this hack in Table 8-1. The first country is the currency you are converting from, and the second is the currency you are converting to. The conversion will relate one unit of currency from country1 to the calculated number of units of country2.

### The Code

As with the other Web Service hacks **[Hacks #53 and #54]**, very few changes other than adjusting variable values are required. Following is the code for the CurrencyService class and its method to convert currencies:

```
import java.util.*;
import samples.client.DynamicInvoker;

public class CurrencyService {

    static String wsdlLocation =
            "http://www.xmethods.net/sd/2001/CurrencyExchangeService.wsdl";
    static String operationName= "getRate";
    static String outputName = "Result";
    static String portName = null;

    public static String convert(String country1, String country2) {
        String[] args =
                new String[] {wsdlLocation, operationName, country1,
country2};
        try {
            DynamicInvoker invoker=new DynamicInvoker(wsdlLocation);
```

```
                HashMap map = invoker.invokeMethod(operationName, portName,
    args);
                return map.get(outputName).toString();
            }catch (Exception e){return null;}
        }
    }
```

You now have a working method for using the Web Service to convert currencies. Like the previous service hacks, it will use PircBot and add code to the onMessage method. You can build this hack on top of the basic example in "IRC with Java and PircBot" [Hack #35] or continue building up a multifunctional Web Services bot based on the previous Web Services hack. The bot will handle two types of messages—users can get the exchange rate or convert a specific amount of currency. To get the exchange rate, the bot will read messages in the following format:

```
WSBot, exchange COUNTRY1 to COUNTRY2
```

To process this request, you begin as with the previous example, using a StringTokenizer to parse the input:

```
String query = t.nextToken();
if (query.equals("exchange")) {
    String response = "";
```

The next step will be to pull out the two country names. This is not trivial because some countries have two words in their names (e.g., Sri Lanka). Thus, you cannot just pull single tokens. The following code shows how to find the names for both countries. Since the word "to" separates the country names, you can concatenate words until you find the "to":

```
String country1 = t.nextToken();
String next = t.nextToken();
while (!next.equals("to")){
    country1 = country1 + " " + next;
    next = t.nextToken();
}

String country2 = t.nextToken();

while (t.hasMoreTokens()) {
    next = t.nextToken();
    country2 = country2 + " " + next;

}
```

With the two country names taken care of, the only steps left are to call the Web Service and print an output message:

```
sendMessage(channel, "Just a moment while I look that up...");
String result = CurrencyService.convert(country1, country2);
response = "1 unit of " + country1 + " currency is equal to ";
```

```
                    response = response + result + " units of " + country2 + "
currency.";
            }
        sendMessage(channel, response);
    }
    ...
```

The second message will have an additional number, providing us with an amount to convert:

```
WSBot, convert AMOUNT COUNTRY1 to COUNTRY2
```

The code for this conversion is almost identical to the exchange rate code. The additional step requires us to get the amount of currency being converted and then multiply it by the exchange rate. The following code is identical to the previous code, except for the bold lines:

```
String query = t.nextToken( );
if (query.equals("convert")) {

        String response = "";
        String amount = t.nextToken( );
        String country1 = t.nextToken( );
        String next = t.nextToken( );
        while (!next.equals("to")){
            country1 = country1 + " " + next;
            next = t.nextToken( );
        }

        String country2 = t.nextToken( );

        while (t.hasMoreTokens( )){
            next = t.nextToken( );
            country2 = country2 + " " + next;

        }

        sendMessage(channel, "Just a moment while I look that up...");
        String result = CurrencyService.convert(country1, country2);

        double converted = Double.valueOf(amount).doubleValue( ) *
            Double.valueOf(result).doubleValue( );

        response = amount + " units of " + country1 + "
            currency is equal to ";
        response += converted + " units of " + country2 + " currency.";
    }
    sendMessage(channel, response);
}
```

## Running the Hack

As with the previous Web Services hacks, you will need to ensure that you have all of the Axis components in your classpath when you compile the bot:

```
% javac -classpath .:pircbot.jar:axis-1_1/lib/axis.jar: \
axis-1_1/lib/axis-ant.jar: \
axis-1_1/lib/commons-discovery.jar:axis-1_1/lib/commons-logging.jar: \
axis-1_1/lib/jaxrpc.jar:axis-1_1/lib/log4j-1.2.8.jar:axis-1_1/lib/saaj.jar:\
axis-1_1/lib/wsdl4j.jar *.java
```

Depending on the name of your main class, you can then run the bot like so:

```
% java -classpath .:pircbot.jar:axis-1_1/lib/axis.jar: \
axis-1_1/lib/axis-ant.jar: \
axis-1_1/lib/commons-discovery.jar:axis-1_1/lib/commons-logging.jar: \
axis-1_1/lib/jaxrpc.jar:axis-1_1/lib/log4j-1.2.8.jar:axis-1_1/lib/saaj.jar:\
axis-1_1/lib/wsdl4j.jar Main
```

Replace *Main* with the correct name for your main class if it is different.

The conversions, shown in Figure 8-7, are quick and easy and can be requested by anyone in the same channel as the bot.

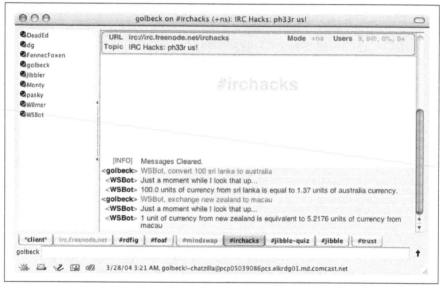

*Figure 8-7. The Web Service bot performing currency conversions*

Table 8-1 shows the list of supported countries for use with the currency conversion bot. For example, to convert 10 U.S. dollars to U.K. pounds, you say:

```
WSBot, convert 10 us to uk
```

and the bot will respond with:

```
<WSBot> Just a moment while I look that up...
<WSBot> 10 units of currency from us is equal to 5.60108 units of uk
currency.
```

*Table 8-1. Country list for currency conversion Web Service*

| | | | |
|---|---|---|---|
| afghanistan | east caribbean | liberia | saudi arabia |
| albania | ecuador | libya | seychelles |
| algeria | egypt | lithuania | sierra leone |
| andorra | el salvador | luxembourg | singapore |
| angola | estonia | macau | slovakia |
| argentina | ethiopia | macedonia | slovenia |
| aruba | euro | malaga | solomon islands |
| australia | falkland islands | malawi kwacha | somalia |
| austria | fiji | malaysia | south africa |
| bahrain | finland | maldives | spain |
| bangladesh | france | malta | sri lanka |
| barbados | gambia | mauritania | st. helena |
| belgium | germany | mauritius | sudan |
| belize | ghana | mexico | suriname |
| bermuda | gibraltar | moldova | swaziland |
| bhutan | greece | mongolia | sweden |
| bolivian | guatemala | morocco | switzerland |
| botswana | guinea | mozambique | syria |
| brazil | guyana | myanmar | taiwan |
| england | haiti | namibia | tanzania |
| united kingdom | honduras | nepal | thailand |
| uk | hong kong | netherlands | tonga |
| great britain | hungary | new zealand | trinidad |
| brunei | iceland | nicaragua | tunisia |
| burundi | india | nigeria | turkey |
| cambodia | indonesia | north korea | united states |
| canada | iraq | norway | us |
| cape verde | ireland | oman | usa |
| cayman islands | israel | pakistan | uae |
| chile | italy | panama | united arab emirates |
| china | jamaica | papua new guinea | uganda |
| colombia | japan | paraguay | uk |
| comoros | jordan | peru | ukraine |
| costa rica | kazakhstan | philippines | uzbekistan |
| croatia | kenya | poland | vanuatu |
| cuba | korea | portugal | venezuela |
| cyprus | kuwait | qatar | vietnam |
| czech republic | laos | romania | yemen |
| denmark | latvia | russia | yugoslavua |
| dijibouti | lebanon | samoa | zambia |
| dominican republic | lesotho | sao tome | zimbabwe |

Now when someone's boasting about how little they paid for a new CD when they were on holiday abroad, you can use this bot to find out what the equivalent amount is in your country.

*—Jennifer Golbeck*

H A C K
**#56**

# Find Out When People Are on the Network

People aren't always connected to IRC 24/7. Find out when they are.

If you're looking for a particular person on IRC, you can tell if she's around by seeing if she's in any of your channels. But what if she's connected to the network but not in any of your channels? Most people resort to a simple /whois *nickname* at this stage. If the user is on the network, then you will be told what public channels she is in, how long she has been connected, and so on. If she doesn't appear to be in any public channels, you can still send a private message directly to that user.

This is all rather inefficient if you plan to do it regularly, so the ISON command was implemented and detailed in the IRC RFC. This provides a quick and efficient way of finding out whether a given nickname is on IRC. At the protocol level, the ISON command takes a list of nicknames as its only parameter, for example:

```
ISON Jibbler golbeck pasky raelity DeadEd
```

There is no limit to the number of nicknames that can be included in the argument, but as with all IRC messages, you cannot exceed the 512-character line-length limit, which includes the return and newline characters at the end.

The server will generate a 303 numeric reply (referred to as RPL_ISON in the IRC RFC), which lists the subset of nicknames that are connected to the network. In this case, everyone except "raelity" was connected, so he is omitted from the returned list:

```
:kornbluth.freenode.net 303 Jibbler :Jibbler golbeck pasky DeadEd
```

This is the best method of finding out who is on a server, as the request is handled locally by the server you are connected to—there is no need for it to get any information from any other servers in the network.

## The Code

With this knowledge of the ISON command, it's easy to write a bot that keeps track of your friends on IRC. All it needs to do is store a set of nicknames to look for and send the ISON command periodically.

The nicknames will be stored in a HashSet, which ensures that no duplicates are stored. Extra nicknames can be added to the bot using the addNick method. The onServerResponse method is overridden to catch the RPL_ISON reply and work out which users are newcomers to the network.

Save the following as *IsonBot.java*:

```
import org.jibble.pircbot.*;
import java.util.*;
```

```
public class IsonBot extends PircBot {

    // Stores the nicknames that were on the server when we last checked.
    private HashSet onServer = new HashSet();
    // Stores the nicknames that we are looking for.
    private HashSet nicks = new HashSet();

    public IsonBot(String name) {
        setName(name);
    }

    public synchronized void addNick(String nick) {
        nicks.add(nick.toLowerCase());
    }

    public HashSet getNicks() {
        return nicks;
    }

    public synchronized void onServerResponse(int code, String response) {
        if (code == RPL_ISON) {
            // Get the list of nicknames returned by the server.
            String nicks = response.substring(response.indexOf(':') + 1);
            String[] tokens = nicks.split("\\s+");

            HashSet newOnServer = new HashSet();

            for (int i = 0; i < tokens.length; i++) {
                String nick = tokens[i];
                String key = nick.toLowerCase();
                newOnServer.add(key);
                if (!onServer.contains(key)) {
                    // If the user wasn't already on, let us know.
                    System.out.println(nick + " is on the server.");
                }
            }

            // Update the set of users who are currently on the network.
            onServer = newOnServer;
        }
    }

}
```

The bot thus far handles ISON replies perfectly and prints out a message each time someone new appears in the reply. A separate thread will be used to perform the task of sending the ISON request every minute. The PircBot class lets you send raw commands to the server with its sendRawLine method, which appends the return and newline characters to the line on your behalf.

Save the following as *IsonThread.java*:

```java
import java.util.*;

public class IsonThread extends Thread {

    IsonBot bot;

    public IsonThread(IsonBot bot) {
        this.bot = bot;
        // Let the program to exit if this is the only thread still running.
        setDaemon(true);
    }

    public void run() {
        boolean running = true;
        while (running) {

            // Build up the contents of the ISON command.
            String command = "ISON";
            synchronized (bot) {
                HashSet nicks = bot.getNicks();
                Iterator it = nicks.iterator();
                while (it.hasNext()) {
                    String nick = (String) it.next();
                    // Append each nickname to the argument list.
                    command += " " + nick;
                }
            }
            bot.sendRawLine(command);

            // Wait for 60 seconds before sending the next request.
            delay(60);
        }
    }

    // Delay for the given number of seconds.
    private void delay (int seconds) {
        try {
            Thread.sleep(1000 * (long) seconds);
        }
        catch (InterruptedException e) {
            // Do nothing.
        }
    }

}
```

The main method has to instantiate the bot, add some nicknames to its search set, and tell the bot to connect to an IRC server. After it has connected, you can then start up the IsonThread so it can send a request every minute.

Save the following as *IsonBotMain.java*:

```
public class IsonBotMain {

    public static void main(String[] args) throws Exception {

        IsonBot bot = new IsonBot("IsonBot");

        // Add any set of nicknames you want...
        bot.addNick("Jibbler");
        bot.addNick("golbeck");
        bot.addNick("pasky");
        bot.addNick("raelity");
        bot.addNick("DeadEd");

        bot.setVerbose(false);
        bot.connect("irc.freenode.net");

        // Start the IsonThread.
        IsonThread thread = new IsonThread(bot);
        thread.start();
    }

}
```

## Running the Hack

Compile the bot like this:

```
C:\java\IsonBot> javac -classpath .;pircbot.jar *.java
```

Run the bot like this:

```
C:\java\IsonBot> java -classpath .;pircbot.jar IsonBotMain
```

## The Results

When the bot receives its first reply to an ISON query, it will let you know straightaway who is connected to the network, for example:

```
Jibbler is on the server.
golbeck is on the server.
pasky is on the server.
DeadEd is on the server.
```

If one of these users disconnects from the network, he or she will be removed from the onServer HashSet the next time an ISON is performed. If the user eventually comes back to the network, the bot will announce his or her reappearance in a similar way, for example:

```
Jibbler is on the server.
```

Adding ISON functionality to the TellBot **[Hack #50]** would allow it to deliver messages to other users even if they don't join the same channels as TellBot.

## HACK #57    Search for Books on Amazon

With the Amazon Web Services Developer's Kit, perform keyword searches and return the results to IRC.

After familiarizing yourself with the previous hacks, you should be well aware of the power of Web Services. Amazon provides a Web Services Developer's Kit, available from *http://www.amazon.com/gp/aws/landing.html*. You can download this for free and use it to search Amazon for books or other items. To use it from a Java program, you will also need to download the Apache Axis SOAP implementation from *http://ws.apache.org/axis*.

When you have installed Axis and Amazon Web Services, you can choose to either use Amazon's WSDL directly or use the more friendly com.amazon.soap.axis package. This hack will show you how to use this package to search for books on Amazon.

Amazon doesn't provide a Java package to use their Web Services, so you must generate the com.amazon.soap.axis package yourself. To do this, you must download the Amazon Web Services WSDL file from *http://soap.amazon.com/schemas2/AmazonWebServices.wsdl*. Now change to the *kit/AmazonWebServices/JavaCodeSample* directory and execute the *client.axis.sh* or *client.axis.bat* script. This will automatically generate the package for you. Make sure all of the *JAR* files in *axis/lib* are included in your classpath, along with your new com.amazon.soap.axis package and *pircbot.jar*.

The IRC bot described in this hack will respond to the !amazon command and use any parameters as keywords when performing a search of Amazon's books. The top three results, if any, will then be returned to the channel.

### The Code

Save the following as *AmazonBot.java*:

```java
import java.net.*;
import com.amazon.soap.axis.*;
import org.jibble.pircbot.*;

public class AmazonBot extends PircBot {

    private AmazonSearchService service = new AmazonSearchServiceLocator();

    public AmazonBot(String name) {
        setName(name);
    }

    public void onMessage(String channel, String sender, String login,
            String hostname, String message) {
```

```
        message = message.trim( );
        String[] parts = message.split("\\s+", 2);
        // Check for the !amazon command and keywords.
        if (parts.length == 2 && parts[0].toLowerCase( ).equals("!amazon")) {
            String keywords = parts[1];
            String results = getBooks(keywords);
            if (results == null) {
                results = "Cannot find any matches.";
            }
            // Send the results back to the channel.
            sendMessage(channel, results);
        }
    }

    public String getBooks(String keywords) {

        String topMatches = "Top matches:";

        try {
            AmazonSearchPort port = service.getAmazonSearchPort( );
            KeywordRequest request = new KeywordRequest( );
            request.setKeyword(URLEncoder.encode(keywords, "utf-8"));
            // Search only for books.
            request.setMode("books");
            request.setType("lite");
            ProductInfo results = port.keywordSearchRequest(request);

            Details[] details = results.getDetails( );
            for (int i = 0; i < details.length && i < 3; i++) {
                Details current = details[i];
                 topMatches += " " + Colors.BOLD + (i + 1) + ". " +
                Colors.NORMAL + current.getProductName( );
                // If the book has an author, include it in brackets.
                if (current.getAuthors( ) != null) {
                    topMatches += " (" + current.getAuthors( )[0] + ")";
                }
            }
        }
        catch (Exception e) {
            return null;
        }

        return topMatches;
    }

}
```

Now create a main method in *AmazonBotMain.java* to launch the bot:

```
public class AmazonBotMain {

    public static void main(String[] args) throws Exception {
```

```
        AmazonBot bot = new AmazonBot("AmazonBot");
        bot.setVerbose(true);
        bot.connect("irc.freenode.net");
        bot.joinChannel("#irchacks");
    }

}
```

## Running the Hack

To compile the bot, you will need to have the Axis JAR files in your class-path, along with *pircbot.jar*. The com.amazon.soap.axis hierarchy can be placed in the current directory, so you won't have to explicitly include it in the classpath.

You can add the relevant entries to your system classpath or specify them on the command line when you compile the bot, for example:

```
% javac -classpath .:pircbot.jar:axis-1_1/lib/axis.jar: \
axis-1_1/lib/axis-ant.jar: \
axis-1_1/lib/commons-discovery.jar:axis-1_1/lib/commons-logging.jar: \
axis-1_1/lib/jaxrpc.jar:axis-1_1/lib/log4j-1.2.8.jar:axis-1_1/lib/saaj.jar:\
axis-1_1/lib/wsdl4j.jar *.java
```

You can then run the bot like so:

```
% java -classpath .:pircbot.jar:axis-1_1/lib/axis.jar: \
axis-1_1/lib/axis-ant.jar: \
axis-1_1/lib/commons-discovery.jar:axis-1_1/lib/commons-logging.jar: \
axis-1_1/lib/jaxrpc.jar:axis-1_1/lib/log4j-1.2.8.jar:axis-1_1/lib/saaj.jar:\
axis-1_1/lib/wsdl4j.jar AmazonBotMain
```

## Using the Bot

As soon as the bot joins your channel, it is ready to start looking up books on Amazon. You can pass whatever keywords you want to it, including parts of the title or even the name of an author. Only the first three results will be shown, for example:

```
<Jibbler> !amazon hacks
<AmazonBot> Top matches: 1. Google Hacks: 100 Industrial-Strength Tips & Tools
(Tara Calishain) 2. The Hack Counter-Hack Training Course: A Desktop Seminar
from Ed Skoudis, with Video (Edward Skoudis) 3. eBay Hacks: 100 Industrial-
Strength Tips and Tools (David A. Karp)
```

Here is another example, which returns three books by the author Eric Dymock:

```
<Jibbler> !amazon eric dymock
```

```
<AmazonBot> Top matches: 1. The Audi File: All Models Since 1888
(Eric Dymock) 2. Jim Clark: Racing Legend (Eric Dymock) 3. The Renault File:
All Models Since 1898 (An Eric Dymock Motor Book) (Eric Dymock)
```

If the bot cannot find any results at all, it will let you know that it could not find any matches.

## Hacking the Hack

At the moment, the bot uses the getProductName and getAuthors methods to display the name of each book and the first author when it displays the results of each search. There are several other methods in the Details class that you may like to include in your results. Here are some of the most useful ones:

getIsbn
> Returns the ISBN for the book. This is a unique identifier and can be used to look up the same product at a later date.

getAgeGroup
> If your IRC channel is designed for use by youngsters, you can use this method to determine whether each search result is suitable for them.

getImageUrlLarge
> Returns a URL pointing to a large image of the book.

getListPrice
> Shows the list price for the book.

getOurPrice
> Shows the price of the book on Amazon.

getSalesRank
> Shows how popular the book is (a lower value means it is more popular).

Using the getListPrice method, you can add prices to your results. For example:

```
<Jibbler> !amazon irc hacks
<AmazonBot> Top matches: 1. $24.95 IRC Hacks (Paul Mutton)
```

Amazon Web Services provide an easy way to get information from the Amazon web site. Without these, making such a bot would have been much more complicated.

# Fun Bots
## Hacks 58–63

Life—even on IRC—can be dull without a little silliness thrown in for good measure. Not all bots have to serve a serious, clearly defined purpose, and this chapter aims to prove that.

Adventure gamers may find the DiceBot useful, as it can be used to simulate dice rolls, allowing the results to be seen by everybody in the channel. This reduces the chance of cheating on Internet-wide games, and bored users can even push their luck with the Russian roulette subgame built into the bot. While they are playing their games, they can use the egg timer bot to help them cook the perfect egg and remind them when to take it off the boil.

A great way of learning (OK, wasting time) on IRC is to join a channel with a trivia bot. These bots ask questions and award points to the first person to guess the correct answer. This chapter shows you how to make your own basic trivia bot, leaving plenty of room for extra features if you want to add them. If any of the questions are of a mathematical nature, you could even use the MathBot described in this chapter to help you out. Just don't rely on an artificial intelligence bot to make too much sense if you ask it for help, as the one described in this chapter is hardly likely to beat the Turing Test.

The last hack in this chapter shows you how to set up a *ComicBot* to sit in your channel and draw comic strips when funny things happen. You can put these comic strips on the Web and show people what a great time you have in your channel.

### HACK #58  A DiceBot

If you're an adventure gamer who likes to use IRC, make your own bot to roll the dice for you and your friends.

Dice are used for many games, such as yahtzee, craps, or even more elaborate adventure games like Warhammer (*http://www.games-workshop.com*).

Some games even require special dice with more than six sides. If you lose your dice, you may become stuck where you are. But with an IRC bot to roll virtual dice for you, you'll always be able to play such games against other players on the Internet without any risk of anyone cheating, as you will be able to see their dice rolls.

This hack will show you how to make a simple IRC bot that rolls a single die with any number of sides.

## The Code

The random numbers will be generated with an instance of the Random class in Java. This can be used to generate a pseudorandom sequence of numbers, which is more than adequate for a dice-rolling application.

The goal is to create a bot that responds to the !roll command by rolling a die and displaying the value.

Create a file called *DiceBot.java*:

```
import org.jibble.pircbot.*;
import java.util.Random;

public class DiceBot extends PircBot {

    private Random random = new Random( );

    public DiceBot(String name) {
        setName(name);
    }

    public void onMessage(String channel, String sender,
            String login, String hostname, String message) {

        message = message.trim().toLowerCase( );

        if (message.equals("!roll")) {
            sendMessage(channel, "I rolled a " + (random.nextInt(6) + 1));
        }
        else if (message.equals("!shoot")) {
            if (random.nextInt(6) == 0) {
                kick(channel, sender, "BANG!");
            }
            else {
                sendMessage(channel, sender + ": click");
            }
        }
    }

}
```

Notice that another feature has been introduced to the bot: a kind of Russian roulette game. If a user sends the message !shoot to the channel, there will be a one in six chance of the bot kicking him from the channel with the reason, "BANG!" If the user manages to escape the bullet, the bot will just send "click" to the channel.

For the Russian roulette feature to work properly, the bot must have channel operator status in the appropriate channels. The bot is capable of running in multiple channels.

A main method is required to tell the bot which server to connect to and which channel or channels to join. Save the following as *DiceBotMain.java*:

```
public class DiceBotMain {

    public static void main(String[] args) throws Exception {
        DiceBot bot = new DiceBot("Dice");
        bot.setVerbose(true);
        bot.connect("irc.freenode.net");
        bot.joinChannel("#irchacks");
    }

}
```

## Running the Hack

You can compile the hack by typing:

```
C:\java\DiceBot> javac -classpath pircbot.jar;. *.java
```

Run the hack with:

```
C:\java\DiceBot> java -classpath pircbot.jar;. DiceBotMain
```

## The Results

Figure 9-1 shows users Jibbler and Monty being lucky with their dice rolling. Jibbler then ends up getting kicked from the channel by pushing his luck with the !shoot command.

Advanced gamers can easily modify this bot to roll dice with more than six sides. If you are feeling adventurous, you could even try to create a bot that takes part in these games.

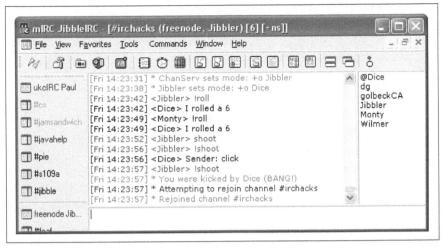

Figure 9-1. Using the DiceBot

# An Egg Timer

## #59

Create an IRC bot that can remind you to do something after a set interval.

Some people spend far too long in front of their computers using IRC. If you are one of those people, here is a hack that may appeal to you. Never again will you forget to do something important, because you'll be able to get an IRC bot to remind you!

This hack shows how to create a simple IRC bot that sits in any number of channels and responds to the !egg command. After three minutes, the bot will remind you that your egg is done, for this is how long it takes to boil the perfect egg.

Scheduling a task for later execution is easy with Java. The java.util.Timer class allows you to schedule tasks that extend java.util.TimerTask. The Timer class is scalable, so the bot should be perfectly capable of scheduling thousands of tasks at the same time. That's a lot of eggs.

### The Code

You will need to create a special class called EggTimerTask that extends TimerTask. When the egg is ready, the run method in this class will be called. In the run method, the bot must send a message to the channel to tell the user that her egg is ready to eat. Instances of this class therefore need to store a reference to the bot, channel, and nickname of the user.

Create the file *EggTimerTask.java*:

```java
import java.util.TimerTask;

public class EggTimerTask extends TimerTask {

    private EggTimerBot bot;
    private String nick;
    private String channel;

    public EggTimerTask(EggTimerBot bot, String nick, String channel) {
        this.bot = bot;
        this.nick = nick;
        this.channel = channel;
    }

    public void run() {
        bot.sendMessage(channel, nick + ": Your egg is ready!");
    }

}
```

Writing the actual bot is rather straightforward, as all you need to do is make it respond to messages that look like "!egg". It needs to create a new EggTimerTask and schedule it for running three minutes later.

Create the file *EggTimerBot.java*:

```java
import org.jibble.pircbot.*;
import java.util.Timer;

public class EggTimerBot extends PircBot {

    public static final long DURATION = 3 * 60 * 1000;
    private Timer timer = new Timer(true);

    public EggTimerBot(String name) {
        setName(name);
    }

    public void onMessage(String channel, String sender,
            String login, String hostname, String message) {

        if (message.trim().toLowerCase().equals("!egg")) {
            sendMessage(channel, sender + ": I am timing your 3 minutes now.
..");
            EggTimerTask timerTask = new EggTimerTask(this, sender,
channel);
            timer.schedule(timerTask, DURATION);
        }
    }

}
```

Finally, you just need a main method to start the bot and tell it to connect to a server and join a channel. If you want, you can ask this bot to join more than one channel, and it will still happily do its job.

Save the following as *EggTimerBotMain.java*:

```java
public class EggTimerBotMain {

    public static void main(String[] args) throws Exception {
        EggTimerBot bot = new EggTimerBot("eggcook");
        bot.setVerbose(true);
        bot.connect("irc.freenode.net");
        bot.joinChannel("#irchacks");
    }

}
```

## Running the Hack

Compile the bot:

```
C:\java\EggTimerBot> javac -classpath .;pircbot.jar *.java
```

Run it like so:

```
C:\java\EggTimerBot> java -classpath .;pircbot.jar EggTimerBotMain
```

## The Results

When someone issues the !egg command, the bot will tell him when three minutes has elapsed, as shown in Figure 9-2. Note that multiple timings can run concurrently. If you want, you could even run this bot in more than one channel [Hack #50].

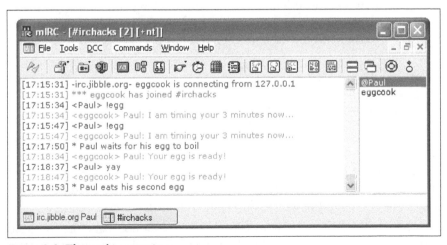

*Figure 9-2. The working egg timer*

## Hacking the Hack

Timing three minutes is fine if you're a fan of boiled eggs, but not every-thing takes three minutes to cook. You could generalize the bot so it is suit-able for other purposes. Modify the body of the onMessage method so it can accept a new command, !timer *duration*, where *duration* is the number of seconds to wait before alerting you:

```
message = message.trim().toLowerCase();
if (message.equals("!egg")) {
    sendMessage(channel, sender + ": I am timing your 3 minutes now...");
    EggTimerTask timerTask = new EggTimerTask(this, sender, channel);
    timer.schedule(timerTask, DURATION);
}
else if (message.startsWith("!timer ")) {
    try {
        int duration = Integer.parseInt(message.substring(7));
        if (duration > 0) {
            EggTimerTask timerTask = new EggTimerTask(this, sender,
channel);
            // Multiply the milliseconds by 1000 to get seconds.
            timer.schedule(timerTask, duration * 1000);
        }
    }
    catch (NumberFormatException e) {
        // Do nothing.
    }
}
```

You can now get the bot to time any period measured in seconds, for example:

**!timer** *30*

would make the bot wait half a minute before telling you your egg's ready. Of course, you may not be using it for cooking eggs by this stage, so you may like to change the message that is output by the EggTimerTask class.

### HACK #60   A Trivia Bot

Turn an IRC bot into an automated quiz show host. Compete with your friends to be first to answer each question.

If your channel ever seems to lack excitement, you can rev up the enjoy-ment factor by introducing a *trivia bot* that asks questions and waits for someone to respond with the correct answer. Most trivia bots ask a single question and wait for someone to give the correct answer. When the correct answer has been given, the bot will ask another question.

This hack will show you how to make a basic trivia bot that stores all of its questions and answers in a text file. More advanced trivia bots can let you store the total scores for each user and may even have time limits for each question.

## The Code

To make your trivia bot easy to extend, you should create a Question class, so each question (and answer) can be stored in a Question object. The Question class also provides an isCorrect method, so you can see if a candidate answer is correct.

Create a file called *Question.java*:

```java
public class Question {

    private String question;
    private String answer;

    public Question(String question, String answer) {
        this.question = question;
        this.answer = answer;
    }

    public String toString( ) {
        return question;
    }

    public String getAnswer( ) {
        return answer;
    }

    public boolean isCorrect(String a) {
        return answer.equalsIgnoreCase(a);
    }

}
```

The TriviaBot class will be used to maintain a collection of Question objects. Each time a new question is asked, it will be chosen randomly from this collection. As soon as the trivia bot joins a channel, it will ask a question.

Whenever someone sends a message to the channel, the trivia bot will check to see if it matches the answer for the current question. If the answer is correct, the trivia bot will announce the sender of that message as being the winner.

This trivia bot will also allow users to say the "clue" command. If anybody says "clue" in the channel, the trivia bot will respond by showing how many letters are in the answer. It does this by replacing each letter in the answer with a * character and sending it to the channel. So if the correct answer is "Internet Relay Chat," the bot will send the following to the channel:

```
<Jibbler> clue
<TriviaBot> Clue: ******** ***** ****
```

This class extends PircBot to connect to IRC and uses the Random class in the java.util package to generate random question numbers.

Create a file called *TriviaBot.java*:

```java
import org.jibble.pircbot.*;
import java.util.*;

public class TriviaBot extends PircBot {

    private Question currentQuestion = null;
    private ArrayList questions = new ArrayList();
    private static Random rand = new Random();

    public TriviaBot(String name) {
        setName(name);
    }

    public void addQuestion(Question question) {
        questions.add(question);
    }

    public void onJoin(String channel, String sender,
            String login, String hostname) {

        if (sender.equals(getNick())) {
            setNextQuestion(channel);
        }
    }

    public void onMessage(String channel, String sender, String login,
            String hostname, String message) {

        message = message.toLowerCase().trim();
        if (currentQuestion.isCorrect(message)) {
            sendMessage(channel, sender + " is the winner, with the correct"
                + "answer of" + currentQuestion.getAnswer());
            setNextQuestion(channel);
        }
        else if (message.equalsIgnoreCase("clue")) {
            String clue = currentQuestion.getAnswer();
            clue = clue.replaceAll("[^\\ ]", "*");
            sendMessage(channel, "Clue: " + clue);
        }
    }

    private void setNextQuestion(String channel) {
        currentQuestion = (Question) questions.get(rand.nextInt(questions.
size()));
        sendMessage(channel, "Next question: " + currentQuestion);
    }

}
```

The `TriviaBot` class uses an `ArrayList` to store each `Question` object. New questions can be added to the bot with the `addQuestion` method. The `setNextQuestion` method is used to pick a random question and announce it to the channel.

The `onJoin` method is overridden and will be called whenever the bot joins a channel. The bot will then ask the first randomly picked question.

The `onMessage` method is overridden and will be called whenever someone sends a message to the channel. If the message matches the correct answer for the current question, the bot will announce that the sender won and it will then pose the next question and carry on as before. If anybody sends the "clue" command, the bot will send the clue to the channel.

## Making Questions

This bot will be near to useless without a large bundle of questions to ask. For now though, you can just make up a few questions to test the bot, then add more later.

Each line of the text file will contain a question and an answer. The | character is used to separate each question and its answer.

Create a file called *quiz.txt* and add some questions:

```
What is the square root of 81?|9
What does IRC stand for?|Internet Relay Chat
What is "bot" short for?|robot
```

To make the bot turn each line of this file into a Question object, you must parse the contents before the bot connects to a server. You can add this little bit of code to the main method, which instantiates the bot.

Create *TriviaBotMain.java*:

```
import java.io.*;

public class TriviaBotMain {

    public static void main(String[] args) throws Exception {
        TriviaBot bot = new TriviaBot("TriviaBot");

        // Read the questions from the file and add them to the bot.
        BufferedReader reader = new BufferedReader(
            new FileReader("./quiz.txt"));
        String line;
        while ((line = reader.readLine()) != null) {
            String[] tokens = line.split("\\|");
            if (tokens.length == 2) {
                Question question = new Question(tokens[0], tokens[1]);
                bot.addQuestion(question);
```

```
            }
        }

        bot.setVerbose(true);
        bot.connect("irc.freenode.net");
        bot.joinChannel("#irchacks");
    }

}
```

## Running the Hack

Compile the hack like so:

```
C:\java\TriviaBot> javac -classpath .;pircbot.jar *.java
```

Run the bot like so:

```
C:\java\TriviaBot> java -classpath .;pircbot.jar TriviaBotMain
```

The bot will then start up.

## The Results

When the bot starts up, it will read the questions from *quiz.txt*, connect to the server, and join the channel #irchacks, as shown in Figure 9-3.

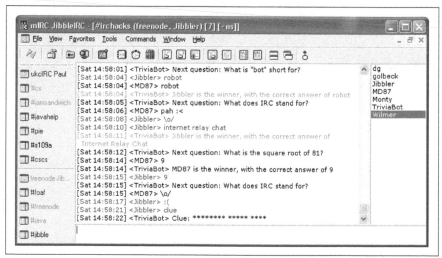

*Figure 9-3. TriviaBot running in #irchacks*

Note that without modification, this bot is suitable only for use in a single channel. This is because it stores the current question in a single field (currentQuestion), while multiple channel support would entail having a different variable for each channel. One way to make it suitable for use in multiple channels is to replace this simple variable with a HashMap, which is indexed by the channel name. This approach is implemented in the WelcomeBot **[Hack #64]**.

## HACK #61 Perform Feats of Math

Lose your calculator. Evaluate mathematical expressions with a bot that uses the Java Expression Parser.

How many times have you been desperate to find out the answer to a simple sum, only to discover that you can't remember where you left your calculator? One solution could be to fire up a calculator application on your computer, but for IRC users, a solution can be found even closer to home.

### Java Expression Parser

The Java Expression Parser (JEP) is an excellent tool for parsing and evaluating mathematical expressions. This is ideal for use by bots, because it can take a string as input, parse it, and evaluate the answer. This hack is based on the 2.24 release, which is available for free at *http://www.singularsys.com/jep*.

JEP input can contain the usual +, -, *, and / symbols, along with ^ to raise powers. JEP contains a set of standard constants, such as pi, e, and i, and a standard set of functions, such as sqrt, sin, abs, and so on. JEP supports implicit multiplication, where 2pi is automatically interpreted as meaning 2 * pi. Expressions like sqrt(-1) will not break JEP, as it can handle complex arithmetic and give answers with both a real and imaginary part.

### The Code

This bot will make use of the JEP and PircBot packages. It will respond to any channel messages of the form calc *expression*. If it is able to parse the expression correctly, it will give the answer; otherwise, it will say it is unable to do so.

Save the following code as *MathBot.java*:

```
import org.jibble.pircbot.*;
import org.nfunk.jep.*;

public class MathBot extends PircBot {

    // This JEP object will be used for the calculations.
    private JEP jep;

    public MathBot(String name) {
        setName(name);
```

```
                // Set up the JEP object's capabilities.
                jep = new JEP();
                jep.addStandardConstants();
                jep.addStandardFunctions();
                jep.setAllowUndeclared(false);
                jep.setImplicitMul(true);
                jep.addComplex();
        }

        public void onMessage(String channel, String sender,
                    String login, String hostname, String message) {

            message = message.trim().toLowerCase();

            // Check for the "calc" command.
            if (message.startsWith("calc ")) {
                String expression = message.substring(5);

                // Default answer.
                String answer = "Unable to parse your input.";

                try {
                    jep.parseExpression(expression);
                    if (!jep.hasError()) {
                        String real = String.valueOf(jep.getValue());
                        String complex = String.valueOf(jep.getComplexValue());
                        answer = real;

                        // Remove the decimal point if the number is integral.
                        if (real.endsWith(".0")) {
                            answer = real.substring(0, real.length() - 2);
                        }

                        if (!complex.endsWith(" 0.0)")) {
                            answer = "Complex " + complex;
                        }
                    }
                }
                catch (Exception e) {
                    // Do nothing.
                }

                sendMessage(channel, sender + ": " + answer);
            }

        }

    }
```

A main method is required to create the bot and tell it to join a channel;
we'll call it *MathBotMain.java*:

```
    public class MathBotMain {
```

```
public static void main(String[] args) throws Exception {
    MathBot bot = new MathBot("MathBot");
    bot.setVerbose(true);
    bot.connect("irc.freenode.net");
    bot.joinChannel("#irchacks");
}

}
```

## Running the Hack

Compile the bot:

C:\java\MathBot> **javac -classpath jep-2.24.jar;pircbot.jar;. *.java**

Run it like so:

C:\java\MathBot> **java -classpath jep-2.24.jar;pircbot.jar;. MathBotMain**

You can see the bot in action in Figure 9-4.

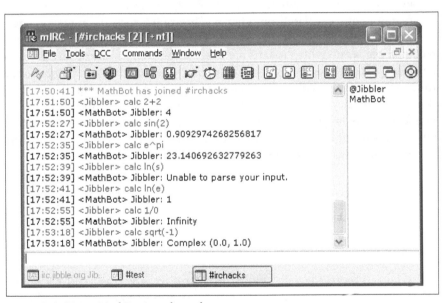

*Figure 9-4. Using MathBot in a channel*

## An Artificial Intelligence Bot

Use the JMegaHal package in a PircBot-based IRC bot that learns from and chats with other users.

IRC is not just a place where people hang out in channels, chatting with one another. It is also a valuable learning zone. Knowledgeable users populate certain channels. Interacting with these users makes it possible to learn new facts and share in a wealth of expert information on a particular subject.

This is obviously useful to human users, but what about bots? Can they too learn from what they see on IRC? Is it possible to mimic the behavior of a human user?

From a learning point of view, one appealing thing about IRC is that you can join a channel and quietly observe real humans talking to one another. You can learn a lot while lurking—and so can a bot. One popular pastime is to try to make conversation bots that respond intelligently to what is being said by the humans around it. What better way could there be of teaching such bots than by leaving them in a busy channel, learning from what real users are saying?

## Markov Modeling

One simple way of modeling each sentence generated by a human user is to break it down into tokens. In the simplest case, each word in the sentence is a token. After several sentences are "learned," an attempt can be made to create new sentences based on what has been observed. As humans generate more sentences, tokens that are used to start and end sentences become recognizable, as do which tokens are likely to precede or follow any particular token. All of these links form a graphlike structure that can be navigated from start to finish, with each random walk generating a different sentence that nearly makes logical sense. Due to the nature of this model, it is independent on the language spoken, although strange results may be observed when it learns more than one language at a time. Figure 9-5 shows the kind of data structures that form in a Markov chain.

> There is a simple Java Applet that demonstrates and visualizes the generation of these graphs at *http://www.jibble.org/dynamicgraph.php*.

## JMegaHal

MegaHal is a more advanced model that improves the quality of the generated sentences by gathering tokens into sequences of four and remembering which tokens precede and follow these sequences. Tokens consist of words and punctuation between words. A full description of the model can be found at *http://www.megahal.net*.

JMegaHal is a simple Java implementation of MegaHal and can be found at *http://www.jibble.org/jmegahal*. This also generates a fourth-order Markov chain to generate sentences in response to user input. It is these higher orders that ensure the output makes more sense than simpler implementations, but, of course, this will also depend on where your bot is learning its sentences.

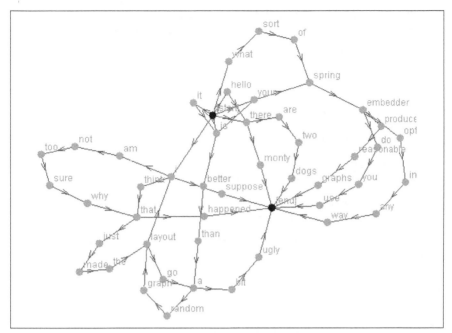

*Figure 9-5. The data structures present in a Markov chain*

Because the token set can include the whitespace and punctuation between words, the model is likely to preserve punctuation styles. However, because IRC channels typically contain more than one user, you probably won't notice any recognizable style, as it will be learning from everybody.

As an example, given the following two sentences to learn from:

```
The dog sat on the mat.
There was a dog sat in the bushes.
```

JMegaHal could possibly come out with four different sentences:

```
The dog sat on the mat.
There was a dog sat in the bushes.
The dog sat in the bushes.
There was a dog sat on the mat.
```

## The Code

In this hack, we use the JMegaHal package to learn sentences and generate replies. We will then combine it with the PircBot package **[Hack #35]** to create an IRC bot that can learn from other IRC users and hold wacky conversations with them.

An Artificial Intelligence Bot

**A simple example.** The JMegaHal package is supplied in a JAR file, so it is easy to integrate into any Java program, including an IRC bot. Make sure you import org.jibble.jmegahal.*; in any classes that will use it.

```
JMegaHal hal = new JMegaHal();

// Teach it some sentences.
hal.add("Hello, my name is Paul.");
hal.add("This is a sentence.");
// Note that the more sentences you add, the more sense it will make...

// Make JMegaHal generate a sentence.
String sentence1 = hal.getSentence();

// Get another sentence, with the word "jibble" in it (if possible).
String sentence2 = hal.getSentence("jibble");
```

Notice the getSentence method can take a String as an optional argument. If you want to generate random sentences all about pie, then you might want to call hal.getSentence("pie"). This ensures that all generated sentences include the word "pie" somewhere. If JMegaHal has not yet learned anything about pie, it will choose some other random token.

One thing to consider with a chat bot is telling it when to respond. If you make it respond to every message, the other users in the channel will very quickly get fed up with it and kick it out. One safe option is to make it respond only to messages that contain its nickname but to learn from all other messages.

**Combining JMegaHal and PircBot.** Combining JMegaHal and PircBot is very easy. If anybody utters the bot's nickname, it should respond with a randomly generated sentence from the JMegaHal object. All other messages that do not contain the bot's nickname will be used to teach it more sentences. In the following simple implementation, the bot is seeded with a starting sentence in the constructor, so it will always be able to respond with this if it has not learned anything else.

Create a file called *JMegaHalBot.java*:

```
import org.jibble.pircbot.*;
import org.jibble.jmegahal.*;

public class JMegaHalBot extends PircBot {

    private String name;
    private JMegaHal hal;

    public JMegaHalBot(String name) {
        setName(name);
        hal = new JMegaHal();
```

```
        // Add at least one sentence so the bot can always form a reply.
        hal.add("What is the weather like today?");
    }

    public void onMessage(String channel, String sender,
            String login, String hostname, String message) {

        if (message.toLowerCase().indexOf(getNick().toLowerCase()) >= 0) {
            // If the bot's nickname was mentioned, generate a random reply.
            String sentence = hal.getSentence();
            sendMessage(channel, sentence);
        }
        else {
            // Otherwise, make the bot learn the message.
            hal.add(message);
        }
    }

}
```

Now you just need to create a main method to construct the bot and tell it what nickname to use. The main method will also tell the bot which server to use and which channel to join.

This bot can run in multiple channels, but bear in mind that sentences learned in one channel could end up appearing in other channels.

Create the file *JMegaHalBotMain.java*:

```
public class JMegaHalBotMain {

    public static void main(String[] args) throws Exception {
        JMegaHalBot bot = new JMegaHalBot("Chatty");
        bot.setVerbose(true);
        bot.connect("irc.freenode.net");
        bot.joinChannel("#irchacks");
    }

}
```

## Running the Hack

To compile and run the hack, you will need both the *JMegaHal.jar* and *pircbot.jar* files. Both of these must be in the classpath when compiling and running. To compile the bot, type the following:

```
C:\java\JMegaHalBot> javac -classpath .;pircbot.jar;JMegaHal.jar *.java
```

To run the bot:

```
C:\java\JMegaHalBot> java -classpath .;pircbot.jar;JMegaHal.jar
JmegaHalBotMain
```

The bot will echo everything it's doing to the standard output, and you can start chatting with it as soon as it's joined the channel.

## The Results

Figure 9-6 shows the JMegaHalBot in action. The bot will obviously learn more if it is placed in a busy channel. Don't expect it to come out with anything too profound or unique until it has learned more than a hundred sentences.

Figure 9-6. *The JMegaHalBot trained with the contents of this hack*

Although you probably want your bot to learn as fast as it can, it's not always a good idea to place it in an enormously busy channel, as it may not get noticed. Be patient and wait for the best results.

## Create Comic Strips

IRC chat certainly has its moments. Wouldn't it be great if you could immortalize some of these moments in the form of a comic strip?

At times, an ordinary conversation on IRC turns into something much more amusing. People take funny quotes (quite often out of context) and plaster them all over the Web so other people can enjoy the humor. One of the most popular IRC quotes web sites is *http://www.bash.org*, which contains thousands of manually approved funny quotes.

Plain text quotes are all very well, but there's no reason they can't be made into comic strips. ComicBot (*http://www.jibble.org/comicbot*) is an IRC bot based on the PircBot framework that sits quietly in a channel and observes what people say. If somebody utters "lol" or suchlike, the bot assumes that something funny has been said and uses the last few lines to fill in a comic strip template.

## Setting Up ComicBot

ComicBot can be downloaded from *http://www.jibble.org/comicbot*. The ZIP file contains the source code, the compiled bytecode, and several comic strip templates.

The first step is to edit the configuration file, so open *bot.ini* in your favorite text editor. You'll find several settings in this file that you will need to change:

```
nick = MyComicBot
login = comicbot
server = irc.freenode.net
channel = #channel
outputDirectory = /home/paul/webpages/comicbot
helpString = Check out the latest cartoon at http://www.jibble.org/comicbot/
```

You can change the nickname of your ComicBot by changing the nick setting. You will need to make sure you set it to something that isn't already in use on the server. The server and channel let you tell the bot what to connect to and which channel to join. When the bot creates a new comic strip, it will write it to the outputDirectory, so make sure this directory is writable by the bot. Finally, the helpString is what the bot says when people ask the bot for help. It is always a good idea to provide a help feature in a bot so that other users can establish what its purpose is, for example:

```
<Paul> ComicBot: help
<ComicBot> Check out the latest cartoon at http://www.jibble.org/comicbot/
```

## Running ComicBot

Windows users can simply double-click on *run.bat* to launch ComicBot (the program is already compiled, so you will only need to run *comp.bat* to compile the source code if you have made any changes to it).

Linux/Unix users can run ComicBot from a terminal window by entering:

```
% java -classpath .:./pircbot.jar CartoonStripBot
```

After the bot has been started, you should see it connect to the IRC server and join the channel specified in *bot.ini*. Leave the bot running for a while and you will see each comic strip generated and stored in the output directory.

## Comic Strip Templates

Each time ComicBot sees something that it believes is funny, it will randomly pick one of the templates stored in the *data* directory and use it to create a comic strip. Each template consists of two files—a configuration file and a background image. For example, the first template in this directory would consist of the files *strip1.ini* and *strip1.png*.

Making your own template is straightforward. The easiest method is to copy an existing template, alter the PNG image, and edit the configuration file in a text editor. The configuration file will start by setting the filename of the background image:

```
background = strip1.png
```

This particular background image looks like Figure 9-7.

*Figure 9-7. A simple background image for a template*

ComicBot will write a date stamp on the output so that you know when each comic strip was generated. The datestamp setting is used to specify the x,y coordinate of where this should be placed, so make sure you know how big your background image is and that there is a suitable area of whitespace for the date stamp to be written. Figure 9-7 provides room for a date stamp along the bottom left.

```
datestamp = 11,261
```

Each template background should contain white regions that can be used to write each part of the IRC quote. The inner bounding box of the first "speech bubble" is defined like so:

```
bubble1 = 29,65,146,82
maxlength1 = 100
```

This means that the first line of text to be placed in the comic strip will be fitted into a rectangle with a top-left coordinate of (29,65), with a width of 146 and height of 82. The ComicBot will shrink the text if necessary so it fits nicely. However, if there is too much text, it could become so small it is unreadable. In this case, the maximum length of the speech bubble has been limited to 100 characters. If there are more than 100 characters, ComicBot will simply give up instead of producing a comic strip with small, unreadable text. The next speech bubble coordinates are specified with bubble2 and so on.

Once you have made the template, you should end up with something like Figure 9-8.

*Figure 9-8. A complete comic strip created from the template*

If you make any interesting comic strips, let me know and I can link to them or even include your templates in future versions of ComicBot.

# CHAPTER TEN

# Announcement Bots
## Hacks 64–67

IRC bots are ideal for making announcements. They can happily sit there and wait for an event to happen without getting bored. Furthermore, when a bot makes an announcement, it will never get involved in the subsequent debate that ensues.

The first hack in this chapter shows you how to make a simple bot that welcomes users to your channel. The hacks steadily become more complex, showing you how to announce the appearance of new newsgroup posts and news items found in RSS feeds. The final hack shows you how to use *MatchEd* to monitor the progress of multiplayer first-person action games from the comfort of IRC.

Beyond the hacks in this chapter, we hope that your imagination can lead you to create your own unique hacks, such as a bot that notifies you when you're low on hard disk space or when it's time to go and watch your favorite TV program.

### HACK
### #64
### Welcome Visitors Automagically
Create a simple bot that welcomes visitors to your IRC channels.

"Can I ask a question?" Users of busy channels will often observe newcomers popping in and asking this. You may wonder why they don't just ask their question, allowing people to choose whether or not to answer it, rather than having to answer the redundant question as well.

### Channel Rules

Many IRC channels have a basic set of ground rules associated with them. The regular inhabitants of the channel generally know these rules and abide by them. A lot of rules are common sense and are put in place to avoid wasting people's time. Busy IRC channels invariably have lots of first-time visitors. Some of these visitors tend to be unaware of the rules, including the ones that you may consider to be common sense! Consider including the rules in a welcome message that is sent as soon as newcomers join the channel.

## Welcome Options

Welcome messages can be sent to people who have just arrived in a channel in a number of ways. Sending a message to the entire channel is definitely one method to avoid, as only the newcomer will find the message relevant—nobody else in the channel will want to keep seeing it again and again. Sending a private message to the newcomer is a better option, as it won't annoy other users. However, most clients display private messages in a different window or tab, so some people opt to send a notice to the user instead. Many clients display notices in the active window that are easily distinguished from normal messages.

Sometimes people aren't around to personally deliver welcome messages in a timely fashion, so a bot comes into play.

## The Code

*WelcomeBot.java* joins multiple channels and uses a unique welcome message for each channel:

```
import org.jibble.pircbot.*;
import java.util.HashMap;

public class WelcomeBot extends PircBot {

    // This maps channel names to welcome messages.
    private HashMap welcomes = new HashMap();
    private static final String defaultWelcome = "Welcome to this channel.";

    public WelcomeBot(String name) {
        setName(name);
    }

    // Adds a new welcome message to the bot.
    public void addWelcome(String channel, String welcome) {
        welcomes.put(channel.toLowerCase(), welcome);
    }

    // Returns a welcome message for the specified channel.
    private String getWelcome(String channel, String nickname) {
        String welcome = (String) welcomes.get(channel.toLowerCase());

        // If there is no welcome message for this channel, use the default.
        if (welcome == null) {
```

```
                welcome = defaultWelcome;
        }

        // Replace $channel and $nickname if they are found.
        welcome = welcome.replaceAll("(?i:\\$channel)", channel);
        welcome = welcome.replaceAll("(?i:\\$nickname)", nickname);

        return welcome;
    }

    // This method gets called whenever someone joins a channel.
    public void onJoin(String channel, String sender,
            String login, String hostname) {

        if (!sender.equalsIgnoreCase(getNick())) {
            // Send a welcome notice to the visitor.
            sendNotice(sender, getWelcome(channel, sender));
        }
    }

}
```

The bot will welcome users to all of the channels into which it has been sent.
In your main method, you can add specific welcome messages for each channel. If you do not specify these, the default welcome message will be used.

Set a custom welcome message for a channel by calling the addWelcome
method:

```
bot.addWelcome("#channel", "Welcome to our channel... behave nicely!");
```

Your welcome message can also make use of the $channel and $nickname
variables, which will be automatically replaced by the bot, for example:

```
bot.addWelcome("#channel", "Welcome to $channel, $nickname.");
```

Create a file called *WelcomeBotMain.java*. You will use this to specify your
welcome messages and tell the bot which channels to join:

```
public class WelcomeBotMain {

    public static void main(String[] args) throws Exception {
        WelcomeBot bot = new WelcomeBot("WelcomeBot");
        bot.setVerbose(true);

        bot.addWelcome("#irchacks", "Welcome to $channel, $nickname");

        bot.connect("irc.freenode.net");
        bot.joinChannel("#irchacks");
        bot.joinChannel("#test");
    }

}
```

## Running the Hack

Compile the bot like so:

```
C:\java\NntpBot> javac -classpath .;pircbot.jar *.java
```

You can then run the bot by entering:

```
C:\java\NntpBot> java -classpath .;pircbot.jar WelcomeBotMain
```

## The Results

Figure 10-1 shows the WelcomeBot in action, delivering welcome notices to two channels. In the top half, you can see the default welcome notice being sent as I join the channel #test. In the bottom half, you can see the custom welcome notice that was specified in *WelcomeBotMain.java*.

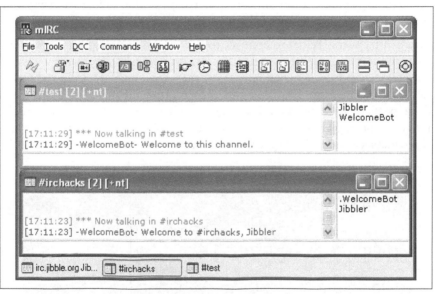

*Figure 10-1. WelcomeBot delivering welcome notices to two channels*

If your IRC network runs a ChanServ service, an alternative approach is to use ChanServ **[Hack #9]** to send welcome notices to users.

## HACK #65 Announce Newsgroup Posts

Moderated newsgroups are updated only every so often. Have an IRC bot check for new posts instead of wasting your time.

Usenet discussion groups (or newsgroups, as some like to call them) form a worldwide bulletin board system that can be accessed through the Internet.

A user can post a message to a newsgroup that will then be seen by anyone else who reads that newsgroup.

Some newsgroups have very infrequent postings or may even be moderated. Moderated newsgroups require a moderator to approve all postings before they end up on the newsgroup. In either case, the only way you can see whether there are new posts is to actually open up your newsreader and take a look. This is a waste of time if there aren't any new messages, so why not make an IRC bot to do it for you?

## Connecting to a News Server

Newsreaders communicate with newsgroup servers with NNTP (Network News Transfer Protocol). This is a text-based protocol and is quite easy to understand, so it's not too difficult to make a bot that talks to a newsgroup server. The default port for NNTP is 119.

You can try using Telnet to connect to port 119 of a newsgroup server and issue the GROUP *newsgroup* command. If the group exists, the server will reply with a 211 response, showing how many messages there are, followed by the range of the message IDs. You can then request information about all of these posts by entering **XOVER *lower-upper***, where ***lower*** and ***upper*** define the range of message IDs to request. Figure 10-2 shows a request for the last three messages from the newsgroup alt.irc:

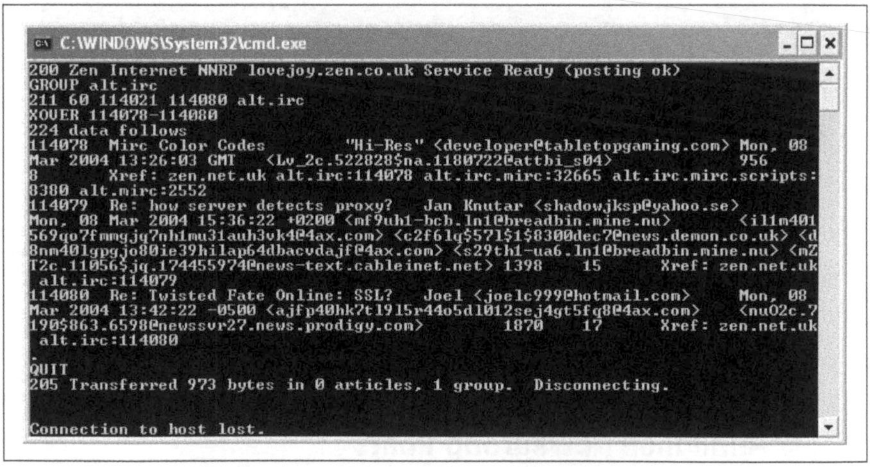

*Figure 10-2. Connecting to a newsgroup server with Telnet*

## The Code

Now that you know how to request message details via NNTP, you can encapsulate this into a separate class that is responsible for getting these details. This class will use its count field to keep track of the most recent message on the newsgroup, so each time it receives a response to the XOVER command, it can tell if new messages have arrived. The getNewSubjects method will then be responsible for returning an array of these new messages.

Create the file *NntpConnection.java*:

```java
import java.util.*;
import java.net.*;
import java.io.*;

public class NntpConnection {

    private BufferedReader reader;
    private BufferedWriter writer;
    private Socket socket;
    private int count = -1;

    public NntpConnection(String server) throws IOException {
        socket = new Socket(server, 119);
        reader = new BufferedReader(
                new InputStreamReader(socket.getInputStream( )));
        writer = new BufferedWriter(
                new OutputStreamWriter(socket.getOutputStream( )));
        reader.readLine( );
        writeLine("MODE READER");
        reader.readLine( );
    }

    public void writeLine(String line) throws IOException {
        writer.write(line + "\r\n");
        writer.flush( );
    }

    public String[] getNewSubjects(String group) throws IOException {
        String[] results = new String[0];

        writeLine("GROUP " + group);
        String[] replyParts = reader.readLine( ).split("\\s+");
        if (replyParts[0].equals("211")) {
            int newCount = Integer.parseInt(replyParts[3]);

            int oldCount = count;
            if (oldCount == -1) {
                oldCount = newCount;
                count = oldCount;
            }
            else if (oldCount < newCount) {
```

```
                            writeLine("XOVER " + (oldCount + 1) + "-" + newCount);
                            if (reader.readLine( ).startsWith("224")) {
                                LinkedList lines = new LinkedList( );
                                String line = null;
                                while (!(line = reader.readLine( )).equals(".")) {
                                    lines.add(line);
                                }
                                results = (String[]) lines.toArray(results);
                                count = newCount;
                            }
                        }
                    }
                    return results;
                }

            }
```

The IRC bot will be written so that it spawns a new Thread to continually poll the newsgroup server. Performing this checking in a new Thread means that the bot is able to carry on doing essential tasks like responding to server pings. This new Thread is able to send messages to the IRC channel, as the sendMessage method in the PircBot class is thread-safe.

The bot will also store the time it last found new articles and made an announcement. If it has been less than 10 minutes since the last announcement, the bot will not bother saying anything. This is useful when lots of messages are arriving on a moderated newsgroup, as these tend to arrive in large clusters in a short time.

Create the bot in a file called *NntpBot.java*:

```java
import org.jibble.pircbot.*;

public class NntpBot extends PircBot {

    private NntpConnection conn;
    private long updateInterval = 10000; // 10 seconds.
    private long lastTime = 0;

    public NntpBot(String ircServer, final String ircChannel, final String
            newsServer, final String newsGroup) throws Exception {
        setName("NntpBot");
        setVerbose(true);
        setMessageDelay(5000);

        conn = new NntpConnection(newsServer);

        connect(ircServer);
        joinChannel(ircChannel);

        new Thread( ) {
            public void run( ) {
```

```
            boolean running = true;
            while (running) {
                try {
                    String[] lines = conn.getNewSubjects(newsGroup);
                    if (lines.length > 0) {
                        long now = System.currentTimeMillis();
                        if (now - lastTime > 600000) {  // 10 minutes.
                            sendMessage(ircChannel, "New articles posted
to " + newsGroup);
                        }
                        lastTime = now;
                    }
                    for (int i = 0; i < lines.length; i++) {
                        String line = lines[i];
                        String[] lineParts = line.split("\\t");
                        String count = lineParts[0];
                        String subject = lineParts[1];
                        String from = lineParts[2];
                        String date = lineParts[3];
                        String id = lineParts[4];
                        // Ignore the other fields.
                        sendMessage(ircChannel, Colors.BOLD +
                                "[" + newsGroup + "] " + subject +
                                Colors.NORMAL + " " + from + " " + id);
                    }
                    try {
                        Thread.sleep(updateInterval);
                    }
                    catch (InterruptedException ie) {
                        // Do nothing.
                    }
                }
                catch (Exception e) {
                    System.out.println("Disconnected from news server.");
                }
            }
        }
    }.start();
}

}
```

Note that the Thread is started from the NntpBot constructor and no PircBot methods are overridden—there is no need for this bot to respond to user input, unless you want to modify it to do so.

The main method now just has to construct an instance of the bot, as the constructor also tells the bot to connect to the IRC server.

Create the main method in *NntpBotMain.java*:

```
public class NntpBotMain {

    public static void main(String[] args) throws Exception {
        NntpBot bot = new NntpBot("irc.freenode.net", "#irchacks",
                "news.kent.ac.uk", "ukc.misc");
    }

}
```

Note that the constructor arguments specify which IRC server to connect to, which channel to join, which newsgroup server to connect to, and which newsgroup to monitor. If you want, you could make the bot more flexible by using the command-line arguments (args) to specify the name of the server, channel, and so forth.

## Running the Hack

Compile the bot like so:

```
C:\java\NntpBot> javac -classpath .;pircbot.jar *.java
```

You can then run the bot by entering:

```
C:\java\NntpBot> java -classpath .;pircbot.jar NntpBotMain
```

## The Results

When you run the bot, it will connect to the IRC server and join the channel you specified. Each time a new post appears in the newsgroup, the bot will announce the post details, as shown in Figure 10-3. These details include title, author, email address, and message ID.

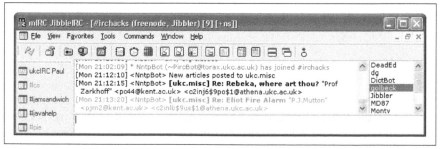

*Figure 10-3. Running NntpBot on a local newsgroup server*

Now you can keep an eye on your moderated newsgroups without having to keep your news client running in the background.

# Feed Syndicated RSS News into IRC Channels

### HACK #66

Have an IRC bot bring home the latest stories from an RSS feed instead of visiting your favorite news web sites every hour.

I like RSS, you like RSS, everyone and their weblogs' visitors like RSS, as well as their favorite news site. Even if you don't know what it is, you'll probably like it when you find out. The abbreviation stands for *RDF Site Summary* (or *Really Simple Syndication*, depending on who you believe), and it is basically a special kind of XML document that is commonly used to describe the latest items appearing on a web site.

This means that you could find the latest software releases from a Freshmeat RSS feed, while Slashdot's RSS feed would keep you informed about the latest published stories. But how does one use it? RSS is utilized behind the scenes of most of the "headlines" sidebars found on a growing number of web pages. People use various dedicated RSS readers to keep track of news and blog entries. *irssi* users can have the latest headlines of chosen RSS feeds cycling in their status bar.

Well, the natural next step would be to announce the latest RSS headlines in an IRC channel, so that people can hang around and watch the show, enjoying the massive information stream. So let's take that step right now with our hack, exploring RSS basics in Perl as well as practicing our usage with Net::IRC.

## The Code

The hack will use the Net::IRC module for the IRC connectivity. It suffers from a horrible incompleteness of documentation, but this is perhaps beneficial for beginner Perl programmers, as they will be forced to dive into the module's source code and absorb it. That will eventually improve your coding skills, and you will get a new surge of experience with How Others Do Things.

For RSS feed fetching and munching, you can use LWP::UserAgent in connection with the XML::RSS module. In order to refresh the RSS feed every $refresh seconds, you must set up an alarm that will raise the SIGALRM signal after the given time interval. Otherwise, the code should be pretty simple and straightforward.

Save the following as *rssbot.pl*:

```
#!/usr/bin/perl -w
# Petr Baudis (c) 2004, public domain
# Slightly inspired by Stefan "tommie" Tomanek's newsline.pl.
# RSS->IRC gateway
```

```perl
use strict;

### Configuration section.
# In our example setup, we are going to deliver Slashdot headlines.
use vars qw ($nick $server $port $channel $rss_url $refresh);

$nick = 'slashrss';
$server = 'irc.freenode.net';
$port = 6667;
$channel = '#irchacks';
$rss_url = 'http://www.slashdot.org/slashdot.rss';
$refresh = 30*60; # in seconds; Slashdot allows refresh max. once per 30
minutes

### Preamble.
use POSIX;
use Net::IRC;
use LWP::UserAgent;
use XML::RSS;

### Connection initialization.
use vars qw ($irc $conn);
$irc = new Net::IRC;
print "Connecting to server ".$server.":".$port." with nick ".$nick."...\n";
$conn = $irc->newconn (Nick => $nick, Server => $server, Port => $port,
                       Ircname => 'RSS->IRC gateway IRC hack');

# Connect event handler - we immediately try to join our channel.
sub on_connect {
  my ($self, $event) = @_;
  print "Joining channel ".$channel."...\n";
  $self->join ($channel);
}
$conn->add_handler ('welcome', \&on_connect);

# Joined the channel, so log that.
sub on_joined {
  my ($self, $event) = @_;
  print "Joined channel ".$channel."...\n";
}
$conn->add_handler ('endofnames', \&on_joined);

# It is a good custom to reply to the CTCP VERSION request.
sub on_cversion {
  my ($self, $event) = @_;
  $self->ctcp_reply ($event->nick, 'VERSION RSS->IRS gateway IRC hack');
}
$conn->add_handler ('cversion', \&on_cversion);

### The RSS feed
use vars qw (@items);
# Fetches the RSS from server and returns a list of RSS items.
sub fetch_rss {
```

```
  my $ua = LWP::UserAgent->new (env_proxy => 1, keep_alive => 1, timeout =>
30);
  my $request = HTTP::Request->new('GET', $rss_url);
  my $response = $ua->request ($request);
  return unless ($response->is_success);
  my $data = $response->content;
  my $rss = new XML::RSS ();
  $rss->parse($data);
  foreach my $item (@{$rss->{items}}) {
    # Make sure to strip any possible newlines and similiar stuff.
    $item->{title} =~ s/\s/ /g;
  }
  return @{$rss->{items}};
}

# Attempts to find some newly appeared RSS items.
sub delta_rss {
  my ($old, $new) = @_;

  # If @$old is empty, it means this is the first run and
    we will therefore not do anything.
  return () unless ($old and @$old);

  # We take the first item of @$old and find it in @$new.
    Then anything before its position in @$new are the
    newly appeared items which we return.
  my $sync = $old->[0];

  # If it is at the start of @$new, nothing has changed.
  return () if ($sync->{title} eq $new->[0]->{title});

  my $item;
  for ($item = 1; $item < @$new; $item++) {
    # We are comparing the titles which might not be 100% reliable but RSS
    # streams really should not contain multiple items with same title.
    last if ($sync->{title} eq $new->[$item]->{title});
  }
  return @$new[0 .. $item - 1];
}

# Check RSS feed periodically.
sub check_rss {
  my (@new_items);
  print "Checking RSS feed [".$rss_url."]...\n";
  @new_items = fetch_rss ();
  if (@new_items) {
    my @delta = delta_rss (\@items, \@new_items);
    foreach my $item (reverse @delta) {
      $conn->privmsg ($channel, '"'.$item->{title}.'"' :: '.$item->{link});
    }
    @items = @new_items;
  }
  alarm $refresh;
}
```

```
$SIG{ALRM} = \&check_rss;
check_rss();

# Fire up the IRC loop.
$irc->start;
```

## Running the Hack

Before running the script, make sure that the configuration suits your needs. Be especially careful with the $refresh value—check the target site first to see if it has a recommended or allowed refresh rate. For example, Slashdot currently does not allow a shorter refresh rate than 30 minutes and is happy to block your access for 72 hours if you violate this rule.

The script takes no additional arguments; you just execute it and watch the results on IRC. The script logs all its interesting activities to stdout, so that you have an idea what it does right now.

You can invoke this Perl script on the command line:

```
% perl rssbot.pl
```

## Hacking the Hack

A similar script is available for *irssi*, which hooks only to the user interface and provides no IRC announcement functionality. It shouldn't be too difficult to add this feature if you adapt the way it announces new stories in your current window. It even supports multiple feeds.

On the other hand, the script presented here is pretty simple and should be easy to customize. You could obviously make the output nicer, perhaps by making it a bit more colorful and easier to take in, as well as providing some more details. You could make it emit the item description or add a timestamp to the message or so on. In particular, one obvious enhancement for the Slashdot newsfeed would be to display the editor's name and department information.

One caveat here is the character set you choose to use. There is no single rule specifying which charset is to be used on IRC, so the safest thing to do is obviously to go with pure ASCII. This is, of course, not always acceptable, so you usually get to choose between a national charset (frequently ISO-8859-n) and UTF-8. Opinions and customs differ wildly between IRC networks, channels, and single individuals, so it is certainly wise to leave that as an option. The XML input will usually be in UTF-8 format, so it is up to you whether you leave it alone or encode it as a different charset. Some trivial charset remapping can be done by Unicode::String, while for a reasonable range of target charsets, you will probably have to use Text::Iconv.

It is always nice to be able to control the script from IRC. Consider implementing a generic module as a Net::IRC extension that would provide a kind of universal administration interface for an IRC bot, and then embed the module into this script. Then you could let users subscribe to the news individually, connect various channels with various RSS feeds, and do other similar grand things.

You may now be wondering what other useful RSS feeds exist. Yes, there are all the popular geek sites and your friends' weblogs, but aside from that, how about trying something a bit more unusual? For example, the Commits Information Agency (*http://cia.navi.cx*) provides RSS feeds of the latest commits for a large number of open source projects.

*—Petr Baudis*

## Watch Online Games with MatchEd

**HACK #67**

Many online gamers use IRC to organize battles and discuss tactics. MatchEd lets you watch the progress of a game from the safety of IRC.

Online gaming is becoming an increasingly popular form of recreational computing. With the widespread introduction of broadband Internet connections for home users, many more people are able to play these online games with acceptable responsiveness. Counter-Strike is one such game and has proven to be very popular among online communities. This team-based game pitches terrorists against counterterrorists. Sets of players often form themselves into clans—groups of people who play as a team against other clans. Clan members may be geographically distant, so IRC provides a suitable way of letting clans discuss their tactics and plan future events.

While clan members are busy chatting away in their IRC channel, they may find it useful to know what is going on while other people play on their Counter-Strike server.

MatchEd is an IRC bot that lets you watch the progress of a game of Counter-Strike, Action Half-Life, Natural Selection, Fire Arms, Death Match Classic, or Front Line Force. MatchEd is designed to be platform independent and can be run on any platform that supports Java. MatchEd uses very little CPU time, which makes it ideal for running on the same machine as the game server, making it permanently available. See it monitoring a game of Counter-Strike in Figure 10-4.

MatchEd works by reading the logs directed via the Half-Life server logaddress command. To use this, you must have rcon access to the server.

You can download MatchEd from *http://www.deaded.com*. To run it, you will need to have a Java Runtime Environment installed.

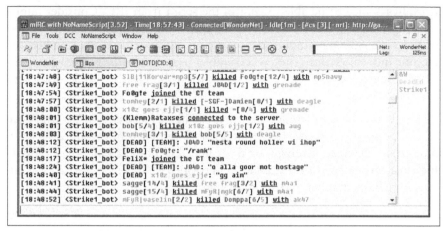

*Figure 10-4. MatchEd reporting on a game of Counter-Strike*

## Configuring MatchEd

Configuration of MatchEd is done in the *MatchEd.properties* file. The following information must be set.

IRCServer

> The IRC server the bot will connect to (e.g., irc.quakenet.org).

BotName

> The nickname the bot will use when connecting to the IRC server.

Channel

> The channel the bot will join when it connects to the IRC server.

AdminPassword

> The password to access the bot's administrations features.

RconAuthPassword

> The password for the game server administrators to use. Note that this is not the actual rcon password.

GameServerIP

> The IP address of the game server to use for reporting.

GameServerPort

> The port number of the game server to use for reporting.

## Starting MatchEd

Let's assume the following variables are set up in the *MatchEd.properties* file:

```
BotName = MatchEd
AdminPassword = power
```

```
RconAuthPassword = fubar
    - etc -
```

Most commands can be accessed only if you have been authorized as an administrator of the bot. Authorization is carried out by sending a private message to MatchEd:

```
/msg MatchEd auth power
```

If you want MatchEd to start reporting the progress of a game of Counter-Strike, you will need to authenticate as an admin or rcon administrator and tell the bot the rcon password for the Counter-Strike server:

```
/msg MatchEd rcon_auth fubar
/msg MatchEd rcon_password real-rcon-password
```

The authenticated user is now able to tell MatchEd to start reporting on the game of Counter-Strike by typing **!startcs** in the channel.

A quick way of checking to see if everything is working properly is to get MatchEd to say something to the Counter-Strike server. First, type **!serversayon** in the channel. This causes the bot to announce all server admin messages that are typed in the game. You can get the bot to send a message to the game with the rcon say command:

```
/msg MatchEd rcon say test
```

If everything worked successfully, you should see MatchEd respond with the following:

```
<MatchEd> [SERVER]: "test"
```

From this point on, any activity in the server will be visible in the IRC channel.

## Message Styles

Most aspects of MatchEd can be customized, including its name and the rate that it sends the messages to IRC. This can be useful to prevent the bot from being killed for flooding the server. It is also possible to change the style of the messages that are used to describe the events happening in the game.

To change any of the message styles, you must edit the *MatchEd.properties* file. As an example, the default output when an rcon say message is displayed is set as the following:

```
CSServerSay = [SERVER]: ${sayMsg}
```

Note the variable ${sayMsg}, which contains the actual message from the game server.

There are some other static variables that can be used to apply some color to the style, such as $RED, $BLUE, $GREEN, and so on. Each time a color is applied, it will affect the rest of the message until it is changed or turned off with the $NORMAL variable. Other formatting, such as $BOLD, $UNDERLINE, and $REVERSE are complementary. Each of these styles can be turned off by repeating the same variable or by using the $NORMAL variable.

To make the rcon say message style stand out a bit more, you can add color and boldness like this:

```
CSServerSay = $RED[SERVER ADMIN SAYS]$NORMAL: $BOLD${sayMsg}$NORMAL
```

**Dynamic configuration.** If you are authorized as an administrator, reload the changes made to any of the game output sections in *MatchEd.properties* while the bot is still running. If you type **!reload** in the channel, the bot will reload its configuration from the file. You can see whether this has worked by telling the bot to send the test message again. The bot should promptly return the following:

```
<MatchEd> [SERVER ADMIN SAYS]: "test"
```

The [SERVER ADMIN SAYS] text will be in red and the actual say message, "test", will be shown in bold in the normal text color.

—*Alex North*

# Network Bots
## Hacks 68–72

You can't use IRC without a connection to the Internet, and if you have a connection to the Internet, you may as well use it to its full potential. This chapter is all about using the Internet to link bots together or access them remotely.

By coincidence of misfortune, similar communities sometimes start channels on different IRC networks. When they realize they share the same interests but exist on different networks, it's not an easy task to get everyone to migrate to the same network. The first hack in this chapter covers one solution, which creates a bot that links channels on different networks and relays messages between them. Communities that run infobots can even share their factoids with one another by bridging them together with a separate bot.

By connecting directly to an IRC bot, you can watch remote log files as they fill or even access a command prompt to enable you to perform maintenance tasks. This chapter shows you how to achieve both of these feats.

The final hack in this chapter shows you how to create a file-sharing bot, allowing you to distribute your favorite music or pictures to people in your IRC channel.

### HACK #68 Link Channels on Multiple Networks

How do you encourage a community on one network to talk to those on another network? Create a bot that can relay messages between the networks.

Most IRC users are happy staying connected to just a single IRC network. Joining more networks inevitably means joining more channels, and, before you know it, you've run out of space on your screen. The problem here is that you might end up missing out on discussions with people who have similar interests on the other networks.

Sometimes there are other reasons for communities to be divided across two (or more) networks. A firewall or other technical constraint may prevent some users from connecting to one of the networks. But as long as someone (or something) can connect to all of them, it will be possible for messages to be relayed to other users. This can be done either manually, such as, "Hey Paul, did you hear about Dave's great idea on the other network?" or automatically with a bot that relays all messages between the servers.

Bots that link channels on different IRC networks are often called *relay bots*, as they are used to relay messages from one network to all the other networks they are connected to. Simple relay bots are straightforward to implement—all they have to do is connect to a few networks, join the same channel on each network, and read all the messages they see. Each time a message is received, it must be passed on to all networks except the one it was received from.

This hack will walk you through the process of creating your own relay bot.

## The Code

This hack will use the PircBot IRC API **[Hack #35]** to connect to each IRC network. Each connection will be dealt with by its own PircBot subclass, with a single Controller class being used to pass on messages to the other connections. The Controller is essentially a collection of separate IRC bots and is used to link them together.

Each bot just has to listen for messages and pass them on to the Controller, so there is not too much code to write. Save the following as *ChannelLinkBot.java*:

```
import org.jibble.pircbot.*;

public class ChannelLinkBot extends PircBot {

    // This is the Controller that we will pass messages to.
    private Controller controller;

    public ChannelLinkBot(Controller c, String server) throws Exception {
        controller = c;
        setName("MyLinkBot");
        setVerbose(true);
        connect(server);
    }

    public void onMessage(String channel, String sender,
            String login, String hostname, String message) {

        // Pass the message on to the Controller.
        controller.shareMessage(this, Colors.BOLD + "<" + sender + "> " +
```

```
                        Colors.NORMAL + message);
        }

    }
```

As you can see from this code, whenever one of the bots receives a message, it shares that message with the Controller. Each bot is passed a reference to the Controller in its constructor, along with the name of the server to connect to.

All the Controller needs to do is maintain a list of all of its bots and allow each of those bots to send messages to all the other bots. A LinkedList is used to store the collection of bots.

Save the following as *Controller.java*:

```java
import java.util.*;

public class Controller {

    private LinkedList bots = new LinkedList();
    private String channel;

    public Controller(String channel) {
        this.channel = channel;
    }

    // Add a new bot to the list and make it join the channel.
    public synchronized void add(ChannelLinkBot bot) {
        bot.joinChannel(channel);
        bots.add(bot);
    }

    // Share a message with all other networks.
    public synchronized void shareMessage(ChannelLinkBot from, String
message) {
        Iterator it = bots.iterator();
        while (it.hasNext()) {
            ChannelLinkBot bot = (ChannelLinkBot) it.next();
            if (bot != from) {
                bot.sendMessage(channel, message);
            }
        }
    }

}
```

The add method in the Controller is used to add a new bot to the LinkedList. Each time a new bot is added, it is told to join the same channel. Note that this method is synchronized, so it is safe to add new bots while the program is running.

The `shareMessage` method can be called by each of the bots and the `Controller` then iterates through the list of bots and tells each bot to send that message to its network. The bot that called this method must not be told to send the message; otherwise, it will simply end up repeating everything that is said on its network.

The main method of this program must create a `Controller` object and add a bot for each network it will connect to. You can supply these arguments through the command line.

Save the following as *ChannelLinkBotMain.java*:

```
public class ChannelLinkBotMain {

    public static void main(String[] args) {
        String channel = args[0];
        Controller controller = new Controller(channel);

        for (int i = 1; i < args.length; i++) {
            try {
                ChannelLinkBot bot = new ChannelLinkBot(controller,
args[i]);
                controller.add(bot);
            }
            catch (Exception e) {
                System.out.println("Could not add a bot: " + e);
            }
        }
    }

}
```

## Running the Hack

Compile the bot like so:

```
C:\java\ChannelLinkBot> javac -classpath .;pircbot.jar *.java
```

When you run the bot, you must specify the channel name as the first command-line argument. All subsequent arguments will be treated as server names, and a bot will be created to connect to each of them.

To make your bot connect to irc.freenode.net and an IRC server running on your own machine, you can run it like this:

```
C:\java\ChannelLinkBot> java -classpath .;pircbot.jar ChannelLinkBotMain
        #irchacks irc.freenode.net localhost
```

As soon as the bot has connected to each server, it will join the channel #irchacks. When it has joined at least two servers, it will be ready to begin relaying messages.

## The Results

When the bot is running, it will relay messages from each network to all other networks. Each message is prefixed with the nickname of the sender and is made bold to make it stand out more than the name of the bot. This gives the impression of everybody being in the same channel on the same IRC network, as shown in Figure 11-1.

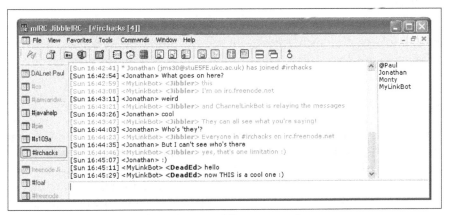

*Figure 11-1. Connecting a channel on two different networks*

This kind of bot is not really suitable for running in very busy channels, as the volume of traffic could cause the server to disconnect it for flooding the server as it relays messages. If channels are large enough for this to be a problem, then there is probably not much to be gained by linking them anyway.

## Get a Remote Shell

**#69** It's great to have remote access to an operating system. Build such features into your own IRC bot!

Having remote access to an operating system is useful, particularly if your IRC bot is running on it. You can check up on the amount of memory it's using, keep an eye on the amount of free disk space, delete files, and so on.

Unix/Linux users can get remote access to their systems using Telnet, SSH, or even graphical tools such as VNC (*http://www.realvnc.com*).

Depending on which version you have installed, you can also telnet to Windows machines and/or access your desktop with the Remote Desktop Connection client (*http://www.microsoft.com/windowsxp/pro/downloads/rdclientdl.asp*).

But it's not always possible to use these methods to gain remote access to a system. For example, you may run your IRC bot from a networked Windows

XP machine that doesn't have Remote Desktop enabled. The solution here is to exploit the fact that your IRC bot is running on that machine and turn IRC into the remote access protocol.

If your IRC bot is running on a particular machine, there is no reason it cannot just start up a local shell process and forward the output to a remote user on IRC. That remote user could then make use of the shell by providing her commands as input.

Providing remote access to a machine has serious security implications, so you should protect such access with a password at the very least. The bot detailed in this hack uses a simple password that is stored as plain text in the source code.

## DCC

DCC stands for Direct Client Connection and falls into two categories: chat and file transfers. DCC connections are negotiated via the IRC network, but once established, all data bypasses the IRC network and travels directly between a pair of clients. This makes DCC suitable for transferring files of any size or chatting with more privacy, without having to worry about the flood protection measures imposed by the IRC network.

The initial negotiation takes place via CTCP [Hack #85]. A file transfer request is made by sending a CTCP message containing the following:

```
DCC type argument address port [size]
```

type must either be SEND or CHAT for a file transfer or chat session, respectively. argument is a filename for the SEND type, with address and port being used to specify the IP address of the sending machine and the port on which the connection will be made. [size] is an optional parameter and can be used to specify the size of the file to be transferred. Extra data can be present after [size] and should be ignored if it is not understood.

Data sent via a CHAT connection should be sent one line at a time, with no prefixes or commands. Each line must be terminated with a newline character. You can find out more about DCC transfers by reading the full CTCP or DCC specifications.

## The Code

Because this bot is going to allow remote access to a shell, it will be called ShellBot. The access password will be stored in the field password, and it will respond to any private message that contains only this password.

When a user sends the correct password, the bot will start up a new ProcessThread in which to handle the shell process.

Save the following as *ShellBot.java*:

```java
import org.jibble.pircbot.*;

public class ShellBot extends PircBot {

    private String password = "password";

    public ShellBot(String name) {
        setName(name);
    }

    public void onPrivateMessage(String sender, String login,
            String hostname, String message) {

        if (message.trim( ).equals(password)) {
            // Password was correct, so create a new thread to handle the shell.
            Thread thread = new ProcessThread(this, sender);
            thread.start( );
        }
    }

}
```

The ProcessThread class launches the shell process in its own thread so that it doesn't block the normal operation of the bot. The thread starts by sending a *DCC CHAT* request to the user and waits for up to 120,000 milliseconds for the recipient to establish the connection to the bot. If the connection is not made in time, the bot gives up and the user will have to resend the correct password and try again.

If the user's IRC client accepts the DCC CHAT request in time, it will establish a direct TCP connection to the bot. This connection will be used to provide the remote shell access, as it is not subject to flood prevention restrictions like normal IRC messages.

This particular bot is set up to run on Windows, so it executes *cmd.exe* to provide shell access. If you are using an older version of Windows, you may have to change this to *command.com*. If you wish to use ShellBot on Unix/ Linux or Mac, you will need to change it to */bin/sh* or suchlike.

Save the following as *ProcessThread.java*:

```java
import org.jibble.pircbot.*;
import java.io.*;

public class ProcessThread extends Thread {

    private PircBot bot;
```

```
        private String nick;

        public ProcessThread(PircBot bot, String nick) {
            this.bot = bot;
            this.nick = nick;
        }

        public void run( ) {
            DccChat chat = null;
            try {
                // Send a DCC CHAT request.
                chat = bot.dccSendChatRequest(nick, 120000);
                if (chat != null) {
                    Runtime runtime = Runtime.getRuntime( );

                    // Use "/bin/sh" on Linux.
                    Process p = runtime.exec("cmd.exe");

                    // Start a new thread to handle input from the client.
                    BufferedWriter writer = new BufferedWriter(
                            new OutputStreamWriter(p.getOutputStream( )));
                    ProcessInputThread inputThread =
                            new ProcessInputThread(chat, writer);
                    inputThread.start( );

                    // Return all lines from the shell.
                    BufferedReader reader = new BufferedReader(
                            new InputStreamReader(p.getInputStream( )));
                    String line;
                    while ((line = reader.readLine( )) != null) {
                        chat.sendLine(line);
                    }
                }
            }
            catch (IOException e) {
                // Chat session ended unexpectedly.
            }

            if (chat != null) {
                try {
                    chat.close( );
                }
                catch (IOException e) {
                    // Do nothing.
                }
            }

        }

    }
```

The ProcessThread runs the shell process and reads all lines that it outputs.
Each line is then sent down the DCC connection to the connected client.

The shell process is running all the time, so you must create another thread
to handle input from the connected client.

Save the following as *ProcessInputThread.java*:

```
import org.jibble.pircbot.*;
import java.io.*;

public class ProcessInputThread extends Thread {

    private DccChat chat;
    private BufferedWriter writer;

    public ProcessInputThread(DccChat chat, BufferedWriter writer) {
        this.chat = chat;
        this.writer = writer;
    }

    public void run( ) {
        try {
            // Kludge... write a blank line to shell so path shows up.
            writer.write("\r\n");
            writer.flush( );

            // Pass each line from the client to the process.
            String line;
            while ((line = chat.readLine( )) != null) {
                writer.write(line + "\r\n\r\n");
                writer.flush( );
            }
        }
        catch (Exception e) {
            // Just let the thread end...
        }
    }

}
```

Because DCC CHAT is designed to send and receive only complete lines,
you will not see the command-line prompt, as it does not end with a newline character. The kludge fix for this is to enter a blank line after every input
from the user. This is implemented in the ProcessInputThread class and
causes the command-line prompt to appear each time the shell is ready to
receive the next command; it also causes it to be echoed a second time when
each command is processed.

The ShellBot doesn't need to join any channels, as it responds only to private messages, but it is sometimes useful to place such a bot in a channel so
that you know it's there.

Save the following as *ShellBotMain.java*:

```
public class ShellBotMain {

    public static void main(String[] args) throws Exception {
        ShellBot bot = new ShellBot("ShellBot");
        bot.setVerbose(true);
        bot.connect("irc.freenode.net");
        bot.joinChannel("#irchacks");
    }

}
```

## Running the Hack

Compile the bot like this:

```
C:\java\ShellBot> javac -classpath .;pircbot.jar *.java
```

Run the bot like this:

```
C:\java\ShellBot> java -classpath .;pircbot.jar ShellBotMain
```

The bot will then start up.

## The Results

You can start using ShellBot as soon as it's running by sending the password as a private message:

```
/msg ShellBot password
```

ShellBot will then request a DCC CHAT session with you. If you accept this, your IRC client will connect directly to ShellBot and you will be presented with a command prompt, as shown in Figure 11-2.

Figure 11-2 shows a DCC CHAT session with ShellBot. The user has executed the `dir` command to get a directory listing, showing the contents of the directory in which the bot is running. As with a normal Windows command prompt, you can use the `cd` command to change to another directory and `del` to delete files.

## DCC CHAT Limitations

Because of the line-by-line nature of the DCC CHAT Protocol, ShellBot will not work too well if you run interactive commands. Any command that requires interactive input is likely to cause the shell to stop responding, as it will be waiting for input that will never arrive.

Another interesting "feature" is that typing **notepad** on a Windows shell will cause the Notepad application to start up and surprise whoever happens to

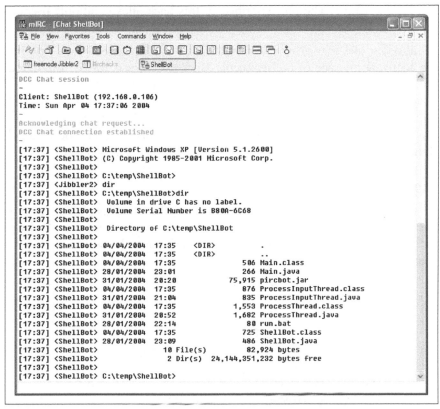

Figure 11-2. ShellBot delivering a Windows XP command prompt

be sitting in front of the computer at the time. ShellBot won't let you interact with applications like this, so you'll have to start a new DCC CHAT session or restart the bot.

## HACK #70 Tail Log Files

Keeping track of your log file activity is even easier when you can view real-time logs over IRC.

Many programs generate log files. If you have direct access to the filesystem, you can *tail* these files in real time using `tail -f filename`. This allows you to see the latest lines being appended to the log file every second. Most IRC bots generate log files so you can keep track of what they've been up to and to see any errors that may have occurred.

If you don't have direct access to the filesystem or if you want to let other people tail your log files, you can create an IRC bot that offers to tail files on the local machine. The bot described in this hack allows multiple users to tail the same log file over separate DCC CHAT connections.

Because log files may grow at a fast rate, you can't just send each new line via a private message to the recipient. Most IRC servers restrict the rate at which messages can be sent and will even disconnect you if you try to send too much too fast. This is why this bot will make use of DCC CHAT—it allows lines to be sent to a recipient over a direct TCP connection, bypassing the servers that make up the IRC network. This lets you send as much data as you want, without having to worry about being disconnected.

## The Code

To restrict access to the log file, a password will be stored as plain text in the bot's source code. If you want to tail the log file, simply send this password to the bot in a private message and it will start a new thread to handle your request.

Save the main bot code as *TailBot.java*:

```
import org.jibble.pircbot.*;

public class TailBot extends PircBot {

    // The top-secret access password.
    private String password = "password";
    // The log file to tail.
    private String filename = "c:/temp/log.txt";

    public TailBot(String name) {
        setName(name);
    }

    public void onPrivateMessage(String sender, String login,
            String hostname, String message) {

        if (message.trim().equals(password)) {
            Thread thread = new TailThread(this, sender, filename);
            thread.start();
        }
    }

}
```

The TailThread class will be responsible for requesting and accepting the DCC CHAT connection. This is done in a separate thread to the main bot, as it could take a long time for this to happen and it would otherwise block the normal operation of the bot.

Once the DCC CHAT connection has been established, the TailThread class
will perform the tailing by checking the size of the file every second. If the
file has grown since the last time it was checked, the new content will be
sent directly to the connected client. If the file size remains the same, no
action needs to be taken. If the file size shrinks, then the log file may have
been rotated or truncated. When this happens, the user is notified and the
tailing continues from the end of the file.

Save the following as *TailThread.java*:

```java
import org.jibble.pircbot.*;
import java.io.*;

public class TailThread extends Thread {

    public static final long delay = 1000;
    private PircBot bot;
    private String nick;
    private File file;

    public TailThread(PircBot bot, String nick, String filename) {
        this.bot = bot;
        this.nick = nick;
        file = new File(filename);
    }

    public void run() {

        try {
            DccChat chat = bot.dccSendChatRequest(nick, 120000);
            if (chat != null) {

                long lastLength = file.length();
                boolean running = true;
                while (running) {
                    long length = file.length();
                    if (length > lastLength) {
                        // Open the file to get the new contents.
                        RandomAccessFile raf = new RandomAccessFile(file,
"r");

                        raf.seek(lastLength);
                        String line = null;
                        // Send each new line to the connected client.
                        while ((line = raf.readLine()) != null) {
                            chat.sendLine(line);
                        }
                        raf.close();
                    }
                    else if (length < lastLength) {
                        chat.sendLine(Colors.RED + Colors.BOLD +
                                "[Log file truncated. Restarting at end.]");
                    }
```

```
                        lastLength = length;

                        // Wait a second before the next check.
                        try {
                            Thread.sleep(delay);
                        }
                        catch (InterruptedException e) {
                            // Do nothing.
                        }
                    }
                }
            }
            catch (IOException e) {
                // Chat session ended unexpectedly.
            }
        }

    }
```

Because this bot responds only to private messages, it's not essential to place it in a channel, but doing so helps to make other people realize its presence. Save the following as *TailBotMain.java*:

```
public class TailBotMain {

    public static void main(String[] args) throws Exception {
        TailBot bot = new TailBot("TailBot");
        bot.setVerbose(true);
        bot.connect("irc.freenode.net");
        bot.joinChannel("#irchacks");
    }

}
```

## Running the Hack

Compile the bot like so:

```
C:\java\TailBot> javac -classpath .;pircbot.jar *.java
```

Run TailBotMain with the following:

```
C:\java\TailBot> java -classpath .;pircbot.jar TailBotMain
```

TailBot will then start up and be ready to receive commands.

## The Results

You will need to send your chosen password to TailBot in order to view the log activity:

```
/msg TailBot password
```

The bot will then send a DCC CHAT request. As soon as you accept this request, you will be connected directly to the bot and will start seeing the output from the tailing. Figure 11-3 shows a simple web server log file being tailed. The timestamps provided by the IRC client provide a useful piece of information that is missing from the log file itself.

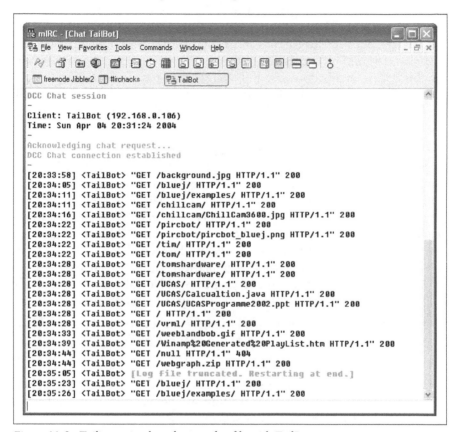

*Figure 11-3. Tailing a simple web server log file with TailBot*

If you have a log file that is appended to very rarely, it may be possible to implement such a tailing system via private messages. This removes any firewall problems, as you no longer have to connect directly to the bot, but at the expense of risking disconnection if the log file updates too rapidly.

### Bridge Two Infobots

**HACK**
**#71**   Combining the knowledge of infobots running on different servers is a useful way of sharing information between two communities.

Infobots are one of the more popular "fun" IRC bots out there. Usually, they are set up so that they create their own database of information nuggets—known as *factoids*—by monitoring conversations in channels. You can also add, delete, and update factoids manually. An infobot configured like this quickly turns into a "community memory," storing hard-to-remember facts like birthdays, email addresses, and references to past embarrassments concerning the members of the IRC community it serves. In this hack, we'll look at how to allow two communities to access each other's memories, by bridging two infobots on different servers.

Let's say that there are two infobots, called Norfolk and Dipsy. Norfolk and Dipsy are connected to different IRC servers. Imagine that the owners of Norfolk want Dipsy to appear on their channel too. What they need is a "bridge bot" on their channel that will be called "Dipsy" on their server, but that will connect to the second server under a different name and talk to the real Dipsy off-channel. Of course, there's no reason that different name can't be "Norfolk," assuming the name is free on the second server. In this case, the bridge bot can be completely symmetrical, sitting on-channel next to Dipsy on the second server and querying the real Norfolk off-channel on the original server. Both channels now appear to have both bots sitting on them.

Note that regardless of how the real infobots are set up, the "dummy" bots will respond only if directly addressed in a channel, like so.

```
dipsy: what is the meaning of life?
```

The format of infobot responses to on-channel and off-channel messages is slightly different, so the bridging isn't always going to be perfect. There's nothing in this hack that is infobot-specific, so it should work with any two bots that respond to off-channel messages in the same way as on-channel ones, or even with real people.

> Don't forget to tell the two infobots to ignore their new companions, or they will end up flooding the channels!

The bridge bot can be implemented in a particularly elegant fashion with Java by creating two instances of the same PircBot-based class and making each instance a member class of the other.

## The Code

The bridge bot lives in *BridgeBot.java* and makes use of the PircBot package
to connect to IRC servers. Note the getName( ) accessor method is used to
get the current name of a bot.

```java
import org.jibble.pircbot.*;

public class BridgeBot extends PircBot {

    public BridgeBot otherBot;
    public String channelName;

    public BridgeBot(String name, String channelName) {
        this.setName(name);
        otherBot = this;
        this.channelName = channelName;
    }

    // Handle on-channel messages.
    public void onMessage(String channel, String sender,
            String login, String hostname, String message) {
        if (!sender.equals(getName()) && message.startsWith(getName())) {
            // Pass the message on to the real version of this bot.
            otherBot.sendMessage(getName( ), message);
        }
    }

    // Handle off-channel messages
    public void onPrivateMessage(String sender, String login,
            String hostname, String message)  {
        if (!sender.equals(getName()) && sender.equals(otherBot.getName( )))
    {

            // Make the otherBot send a message to its channel.
            otherBot.sendMessage(otherBot.channelName, message);
        }
    }

}
```

To kick the bridge bot into life, you will need to create a main method that
creates two instances of the BridgeBot class. You could place this main
method in a new file, *BridgeBotMain.java*. After each bridge bot is instanti-
ated, it is supplied with a reference to the other BridgeBot object to allow
messages to be passed on.

```java
public class BridgeBotMain {

    // Configuration settings for each BridgeBot.
    public static final String firstServerName = "ircserver.domain.com";
    public static final String firstBotName = "Norfolk";
    public static final String firstChannel = "#channel1";
```

```
        public static final String secondServerName = "ircserver.anotherdomain.
com";
        public static final String secondBotName = "Dipsy";
        public static final String secondChannel = "#channel2";

        public static void main(String[] args) throws Exception {

        BridgeBot firstBot = new BridgeBot(firstBotName, firstChannel);
          BridgeBot secondBot = new BridgeBot(secondBotName, secondChannel);

            // Supply each BridgeBot with a reference to its partner.
            firstBot.otherBot = secondBot;
            secondBot.otherBot = firstBot;

            // Make the bots join servers and channels.
            firstBot.connect(firstServerName);
            firstBot.joinChannel(firstChannel);
            firstBot.channelName = firstChannel;

            secondBot.connect(secondServerName);
            secondBot.joinChannel(secondChannel);
            secondBot.channelName = secondChannel;
        }
    }
```

## Running the Hack

Compile the classes with the javac command:

```
C:\java\BridgeBot> javac -classpath .;pircbot.jar *.java
```

Launch the two bots by running the main method in the `BridgeBotMain` class:

```
C:\java\BridgeBot> java -classpath .;pircbot.jar BridgeBotMain
```

*—Steve Jolly*

## HACK #72    A File-Sharing Bot

Want to share files on IRC without the hassle of having to send anything manually? Use this IRC bot to tell people what files you're sharing and automatically offer them for download.

IRC provides a convenient way to distribute your band's music, lyrics, videos, or whatever else you may want to share with members of your channel. This hack will show you how to make a simple IRC bot that will tell people what files the bot has to offer, as well as letting them download any of those files.

This bot will respond to the commands !files and !get. The !files command will show a list of the files available in the current runtime directory. The !get command will allow a user to download a file using DCC send.

## The Code

Save the following as *FileBot.java*:

```java
import java.io.*;
import java.net.*;
import org.jibble.pircbot.PircBot;

public class FileBot extends PircBot {

    private static final String COMMAND_FILES = "!files";
    private static final String COMMAND_GET = "!get";
    private static final int DCC_TIMEOUT = 120000;

    public FileBot() {
        this.setName("FileBot");
    }

    public void onMessage(String channel, String sender, String login,
            String hostname, String message) {

        if(message.equalsIgnoreCase(COMMAND_FILES)) {
            // Get the current directory.
            File dir = new File(".");

            // Get all files (not directories) in the directory.
            File[] fileList = dir.listFiles();
            if (fileList == null || fileList.length == 0) {
                sendMessage(channel, "Sorry, no files available right now.
");
            } else {
                // List the files.
                for (int i = 0; i < fileList.length; i++) {
                    if(fileList[i].isFile()) {
                        sendMessage(channel, fileList[i].getName());
                    }
                }
            }
        } else if(message.toLowerCase().startsWith(COMMAND_GET + " ")) {
            String fileToGet = message.substring(COMMAND_GET.length()).trim(
);

            // Send the requested file over DCC.
            dccSendFile(new File(fileToGet), sender, DCC_TIMEOUT);
        }
    }

}
```

Now you just need a main method to tell the bot to connect to a server and join a channel. Save the following as *FileBotMain.java*:

```java
public class FileBotMain {

    public static void main(String[] args) throws Exception {
```

```
                FileBot fBot = new FileBot( );
                fBot.setVerbose(true);
                fBot.connect("irc.freenode.net");
                fBot.joinChannel("#irchacks");
        }


    }
```

## Running the Hack

Compile the bot with the following command:

```
C:\java\FileBot> javac -classpath pircbot.jar;. *.java
```

Run the bot like so:

```
C:\java\FileBot> java -classpath pircbot.jar;. FileBotMain
```

The bot will then start up and be ready to serve files.

## Hacking the Hack

Sometimes people are unable to use DCC. Firewalls are a common reason for this, so an alternative method of transport must be found. This can be achieved quite simply by incorporating a very basic web server into the IRC bot, such as the one found at *http://www.jibble.org/miniwebserver*.

To use this, you must add the following import statement to *FileBot.java*:

```
import org.jibble.simplewebserver.SimpleWebServer;
```

To allow access to the new feature, you must provide another field to store the command name:

```
private static final String COMMAND_GETHTTP = "!gethttp";
```

In the constructor, you can create the web server instance:

```
try {
    SimpleWebServer server = new SimpleWebServer(new File("./"), 80);
} catch (IOException e) {
    e.printStackTrace( );
}
```

In the onMessage method, you can now add handling for the new command:

```
    ...
    } else if(message.toLowerCase( ).startsWith(COMMAND_GETHTTP + " ")) {
        String fileToGet = message.substring(COMMAND_GETHTTP.length( )).trim(
);

        try {
            sendMessage(channel, "http://" +
                    InetAddress.getLocalHost().getHostAddress( ) + "/" +
fileToGet);
```

```
    } catch (UnknownHostException e) {
        e.printStackTrace( );
    }
}
```

## The Results

When you send the !files command, the bot will list all of the files in the current directory, for example:

```
<DeadEd> !files
<FileBot> Image1.gif
<FileBot> Snd2.wav
<FileBot> Report.doc
<FileBot> FileBot.txt
```

If you want one of these files, you can use the !get *filename* command, for example:

```
<DeadEd> !get FileBot.txt
```

FileBot will now try and send the file via DCC send. If this fails for some reason, you can try the last resort—download the file over HTTP:

```
<DeadEd> !gethttp FileBot.txt
<FileBot> http://123.456.123.456/FileBot.txt
```

Follow that link in your browser and the file should start downloading—assuming, of course, that the web server on which FileBot is running is accessible to you over the Web.

*—Alex North*

# CHAPTER TWELVE

# Channel Management Bots
## Hacks 73–77

Channel management is a high priority for some people. The last thing you want is to have your channel attacked by malicious users who are intent on leaving their mark in any way they can. Fortunately, this happens quite rarely, but you should be ready for it when it does happen.

All IRC channels have a topic, which can usually be changed by anybody. The first hack in this chapter shows how to restrict the ability to change the topic and how to implement a simple bot that can look after the topic for you.

Another way to protect your channel is to make it "invite-only" and use a bot to invite users into it. If you are a channel operator, you have the ability to kick people out of your channel; so one of the hacks also shows you how to create a bot that can hand out operator status to other users.

Eggdrops are one of the oldest types of bot still in active development. These are typically used to manage channels, so this chapter shows you how to set one up and get it to manage your channels for you.

### HACK #73 Protect the Channel Topic

Set your channel's topic to something inviting and friendly—and make sure it stays that way.

The topic of a channel is surprisingly important. Not only is it the first thing people will see when they join the channel, but it is also visible when users perform the /list command (see "Filter Channel Lists" [Hack #16]). If users don't like the look of the topic, they certainly aren't going to consider joining your channel. For this reason, some people make efforts to ensure that the topic does not get tampered with. It is obviously desirable to stop people setting the topic to something that is abusive, but on the other hand, it is useful to let people change the topic so they can announce some important news to other users in the channel.

## Topic Protection Mode

The simplest form of topic protection can be achieved by setting the mode of the channel to +t. If you are a channel operator, you can do this in most IRC clients by entering /mode *#channel* +t. Once this mode has been set, only other channel operators will be able to set the topic. Topic protection can be removed by entering /mode *#channel* -t.

Allowing the topic to be changed only by channel operators is generally safe, as it is assumed that only responsible users will ever be granted operator status. However, this is not very friendly to the nonoperator users of that channel; the majority of which will be well behaved and may even want to add important information to the topic. Of course, they could just ask a channel operator to add something to the topic, but this gets rather annoying after a while, and no operators may be watching the channel at that moment.

## Topic Erasure

Using an IRC bot or script to manage topic changes is a better way of handling things, as it can be present all the time and do everything automatically. Opening up the channel by applying mode -t will allow anybody to set the topic under the watchful guise of the bot. A trivial task that a bot can carry out is to make it easy to ensure that nobody erases the topic completely. If a rogue user were to erase the topic, all the bot would have to do is set it back to what the topic used to be. The rogue user would be free to erase the topic again, but the bot would just keep resetting the old topic until he got bored and left. An alternative action would be for the bot to apply mode +t for a short period.

## Formatting and Colors

Some users are put off by a channel that is brightly colored or heavily formatted. The use of these features certainly makes the topic stand out more, but they often have an adverse effect on legibility—and can make your channel seem cheesy. An IRC bot can easily sit in a channel and ensure that topics never contain any strange formatting or colors. This can be done by refusing to accept the topic completely or by reformatting it without formats and colors.

## Profanity Filtering

IRC bots are ideal for ensuring that topics never contain any rude words. If a user changes the topic to something that includes rude words, the bot could set the topic back to what it used to be, or some wildcard character could replace the rude words. Although the detection of rude words is difficult to achieve with the same accuracy as a human observer, a bot nonetheless has the advantage of being able to do it automatically.

## The Code

This bot will perform the filtering and erasure protection described so you don't have to.

Save the following code as *TopicBot.java*:

```java
import org.jibble.pircbot.*;
import java.util.*;

public class TopicBot extends PircBot {

    private String oldTopic = null;
    private ArrayList badWords = new ArrayList();

    public TopicBot(String name) {
        setName(name);
    }

    public void onTopic(String channel, String topic,
            String setBy, long date, boolean changed) {

        if (changed && !setBy.equalsIgnoreCase(getNick())) {

            topic = topic.trim();
            String unformatted = Colors.removeFormattingAndColors(topic);

            if (topic.length() == 0) {
                // Prevent the topic from being removed.
                setTopic(channel, oldTopic);
            }
            else if (!unformatted.equals(topic)) {
                // Remove strange formatting from the topic.
                setTopic(channel, unformatted);
            }
            else if (containsBadWord(topic)) {
                // Set the old topic if the new one contains bad words.
                setTopic(channel, oldTopic);
            }

        }

        oldTopic = topic;
    }

    public void addBadWord(String word) {
        badWords.add(word.trim().toLowerCase());
    }
```

```
    // Returns true if the topic contains any bad words.
    public boolean containsBadWord(String topic) {
        topic = topic.toLowerCase();
        for (int i = 0; i < badWords.size(); i++) {
            String word = (String) badWords.get(i);
            if (topic.indexOf(word) >= 0) {
                return true;
            }
        }
        return false;
    }

}
```

TopicBot observes topic changes in a channel by overriding the onTopic
method and then checks to see if they are allowed. When the bot joins a
channel, this method is called with the changed variable set to false. This is
because the topic has not actually been changed as such, but is merely being
sent to us by the IRC server. Whenever a user changes this topic, it will be
set to true. Each time the topic changes, the bot will store the topic in the
oldTopic field.

If somebody tries to set an empty topic, the bot will immediately set the
topic back to the old topic. If a user sets a topic that includes formatting or
color, the bot will respond by setting the topic to the same text, but without
the formatting or color. This preserves the content of the topic while also
making it easier to read. If a topic contains "bad" words, the bot will set the
old topic.

The containsBadWord method is responsible for checking a String to see if it
contains any of the bad words in the badWords list. Words must be added to
this list with the addBadWord method.

Create a file called *TopicBotMain.java* that will be used to connect to the
IRC server and specify which bad words to use:

```
public class TopicBotMain {

    public static void main(String[] args) throws Exception {
        TopicBot bot = new TopicBot("TopicBot");
        bot.setVerbose(true);
        bot.connect("irc.freenode.net");

        // Add some bad words. These are not allowed in topics.
        bot.addBadWord("bottoms");
        bot.addBadWord("fudge");
        bot.addBadWord("unix");

        bot.joinChannel("#irchacks");
    }

}
```

Notice that for simplicity, TopicBot stores the old topic as a String. This bot is therefore suitable for use only in a single channel. You could add support for multiple channels by replacing this String with a HashMap that maps a channel name to its topic, as with the WelcomeBot [Hack #64].

## Running the Hack

Compile the bot like so:

```
C:\java\TopicBot> javac -classpath pircbot.jar;. *.java
```

And run it:

```
C:\java\TopicBot> java -classpath pircbot.jar;. TopicBotMain
```

The bot will then leap into life and protect your channel topic from users who try to deface it.

## HACK #74 Invite Users into Channels

The safest way to keep a channel under control and free from unwanted intruders is to mark it as invite-only. Of course, you need a nice way of letting the regular users in.

Marking a channel as invite-only means that you can join that channel only if an operator in that channel invites you. This is a great way of keeping out unwanted or abusive visitors. To mark a channel as being invite-only, you must be a channel operator to apply the mode +i, for example:

/mode #irchacks **+i**

If a user now tries to join this channel, she will be told that she cannot do so because it is invite-only. To send an invitation to another user, you can use the /invite command, for example:

/invite Jibbler #irchacks

Marking your channel as secret (+s) can also help to avoid unwanted attention. This prevents the channel being listed when users execute the /list command. If people don't even know your channel exists, they can't even begin to contemplate causing any trouble there.

Of course, the whole invite-only solution is not perfect. If you have just connected to the server, the only way you would be able to join the channel is if you get invited. To get invited, you would probably need to send a private message to an operator in the channel and ask to be invited. The operator then invites you into the channel, and you are able to join it. But what if the operator isn't there to invite you? And how can you tell who's an operator in that channel if you can't see who's in it?

## Create an InviteBot

One obvious solution is to create an IRC bot that is responsible for handing out invitations. This will be called *InviteBot*. The bot will sit in the channel and accept invitation requests via private message. To ensure that only valid users are able to use the bot, the invitation request will actually be a password. You can define what this password is and then share it with everybody who is allowed to use the channel. If you send the bot the correct password, it will send you an invitation.

Remember to make sure the bot is a channel operator, otherwise it won't be able to send any invitations.

## The Code

Save the following as *InviteBot.java*:

```java
import org.jibble.pircbot.*;
import java.util.*;

public class InviteBot extends PircBot {

    private String channel;
    // The invitation request password.
    private String password = "password";

    public InviteBot(String name, String channel) {
        setName(name);
        this.channel = channel;
    }

    // Return the channel that this bot lives in.
    public String getChannel() {
        return channel;
    }

    // Accept private messages.
    public void onPrivateMessage(String sender, String login,
            String hostname, String message) {

        // Send an invitation if the password was correct.
        if (message.trim().equals(password)) {
            sendInvite(sender, getChannel());
        }
    }

}
```

This is quite a simple bot. You will notice that the password is set and stored in the password field. Feel free to change this to whatever you want, but remember not to use a sensitive password, as you will be sharing this with other users!

When the bot receives a private message, the onPrivateMessage method gets called. The bot then checks to see if the message matches the password. If it does, the sender of the message is sent an invitation to join the channel. The sender can then join the channel.

Now you need a main method to launch InviteBot. When you construct InviteBot, you must tell it which channel it is going to live in (#irchacks in this case). Save the following as *InviteBotMain.java*:

```
public class InviteBotMain {

    public static void main(String[] args) throws Exception {
        InviteBot bot = new InviteBot("InviteBot", "#irchacks");
        bot.setVerbose(true);
        bot.connect("irc.freenode.net");
        bot.joinChannel(bot.getChannel());
    }

}
```

## Running the Hack

Compile the bot like this:

```
C:\java\InviteBot> javac -classpath .;pircbot.jar *.java
```

You can then run the bot like this:

```
C:\java\InviteBot> java -classpath .;pircbot.jar InviteBotMain
```

## The Results

In the channel, Paul sets the bot up with operator privileges and sets the channel as invite-only:

```
* Paul sets mode: +o InviteBot
* Paul sets mode: +i
```

Jibbler comes along and tries to join the channel, but is told he can't:

```
/join #irchacks
#irchacks unable to join channel (invite only)
```

Now, rather than pestering a channel operator and asking her to invite him in, Jibbler can now just send the password to InviteBot:

```
/msg InviteBot password
```

If Jibbler got the right password, he will receive a message similar to this:

```
* InviteBot (identd@registered.freenode) invites you to join #irchacks
```

Jibbler is now able to join the channel. If Jibbler's IRC client was set up to automatically join a channel when invited, he won't even need to type **/join #irchacks**.

## Maintain Operator Status

**#75**  Losing operator status in your own channel can be a nuisance. Create an IRC bot that automatically grants operator status to those who deserve it.

Running an IRC channel can be a frustrating experience if you have to manage the ops yourself. Some networks implement IRC Services such as Nick-Serv **[Hack #8]** and ChanServ **[Hack #9]** to bring some order to the chaos, but there are plenty that don't. A popular solution is to run an *op bot* to handle things for you. It will sit on your channel tirelessly, granting status to those it trusts and placidly ignoring the cries of "opme!" from those it doesn't. Barring ping time outs, server downtime, and the wrath of the IRC admins, it will save you from the vexation of discovering that everyone with ops has just quit.

> Always check your IRC network's policy on bots before running one. Some disallow bots, particularly if they are used for the purpose of *opping* and *de-opping* users.

There are some ready-made op bots out there, but let's face it—it's far more fun to write your own, and you'll learn something along the way. This hack shows how to make a simple op bot that you could extend to get something a bit more fully featured. It runs on a single channel and contains a single list of trusted people, who get opped when they join the channel and who can add or remove other people from the list. For convenience, the bot saves a copy of the list to a file in its working directory whenever it's updated, so make sure it runs with the necessary file permissions.

You can add nicknames to the bot's list by editing the *trustedlist.txt* file before the bot is started. Create this file and add your own nickname to it. If you are in this list and you join the same channel as the bot, it will op you. You can also add nicknames while the bot is running. To add a nickname, you can send a private message to the bot:

    /msg opbot add nickname

Likewise, you can also remove nicknames from the bot's list at runtime:

    /msg opbot remove nickname

> The bot will be able to op people only if it has operator status itself. On IRC servers that do not run any channel services, the bot can get such status only if it is the first client to join a channel or if an existing op in the channel ops it.

## The Code

Create a source file called *OpBot.java*:

```java
import org.jibble.pircbot.*;
import java.io.*;
import java.util.*;

public class OpBot extends PircBot {

    private File file = new File("trustedlist.txt");
    private Vector trustedlist = new Vector();

    public OpBot(String botName) {
        setName(botName);
        setLogin(botName);
        // Try to read in the trusted list from the file.
        try {
            FileReader fileReader = new FileReader(file);
            BufferedReader reader = new BufferedReader(fileReader);
            String nickname = null;
            while ((nickname = reader.readLine()) != null) {
                trustedlist.add(nickname);
            }
            reader.close();
        }
        catch (Exception e) {
            System.err.println("Problem reading from " + file + ": " + e);
        }
    }

    public void onPrivateMessage(String sender, String login,
            String hostname, String message) {
        String nickname;

        // Only authorized users can send commands to the bot.
        if (trustedlist.contains(sender)) {
            if (message.startsWith("add ")) {
                nickname = message.substring(4);
                // Add the user to the trusted list and save.
                trustedlist.add(nickname);
                sendMessage(sender,"added " + nickname);
                saveTrustedList();
            }
            else if (message.startsWith("remove ")) {
                nickname = message.substring(7);
                if (trustedlist.contains(nickname)) {
                    // Remove the user from the trusted list and save.
                    trustedlist.remove(nickname);
                    sendMessage(sender,"removed " + nickname);
                    saveTrustedList();
                } else {
                    sendMessage(sender, "nickname not in list");
```

```
            }
        }
        else {
            sendMessage(sender, "invalid command");
        }
    }
}

public void onJoin(String channel, String sender,
        String login, String hostname) {
    if (trustedlist.contains(sender)) {
        // Op the user if he is on the trusted list.
        op(channel, sender);
    }
}

private void saveTrustedList( ) {
    try {
        FileWriter writer = new FileWriter(file);
        Iterator it = trustedlist.iterator( );
        while (it.hasNext( )) {
            writer.write(it.next( ) + "\n");
        }
        writer.flush( );
        writer.close( );
    }
    catch (Exception e){
        System.out.println("Error saving trustedlist: " + e);
    }
}
}
```

You'll need a main method to instantiate the bot and tell it which server to connect to and which channels to join. You can save this as *OpBotMain.java*:

```
public class OpBotMain {

    public static void main(String[] args) throws Exception {
        OpBot bot = new OpBot("opbot");
        bot.setVerbose(true);
        bot.connect("irc.freenode.net");
        bot.joinChannel("#irchacks");
    }
}
```

## Running the Hack

Compile the bot like so:

```
C:\java\OpBot> javac -classpath pircbot.jar;. *.java
```

And run it:

```
C:\java\OpBot> java –classpath pircbot.jar;. OpBotMain
```

The bot will start up and get ready to op people in your channel.

## Hacking the Hack

This is a pretty simple op bot. There are a few eventualities that it does not currently deal with. For example, what if you change your nickname while you are in the channel—should it de-op you? Worse still, what if someone else tries to use your nickname to get operator status in your channel? This hack forms the basis of something better—you could modify it to op only users with the correct host masks and nickname or even accept passwords through private messages from users who wish to be opped, as with the InviteBot **[Hack #74]**.

*—Steve Jolly*

### HACK   **Set Up an Eggdrop Bot**
### #76
Eggdrops have been around for quite a few years, so plenty of authors have had time to write Tcl scripts or C modules that make these kinds of bots very powerful. This hack shows you how to install and set up a simple Eggdrop.

Eggdrop is the oldest IRC bot still in active development. It supports multiple channels and can be extended using Tcl scripts or C modules—thousands of which can be downloaded freely to perform common tasks, which Eggdrop does not support natively.

Downloading, installing, and configuring Eggdrop is relatively simple. The first step is to connect to the server you will run the bot on, probably via SSH or Telnet. When you are connected, you can obtain a copy of the Eggdrop source code. The easiest way to obtain the latest version of the source code is to use wget. If you type **wget  eggheads.org**, the current (stable) version of the Eggdrop code will be downloaded to the current directory, as shown in Figure 12-1.

If your server does not have wget installed or you would rather not use it, you can download the files manually from *http://www.eggheads.org* and upload the files to the server via FTP or SCP.

The Eggdrop source code is distributed as a tarball, so the next thing to do is "untar" it. This is done using the tar command, like so:

```
% tar zxvf eggdrop1.6.15.tar.gz
```

You may need to change the filename if you have downloaded a more recent version.

This will copy all of the files in the tarball to a new directory, as shown in Figure 12-2.

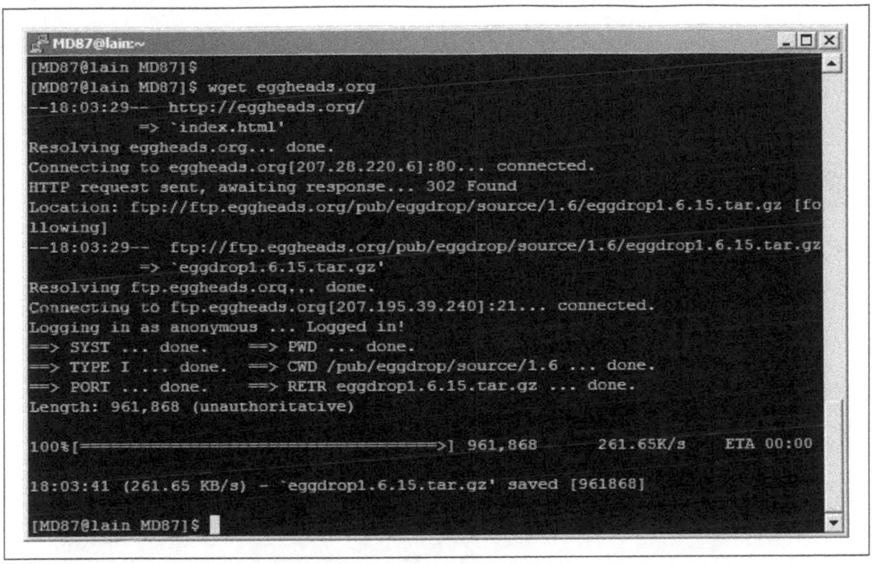

Figure 12-1. Using wget to get the Eggdrop source code

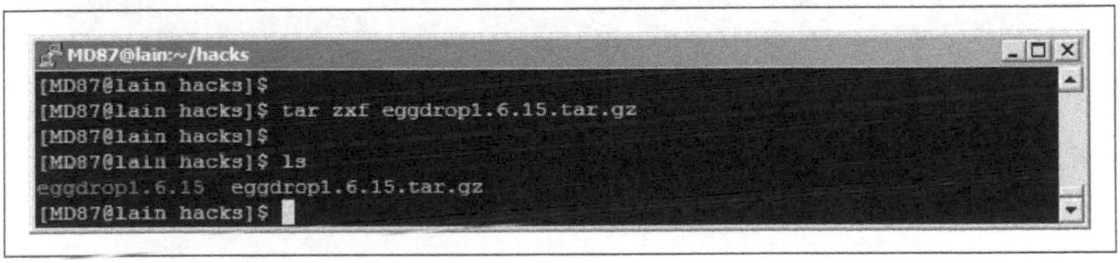

Figure 12-2. Eggdrop extracted into its own directory

Now change to the new directory:

```
% cd eggdrop1.6.15
```

If you are curious about Eggdrop, you may want to read the README and INSTALL files. They contain information on installing and running Eggdrop. When you have read these files, you can run Eggdrop's configure script:

```
% ./configure
```

This allows Eggdrop to adjust its settings so it can work correctly on your system. When this has finished, type:

```
% make config
```

This allows Eggdrop to configure the modules it needs. When the default modules have finished compiling, you should see something like Figure 12-3.

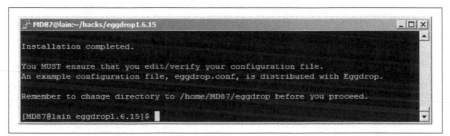

*Figure 12-3. Configuring the required modules with make config*

Next, you can type:

```
% make
```

This will compile the bot, but it may take a few minutes depending on the speed of your server. Now you're ready to install the bot. Type this:

```
% make install
```

and you should see something like Figure 12-4.

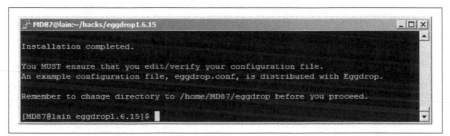

*Figure 12-4. Installing Eggdrop*

This will install Eggdrop into ~/eggdrop—that is, it will create an *eggdrop* directory in your home directory. cd to this folder, and you are now ready to edit the configuration file for your Eggdrop.

## Configuring Eggdrop

The first step is to open the config file in your favorite editor, for example:

```
% pico -w eggdrop.conf
```

As you look through the file, remember that all the lines that begin with a hash (#) are comments and will not be interpreted by Eggdrop. You can safely ignore most of these if you're in a rush, but they can often provide valuable help when it comes to setting up the more exotic features.

Most of Eggdrop's settings are in the form of set variable "value", which assigns the "value" to the variable. For example set nick "Hacky" would set the Eggdrop's nickname to "Hacky." The most important settings follow:

username

> This is the login that Eggdrop will use as its Ident if there is no *identd* running.

admin

> This should tell users how to contact the administrator of the bot (most likely you). The information is given out when a user types **/msg bot help**.

network

> This is used only if you are linking your Eggdrop to another bot and allows the bots to establish a connection whether they are on the same network or not. It should be either the name of the network (for example, "freenode") or a server name.

timezone

> This controls which time zone the bot will be running in and should probably be set to the same time zone as the server.

userfile

> This determines where Eggdrop will look for its user file. This contains details about all of the users known to the bot. It can be named anything you like. Something like *hacky.users* is the easiest to keep track of, however.

listen

> This command takes a different format than most others. The syntax is listen port type, and it needs to be uncommented and altered if you wish to link your Eggdrop to other bots or if you wish to telnet to it. Chose a number for the port, somewhere between 1024 and 10000, and make sure the # is removed from the line.

owner

> This command is required for your bot to recognize you as its owner. Uncomment the line, and replace the value with the nickname you use on IRC.

die

> A few lines beneath the owner setting is a line beginning with die. This must be removed or commented out; otherwise your bot will not start. This is cunningly placed there to ensure that people edit the config file fully before using the bot.

chanfile

> This is the file that Eggdrop will store its channels and settings in. You may like to name it in a similar fashion to the user file.

net-type

> This setting allows the bot to determine which commands it can use on the server it is connecting to. Most networks will probably be of type "other."

nick

> This is the nickname the bot uses on IRC. It can be anything you like, as long as the IRC server allows it. Most servers will not allow a nickname beginning with numbers, for example.

altnick

> This is the nickname the bot will try to use if its preferred nickname is in use. It can contain a question mark, which tells Eggdrop to insert a random number at that point. For example, setting this to "Hacky?" could result in the nick ending up as "Hacky123."

realname

> This is what will be displayed as the bot's real name on IRC. Most people set this to "/msg botname hello" or list the bot's primary channel. Other users are then able to view this information when they type **/whois hacky**.

servers

> This is a list of servers the bot will try to connect to. Delete the two examples and add the addresses of one or more servers on the network you want the bot to connect to.

learn-users

> This controls whether users can create their own account on the bot by saying "hello" to it. Setting it to "1" will make it easier to set up the bot via IRC.

notefile

> This is the file in which the bot will store notes (messages from one user to another). This should probably be named similarly to the user file.

die

> Shortly after the notefile setting is another die command that needs to be commented out.

blowfish

> This is a commented-out loadmodule command. You must uncomment this line, as blowfish is required to encrypt the passwords in the bot's user file.

When you have finished editing the file, save the changes and quit back to the shell. You can now start the bot by typing:

```
% ./eggdrop -m eggdrop.conf
```

This launches the bot for the first time. To run it again, type:

```
% ./eggdrop eggdrop.conf
```

*—Chris Smith*

## Manage Channels with an Eggdrop

**#77** Eggdrops are pretty neat bots for handling channels. Use one to prevent people flooding and to give out ops and voice.

Once you have set up and run Eggdrop for the first time, you will need to say "hello" to it.

This is done by simply sending the word "hello" to the bot in a private message:

```
/msg Hacky hello
```

The bot should reply with some basic information and explain how to set a password:

```
-Hacky- Hi MD87!  I'm Hacky, an eggdrop bot.
-Hacky- I'll recognize you by hostmask '*!MD87@caduceus' from now on.
-Hacky- YOU ARE THE OWNER ON THIS BOT NOW
-Hacky- As master you really need to set a password: with /MSG Hacky pass
<your-chosen-password>.
-Hacky- All major commands are used from DCC chat. From now on, you don't
need to use the -m option when starting the bot.  Enjoy !!!
```

You can then tell the Eggdrop what your password is:

```
/msg Hacky pass password
```

The bot will respond by confirming your choice of password:

```
-Hacky- Password set to: 'password'.
```

After you've set the password, you can start a DCC chat session with the bot. The command to do this may vary from client to client, but it will usually be similar to:

```
/dcc chat Hacky
```

The DCC chat session works by letting the Eggdrop connect directly to your IRC client, so you will need to make sure the bot is able to do this—check that you do not have a firewall blocking these sorts of connections. When the DCC chat is established, enter your username and password if the bot asks for them:

```
<Hacky> Enter your password.
<MD87> password
<Hacky>
<Hacky> Connected to Hacky, running eggdrop v1.6.16+notesfix
```

You are now connected to the bot's "partyline." From here you can issue commands to the bot, monitor events, and talk to other users who are connected to the partyline.

## Joining Channels

The command to make an Eggdrop join a channel is .+chan. This is done within the partyline, for example:

**.+chan** *#irchacks*

When you issue this command, the bot should tell you that it is joining the channel and will eventually confirm when it has joined:

```
<Hacky> [12:41] #MD87# +chan #irchacks
<Hacky> [12:41] Hacky joined #irchacks.
```

Now that the bot is in the channel, you can begin configuring it. The main command used to alter channel settings is the .chanset command. To get the Eggdrop to list all of its available options for the channel #irchacks, you can type:

**.chaninfo** *#irchacks*

The Eggdrop will then respond with something similar to this:

```
<Hacky> Settings for dynamic channel #irchacks:
<Hacky> Protect modes (chanmode): +tn
<Hacky> Idle Kick after (idle-kick): DON'T!
<Hacky> stopnethack: DON'T!
<Hacky> aop-delay: 5:30
<Hacky> revenge-mode: 0
<Hacky> ban-time: 120
<Hacky> exempt-time: 60
<Hacky> invite-time: 60
<Hacky> Other modes:
<Hacky>      -inactive      +statuslog      -secret      +shared
<Hacky>      +greet         -seen           +cycle       +dontkickops
<Hacky>      +protectops    -protectfriends -revenge     -revengebot
<Hacky>      -bitch         -autoop         -autovoice   -nodesynch
<Hacky>      -enforcebans   +dynamicbans    +userbans    -autohalfop
<Hacky>      -protecthalfops
<Hacky>      +dynamicexempts +userexempts   +dynamicinvites +userinvites
<Hacky> flood settings: chan ctcp join kick deop nick
<Hacky> number:         10   3    5    3    3    5
<Hacky> time  :         60   60   60   10   10   60
```

Each option is explained in the bot's help file, which is available by typing:

**.help chaninfo**

The first thing you can play with is the "revenge" mode. This makes the bot take revenge on people who de-op or kick known operators or Eggdrop owners. To enable this, you must type:

**.chanset** *#foo* **+revenge**

Other settings can be activated in a similar way.

You also need to change the revenge mode setting. This defines what sort of punishment the bot will give. The online help describes the various levels:

```
<Hacky>       revenge-mode      This setting defines how the bot should punish
<Hacky>                         bad users when revenging. There are four possible
<Hacky>                         settings:
<Hacky>                             0 Deop the user.
<Hacky>                             1 Deop the user and give them the +d flag for the
<Hacky>                               channel.
<Hacky>                             2 Deop the user, give them the +d flag for the
<Hacky>                               channel, and kick them.
<Hacky>                             3 Deop the user, give them the +d flag for the
<Hacky>                               channel, kick, and ban them.
```

The +d flag mentioned is the de-op flag. This will make the bot de-op the user whenever she is opped. To change the setting so that a user is de-opped and also de-opped again each time she is opped, you should set option 1, like so:

```
.chanset #irchacks revenge-mode 1
```

Now, if someone de-ops you, the bot will de-op him and make sure he stays de-opped:

```
* Lamer sets mode: -o MD87
* Hacky sets mode: -o Lamer
```

Likewise, the bot will de-op somebody if he kicks you from the channel:

```
* MD87 was kicked by Lamer (MD87)
* Hacky sets mode: -o Lamer
```

## Adding Users

Adding another user to the Eggdrop is also simple. She can either say "hello" to the bot as you did when you were setting it up, or you can add her from the partyline. The syntax for this is .+user *handle hostmask*. *handle* is the name the bot will know the user by. This can be anything you like, but it's probably best to keep it similar to the user's nickname. *hostmask* is a mask to match the user's address on IRC, in the form of *ident@host*. If you /whois the user, you should see this on the first line. You may include the wildcard * to match any number of characters, so if the user has a dynamic IP address like 123-123-123-123.isp.com, you can match it with *.isp.com.

After you've added a user, you can make the bot automatically op that user. This is done with the .chattr command. Eggdrop bots use a "flags" system—each handle has both global flags and channel-specific flags.

To add, remove, and view a user's flag, type **.chattr** *handle*. Most of the flags are explained in the bot's online help, which you can get by entering **.help whois**. The flag for auto-op is +a, so to give user "foo" auto-op on channel #irchacks, you should type:

```
.chattr foo +a #irchacks
```

If you want the bot to op foo on all channels, just type:

```
.chattr foo +a
```

When foo joins a channel, he will be opped after a short delay. You can alter the length of this delay using the "aop-delay" channel setting.

## Flood Protection

Another useful feature of Eggdrop bots is that they can protect channels from flooders. Flooders are users or bots that repeatedly send nonsense messages to a channel. These settings are listed at the bottom of the output from the .chaninfo command:

```
<Hacky> flood settings: chan ctcp join kick deop nick
<Hacky> number:          10   3    5    3    3    5
<Hacky> time  :          60  60   60   10   10   60
```

These settings show how many times a user can do something (number) in a given number of seconds (time). In this example, you can see that anyone sending more than 10 channel messages in 60 seconds will be kicked.

To alter these settings, like all others, use the .chanset command. The format for this is .chanset #channel flood-type number:time, where type is the type of flood (this must match one of the entries on the first line of the preceding output), number is the number of times a user can do it, and time is the time in seconds.

For example, setting the nick flood setting to 2 nick changes in 10 seconds would be done like so:

```
.chanset #irchacks flood-nick 2:10
```

This results in the bot banning and then kicking any user who changes nicks more than two times in 10 seconds, for example:

```
* Lame is now known as Lamer
* Lamer is now known as Lame2
* Lame2 is now known as LameSquared
* Hacky sets mode: +b *!*@Lame.users.network.com
* LameSquared was kicked by Hacky (nick flood)
```

All of the other flood settings can be changed in a similar way.

Eggdrop has lots of other built-in features, as well as a complete online documentation system. Typing **.help** in the partyline will allow you to access this online help, which is invaluable for anyone who wants to do more with her Eggdrop.

*—Chris Smith*

# CHAPTER THIRTEEN

# The IRC Protocol
## Hacks 78–85

You need to become more familiar with the underlying IRC protocol to get the most out of your bot hacking. The protocol imposes restrictions on the lengths of your messages—if you don't know about this, you may make a bot that sends too much data in one go and run the risk of truncating your valuable messages.

To ascertain the authenticity of who you claim to be, a lot of IRC servers try to contact your machine and ask it who you are. The Ident Protocol is used to handle this request, but Windows machines do not run an Ident server. Most Windows IRC clients therefore create their own temporary Ident server that runs while the client is connecting to an IRC server. In case you need to add such a feature to one of your bots, one of the hacks shows you how to create your own disposable Ident server.

In Chapter 4, you were shown how to add color and formatting to your IRC messages. When parsing these messages within the brain of an IRC bot, the extra formatting characters may cause problems. This chapter shows you how to remove colors and formatting from IRC messages, thus alleviating the problem.

The IRC protocol is text based, so the only way you can ensure total privacy is to encrypt your messages before they leave your IRC client and decrypt them when another client receives them. One hack shows you how to create a proof-of-concept bot that encrypts messages using a shared pass phrase or key. Only people who know the key will be able to decrypt the messages.

*Netsplits* occur frequently on IRC. A netsplit is a link breaking between a pair of servers that make up the IRC network. If you're wondering how IRC servers cope when a netsplit occurs, the TS Protocol gives you an interesting insight into the problems and how they are solved.

## Understanding the IRC Protocol

**#78**    The IRC protocol is a text-based protocol. Exploit it with just a little knowledge of its features and restrictions.

Because the IRC protocol is text based, you can easily look at it and see what's going on. You can do this either by creating a raw Telnet connection to an IRC server and typing the commands manually or by running a packet sniffer that displays all of the traffic going in and out of your IRC client.

Some IRC clients even let you see what's going on at the protocol level. For example, in mIRC, you can type **/debug @output** to make a new window that displays all raw lines being sent to and from the IRC server. The output looks something like Figure 13-1.

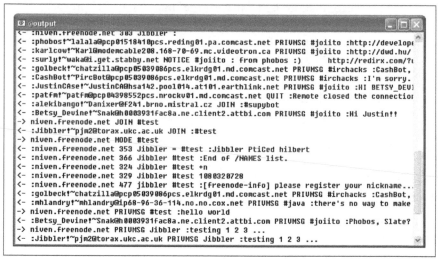

*Figure 13-1. mIRC debug window showing the raw IRC messages*

### Asynchronous by Nature

The IRC protocol is *asynchronous*, consisting of a series of events about which you are notified. All these events come through on the same connection, line by line regardless of their content; messages from one channel are interleaved with those of another channel, private messages, server notices, and more.

If you wish the server to send you a list of names on a channel, the server will happily oblige. However, the data will be sent like any other data. If you want to interpret the data and include it in, say, a user list in the IRC client you're programming (or perhaps a user list for a channel bot), you will need to set it up to expect that data. The data must be received one line at a time and be redirected to some sort of data structure that will hold it until the list is complete.

You cannot simply request the list and expect that its content will immediately follow. Some other data might come through first, or there might be a channel message in the middle of the list. On a related note, you should not wait forever for a reply—there is always the possibility that it will never come.

Furthermore, the IRC server will *not* confirm your actions. If you send a message to a channel, you can only assume that it made it to the channel. The IRC server will not send anything in reply if it did. Therefore, if you're programming some sort of IRC client, you can only assume that whatever you type is going through and display it on screen. If you ask to join a channel, you cannot assume that you have joined it until the server tells you so. This asynchronous nature makes it possible for IRC servers to force IRC clients to join a particular channel, as most IRC clients will be unaware that they haven't actually asked to join that channel.

On a related note, you should be prepared to expect the unexpected from the IRC server. Although it doesn't generally happen, by virtue of the IRC protocol, you could be sent username lists, have your nickname changed without even asking for it, have words put into your mouth, be summoned into random channels, and so on.

As a general rule, you should always listen to the IRC server and accept what it tells you. For example, some servers can be set up to make you automatically join a channel when you connect, and your IRC client must accept this, even if it knows it has never asked to join that channel. Strange events like this rarely happen but become more common when you try to share the same IRC connection among several IRC clients at the same time. JBouncer (*http://www.jibble.org/jbouncer*) is an IRC proxy that lets you resume proxy sessions—even if other clients are already using them—resulting in multiple replies when you /VERSION the proxy user (see "Understanding CTCP Messages" **[Hack #85]**).

## The Protocol

The IRC protocol is defined in RFC 1459 and updated in RFC 2812. These are both good references and explain the protocol in augmented BNF format. If you don't know what that means, you'll be glad to know a few examples of each message type follow.

**Message.** Messages have the following format:

```
prefix command command-parameters\r\n
```

The line must end with an ASCII carriage return and linefeed (\r\n). The line is not allowed to be more than 512 characters long, including the CR+LF at the end.

The *prefix* is optional and is generally used only in incoming messages. If there is a prefix, the message will start with a colon character (:). It will contain either the name of an IRC server, an IRC nickname, or an IRC nickname and host mask (nick!ident@host). This identifies the source of the message; if there is no prefix, you should assume the message came from your client.

The *command* is either one of the IRC text-based commands or, in some incoming messages, a three-digit response code.

The *command-parameters* are also optional. In many commands, the parameters will consist of a destination and a message. The message is prefixed with a : to separate it from the rest of the command parameters.

**PRIVMSG.** The most common command sent to an IRC server is PRIVMSG. Although it might seem that this command would be limited to private conversations between users, it is in fact used to send messages to channels as well. Its format is:

```
prefix PRIVMSG destination :message-contents
```

For example, a message sent to a channel could end up looking like this when it is received:

```
:Tracey`^!me@68.178.52.73 PRIVMSG #game1 :She's dead. Keep laughing.
```

A message sent to another user would look like this when he receives it:

```
:AlcarGM!alcar@g42-70-262-54.ok.comcast.net PRIVMSG Brisby :And no, Tracey
    doesn't know Oscar.
```

Of course, when you send a message, you can make things a bit simpler by not having to specify your own host mask. So to send a message to a channel, your client would simply have to send:

```
PRIVMSG #game1 :(( Keep laughing?!? YOU INSENSITIVE CLOD!!! ))
```

Likewise, to send a message to another user (in this case, Gandalf[bot]), you could just do this:

```
PRIVMSG Gandalf[bot] :Note to Fennec: Where have you been?!?!?!
```

You can also send private messages by specifying the fully qualified host mask for the user, for example:

```
PRIVMSG JacobRiis!~fennec@fennec.computer.wfu.edu :I know where you sleep!!!
```

Note also that there is no IRC command for an *action*. These commands are handled by the CTCP command ACTION, and are transported via PRIVMSG commands, as shown in "Understanding CTCP Messages" **[Hack #85]**.

**NOTICE.** A NOTICE is much like a PRIVMSG, but RFC 2812 absolutely forbids that any automated reply be sent to a NOTICE. This restriction is designed to prevent infinite loops between automatic systems such as IRC bots. The syntax is the same as for PRIVMSG. The NOTICE command is not used very often, although you may see it coming from IRC service commands such as Nick-Serv [Hack #8] and ChanServ [Hack #9].

People may be upset if you send many NOTICE messages to a channel because, depending on the nature of the IRC client, NOTICE messages are seldom displayed or interpreted as nicely as normal PRIVMSG commands.

**PING/PONG.** Every so often, the server may check to see if you're still connected. It does this by sending a PING message. This message should be immediately replied to with a PONG command with the same parameters. Failure to do so could result in a *ping timeout*, which will result in the server disconnecting you.

Example:

```
PING 1079550066
```

Reply:

```
PONG 1079550066
```

*—Thomas Whaples*

## Text Over Multiple Lines

**#79** If you send a message that is too long, the end of it could get chopped off, leaving the recipient wondering in anticipation what you meant to say. Why is this a problem and how can you solve it?

The IRC RFC states that all lines sent to and from the server cannot be longer than 512 bytes, including the trailing carriage return and linefeed pair (\r\n). In practice, this means that the maximum length of any message will be approximately 460 bytes, as there will also be bytes used at the start of the line to say who the sender is and to whom the message is being sent.

If your nickname is Jibbler, you can send yourself the message "message" by typing this:

```
/msg Jibbler message
```

The message will then be sent to the IRC server before being returned to your IRC client. Your IRC client will end up sending something like this to the server:

```
PRIVMSG Jibbler :message\r\n
```

Including the two trailing \r\n characters, this line takes up 26 characters when you send it to the server. The simple 7-byte message has grown quite a bit already, but when this line arrives back from the server, you will see that it now looks even longer:

```
:Jibbler!~pjm2@torax.ukc.ac.uk PRIVMSG Jibbler :message\r\n
```

The line has now grown by 31 characters, to a size of 57 bytes. The extra characters appended to the beginning of the line say who the message is from. So in this case, you end up with a 50-byte overhead to any message that you send to yourself. This overhead will be even larger if you have a longer nickname, username, or hostname.

Also remember to take into account the length of channel names. Some servers allow ridiculously long channel names, and the length of your lines will reflect this when the channel inhabitants receive your messages, for example:

```
:Jibbler!~pjm2@torax.ukc.ac.uk PRIVMSG #arediculouslylongchannelname :
message\r\n
```

## Avoiding the Problem

There are many IRC clients out there, and each one has its own way of dealing with large messages. Some truncate the message and lose the end of it, while some will try to split it up and send it over multiple lines. If you are implementing your own client or bot, there is a simple way of spreading text over multiple lines while making each line as long as possible.

The first step is to send yourself a private message so you can see how long your message prefix will be. If you send the message "FLOODCHECK" to yourself, you will be expecting to see something like this back from the server:

```
:Jibbler!~pjm2@torax.ukc.ac.uk PRIVMSG Jibbler :FLOODCHECK\r\n
```

You could program your client or bot so that it doesn't display private messages from yourself. Take note of the length of the first part, as when you send a message to another user or channel, the only difference will be the target of the message. For example, when you send a message to #irchacks, the users in the channel will receive this line:

```
:Jibbler!~pjm2@torax.ukc.ac.uk PRIVMSG #irchacks :Hi guys\r\n
```

You can split this message up into four parts, as shown in Table 13-1.

*Table 13-1. The four components of a message*

| Component | Example |
|-----------|---------|
| Prefix | :Jibbler!~pjm2@torax.ukc.ac.uk |
| Type | PRIVMSG |
| Target | #irchacks |
| Message | Hi guys |

When you send messages to other users or channels, you can assume that the length of the prefix will remain constant. If you are sending channel or private messages, you can also assume that the length of the type will remain the same. So the only parts that can change in length are the target and message.

You can now work out how long your received lines will be before you even send them. In the previous example, the prefix will take up 30 bytes and the type will take up 7 bytes. Add to this the three spaces that separate the parts of the line, the colon at the start of the message, and the trailing \r\n, and you end up with a minimum line length of 43 bytes.

You can now include the variable aspects of the line. If the target for your message is #irchacks, you can add another 9 bytes to accommodate that. Finally, you add on the length of your message. The message "Hi guys" increases the total line length by another 7 bytes, taking it to a total of 59.

Because this length of 59 is less than the maximum length of 512, you can tell straightaway that it is safe to send this message without its being truncated by the server. In fact, based on our previous reasoning, the longest message Jibbler can send to #irchacks is exactly 460 bytes (512-52).

If your message is greater than 460 bytes in length, you can chop it up and send it as separate messages, each being no longer than 460 bytes of course. Don't forget that longer nicknames, usernames, hostnames, and channel names will reduce this maximum message length.

Taking everything into account, it's pretty much safe to assume that messages less than 400 bytes in length can be sent without being truncated. The performance gains to be had by squeezing in a few more bytes per message is insignificant, so it's not really worth losing too much sleep about. If you do find yourself sending several huge lines of text in a row, then you should be asking yourself if IRC is really the most suitable medium for the output.

# Fake an Ident Response

**#80**    Fake a simple Identification Protocol server to convince IRC servers who you
are.

In the Unix world, it is generally taken for granted that it is possible to determine the ownership of a TCP connection by querying the *Ident* server. A process called *identd* runs in the background and accepts queries from remote machines. The Ident server then responds with information that identifies the user of that connection.

Most IRC servers attempt to use the Identification Protocol to establish the identity of each user that connects to it. When you connect to the IRC server, it will establish a separate connection to the Ident server on the machine you are connecting from. The IRC server will then ask to whom the connection belongs. If all goes well, the Ident server will respond correctly, the IRC server will be happy, and you'll be allowed to chat away.

One curious thing about the Ident Protocol is that nearly all IRC servers make use of it, yet a huge number of users do not run a permanent Ident server. In particular, users of Microsoft Windows will find that their operating system does not run an Ident server unless they have specifically downloaded and installed one. For this reason, most IRC clients come with their own implementation of an Ident server built in. When you instruct your client to connect to an IRC server, it can turn on the temporary Ident server to accept the Ident query. Once this has been done, there is no need to leave the Ident server running, so it can be closed.

The Identification Protocol runs on TCP port 113. On Unix-based systems, "normal" users will not have permission to run processes that create server sockets on this low port number. As the *identd* process is normally already running as root on most Unix systems, this is not so much of a problem. On other operating systems where an Ident server is not already running, such as Windows, there are often no restrictions on creating such processes. If you *do* have permission to create a server socket that accepts connections on port 113, it is worth remembering that there can only be one process at a time that does this.

The Identification Protocol is fairly simple, and you need to know only a little bit about it to fool an IRC server. However, if you want to know more, the protocol is defined in RFC 1413. The full contents of this RFC document can be found at *http://www.faqs.org/rfcs/rfc1413.html*.

When a client (or in our case, an IRC server) wants to query our Ident server, it will do so by connecting to it and sending a line of text. For the purpose of hacking together a quick program to satisfy an IRC server, you do not even need to know what this line of text is—all you have to do is make sure it's used as part of your response. The expected response must start with this line and end with your desired login. Here is an example of an Ident request from an IRC server:

```
3408, 6667
```

The request is simply asking who is connecting to port 6667 from port 3408 on the local machine. If you want to tell the IRC server that your login is "paul," you simply respond with:

```
3408, 6667 : USERID : UNIX : paul
```

You can now close the connection and shut down the Ident server. Note that each line sent via the Identification Protocol must be terminated with a trailing return and new line (i.e., \r\n).

## The Code

Save the following in a file called *IdentServer.java*:

```java
import java.net.*;
import java.io.*;

public class IdentServer {

    public static void ident(String login) throws IOException {

        // Wait for a connection on port 113.
        ServerSocket ss = new ServerSocket(113);
        Socket socket = ss.accept();

        BufferedReader reader = new BufferedReader(
                new InputStreamReader(socket.getInputStream()));
        BufferedWriter writer = new BufferedWriter(
                new OutputStreamWriter(socket.getOutputStream()));

        // Read the line from the connecting client.
        String line = reader.readLine();
        if (line != null) {
            System.out.println(line);

            // Create our line of reply and send it back.
            line = line + " : USERID : UNIX : " + login;
            System.out.println(line);
            writer.write(line + "\r\n");
            writer.flush();
        }

        // Close the connection and let the program end.
        writer.close();
        ss.close();
```

```
        }

        public static void main(String[] args) {
            try {
                // Tell the ident server to respond with the login "paul".
                ident("paul");
            }
            catch (IOException e) {
                // If anything goes wrong, print it to the standard output.
                e.printStackTrace( );
            }
        }

    }
```

## Running the Hack

Compile the program with the `javac` command:

    % **javac IdentServer.java**

After compiling the program, run it with the `java` command:

    % **java IdentServer**

This hack is standalone and can be run as a temporary one-shot Ident server.
While the IdentServer is running, you can connect to an IRC server and let it
respond to the Ident request. After the response has been sent, the program
will end.

As you can see from this hack, implementing a simple Ident server is not
particularly difficult. This standalone program could be modified and used
within your own Java applications, including IRC clients or bots.

> PircBot comes with its own built-in Ident server. This is dis-
> abled by default, but can be started with the
> startIdentServer( ) method. You should start the Ident
> server before trying to connect to an IRC server. The Ident
> server will respond with the login of the bot and then shut
> down. It will also shut down if it has not been used within
> 60 seconds of starting.

## Firewalls and Ident

Take care when using Ident from behind a firewall or Network Address
Translation (NAT). If the IRC server you are connecting to is unable to see
your Ident server, there is no point running it in the first place. Remote
machines must be able to connect to port 113 of your machine to use your
Ident server. To allow this to happen through a firewall, you may need to
explicitly open this port or allow it to be forwarded from another machine.

# Strip Formatting from Messages

Parsing the content of a message is difficult if it contains strange formatting characters. Make it easier for IRC bots to parse these messages by removing those characters.

When you are writing a bot that needs to parse the input from other users, it is all too easy to write code that can break when users apply formatting to their messages. In some cases, this formatting is automatically added by a user's IRC client—possibly without the user being aware of it.

## TimeBot Scenario

Let's take a look at a simple scenario. Charlotte writes a simple Perl bot called TimeBot. Charlotte programs the bot to say what the time is whenever somebody says "time." This soon starts to annoy the users in the channel, because they sometimes find themselves saying "time" in response to messages from other users. Although each utterance of "time" is not necessarily a request to know what the time is, TimeBot nonetheless assumes the user is asking for the time and responds.

Charlotte decides to fix this problem by requiring the bot to be addressed directly. All this means is that the line must start with the bot's name. This prevents people accidentally interacting with TimeBot.

There are many different styles of direct addressing:

```
<Charlotte> TimeBot time
<Charlotte> TimeBot, time
<Charlotte> TimeBot: time
<Charlotte> timebot time?
   ...etc.
```

TimeBot should respond to all of the preceding styles of addressing, along with all permutations. Charlotte whips up a simple Perl regular expression to deal with these new styles:

```
$input = ...
if ($input =~ /^timebot[:,]?\s+time\??$/i) {
    tell_time();
}
```

Charlotte tests this new regular expression in her bot and finds that it works. A few minutes later, she notices that several users are being ignored by the bot. A little investigation reveals that these users are running IRC clients that automatically add formatting characters to the end of autocompleted nicknames. Some IRC clients, and even some add-on scripts, are designed to do this sort of thing on purpose—presumably to try to make the message stand out better.

```
<Charlotte> TimeBot: time
<TimeBot> The time is 13:40
<Paul> TimeBot: time
<Paul> hello?
```

In Charlotte's case, she was observing the "bold colon" effect. The IRC client was adding a colon character to the end of the autocompleted nickname. This should not pose a problem, as the regular expression can cope with this. However, the colon was prefixed with a bold control character and followed by a "normal" control character to remove the boldness from the rest of the message. These extra characters are not accounted for in the regular expression, so the test in the if statement will never return true.

As a temporary measure, Charlotte fixes the problem by adding the extra characters to the regular expression:

```
$input = ...
if ($input =~ /^timebot(\x02:\x0f|[:,])?\s+time\??$/i) {
    tell_time();
}
```

This is clearly not the best way to fix the problem. What might happen if you encounter another type of IRC client that applies formatting somewhere else—for instance, making the entire nickname bold? The best solution is to remove all formatting and then parse the message as before.

## Removing All Formatting

Removing formatting characters is remarkably easy if your programming language is suited to the task. Each style of formatting requires only one control character, so you can simply hunt them down and remove them from the message. The message will then contain exactly the same text as before, but without any formatting, so it can be easily parsed for commands.

**Perl solution.** A simple regular expression replacement is all that is needed to remove the control characters used for formatting. You can then go ahead and use the string as normal without having to worry about taking special account of any formatting.

This single line of Perl will remove all formatting characters from a string:

```
$input =~ s/[\x02\x1f\x16\x0f]//g;
```

**Python solution.** Importing the regular expression module allows you to do a similar replacement in Python:

```
import re
re.compile("[\x02\x1f\x16\x0f]").sub("", input)
```

**Java solution.** In Java 1.4 and later, the static method replaceAll in the String class can be used to do the same thing. This method accepts two String arguments: a regular expression to match and the replacement:

```
input = input.replaceAll("[\u0002\u001f\u0016\u000f]", "");
```

**Java Applet solution.** Removing formatting characters in a Java Applet [Hack #90] is a little trickier. The String class allows us to use the same approach as the Perl solution, but there are problems using this from Applets. The replaceAll method makes use of the java.util.regex package, and neither of these exists in any version of Java prior to 1.4. The obvious problem here is that Java Applets run in web browsers that commonly have only a 1.1-compatible Virtual Machine installed. If you want to remove formatting characters from within a Java Applet, you would therefore be wise to make use only of classes present in the 1.1 releases.

Here is an efficient method that removes all formatting characters within a Java Applet:

```
public static String removeFormatting(String message) {
    int length = message.length();
    StringBuffer buffer = new StringBuffer();
    for (int i = 0; i < length; i++) {
        char ch = message.charAt(i);
        if (ch == '\u000f' || ch == '\u0002' || ch == '\u001f' || ch == '\
u0016') {
            // Don't add this character.
        }
        else {
            buffer.append(ch);
        }
    }
    return buffer.toString();
}
```

There is a removeFormatting method present in the Colors class of PircBot. Both formatting and colors can be removed with the removeFormattingAndColors method. Both of these methods are compatible with Java 1.1.

# Remove Color from Messages

**Parsing messages is difficult when they contain color characters. Make messages easier to store and parse by removing these characters.**

Whether you are trying to parse messages on the fly or store them in a different format, you will notice that people who use colored messages throw a monkey wrench in the works. Adding color to messages means adding lots of spurious control characters. These have to be removed for the message to make sense to anything that isn't an IRC client.

If you take a raw message from an IRC channel and paste it directly onto a web page, it will appear quite different from the colored version in your IRC client. You will see no color at all. Instead, you will see the message with some extra characters sprinkled along it.

One particular situation in which it is useful to remove colors is when you are running an artificial intelligence bot, which learns by reading what other users send to the channel. Removing the special color characters is essential here; otherwise, the bot will get confused and end up speaking multicolored gibberish.

## Simple Color Removal

Let's create some code to remove simple colors. Simple colors are marked by the control character 0x03 and are followed by one or two digits. The number after the control character should be between 0 and 15 inclusive, but may contain an optional leading zero to bulk it up to two digits. Most IRC clients treat any value (00–99) as a valid color, although only 0–15 are clearly defined.

An optional background color may be specified by appending a comma to the foreground color code. This is followed by another one- or two-digit code to specify the background color. You must also take this into account when you remove color codes from a message.

**Perl solution.**  Using regular expressions, this is a trivial one-liner. The following line removes simple coloring from the input:

```
$input =~ s/ \x03[0-9]{1,2}(,[0-9]{1,2})?//g;
```

**Python solution.**  The Python regular expression module lets you apply the same replacement to a Python variable:

```
import re
re.compile(" \x03[0-9]{1,2}(,[0-9]{1,2})?").sub("", input)
```

**Java solution.**  Again, with regular expressions available in Java 1.4 and beyond, this is easy. To remove simple coloring from the input, just do this:

```
input = input.replaceAll(" \u0003[0-9]{1,2}(,[0-9]{1,2})?", "");
```

**Java Applet solution.**  All good Applets should run in Java 1.1, as there is rarely any guarantee that an end user will have anything more recent. Most browsers are supplied with a 1.1-compatible Virtual Machine without the user having to apply any updates.

Being restricted to Java 1.1 makes the process of color removal much more verbose. Although there are more lines of code, it is no less efficient than using regular expressions—if they were available!

This method can be used to remove simple coloring from within a Java Applet:

```java
// A rather long but efficient way of removing colors in Java 1.1.
public static String removeColors(String message) {
    int length = message.length( );
    StringBuffer buffer = new StringBuffer( );
    int i = 0;
    while (i < length) {
        char ch = message.charAt(i);
        if (ch == '\u0003') {
            i++;
            // Skip "x" or "xy" (foreground color).
            if (i < length) {
                ch = message.charAt(i);
                if (Character.isDigit(ch)) {
                    i++;
                    if (i < length) {
                        ch = message.charAt(i);
                        if (Character.isDigit(ch)) {
                            i++;
                        }
                    }
                }
                // Now skip ",x" or ",xy" (background color).
                if (i < length) {
                    ch = message.charAt(i);
                    if (ch == ',') {
                        i++;
                        if (i < length) {
                            ch = message.charAt(i);
                            if (Character.isDigit(ch)) {
                                i++;
                                if (i < length) {
                                    ch = message.charAt(i);
                                    if (Character.isDigit(ch)) {
                                        i++;
                                    }
                                }
                            }
                            else {
                                // Keep the comma.
                                i--;
                            }
                        }
                    }
                    else {
                        // Keep the comma.
                        i--;
                    }
                }
```

```
                    }
                }
            }
        }
    }
    else if (ch == '\u000f') {
        i++;
    }
    else {
        buffer.append(ch);
        i++;
    }
}
return buffer.toString( );
}
```

The PircBot API contains a removeColors method in the Colors class.

## Hacking the Hack

If you have created an IRC bot that writes channel logs to a web page, why not try to retain the information contained in the coloring? One adventurous task would be to modify the methods here to create colored HTML from a message instead of simply removing all color. This is a much harder task than it first seems, so make sure you think about it before you start implementing anything.

## HACK #83   Encrypt Messages

Privacy is very important to some people. The only way to ensure that other people cannot read your messages is to encrypt them.

When you send private messages to another IRC user, those messages are vulnerable to snooping. The messages are being sent as plain text and can therefore be sniffed while they travel from your client to the IRC server and finally to the recipient. Don't forget that the IRC server can obviously see what your messages are—so be careful what you say on untrustworthy IRC servers.

Using DCC chat [Hack #69] solves the server trust problem. DCC chat establishes a connection straight to the recipient and messages are sent along this connection. This is obviously still vulnerable, as plain text messages can still be sniffed on the Internet.

The Internet sniffing issue can be solved by using SSL (Secure Sockets Layer) to connect to the IRC server. While this will prevent your housemates sniffing your messages, it won't prevent the IRC server from seeing what your messages are, as they are decrypted when they arrive. Nor will it prevent your messages being sniffed if the recipient is not using a secure connection. You may also want to take into account the fact that traffic between IRC servers on the same network may not be encrypted.

## Key Encryption

The only way to ensure that your messages cannot be intercepted is to ensure that they are encrypted as soon as they leave your IRC client. Rather than using private and public key cryptography techniques, the simplest way is to use a shared pass phrase or *key*. This means that anyone who knows the key can decrypt the messages. You will obviously need to tell the recipient what the key is, but for obvious reasons, you shouldn't tell them over IRC!

This hack will show you how to use Java to make two simple bots that can send and receive encrypted messages to and from each other. The bots will use a Cipher object to encode and decode arrays of bytes. Both bots must be supplied with the same key, otherwise one won't be able to tell what the other is saying.

## The Code

Create a file called *CryptBot.java* with the following imports and fields:

```
import org.jibble.pircbot.*;
import java.security.*;
import javax.crypto.*;
import javax.crypto.spec.*;

public class CryptBot extends PircBot {

    private Cipher cipher;
    private SecretKey key;
    private IvParameterSpec p;
```

Now define the constructor for CryptBot. If you want to use two of these bots on the same server, they will have to have different nicknames, so the first argument to the constructor will be for the bot's name. Each bot will need to be told what the pass phrase or key is, so the second argument key-String is used to take this. The first 24 bytes of the keyString will be used to make a DES-EDE ("triple-DES") key, so it is padded with zero bytes if it is too short.

The constructor will also initialize the instance fields used to encrypt and decrypt messages. Append this to the CryptBot class:

```
    public CryptBot(String name, String keyString) throws
GeneralSecurityException {
```

```
            setName(name);

            byte[] keyBytes = new byte[24];
            int length = Math.min(keyBytes.length, keyString.length());
            System.arraycopy(keyString.getBytes(), 0, keyBytes, 0, length);

            DESedeKeySpec spec = new DESedeKeySpec(keyBytes);
            SecretKeyFactory keyFactory =
            SecretKeyFactory.getInstance("DESede");
            key = keyFactory.generateSecret(spec);
            cipher = Cipher.getInstance("DESede/CBC/PKCS5Padding");
            p = new IvParameterSpec(keyBytes);
        }
```

Now to make a simple method to encrypt or decrypt an array of bytes. The parameter encrypt is set to true if the array is to be encrypted; otherwise, it will try to decrypt the array. The resulting array is returned by the method. If the message could not be decrypted, the original array is returned. Append the following method to the CryptBot class:

```
        public byte[] crypt(byte[] input, boolean encrypt) {

            byte[] output = input;
            try {
                cipher.init(encrypt ? Cipher.ENCRYPT_MODE:Cipher.DECRYPT_MODE,
        key, p);
                output = cipher.doFinal(input);
            }
            catch (GeneralSecurityException e) {
                // Unable to encrypt or decrypt. Leave the input as it was.
            }
            return output;
        }
```

The sendEncryptedMessage method will allow us to send an encrypted message from the bot. The key will be used to encrypt the message, allowing it to be read by anyone else who holds a copy of the key. The first parameter is used to specify the target, which can be a nickname or a channel. The second parameter specifies the message, which gets encrypted, and the resulting bytes are sent encoded as hexadecimal digits. Append this method to the CryptBot class:

```
        public void sendEncryptedMessage(String target, String message) {
            byte[] plainText = message.getBytes();
            byte[] encrypted = crypt(plainText, true);

            StringBuffer buffer = new StringBuffer();
            for (int i = 0; i < encrypted.length; i++) {
                String hex = Integer.toString(
                        (encrypted[i] & 0xff) + 0x100, 16).substring(1);
                buffer.append(hex);
            }
```

```
            System.out.println("Sending encrypted message: " + new
    String(encrypted));

            sendMessage(target, buffer.toString( ));
        }
```

Now you can add one final method to allow each bot to receive private messages. This method overrides the onPrivateMessage method in the PircBot abstract class. When private messages are received, the bot will try to decrypt them and print out the decrypted message. Append this method to the CryptBot class:

```
        public void onPrivateMessage(String sender, String login,
                String hostname, String message) {

            try {
                byte[] encrypted = new byte[message.length( ) / 2];
                for (int i = 0; i < message.length( ); i += 2) {
                    String hex = message.substring(i, i + 2);
                    encrypted[i / 2] = (byte) Integer.parseInt(hex, 16);
                }

                byte[] plainText = crypt(encrypted, false);
                message = new String(plainText);

                System.out.println("Plain text from " + sender + ": " +
    message);
            }
            catch (Exception e) {
                // Message was not in a suitable format.
            }

        }

    }
```

Piecing together all of the preceding code, you end up with the complete CryptBot class. All you need to do now is write a main method to instantiate a couple of them and tell them to talk to each other.

Save this in a file called *CryptBotMain.java*:

```
    public class CryptBotMain {

        public static void main(String[] args) throws Exception {

            String keyString = "my top secret key";

            CryptBot bot1 = new CryptBot("CryptBot1", keyString);
            CryptBot bot2 = new CryptBot("CryptBot2", keyString);

            bot1.connect("irc.freenode.net");
```

```
        bot2.connect("irc.freenode.net");

        bot1.sendEncryptedMessage("CryptBot2", "Hello");
        bot1.sendEncryptedMessage("CryptBot2", "freenode rocks");
        bot1.sendEncryptedMessage("CryptBot2", "This is a secret message!");

    }

}
```

Note that both bots are constructed with different nicknames so they can join the same server. Both bots are given the same keyString, so they will be able to decrypt messages from each other.

### Running the Hack

Compile the hack with:

```
C:\java\CryptBot> javac -classpath .;pircbot.jar *.java
```

Run the hack with:

```
C:\java\CryptBot> java -classpath .;pircbot.jar CryptBotMain
```

### The Results

After the bots have connected to the IRC server, the main method tells the first bot to send some private messages to the second bot. If all goes well, you should see the second bot correctly decrypting the messages from the first bot:

```
Sending encrypted message: Hello
Sending encrypted message: freenode rocks
Sending encrypted message: This is a secret message!
Encrypted text from CryptBot1: 48656c6c6f
Plain text received from CryptBot1: Hello
Encrypted text from CryptBot1: 667265656e6f6465520726f636b73
Plain text received from CryptBot1: freenode rocks
Encrypted text from CryptBot1:
546869732069732061207365637265574206d65737361676521
Plain text received from CryptBot1: This is a secret message!
```

Now you can feel safe in the knowledge that nobody can read your messages as you send them through unfamiliar servers.

### Timestamp with the TS Protocol

### #84

Master the TS Protocol to prevent people from exploiting the situation when servers relink after a netsplit has broken the IRC network into separate parts.

Any large global network experiences occasional problems. In the case of IRC, they're seen on a regular basis. All it requires is a route flap out of MCI in New York, a fiber-optic cable cut from SBC in Chicago, or an ATT core router crash in London, and you've got problems getting packets from one server to another.

When a server can't talk to another, they sever their connection and create a *netsplit*. Sometimes a netsplit can affect a single server that splits from its hub, but sometimes a netsplit is between two hubs, leaving two large chunks of the IRC network disconnected.

In either case, life goes on regardless of which side of that split you're on. People keep chatting; mode changes keep happening; nick changes keep occurring. The real problem comes when the network comes back together and anything that's changed on the other side of the split has to be reconciled and the data resynced.

The Timestamp, or TS, Protocol was first written and released by Carlo "Run" Wood on June 28, 1993, and was first implemented on Undernet on July 1, 1993. Its purpose was to ease that reconciliation process and reduce the possibility of someone taking over channels and nicks through netsplit hacks and nick collisions.

## Before TS

Anarchy ruled in the days before TS. You could have whatever channel or nick you wanted, with the exercise of resources and ingenuity. Simply wait for a netsplit (or create your own by splitting a server), change to the nick you wanted, or re-create the channel you wanted ops in on your side of the split, and be ready to get your nick or perform a mass de-op when the servers rejoined.

Here's an example of a nick collision attack:

```
<MeanGuy> I'm going to take your nick!
<BBS> No, it's mine.
<Otherguy> That's not nice.
<MeanGjupe> This is my clone, it will help.
```

Then sometime later, a netsplit occurs:

```
*** BBS has left IRC (irc.choopa.net remote.server.com)
*** Otherguy has left IRC (irc.choopa.net remote.server.com)
* MeanGjupe is now known as BBS
<MeanGuy> Haha, now my evil minion, you will sacrifice yourself in the
reconnect!
*** BBS has left IRC (Killed (Nick Collision))
* Otherguy (og!some.where.com) has joined #windows
* MeanGuy is now known as BBS
<BBS> Haha! I am victorious!
<Otherguy> You really are mean :(
* RealBBS (BBS!bbs.choopa.net) has joined #windows
```

```
* MeanGjupe (mean!evil.minion.org) has joined #windows
<RealBBS> Hey! I got killed by remote.server.com for nick collision!
<BBS> You did well my evil jupe bot, this nick is now mine!
```

Note that the nick collision of BBS happened on both sides of the network, so the first person to grab the nick after the KILL was issued gets the nick and can keep it.

Now, on to an example of a channel takeover:

```
<MeanGuy> You may have gotten your nick back, but now I will take the
channel!
<BBS> This again, don't you quit?
<MeanGdeop> This is my mass de-op bot, it will help me rule the world!
```

Then sometime later, the inevitable netsplit occurs:

```
*** BBS has left IRC (irc.choopa.net remote.server.com)
*** Otherguy has left IRC (irc.choopa.net remote.server.com)
<MeanGuy> Go my minion, it's time to cycle the channel!
* MeanGdeop (mean!evil.minion.org) has left #windows
* MeanGuy (mean!doctor.evil.edu) has left #windows
* MeanGuy (mean!doctor.evil.edu) has joined #windows
* irc.choopa.net sets mode: +nt
* irc.choopa.net sets mode: +o MeanGuy
* MeanGdeop (mean!evil.minion.org) has joined #windows
* MeanGuy sets mode: +o MeanGdeop
<MeanGuy> Now we have ops on this side of the split. Prepare for mass de-op!
<MeanGdeop> Yes, my evil master.
* Otherguy (og!some.where.com) has joined #windows
* BBS (BBS!bbs.choopa.net) has joined #windows
* irc.choopa.net sets mode: +oo BBS Otherguy
* MeanGdeop sets mode: -oo Otherguy BBS
<MeanGuy> Mwahaha! The channel is now mine!
<BBS> My lord, you're mean! :(
```

With an automated client set to de-op everyone except its master, taking the channel was child's play.

## TS Saves the Day

Two ideas were thought up for combating nick and channel wars. These were Delay and TS.

Delay required the individual servers to keep track of what channels and nicks were in use during a split and set a delay before someone could re-create the channel or use the nick. In the end, the idea was turned down for many reasons, not the least of which was that a small leaf server that normally handled 500 clients could, all of a sudden, be required to track 15,000 nicks on a large network. Frankly, it was a resource hog.

The second idea, which was widely adopted, is TS, or timestamping. Every time a nick or channel is created, it's assigned a timestamp correlating to the time of creation. If you started a channel on July 23, 1998, the channel was never closed, and at least one server was always around to keep it alive, it would retain that timestamp forever.

Upon a server splitting, instead of a server having to keep track of every nick and channel on the network, the server has to manage only the timestamps on the local server. When the servers relink and reconciliation is performed, the TS of the local nick/channel is compared to the TS of the remote nick/channel, and whichever has the older TS takes precedence.

Now, let's replay the preceding nick collision after the implementation of TS:

```
<MeanGuy> I'm going to take your nick!
<BBS> No, it's mine.
<Otherguy> That's not nice.
<MeanGjupe> This is my clone, it will help.
*** BBS has left IRC (irc.choopa.net remote.server.com)
*** Otherguy has left IRC (irc.choopa.net remote.server.com)
* MeanGjupe is now known as BBS
<MeanGuy> Haha, now my evil minion, you will sacrifice yourself in the
reconnect!
*** BBS has left IRC (Killed (new))
* BBS (BBS!bbs.choopa.net) has joined #windows
* Otherguy (og!some.where.com) has joined #windows
<MeanGuy> No! My minion has been killed and I have been defeated!
<BBS> Stealing isn't the way to win MeanGuy, get your own three-letter nick!
<Otherguy> Yay! The side of good wins!
<MeanGuy> I would have succeeded if it wasn't for that meddling TS!
* MeanGuy (mean!doctor.evil.edu) has left #windows
```

With TS, only the newer version of BBS was killed. The original gets to keep her nick and keep on chatting without having to reconnect.

Now, let's take a look at that channel takeover:

```
<MeanGuy> I may have failed at getting your nick, so instead I'll take your
    entire channel!
<BBS> This again, don't you quit?
<MeanGdeop> This is my mass de-op bot, it will help me rule the world!
*** BBS has left IRC (irc.choopa.net remote.server.com)
*** Otherguy has left IRC (irc.choopa.net remote.server.com)
<MeanGuy> Go my minion, it's time to cycle the channel!
* MeanGdeop (mean!evil.minion.org) has left #windows
* MeanGuy (mean!doctor.evil.edu) has left #windows
* MeanGuy (mean!doctor.evil.edu) has joined #windows
* irc.choopa.net sets mode: +nt
* irc.choopa.net sets mode: +o MeanGuy
* MeanGdeop (mean!evil.minion.org) has joined #windows
* MeanGuy sets mode: +o MeanGdeop
```

```
<MeanGuy> Now we have ops on this side of the split. Prepare for mass de-op!
<MeanGdeop> Yes, my evil master.
* irc.choopa.net sets mode: -oo MeanGuy MeanGdeop
-irc.choopa.net:#windows- *** Notice -- TS for #windows changed from
     1078875452 to 1078875451
* Otherguy (og!some.where.com) has joined #windows
* BBS (BBS!bbs.choopa.net) has joined #windows
* irc.choopa.net sets mode: +oo Otherguy BBS
<MeanGuy> Foiled again! I hate you TS!
<BBS> The good guys win again.
<OtherGuy> Yeah, go start your own channel, evildoer!
<MeanGuy> You may have won this time, but I'll be back!
<MeanGuy> Come, my evil minion!
* MeanGuy (mean!doctor.evil.edu) has left #windows
* MeanGdeop (mean!evil.minion.org) has left #windows
```

This time, the channel takeover never had a chance. TS did exactly what it was supposed to do, and the channel goes on its happy existence.

## Interesting TS Facts

You can see the timestamp of a channel by issuing a /mode #*channel* command with no arguments:

```
/mode #windows
#windows +tnl 111
#windows created on Thu Jul 12 08:04:37 2001
```

TS is based on Unix timestamps, which use a decimal number to represent the number of seconds that have elapsed since midnight of January 1, 1970, GMT. IRC servers are required to use a time sync protocol like NTP. Modern *ircd*s won't even link if the time on both servers differs by more than a second.

TS was not always impossible to get around. In versions of TS up until about 2002, it was possible to join a channel at the exact moment a network rejoin was being reconciled and be given ops in the channel. Many channels were taken that way, or opless channels were restored with ops.

In at least one case on EFnet, a server was hacked and reintroduced to the network after the time on the server had been rolled back to January 1. Upon relinking to EFnet, any channel the hackers wanted was literally handed to them by the servers that saw the hacked server with the older TS. #twilight_zone, an old operator channel on EFnet still has a TS of 1 from the incident:

```
/mode #twilight_zone
#twilight_zone +stin
#twilight_zone created on Thu Jan 1 00:00:01 1970
```

A great deal of information on the technical aspects of TS can be found on Roger Espel's site at *http://www.iagora.com/~espel/ircd/Undernet-TS*. He played a major part in developing some of the later versions of TS.

If you're looking for TS for your IRC network, it's now used in every modern *ircd*. I prefer *ircd-ratbox*, which you can get at *http://www.ircd-ratbox.org*.

*—Hunter Pine*

## H A C K    #85    Understanding CTCP Messages

CTCP messages are used quite frequently on IRC. Learn what they mean so you can use them effectively.

CTCP is the Client-to-Client Protocol, which is used over IRC to send structured data. In general, a CTCP request will be sent as part of a PRIVMSG message **[Hack #78]** to a user or to a channel. This message consists of a string of text between two ASCII 0x01 characters (ASCII character 1). There are two forms of CTCP messages: tagged data and queries. Queries are also used to set up DCC connections **[Hack #69]**.

### Tagged Data

Tagged data consists of specially tagged and formatted data used to send special messages between clients. This is seldom used with modern IRC clients, with the exception of the CTCP ACTION command.

The original CTCP specification spoke of actions as being "used by losers on IRC to simulate 'role-playing' games." Actions are behind the /me  action command. The string is fairly simple and consists of the ACTION command (all uppercase) followed by the text of the action. For example:

```
\001ACTION jumps for joy!\001
\001ACTION is considering switching to Gentoo.\001
\001ACTION tries to recompile his kernel, but fails.\001
```

If the user Fennec is sending these messages, most IRC clients will render these actions similar to this:

```
* Fennec jumps for joy!
* Fennec is considering switching to Gentoo.
* Fennec tries to recompile his kernel, but fails.
```

### Queries

Several simple CTCP commands request information from someone else. When a client receives these, it should reply with a CTCP command of the same name sent to the originator via NOTICE (and not via PRIVMSG). If your client does not understand a CTCP query, it can be safely ignored.

Generally, a CTCP query is sent to an individual user. If you send a CTCP command to a channel, you can expect a response from all the clients on that channel. Doing this repeatedly is seldom appreciated or advisable. If you receive a CTCP query from a channel, however, you should reply only to the original sender.

An example command would be the following sent as a PRIVMSG:

```
\001TIME\001
```

This would be the reply, but note that it would be sent as a NOTICE:

```
\001TIME Sat Nov 12 1955 22:04:00 PST\001
```

Here are some valid CTCP queries:

CTCP VERSION
> Requests the name and version of your IRC client. Replies should be of the form CLIENT NAME:VERSION:ENVIRONMENT; however, this exact format is often ignored—for example: mIRC v6.14 Khaled Mardam-Bey.

CTCP SOURCE
> Rarely used and primarily historical, but it should return the location of the source code for the IRC client.

CTCP PING
> Used as a way to ping an individual client. Typically, the sending machine will use the PING command with some representation of the current time; the receiving machine is expected to reply with an identical PING command, so it is possible to work out how long it took to get the reply.

CTCP TIME
> Requests the time. It should be replied to with a human-readable string informing the user of the client's current local time.

CTCP USERINFO
> Should return a string set by the IRC user, presumably giving information about the user.

CTCP CLIENTINFO
> Should tell what tagged data a client is capable of handling. See RFC 1459 for more information on how this command should be used.

CTCP ERRMSG
> Used to reply to a CTCP request that produces an error. When used as a query, the reply should echo back the exact data produced by the query, followed with an indication that no error has happened.

If you are running a PircBot-based bot, you may notice that it automatically responds to some of these queries, such as VERSION, PING, and TIME. You can override the methods that are responsible for replying, although it is a good idea to call the same method in the superclass to ensure that the bot still responds appropriately, for example:

```
public void onPing(String sourceNick, String sourceLogin,
        String sourceHostname, String target, String pingValue) {

    System.out.println("I got pinged by " + sourceNick);

    // Make the PircBot super class perform its normal response to the PING.
    super.onPing(sourceNick, sourceLogin, sourceHostname, target,
pingValue);
}
```

You can override methods like this to find out which users are interested in your bot.

*—Thomas Whaples*

# CHAPTER FOURTEEN

# Other Ways to Connect to IRC
## Hacks 86–94

Way back in Chapter 1, you were shown how to connect to IRC using a variety of clients. This chapter aims to show you a multitude of alternative ways to connect to IRC, or at least make the process a bit easier.

To make it easier for other people to connect to your IRC network and join your IRC channel, you can place convenient links on your web pages. If a user has an IRC client installed, he can just click on such a link to be transported into your channel. If he doesn't have an IRC client installed, that's not a problem—Java Applets embedded in a web page, or even a pure HTTP client, can also be used to connect to IRC.

You don't have to be near a computer to use IRC. This chapter also contains hacks relevant to those who wish to access IRC from their mobile phones or Pocket PC devices.

For those of you who are concerned about missing out on the action while you're away, you can also explore the possibility of setting up an IRC proxy, which will let you access IRC from anywhere in the world without missing any messages that were sent while you were disconnected.

### HACK #86 Hypertext Links to IRC Channels

Looking for an easy way to get people to join your channel? Add IRC hyperlinks to your web pages.

One way of making your IRC channel easily accessible is to increase the number of ways people can join it. Creating an HTML hyperlink that points to your IRC channel is a convenient way of letting people know the server details and channel name.

To be able to use these links, you must have an IRC client installed that has chat link support enabled. If you have the ChatZilla IRC client installed, you can expect to be able to just click on IRC links to connect to the server and join the specified channel. In some other clients, such as mIRC, you will need to enable support for chat links, as shown in Figure 14-1.

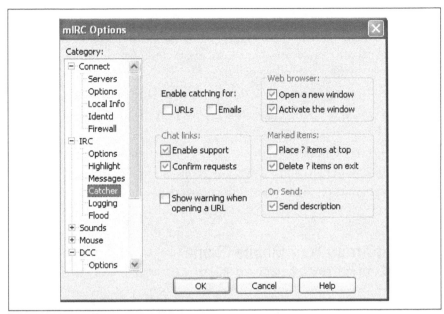

*Figure 14-1. Enabling chat links in mIRC*

## HTML IRC Links

IRC links are specified like any other hyperlink, but with `irc` as the protocol. Valid IRC links look like this:

```
<a href="irc://irc-server:port/channel?key>Click to join</a>
```

Each IRC URL can be broken up into four parts:

*irc-server*
 The IRC server to connect to.

*port*
 The port number to connect to. This is optional and must be preceded by a colon character if you use it. If you do not specify a port number, the default of 6667 will be used.

*channel*
 When your IRC client connects to the server, it will automatically join this channel. Note that you must not include the # character.

*key*
 If the channel is password protected, you can specify the key. This is also optional and must be preceded by a question mark character.

## Example Links

If you just want people to be able to connect to your IRC network in a hurry, you needn't bother specifying a channel to join:

```
<a href="irc://irc.your-irc-server.com">Connect to my IRC server</a>
```

If you have a channel on the freenode IRC network (irc.freenode.net) called #mychan and it has a key of "password", you could let web users visit your channel by providing the following link:

```
<a href="irc://irc.freenode.net/mychan?password">Join my private channel</a>
```

The most typical example you will see in use on the Web would be a link that points at a public channel, such as:

```
<a href="irc://irc.freenode.net/irchacks">IRC Hacks Channel</a>
```

Clicking on this hyperlink will launch your IRC client and join the #irchacks channel on the freenode IRC network.

*—Alex North*

### HACK #87    IRC from Your Mobile Phone

Get out from behind the desk, and IRC from your mobile phone. Everywhere you go, you can take the channels with you.

Why restrict yourself to being able to IRC only from your PC or laptop? If you've got a smart mobile phone, you can IRC from pretty much anywhere you can get a signal. Here are a few tips on how to use IRC with a Symbian- or J2ME-equipped mobile phone.

At the top of the evolutionary tree for mobile phones right now are those with the Symbian operating system. This includes the SonyEricsson P800 and P900; the Nokia 7700, 6600, 3650, and N-Gage; and a handful of more eclectic phones shipped by another four or five phone manufacturers. Symbian phones that are currently shipping can be split into two families: Series 60 (6600, 3650, N-Gage) and UIQ (P800, P900); apps written for one family of devices will usually not run on the other.

Series 60 has a number of IRC apps, my favorite being WirelessIRC (*http://mobileways.de/M/1/4/0*), which has almost all the capabilities of a desktop IRC client: private messages, multiple channels, DCC, and so forth. UIQ users also have many choices, with SymIRC being one of the more popular options (*http://sulaco.mureakuha.com/symirc*). This application also has the advantage of being licensed under the free GNU General Public License (GPL), meaning that if you've got the programming skills, you can take the existing source code and add extra features and functionality.

IRC on a Symbian phone can be a great experience; you can still use the phone as usual for voice calls, SMS, calendar lookup, address book checking, playing games, listening to the radio or MP3s, and so on. It's a multitasking networked computer, so IRC is just another application within it.

If you haven't got a Symbian phone, there's still hope if your phone can run Sun's Java applications. The bare-bones but powerful Virca (GPL-licensed) J2ME app offers good functionality (*http://www.vidarholen.net/contents/virca*).

The one fly in the Java soup is that many phones have poor compatibility with the J2ME specifications, and the sockets-based networking functions are often broken; the popular Nokia 3650 and SonyEricsson T610 are just two phones in this category. Phones like these won't run applications like Virca, but can generally run HTTP-based IRC applications like WLIrc (*http://wirelessirc.sourceforge.net*), which is also licensed under the GPL. These rely on connecting via an external HTTP gateway running elsewhere for connectivity to an IRC server.

Of course, to get one of these applications working, you need connectivity. On a GSM network, GPRS is generally the best option. With GPRS, most operators charge a traffic-based rather than time-based fee for usage, and a slow-paced hour of IRC will often use only 30–40 KB; with U.K. pricing around £2 per MB, this can be cheaper than a single SMS and certainly cheaper than an hour-long voice call. If you have an unlimited GPRS usage tariff as offered by some of the U.S. operators, mobile IRC looks even more attractive. A word of warning though—some operators charge a flat fee for any GPRS connection, and the default GPRS pricing on some networks can be very high, so make sure you understand your tariff before running up huge bills! Many of the IRC clients display a traffic counter so that you can keep track of your usage.

*—Jim Hughes*

## HACK #88   Enemies of Mobile IRC

Mobile IRC has different limitations than the normal experience. Meet eight enemies of mobile IRC, and learn how to defeat them.

I'm the first to admit there are downsides to the mobile IRC experience; some of the things that make a mobile phone so much easier to carry than a PC or laptop can also be a slight hindrance in usage. However, judicious application of Sun Tzu's dictum, "Know your enemy and know yourself and you can fight a hundred battles without disaster," should help you to IRC on the move without disaster.

## The Phone Keypad

Unless you have a device like the Treo 600 or the Nokia 6800, you are unlikely to have a full QWERTY keyboard on your phone, and even with these devices, the constrained dimensions means that full touch typing is unlikely. One or two thumbs on a phone keypad will never approach the speed of 10 fingers on a QWERTY. Accept this fact and use this knowledge to your advantage.

Slow text entry has benefits. It makes you think about what you're writing, and it can improve your writing skills; being able to convey a message concisely and coherently is a skill worth attaining in "real" life as well as on IRC. Be aware that slow entry has its hazards, avoid using words like "it" or "that" because the conversation may have moved on, and the "it" or "that" that you appear to be talking about may now be something completely different. For example, the conversation:

```
<Joe> did you see the game last night on TV?
<You> yeah, it was rubbish
```

could easily turn into the following if you're a bit too slow:

```
<Joe> did you see the game last night on TV?
<Steve> no I was hacking some code together, incidentally did you try my new
app?
<You> yeah, it was rubbish
```

Some mobile IRC apps like Virca allow you to pre-enter common phrases (it calls these favorites), which you can select and reuse time after time. This is very useful for common actions like talking to bots or for giving a quick disclaimer like, "Sorry, I can't type very quickly because I'm using IRC on a mobile phone."

## Predictive Text Entry

If your phone has predictive text entry like the T9 system, one can enter the word "horse" by pressing 4-6-7-7-3 rather than the multitap approach in which one presses 44-666-777-7777-33. This has an obvious benefit in reducing the number of keystrokes required, but predictive text entry is not without its foibles. Sometimes the word you intend to enter is not in the dictionary, or it is not the first- or even the second-choice word for a particular sequence of keystrokes. For example, the name Russ is the ninth choice for the 7-8-7-7 combination of key presses, so at 12 keystrokes—4 for the letters, plus 8 steps through the dictionary—this word is only barely quicker than using the multitap solution of 777-88-7777-7777.

Many words are not in the dictionary of your predictive text entry software. There are at least three ways around this problem. You could add the words to the dictionary so that they're remembered for future use. If you do not want to enter a word into your dictionary, you could enter it in a composite form (i.e., you could enter the words comp-o-site for composite), or you could even turn off predictive text entry for that word. Good words to add to your dictionary are common words that you use frequently; I've added unusual nicknames, technical acronyms, and swear words.

One thing that predictive text entry doesn't help with is bad spelling; if you can't spell, you're going to be hunting for words quite frequently, so think about your spelling.

Numeric entry is simple once you know the tricks. You can either switch from text entry to numeric, or you can usually hold down the intended digit key for about half a second and the numeral will appear instead of a letter. One big benefit of predictive text entry is that "l33t sp34k" is even more tedious to enter than it is read, so even if you are a 14-year-old script kiddy, predictive text entry will at least make you appear more like an intelligent human being on IRC.

## Small Screen Size

Get used to it—no one is going to produce a megapixel resolution phone display in the near future, so this isn't a battle you're going to win, but you can mitigate the damage. On a 128x128-sized display, things can start scrolling past very swiftly. If this happens, you're going to have to stick to lurking for a while until the conversation calms down. If a channel gets too fast for you to follow consistently, it's probably worth leaving it. Keep your channel count low, to keep your stress levels down.

## Street Traffic and Street Furniture

Maybe this should be enemy number 1 if you're the sort of person who tries to walk and IRC. It certainly requires a skill level far above simultaneous walking and gum chewing. Be careful out there. If a conversation gets fast moving, heated, or involved, slow down or even stop walking. Let's face it, IRC has rarely been called a time-saver, so a few extra seconds on your journey is far less serious a problem than your walking in front of a truck. Also, if you are that involved in looking at your phone, you are not going to notice someone running up behind you to steal it until it's far too late.

## Dropped Connections

If you're moving around with a mobile phone, you're going to find areas with limited coverage. If you're using GPRS, this can be interesting as the "connection" can appear to stay up for quite an extended period of no coverage (more than 30 seconds is not unusual). One way to kill your GPRS session is trying to send a message when you are in an area without coverage, so check the signal strength before you hit the Enter key!

## Others Unaware Your Client Is Limited

This can be a problem, as other users will sometimes ask you to send them an email, or they will try to DCC you a huge file or just ask you to check a web page. Some simple J2ME phones will even kill the Java session when you receive an incoming phone call. With some clients and phones, you will be limited in whether you can do these actions as well as use IRC. Your best bet is to let people know you are using a limited client. You could do this by changing your nick from, say, "Steve" to "Steve_3650," or by having a prewritten disclaimer—like a Virca favorite.

## The Ephemeral Nature of Sessions

This will be a shock to those used to using a screen and having channel logs going back for years, but with most mobile IRC clients, you'll be able to see what's gone on in only the current session. Get used to it; it's not such a big disadvantage. Maybe you will have to lurk for a minute or so to find out what's going on when you join a channel, but it's no big deal. If you can't cope with this, use channels with public logs, or run another IRC session elsewhere, logging the channel for later perusal. The mobibot that runs in #mobitopia on the freenode IRC network has been modified to include a recap function that replays the last 10 items of traffic via private message. Sure, it's not extensive, but it's very useful to catch up on the last snippets of a conversation without having to ask someone.

## Battery Life

Modern mobile phones get their impressive standby durations by being very miserly with power consumption when they're not active. The clock speed of the main processor is reduced, the screen backlight is turned off, and all nonessential hardware is powered down. However, when you're tapping away on the keypad, your phone is using as much power as if you were making a voice call or maybe even more. Suddenly, instead of 200 hours between charges, you may be looking at 5 hours or less. You can either accept this as inevitable and ensure that you recharge frequently, or you can mitigate this effect by thinking about your IRC usage.

There are (at least) eight enemies—none serious though. If you're aware of these enemies and their workarounds, mobile IRC isn't going to be a disaster for you.

*—Jim Hughes*

# IRC from a Pocket PC

#89

If you're constantly on the move, whether it be roaming around your home or trekking in the mountains, IRC is only a few taps away on your Pocket PC.

Owners of Pocket PCs are not left in the dark when it comes to IRC connectivity. Pocket IRC (*http://www.pocketirc.com*) is a great little IRC client that lets you use IRC from your handheld device. It is available for free download, and you currently can register your trial version for $14.95.

There are a variety of methods for connecting to an IRC server from your Pocket PC. The simplest is to plug it into its docking station and piggyback your computer's Internet connection. This does seem rather limiting, as you are unable to wander around with your Pocket PC. But nonetheless, this can still be quite useful, as you can use your Pocket PC to keep an eye on IRC while you're playing a full-screen game on your computer.

As you get more adventurous, you can start moving away from your computer. Most Pocket PCs will allow you to connect to a remote device via infrared or Bluetooth. If you have a suitable receiver plugged into your computer, you can use it to gain a bit of IRC freedom as you wander around your office or part of your home.

Going one step further, you can even use the infrared or Bluetooth to get your mobile phone to establish a dialup or GPRS connection to the Internet. This will let you use IRC from anywhere you can receive a signal on your phone: on the bus, on the train, even while walking home if you have a steady pair of hands!

An even better solution is to use something like the O2 XDA II, which is essentially a full-fledged Pocket PC with a built-in mobile phone. With just one device, you can access IRC from anywhere. See it in action in Figure 14-2.

Pocket IRC provides a convenient and usable way of interacting with IRC on a Pocket PC. When you start using it, you will immediately notice that it has been designed to save on the amount of typing you have to do. For example, instead of typing **/join #foo**, you can join the channel just by typing **#foo** and then tapping IRC → Server → Join....

In fact, all */command* commands have been removed and replaced by either a single tap or a tap-and-hold to bring up a menu. It takes only a few minutes to get used to this new style of input, but it is worth it in the long run, as typing on a Pocket PC without a keyboard is not the fastest thing in the world. If you want to type a word that is already visible in the large text area, you simply have to tap that word, and it will be automagically entered into the input box for you.

*Figure 14-2. Accessing IRC from an O2 XDA II with Pocket IRC*

To save screen space, the input box is embedded directly into the standard menu bar at the bottom of the display. Pocket IRC even gives you a full-screen option, which removes the navigation bar from the top of the display.

If you need to fit even more text on the display, you can delve into the vast number of options provided by Pocket IRC, as shown in Figure 14-3. Lowering the font size will help out here, but making it too small will obviously make it unreadable.

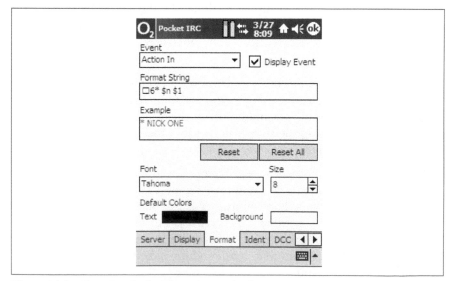

*Figure 14-3. Changing the font face, size, and colors*

ClearType is a technology that makes smaller text more readable by smoothing the edges of screen fonts. You can enable this on your Pocket PC device by going into Settings → System → Screen. Check the *Enable ClearType* box, and you'll notice the difference next time you perform a soft reset.

Getting Pocket IRC to connect to a server takes just two taps (IRC → Connect), but first, you must visit the Server tab in the Options section and tell it which server you want to connect to, as shown in Figure 14-4. Notice that the server has been set to localhost so it can use an SSH tunnel to connect to a private IRC server (see "Tunnel Your IRC Connection with SSH" [Hack #27]), but you can also connect directly to a public IRC network such as irc.freenode.net.

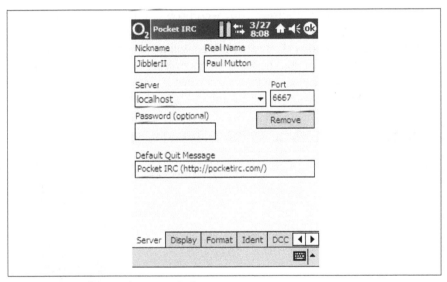

*Figure 14-4. Telling Pocket IRC which server to connect to*

If you have trouble connecting to a server because it wants an Ident response, you can go back into Options and enable the Ident server from the Ident tab. You can tell it to use whatever username you want. Another nice feature is that Pocket IRC even lets you send and receive files over DCC, so if you're stuck on the train and suddenly realize you've forgotten an important file, you can hop onto IRC and ask your colleagues if they can send it to you.

### Access IRC with Java Applets

Even if visitors to your web site don't have an IRC client installed, you can still try to persuade them to join your IRC channel by using a Java Applet client.

PJIRC (*http://www.pjirc.com*) is an IRC client that can be run as a Java Applet. This means you can embed it on web pages and most people will be able to run it through their web browser without having to install a standalone IRC client.

Before you upload PJIRC to your web server, you should edit the HTML in *SimpleApplet.html* to tell it to join the server that you want. The only line that you have to change is the one specifying the host:

```
<param name="host" value="irc.freenode.net">
```

Now you can run it by pointing your web browser at *http://yourserver.com/ pjirc-installation/SimpleApplet.html*. This will cause the PJIRC client to connect you to the freenode IRC network. You will need to join channels manually (for example, /join #irchacks). At this point, you can do anything you like: join channels, message people, notice people, and even change to a different server. You can see PJIRC running in Figure 14-5.

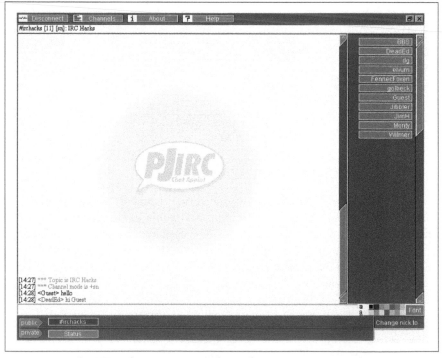

*Figure 14-5. The PJIRC client running inside a web page*

## Customizing PJIRC

If you want people to be able to connect to your server *and* join a channel automatically, a little customization is needed. This is done by passing parameters to the Applet in *SimpleApplet.html*.

**nick.** When somebody uses PJIRC to connect to the chosen IRC network, the nick parameter specifies which nickname to use. On web-based IRC clients, it is common to use the nickname "Guest" to indicate the temporary nature of the IRC client—more regular users of IRC tend to install their own standalone IRC clients.

```
<param name="nick" value="Guest">
```

**alternativenick.** Because all nicknames used on an IRC network must be unique, you must specify an alternative nickname in case "Guest" is already in use. The alternativenick parameter is used to specify this. Using ? in the name will allow PJIRC to replace this with a random number so that a name can be found that is not in use, for example:

```
<param name="alternatenick" value="Guest???">
```

**host.** If you want to make the PJIRC client connect to a different server, just change the host parameter as shown earlier:

```
<param name="host" value="irc.darkmyst.org">
```

**alternativeserver.** If the IRC server could not be found, you can specify a list of additional servers to try. These must be numbered in ascending order, for example:

```
<param name="alternateserver1" value="irc.us.freenode.net 6667">
<param name="alternateserver2" value="irc.eu.freenode.net 6667">
```

**command.** You can tell the PJIRC client to automatically execute a list of commands when it successfully connects to an IRC server. These must be numbered in ascending order. This is a useful way of making the client automatically join a channel, for example:

```
<param name="command1" value="/join #irchacks">
```

**authorizedjoinlist.** If you want to restrict the list of channels that the client can join, you can change the authorizedjoinlist parameter. In this example, the client will be allowed to join only the channel #irchacks:

```
<param name="authorizedjoinlist" value="none+#irchacks">
```

**authorizedcommandlist.** You can even restrict the set of commands that the client is allowed to use. In this case, the user will be able to use only the /me and /msg commands:

```
<param name="authorizedcommandlist" value="none+me+msg">
```

### The Results

Now you have a customized IRC client that people can use from your web site. They will be allowed only in your channel, and they can only chat with the people in the channel, send private messages, or perform specified actions.

*—Alex North*

**H A C K**

**#91**

## Use IRC from a Web Page Without Java

Use IRC from any browser—even mobile devices that don't support Java!

Many reasons may stop you from using a normal IRC client—maybe you can't install one on the computer or device you're using, or maybe a firewall blocks your access to IRC. Alternatively, you may want to provide an easy way for web page visitors to get to your IRC channel.

CGI:IRC provides a nearly full featured IRC client in a web browser. It makes use of JavaScript and DHTML features if they are available. The main omissions are support for scripting, DCC chat, and file transfers, but that's not the end of the world.

You will need a web server that can run Perl CGI scripts and, more importantly, supports Unix domain sockets. This rules out Windows, but Linux, any BSD, and even Mac OS X should work fine. The web server will also need to be able to connect to IRC.

The following instructions assume you are using Apache, as it is the most common web server in use. However, CGI:IRC should work on any web server that supports CGI.

How does it work?

CGI:IRC makes use of a streaming connection to the web server. This is a special HTTP request that never ends and sends data as it becomes available. This means the bandwidth usage is kept to a minimum because the page is not constantly being refreshed. This doesn't work with all browsers and proxies—two of the most common programs that currently have problems with streaming are the Novell BorderManager proxy and Apple's Safari browser. It is also possible the server will not support streaming. For example, mod_gzip on Apache will not work unless the CGI script is excluded from compression.

## Installing CGI:IRC

Download CGI:IRC from its web site at *http://cgiirc.sourceforge.net*, and extract the files to somewhere convenient. The two main steps to installing CGI:IRC are setting up the configuration and uploading the files to the web server.

Two configuration files are supplied with CGI:IRC. One is limited to a single channel and server and has fewer options. The other will allow users to connect to any server and contains a greater number of options. If you want to use the full configuration file, copy *cgiirc.config.full* over *cgiirc.config*. You can also copy and paste lines from the full configuration into the smaller one to make the configuration easier to manage. The file format follows fairly standard conventions. A line beginning with a # is a comment, while other lines set various options to specific values.

The main settings to configure are the server, the channel, and where the images are stored. The default_server and default_channel options should be set to the server you want to connect to and the channel you want to join. If you want to join multiple channels, you can specify a comma-separated list of channel names.

If Apache is configured to use the ExecCGI option (so you can run CGI scripts from anywhere), the default setup will work fine with the images. However, if it is configured with ScriptAlias (where you have a separate *cgi-bin* directory), the images will have to be put elsewhere. The place they are put must be able to display static files, and image_path in the CGI:IRC configuration file will need to be updated to point to this location. For example, if you put the images directory at the root of a virtual host, image_path would be /images. The key thing to remember is that image_path is what is sent to the browser, so this should not contain a full local filesystem path.

Apart from the images, all the files should be uploaded into the same directory. It is recommended that you put them inside a directory called *cgiirc*, as this makes it easier to see which files belong to CGI:IRC. If you use a local server, you just need to move the files into the correct location rather than uploading them. How you upload the files does not matter—you can use FTP/SFTP to the server or any other method that is convenient. You should upload all of the text files in ASCII mode; otherwise, they may not run correctly on the server. Conversely, make sure you upload the images in binary mode.

Once you have uploaded the files, it is a good idea to check the permissions on the .cgi files: *irc.cgi*, *nph-irc.cgi*, and *client-perl.cgi*. They need to have at least read and execute permissions for user, group, and other, that is, r-xr-xr-x. If you aren't sure what the current permissions are, you can either use your FTP client to change the permissions of the files to r-xr-xr-x or log in to the web server and type the following into the shell:

```
% chmod 755 *.cgi
```

Hopefully, all the necessary files will now be on the server and have the correct permissions. If all has gone well, when you visit the location of irc.cgi (for example, *http://localhost/cgi-bin/cgiirc/irc.cgi*), you will see the login page shown in Figure 14-6.

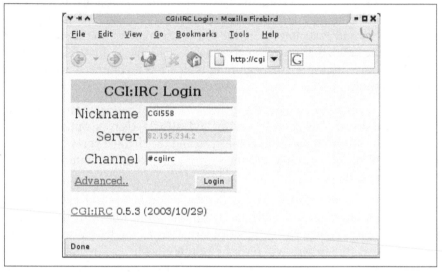

*Figure 14-6. The CGI:IRC login page*

Once you have logged in, you'll see something similar to the screenshot in Figure 14-7. The layout is similar to most graphical IRC clients. Along the top is a list of the channels you are in, with the text color indicating the activity in the window. The buttons on the right will access the online help, open the options, and close the current window. On the right you see the user list. Double-clicking on a name will open a query to let you send private messages. The rest of the screen should be fairly obvious; the only other thing that needs explaining is the << symbol, which causes CGI:IRC to display some extra buttons to allow the input of colors and formatting characters.

There are some limitations in CGI:IRC. Because CGI:IRC acts as a client, connections from it appear to be coming from the web server's address. This allows it to get past firewalls, but, unfortunately, if several clients are connecting from the same address, some IRC servers will refuse to accept additional connections beyond a certain limit. The other main limitation is that it is written in Perl and uses CGI, so quite a lot of memory is used per user.

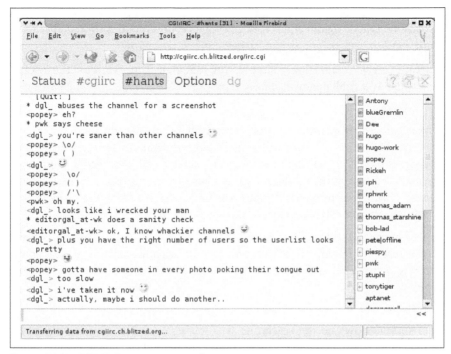

*Figure 14-7. CGI:IRC running in a web page*

This isn't too much of an issue for single users using it to get past firewalls, but for a web site with lots of users, it isn't ideal.

*—David Leadbeater*

## Use IRC Within screen

#92 If you're regularly on the move, you need a way to keep track of IRC while away from your computer. Run a console-based IRC client in screen as a simple yet powerful solution.

If you're running a text mode (console) IRC client on a remote system, it can be annoying having to reconnect if your connection drops or if you have to move to another machine. When you reconnect, you will no longer see the messages that were sent when you were last connected.

GNU *screen* provides a neat solution to this problem. It allows you to disconnect from a terminal session without quitting your running programs. You can then log in and resume the *screen* session at a later time, giving the appearance that you never disconnected.

*screen* is provided as a package on most Unix-based systems. If it isn't already installed, install the *screen* package or download and install it from source at *http://www.gnu.org/software/screen/screen.html*.

Starting *screen* is amazingly simple, yet many people overlook the usefulness of it. At a shell prompt, simply type:

```
% screen
```

If you get a startup message, just press Enter. You should then see a shell prompt. This is just like any other shell, but with one difference—every time you press Ctrl-A, it will be intercepted by *screen*. All of *screen*'s commands are accessed by typing a different letter after this key. *screen* provides a short summary of the commands if you press Ctrl-A followed by the ? key. These combinations are often abbreviated to the form **^A ?**.

Probably the most useful command is the one that lets you "detach" from a *screen* session. Typing **^A d** will detach your session, leaving the programs running inside the *screen* just as they were. To reattach to the session, just type:

```
% screen -r
```

You should now see the screen as you left it. You can also log out completely, and later log back in and reattach. By default, *screen* will also detach sessions when the terminal is closed, so *screen* sessions survive network connections dying and closing the terminal window. If for some reason your connection dies and the *screen* isn't detached, screen -r is not enough to reattach. You will need to run the command screen -r -d to detach and then reattach. Also, if you are running more than one *screen*, you need to give the pid (process ID) or name of the *screen* process that you want to reattach to after the -r parameter.

 If you are using the BitchX IRC client, detaching is even easier. Simply type **/detach** to detach your client, then run the scr-bx command to bring your session back again. However, this feature is nowhere near as powerful as *screen* and won't detach automatically.

*screen*'s other great strength is that it lets you run more than one program inside one terminal window. This makes it easy to leave several programs running and access all of them from another location, even if you are restricted to a very slow connection. This is achieved by supporting virtual windows inside the *screen* session. You can create a new window by pressing **^A c**. Once you have more than one window, you can use **^A n** or **^A** <space> to go to the next window, and **^A p** to go to the previous window.

This feature is made even more flexible because *screen* allows windows to be split. This means you can see more than one window on the screen at a time. To split the screen, type ^A S. This one is case sensitive, so you will need to hold down the Shift key as well. This splits the window into two, and you should see a new blank window in the bottom half of the screen. Pressing ^A <tab> will change to this new window, and you can either change to another existing window by pressing ^A n, or you can create a new window. If you want to get rid of the split windows, ^A Q will hide all the inactive windows.

The screenshot in Figure 14-8 shows *screen* with a split window, displaying *irssi* in a channel where system logs are sent to IRC, and the *screen* manual page in the bottom half.

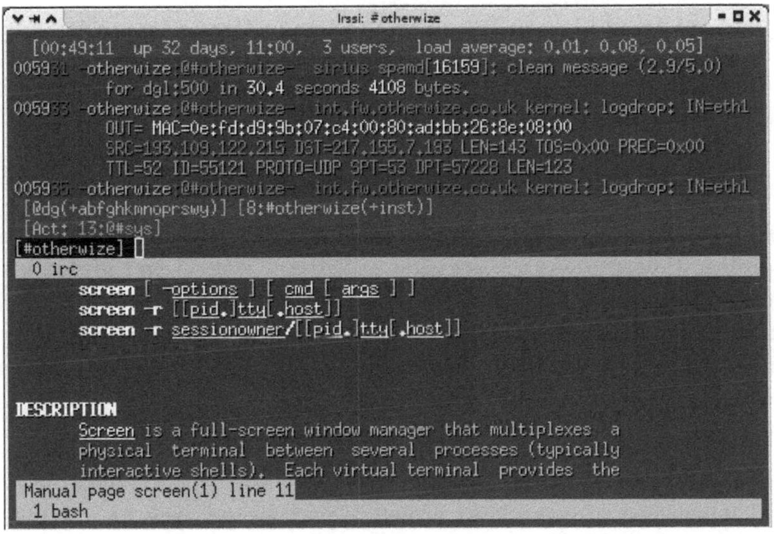

*Figure 14-8. Screen with a split window*

If you have played with the split-window feature, you may have noticed you can have a window visible in several split windows at the same time. This is actually a very useful feature because *screen* allows you to attach to a *screen* session more than once. This is called multiple display mode, and you can use it to display the same window on multiple terminals, or you can display a different window on different terminals. To use it, simply add the -x option to the reattach command, so it becomes:

```
% screen -r -x
```

*screen* also has support for copy and paste from one window to another. Type ^A [ to start the copy, move the cursor with the arrow keys, and press Enter to start copying; then move the cursor to the end of the text you want to copy and press Enter again. The text that you have copied will be stored in memory until you use ^A ] to paste it. When you are selecting the text, there are some other keys that you can use. For example, pressing / will allow you to search within the text buffer, and Page Up and Page Down will scroll a full screen.

More relevant to IRC is a script that checks that your IRC client is running so you don't even have to manually restart if it crashes or if the system you're running it on is rebooted.

This makes use of the cron facility found on most Unix systems, along with a little bit of Bourne shell scripting.

To edit your user's crontab, run this command:

```
% crontab -e
```

You can then create a new line in your crontab:

```
*/5 * * * * IRC=`screen -ls | grep -v Dead | grep "\\.irc"`;
    if [ "x$IRC" = "x" ]; then screen -dmS irc irssi;fi
```

This causes the script to be run every five minutes. When it runs, it checks the output of screen -ls for a session called irc. If it doesn't find it, it starts *screen* in detached mode (with the options -dm) and names the session irc (option -S). *screen* will run the command irssi once it has started. If you want to use a different IRC client, you could replace the irssi with whatever you use to start your IRC client.

*screen* also has a command line as well as key shortcuts. You can access the command line via ^A :. For example, to change the title of a window (this is useful when you're using split screens), you would type ^A :title *new-title*.

If you are paranoid about security, you can password-protect reattaching to your screen by running the password command on the *screen* command line. You can do this by typing ^A :*password* and following the prompts. If you want to make this permanent after setting the password, edit the file *~/.screenrc* (create it if it doesn't exist) and type **password** followed by ^A ] (this pastes the contents of the paste buffer). Your line should look something like password NSQuRKGNxIEbw. Whenever someone runs *screen -r* from now on, they will be prompted for the password. The security provided by this is in addition to that provided by your login password, but it won't deter someone who is determined to get past if they have access to your system account.

There isn't enough room to cover all of *screen*'s features here; however, *screen* has a very good manual page so **man** **screen** will tell you lots more, such as how to remap keys to suit your tastes and how to allow multiple users to share a *screen* session. With *screen*, it's easy to run multiple IRC clients and access them from anywhere in the world.

Quick key reference:

^A c
>   Create window.

^A d
>   Detach.

^A n *or* ^A <space>
>   Next window.

^A p *or* ^A <backspace>
>   Previous window.

^A <number key>
>   Change to that window number.

^A [ *or* ^A <escape>
>   Start a copy.

^A ]
>   Paste copy buffer.

^A S
>   Split window.

^A Q
>   Hide inactive windows.

^A :
>   Enter a *screen* command.

To get a quick list of all of *screen*'s key bindings, press ^A? at any time.

—*David Leadbeater*

### Set Up an IRC Proxy

**#93**  IRC everywhere and never miss anything with an IRC proxy/bouncer.

First of all, you might wonder what a bouncer actually is. The word "proxy" is probably a more accurate description. A bouncer, like a proxy, is a program that connects you to a service (it's IRC in this context, but there are proxies for many different services) and acts as some sort of buffer. Also, like many web proxies, most bouncers cache data. Sometimes they also allow you to hide your real location, particularly if the proxy runs in a completely different place from where you are. People will see that your connection comes from the proxy host and will not be able to see where you are connecting to the proxy from.

CtrlProxy is a good example of an IRC proxy. It connects to your IRC servers and channels and accepts connections from you. Although CtrlProxy is not the only IRC bouncer available, it is one of the more advanced. Like most bouncers, it caches all your received messages while you're away, and, as soon as you connect to CtrlProxy, you'll get them sent to you. Another interesting feature is that CtrlProxy allows you to connect from multiple places. So when you leave home, you can keep your IRC client running on your desktop machine. At work, you can connect to CtrlProxy, and you'll get exactly the same session you left at home. Or if you have multiple machines at home, you can run your IRC client on all of them without being in the channel with three clones. And of course, if you fear the mess when you have your chat logs on lots of separate machines, CtrlProxy can keep them on your server too.

## Setting Up CtrlProxy

CtrlProxy is supported on Unix platforms only. With some work, it's possible to get it working on Windows machines, but you're on your own then.

There are two ways to get hold of CtrlProxy. You can either use the package manager for your operating system, or you can compile it from source. A ctrlproxy package is available for most Linux distributions and the BSD port collections. You can get the source from *http://ctrlproxy.vernstok.nl*. After unpacking the tarball contents, run ./Configure and then run make install. Before you run CtrlProxy, you will have to create a configuration file. At the moment, there are two ways to do this.

The first way to configure CtrlProxy is to take the example file ctrlproxyrc. example from the source tree and adapt it to your setup. It's an XML-formatted file, so it is quite logical to read and understand.

The example contains a list of modules to load. It's usually a good idea to leave those as they are, unless you know exactly what the modules do. Then there is the list of the IRC networks you're on. For every network, you have to specify things like a nickname, an IRC name, and some other details that don't really require any further explanation. In the configuration, you must also set up a listener. A listener is something that allows you to connect to CtrlProxy with your IRC client. When creating multiple IRC networks, make sure each listener listens on a different port. Then you get a list of servers and the channels you want to join. If you want to, you can specify more than one server. CtrlProxy will switch to the next server when a server connection fails. When you start CtrlProxy, it will join each channel automatically. Of course, if you want to join other channels, you can do so with your IRC client when it is connected to the listener.

If the XML configuration file confuses you, there's always the second option. There's a little configuration wizard, called ctrlproxy-setup, inside the CtrlProxy source tree. This generates a ready-to-use configuration file after asking a few questions.

Here's a little sample configuration file, which connects you to the freenode IRC network (and two channels: #ctrlproxy and #irchacks) and a public BitlBee server:

```xml
<?xml version="1.0"?>
<ctrlproxy>
    <plugins>
        <plugin autoload="1" file="libsocket"/>
        <plugin autoload="1" file="librepl_memory"/>
        <plugin autoload="1" file="libadmin"/>
        <plugin autoload="1" file="liblog_irssi">
            <logfile>/home/wilmer/irclogs/</logfile>
        </plugin>
        <plugin autoload="1" file="libctcp"/>
        <plugin autoload="1" file="libstrip"/>
        <plugin autoload="1" file="libnickserv"/>
        <plugin autoload="1" file="libantiflood"/>
        <plugin autoload="1" file="libauto-away">
            <message time="300">I'm currently away, sorry!</message>
        </plugin>
    </plugins>
    <networks>
        <network autoconnect="1" client_pass="secret" name="FREENODE"
            nick="wilmer" username="wilmer" fullname="Wilmer van der Gaast">
            <listen>
                <ipv4 port="6667"/>
            </listen>
            <servers>
                <ipv4 host="irc.freenode.net"/>
                <ipv4 host="sterling.freenode.net"/>
                <ipv6 host="gerrold.freenode.net"/>
            </servers>
            <channel name="#ctrlproxy" autojoin="1"/>
            <channel name="#irchacks" autojoin="1"/>
        </network>
        <network autoconnect="1" client_pass="secret" name="BEE">
            <listen>
                <ipv4 port="6668"/>
            </listen>
            <servers>
                <ipv4 host="im.bitlbee.org"/>
            </servers>
        </network>
    </networks>
</ctrlproxy>
```

## Running the Hack

By default, CtrlProxy reads its configuration from a file called *.ctrlproxyrc* in your home directory. If you want to put the configuration somewhere else, you have to specify the location when you start CtrlProxy. You will probably also want to run CtrlProxy in daemon mode so it will continue running when you log out. To start CtrlProxy in daemon mode using the configuration file *~/.ctrlproxy/ctrlproxyrc*, type this:

```
% ctrlproxy -D -r ~/.ctrlproxy/ctrlproxy
```

CtrlProxy will start, and now you can connect to it by pointing your favorite IRC client at the CtrlProxy listeners. Connect to port 6668 on the host running CtrlProxy (you can use localhost if you are running your client on the same machine), and you'll see the BitlBee session. Connect to port 6667 on the CtrlProxy host, and you'll notice you appear to have been in the two channels for some time already. Don't forget to specify the server password if you put one in the configuration file. If anybody said anything between the moment you started CtrlProxy and the moment you connected to the listener, you'll get those messages too.

Now you can try to make two connections to one listener. As if by magic, you'll find that it just works, and you'll get all the messages on both machines. Of course, when you say something, you'll see that on your other clients too. To some extent, this may depend on how your IRC client behaves—some clients get very confused when they receive messages from their own nick!

## Advanced Features

CtrlProxy has some other quite interesting features. Automatic identification to NickServ is one particularly useful feature. It can also be used to generate pisg-like statistics **[Hack #14]** automatically. By the time you read this hack, several other new features will probably be available. If you want to get more information about them, it's a good idea to read the documentation that comes with CtrlProxy. You can do a lot with this program. Explaining all of it is beyond the scope of this book, but hopefully this is enough to give you some idea of what it can do.

—*Wilmer van der Gaast*

## Use irssi and Its Proxy

irssi is a highly configurable and scriptable IRC client for Unix. Its proxy
feature can open the doors to more advanced use.

This hack shows you how to configure the *irssi* IRC client and set up its
proxy features so you can resume your IRC session while on the move. *irssi*
can be compiled and installed from source code or it can be installed from a
package. There are source and package downloads available from the *irssi*
web site at *http://www.irssi.org*. If you do compile from source, make sure
you add the --with-proxy option to configure, as the final part of this hack
needs it. On Debian systems, the package is named irssi-text. This is
because there is an older version of *irssi*, which has a graphical frontend, but
it hasn't been maintained for a few years.

When you start *irssi* by running the command irssi, it will print a message
telling you to read some of the documentation. You'll find the startup-HOWTO
on the *irssi* web site, although it is also provided in the *docs* directory with
the *irssi* source. You can skip reading it if you like, as this hack will summa-
rize the important points and walk you through the process of using the
proxy.

*irssi* supports multiple servers and deals with connecting to them automatically, but to get the best support, you really need to define the servers. To do
this, you must use the ircnet and the server commands. As an example,
we'll set up the IRC network freenode with one server, irc.freenode.net:

```
/ircnet add freenode
/server add -auto -ircnet freenode irc.freenode.net
```

*ircnet* is the friendly name by which the connection will be referred to in
*irssi*, but the server could be one of many. It's possible to add several servers, so the alternative ones can be tried if there is a problem connecting to
the first. The -auto parameter to /server means to automatically connect to
this server, and the -ircnet associates it with the correct IRC network. If you
want to add extra information such as a password for connecting to a server,
/help server will tell you the syntax. The Page Up key should allow you to
scroll up when you are viewing this documentation. The ircnet command
can also accept some options, for example:

```
/ircnet add -autosendcmd "/^msg NickServ identify password;wait -freenode
    2000" freenode
```

This command will automatically message NickServ with your password
and then wait two seconds before trying to join a channel. The ^ character
before msg means to hide the sending of the message so your password won't
be seen by anyone else who happens to be looking at your screen.

Next you need to decide which channels you want to join. This is very much the same as with servers, the only real difference being that the -ircnet parameter has changed:

```
/channel add -auto #irchacks freenode
```

This means *irssi* will automatically join #irchacks when it connects to freenode.

Before you connect, you might like to change your nickname and real name that are sent to IRC—by default, these will be your login details. They can be changed via the /set command:

```
/set nick Nickname
/set real_name Real Name
```

It's worth noting at this point that the /set command has a useful feature: if you write only part of a setting name, it will show all possible settings that match. The documentation of settings in *irssi* isn't brilliant, so this method is a good way to find undocumented settings. For example, try /set nick and you will see lots of settings related to nicknames.

## Connecting to a Server

There are two ways you can connect with *irssi*. The first is to quit from *irssi* (/quit) and start it again. Because the server is set to automatically connect, it will do so upon startup. The second way is to type **/connect freenode**. Figure 14-9 shows *irssi* connected to the freenode IRC network.

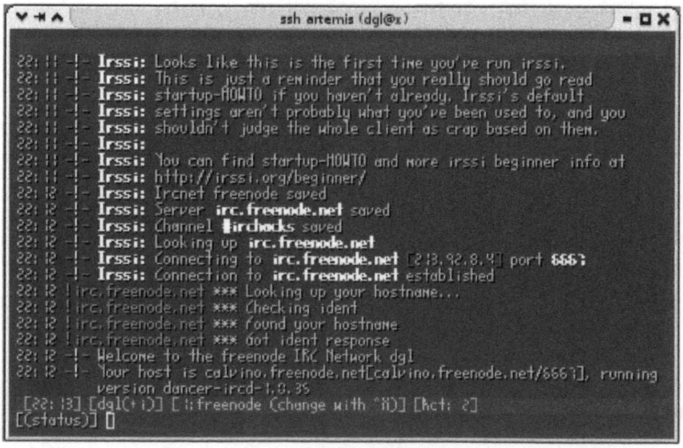

*Figure 14-9. Using irssi to connect to a server for the first time*

Once you have connected and automatically joined a channel, *irssi* will have created a new "window" for the channel. Along the bottom on the status bar you will see [Act: 2]. This means there is activity in window number 2. You can change between windows using various keyboard combinations: Alt-number will change to that window number, Alt-A will change to a window with activity, and Alt-left arrow and Alt-right arrow will go to the window to the left and right. If the Alt combination doesn't work, you will need to change the keyboard mapping of your terminal. startup-HOWTO has details about this.

By now, you may have started chatting with the people in the channel you joined. If you want to ask someone a question or you want to write something directed at someone, you can type part of her nickname and press the Tab key. *irssi* should complete the nickname and add a colon on the end. Tab completion doesn't end there though; / commands will also tab-complete, as will their parameters and even channel and server names.

If you have joined several channels, you may want to keep them in a particular order. You can move the current window to the second location with the /window command:

```
/window move 2
```

Once you have the windows in an order you like, you should run the command:

```
/layout save
```

This will save them and remember the order next time you start *irssi*. Another useful feature is split windows. This means you can display more than one channel at the same time within the same terminal session. For example, in a channel window, you can type:

```
/window show 1
```

This will show the Status window along the top. You can change to it with Alt-1 as usual or with Alt-Up.

Connecting to multiple servers with *irssi* is very easy. You simply need to define another ircnet and another set of servers and channel, as demonstrated by the freenode example earlier. *irssi* will then automatically connect to all the servers on startup. Each server connection is given a tag. This tag is usually the same as the ircnet, but if you connect to a server manually or have multiple connections to one ircnet, it will be different. If you want to execute a command on a specific server connection, you can add the -tag parameter to most commands. For example, to join the channel #foo on the server with the tag private, you would type:

```
/join -private #foo
```

You can also use Ctrl-X to change between servers in a window that does not have any items, such as the Status window.

The /bind command allows you to change what the keys do. You can assign them to any command or a few special commands (see /help bind). By default, the keys Alt-q to Alt-o (along the top line of a QWERTY keyboard) jump to the windows 11 to 19, but if you have a different keyboard layout, you may want to change this.

*irssi* supports embedded Perl scripting. Perl scripts can control nearly all the aspects of *irssi*, so there are lots of possibilities here if you fancy getting into it. The *irssi* script archive at *http://irssi.org/scripts* has a lot of scripts available for download. One script will even automatically install scripts for you from the script archive. To use this, simply type:

```
/script load scriptassist
```

If there is a problem loading the script, you may not have the LWP Perl modules installed. They should be available as a package for most distributions; the name will be something like libwww-perl or LWP.

Once scriptassist is loaded, you will see several new script commands. Typing **/script help** will give you a list of all of these.

As an example, if you want to install the title script that sets the window title in a graphical terminal, type:

```
/script install title
```

To run it automatically whenever you start *irssi*, type:

```
/script autorun title
```

It's also a good idea to do this for scriptassist to ensure that it is always loaded.

The title script also adds some settings. You can see these by typing:

```
/set title
```

Figure 14-10 shows *irssi* running in a graphical terminal with the title script. Note that the window title displays the nickname, network, and current channel.

The status bar at the bottom of the window contains a lot of information, including your current nickname, channel, or server, as well as the modes set on them. As mentioned previously, there is an item that contains the activity in all the windows you have joined. The window number will change color to white if there are messages in the channel, or it will turn red if someone has mentioned your nickname. You can add extra highlight words with the /hilight command.

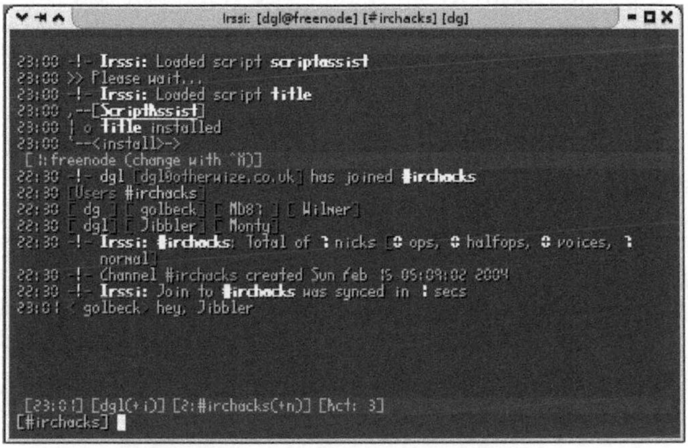

Figure 14-10. *irssi showing scriptassist installing the title script*

It is also possible to script status bar items. For example, *irssi* comes with a script called *usercount* that will display the number of users in a channel. To load it, run /script load usercount. To get the status bar item, you need to use the /statusbar command. The syntax is a little confusing, and you need to remember that the first parameter is always the name of the status bar. You can add the user count to the right of the status bar on the bottom (the window status bar) with the following command:

```
/statusbar window add -alignment right usercount
```

## Using the irssi Proxy

If you're frequently on the move and end up connecting to IRC from different places, it's nice to be able to access it from the same client every time. This not only ensures that you remain permanently connected to the IRC network, but you will be able to keep all your log files in one place. *irssi* allows you achieve this feat by providing a proxy, which lets you use another IRC client to connect to your *irssi* instance.

For those familiar with bouncers (if not, see "Set Up an IRC Proxy" [Hack #93]), this is very similar. The only real difference here is this all happens inside an IRC client, so if you use *irssi inside* screen [Hack #92], you don't always need an IRC client to connect (although you can use one if you want to).

To load the proxy module, type:

```
/load proxy
```

If you want to load the proxy every time you start *irssi*, edit the file *~/.irssi/ startup*, creating it if it doesn't already exist. You can then add the line /load proxy to the file, and this command will be executed automatically every time you start up *irssi*.

The proxy module will tell you to set a password when you load it. To set your password to "password", you must type:

```
/set irssiproxy_password password
```

You will now need to set a port number for each IRC network. These are the port numbers that you will connect to from another IRC client. Valid port numbers range from 1024–65535. It's a good idea to avoid the normal IRC port (6667), as other people may accidentally connect to you and think you're running an IRC server.

For example, you may have two IRC networks you want to proxy: freenode on port 4050 and blitzed on port 4051. Assuming both of these have been set up correctly with the ircnet command, you can type:

```
/set irssiproxy_ports freenode=4050 blitzed=4051
```

This will enable access to these networks via the proxy.

Now you should be able to use another IRC client to connect to port 4050 of the host where *irssi* is running. If you use the correct password, you will appear to join the channels the *irssi* client is in. This connection can now be treated as if you were actually connected to the server, with one minor difference—you will see yourself speaking in the other IRC client when you speak in one.

*—David Leadbeater*

# CHAPTER FIFTEEN

# Servers and Services

## Hacks 95–100

If you're testing out your earlier hacks, you may find it convenient to perform the tests locally, using your own IRC server. Setting up your own IRC server gives you ultimate power over how it behaves, and you can even let other people connect to it from the Internet.

If you already have a server up and running, you may find it useful to add *Services* to it. This lets you add NickServ and ChanServ features to your network, which are welcomed by users who wish to protect their nicknames and stop other people from stealing them.

If you want to expand your IRC network, you can also find out how to link two IRC servers together. This is the secret to the success of IRC, with several servers connected to form a network, providing greater resilience and the ability to allow more users to connect.

As you near the end of this book, you may be getting accustomed to the look-and-feel of IRC. If you really like it, you can find out how to set up the unique *BitlBee* program to combine all of your MSN, ICQ, and AIM contacts into an interface that is transparently presented as a single IRC channel. The final hack in this book then shows you a neat way of combining BitlBee with the IRC proxy described in Chapter 14.

 **HACK** **#95** Set Up Your Own IRC Server for Unix/Linux

Whether it's for testing bots or chatting with your mates, set up your own server for the ultimate power and sense of achievement.

At some point you may want to run your own server—maybe to test a bot without disturbing other users, to learn how the IRC operator commands work, or as a place for your friends to chat. It isn't easy to run your own server, as there is a lot to understand and configure, but it is a good learning experience and quite good fun too!

IRC servers are often called IRC daemons, which are also typically abbreviated as ircds. The code that most IRC servers are based on dates back to the original ircd. Jarkko Oikarinen wrote this in 1988 at the University of Oulu in Finland. The code is licensed under the GPL, and therefore developers are free to extend it under that license.

You have a large choice of ircds. Many of these are listed on *http://directory. google.com/Top/Computers/Software/Internet/Servers/Chat/IRC*. A lot of IRC networks have their own ircd. Some make small modifications to another ircd, while others may add major new features. Although the server-to-server communication format is documented in RFC 1459, modern IRC servers do not strictly adhere to it, as many extensions have been made (and continue to be made). If you are connecting to an existing IRC network, you will have to use an ircd that is compatible.

One of the most popular and full-featured ircds is Unreal. It has versions for both Windows and Unix operating systems. This hack will guide you through installing and configuring it. There is a lot to learn, so this hack will just help you with the basics—setting up a single server with the most basic configuration needed to run. You should read the Unreal documentation and learn about all the features if you are serious about running an ircd for public use.

## Installing Unreal

Download Unreal from *http://www.unrealircd.com*. If you have downloaded the version for Windows, it should be already compiled, and you can skip to the configuration stage. Although you can compile it under Windows, it is much easier to use the precompiled version, so this section will focus on Unix-based systems.

You may need to change some of the filenames depending on which version you download. Extract the source with the tar command:

```
% tar zxvf Unreal3.2.tar.gz
```

Then change directory to the extracted directory:

```
% cd Unreal3.2
```

To compile the ircd, you first need to configure it. This is so you can choose where to install it and set some compile-time options:

```
% ./Config
```

This will ask you some questions and then run the configure script for you. Accepting the defaults is fine, unless you want one of the features that are disabled by default.

Then to compile the ircd:

```
% make
```

Normally, the ircd is run from within the source directory; however, if you specified a different location when you ran the ./Config command, you will also need to run make install like so:

```
% make install
```

Traditional ircd configuration files have followed a format in which each line is identified by a single letter and followed by fields separated by colons. The advantage of this is it is easy to write the parser for the file. Unfortunately, it leads to rather cryptic configuration files, because you need to know what each letter stands for and what order the fields should be in. Some of these are easy to remember, as some letters are commonly used—even by users who may have no idea of their true origin. For example, K-lines (server bans on an address) are named after their format in the configuration file.

Fortunately, Unreal 3.2 has a new-style configuration format that is much more verbose, allowing a clearer configuration file.

To make a configuration file, copy the file *doc/example.conf* to *unrealircd.conf*. Open this file with your favorite text editor. The configuration file may seem very long and scary at first. Well, it is a bit scary, but a lot of the file is full of comments that explain what all of the options do. Comments are text enclosed with /* */, like C comments.

Each part of the configuration is separated into blocks. A block is a set of configuration variables that are related. Taking the "me" block as an example, the format of the configuration file can be explained:

```
me {
    name "irc.example.com";
    info "An example server";
    numeric 1;
};
```

The first line has the name of the block and a { symbol to show it is the start of the block. The next line sets the variable name to the string irc.example.com. Strings must be enclosed in quotation marks, as shown in the code block. All statements must end with a semicolon. Numbers—unlike strings—should not be quoted, as shown by the numeric variable 1. A closing } is used to end the block—notice that the block requires a semicolon at the end. Each line with a variable on it is indented for clarity. While not essential, this makes it much easier to read the file when you have blocks nested within other blocks.

The first block in the example configuration file is the previously mentioned "me" block. The name should be a valid DNS hostname. This could be the hostname of the machine the ircd will run on or a name such as irc.example.com. The info is a description of the server and can be seen by clients when they execute the /whois command on a connected user, among other places. The numeric is a number between 1 and 255 that is unique to this server in a network; 1 is fine if this is the only or the first server in a network. You should change the value of these to ones suitable for your network.

The "admin" block specifies what gets shown when a user runs the /admin command. It is common practice to put contact information here.

Class blocks define various values such as times and the number of clients that can connect. They are referred to by other blocks, such as server connections and client allow blocks. They are the first blocks that can exist more than once—they must also be given a name on the same line as the block name. However, this name is not quoted like other strings. The default classes should be fine to start with, so there is no need to change anything.

The "allow" blocks allow clients to connect. Unless you want to limit your server to specific users, the default is fine.

Each IRC operator on the server must have an "oper" block; you can edit the example for the first operator. The account name goes after the oper in the block name. The "from" is a list of user hosts allowed to use this operator block. This is a standard IRC host mask (without a nickname) and can include the * wildcard. It is a good idea to change the password to something more secure. Flags specify what the operator is allowed to do—a netadmin is allowed to do most things and is probably what you want for yourself. It's up to you what permissions you give to other users. To become an IRC operator, you should connect with your IRC client and type:

```
/oper account-name password
```

The "listen" block defines the ports the IRC server will listen on. Port 6667 is the standard IRC port and what most people expect to connect to, so it's a good idea to leave this as it is. Obviously, you can open extra ports for whatever reason—maybe some institutions block traffic on port 6667, so you can be kind and open up another port number as well. If you chose to enable SSL during the ./Config process, you will also need to specify an SSL port.

The "link" and "ulines" blocks are used for linking other servers and Services to the server. The link defines the password and remote address of the server and will be covered in the next hack on Services, so you can comment out the link block for now. A ulines block allows Services to change modes on channels.

The "drpass" block defines passwords for the /restart and /die commands, which restart and stop the ircd, respectively. The main purpose of each password is merely to prevent accidental usage of the commands, as the user must be an IRC operator to be able to run these commands.

Several other blocks provide extra functionality. The defaults for these should be fine, so don't worry too much. These options cover logging, aliases, tld (display different MOTDs to different users), banning, exceptions, deny (block some DCC file types), and vhost (allow users to change host via a password system). You should comment out features you don't intend to use—at the very least, you will need to remove tld or create the files it needs and remove the default exception.

At the end of the example configuration file, you'll find the "set" blocks. There are some very important settings to make here. The first set block is network settings. The network settings in the example configuration file are for a network called ROXnet, and you should change the names to something more appropriate. It's best to use a valid domain name for the hostnames. However, apart from the default-server setting, the hostnames themselves do not need to be valid hostnames, as they are used only within IRC. The cloak-keys should be set to three different random values greater than 10000—they are needed so that Unreal's masked hosts are secure.

The second set block deals with settings specific to the server. The "kline" address should be set to something valid, and the DNS server should be set to the IP address of your DNS server. If you are unsure what the IP address of your DNS server is, look at the file /etc/resolv.conf on a Unix system. On Windows 2000 and later versions, you can open a command prompt and run the command ipconfig /all. Older Windows machines will display their IP address and DNS server if you run winipcfg.

Now you have most of the settings sorted out, so the server should be ready to run. To test it on a Unix system, run:

```
% ./unreal start
```

When the server starts up, you should see something like Figure 15-1.

Windows users can just start the Unreal ircd program on Windows. When it starts, it will display a control panel as in Figure 15-2. If there is an error, it should give you some idea of the problem, so check the configuration file carefully to see if you can fix it. If the server has started correctly, you should be able to connect to the server by connecting to localhost:6667 with any IRC client.

Once you have connected, you should be able to become an IRC operator using the /oper command, with the username and password that you set in

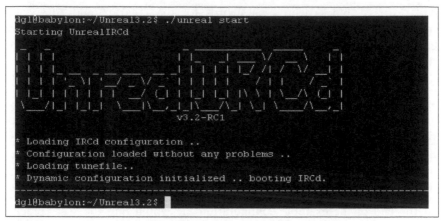

Figure 15-1.  Running Unreal under Linux

Figure 15-2.  Unreal for Windows has a control panel when running

the file. There are lots of IRC operator commands. Typing **/helpop opercmd**
will show a listing, and then **/helpop** *command* will show help on that particular command.

—*David Leadbeater*

## HACK #96 Install Services

You've used the so-called "Services" on various IRC networks, but have you
ever wondered how to set them up for your own IRC server?

A Services package provides the NickServ, ChanServ, MemoServ, and
OperServ features found on many IRC networks. This hack assumes that
you already have an ircd set up, such as that shown in the previous hack.
Just as there are many different types of ircds, there are lots of different Ser-

vices packages, although they vary much more than ircds. The NickServ and ChanServ formats are probably the most common, but there are also bots such as X on Undernet and Q on QuakeNet that provide similar functionality. See "Register Your Channel with ChanServ" **[Hack #9]** for more details on using ChanServ.

IRC Services was one of the first open source ChanServ packages. The first ChanServ was actually used on DALnet, but their version hasn't been released. Ever since Version 5 was released, IRC Services has been modular, so you can choose what functionality you want—it even includes the option of a web server to access data.

Although Services are seen as several clients by users (ChanServ, NickServ, etc.), the Services package itself links to the network as another server. This allows it to see all the clients connected to IRC, see the state of the channels, and change modes that normal clients (and usually operators) are unable to change.

IRC Services is really supported only under Unix-like systems, including Linux and FreeBSD. It should compile under the Cygwin Unix emulation environment on Windows, but the *README* states it isn't supported.

IRC Services can be downloaded from *http://www.ircservices.za.net*. Once you have downloaded the archive file, extract it with the following command:

```
% tar zxvf ircservices-5.0.23.tar.gz
```

You may need to change the version number if you have a more recent version. Now change to the new directory that has appeared and run the configure script:

```
% cd ircservices-5.0.23
% ./configure
```

The configure script asks some questions and configures the Services ready to be compiled. It will ask you the path where the *sbin* directory should be placed. Unless you have root access, you'll need to put this in your home directory, for example in */home/user/services/sbin/*. It will ask you if you want to create the directory if it doesn't already exist. The path for the data should automatically update, so just press Enter. After this, the configure script will check your system for various features. It will then tell you to edit *defs.h* and run make. You shouldn't need to edit *defs.h*, as the default settings will suffice. To compile Services, run:

```
% make
```

It will then tell you to run make install to install Services:

```
% make install
```

## Configuring the IRC Server

The ircd that you are going to link the Services to must be configured to allow this and to also allow Services to change the channel modes. On Unreal 3.2, the configuration blocks are link and ulines. On other ircds, the lines are C: and N: for linking and U: for ulines. For example, if your Services are called services.example.com (you'll be able to set this later), then you need a link for them and a uline for them.

If you are using Unreal, you will need to add something like this to the configuration file, *unrealircd.conf*:

```
link services.example.com {
    username *;
    hostname 127.0.0.1;
    bind-ip *;
    hub *;
    password-connect "password";
    password-receive "password";
};

ulines {
    services.example.com;
};
```

The important thing here is the hostname of Services. This should match the setting you used in the services-server setting in *unrealircd.conf*. The IP address 127.0.0.1 is localhost—if you run Services on the same machine as the ircd, this is fine as it is. The password should be changed to something better than "password". If you compare this to another link block, you will notice the lack of the options section. This is because Services does not support any extra options and is not actually an IRC server, so it cannot be connected to. You don't need to restart the ircd to apply these changes. Simply type **/rehash** when connected to the server as an IRC operator, and it will reread the configuration file.

## Configuring Services

The next step is to edit the configuration files for Services. To do this, change into the *lib/ircservices* directory where you installed IRC Services:

```
% cd ~/services/lib/ircservices
```

There are two configuration files. One is the main configuration for Services, including the server to connect to and the modules to load. The modules configuration file has the settings for each of the modules. These two files are provided as *example-ircservices.conf* and *example-modules.conf*, respectively. A lot of the configuration is up to personal preference and the features you need—this hack will show you how to change only the settings that are needed to get Services running.

Copy *example-ircservices.conf* to *ircservices.conf* and open it in a plain text editor. Lines that start with a # character are comments. There are a lot of useful comments, but some of the settings you will need are also commented out. Each option is described with a word such as REQUIRED or RECOMMENDED. For any setting that is not required, the default value will normally work.

Find the line that sets the option RemoteServer. It will be commented out, so you should remove the # and change the password to the password you used in the link block earlier. ServerName is the hostname that Services should use and should match the name used in the link and ulines blocks. ServiceUser is the username that Services will appear to have when it's on IRC. This should be something like *services@domain*, where *domain* is the domain you chose to use.

Finally, find the line that reads #LoadModule protocol/(insert protocol name here). The protocol name is the type of IRC server in use; this should be changed to unreal if you are using Unreal. The comments explain what to use for other ircds. Remember to remove the # from this line as well. Now save *ircservices.conf*.

The next file that needs editing is *example-modules.conf*. Copy it to *modules.conf* and open it in your text editor. The main aspect is the protocol module. Change the module name where it says Module protocol/(insert protocol name here) to unreal. Each of the protocol options explains the protocols it works with. If you set an option that is not needed for a protocol, you will get an error. On Unreal, you should set the ServerNumeric option. This is the same as the numeric in the "me" block discussed in the previous IRC server hack. Uncomment the ServerNumeric and NSRequireEmail settings by removing the # character from the start of both lines. You will also need to uncomment one of the ListenTo lines so that it reads something like:

    ListenTo *:80

Services can send emails to allow users to retrieve passwords and so on, so you will need to set various email options. The FromAddress and FromName should be changed to values suitable for your domain name. RelayHost should be changed to the name of an SMTP server, and SMTPName should be changed to the hostname of the machine running Services.

Finally the ServicesRoot option should be set to your nickname on IRC. The person who registers this nickname will get full control over Services.

## Running the Services

To start Services, run:

```
% ~/services/sbin/ircservices
```

Services will start and connect to the IRC server. If you get any errors, there is most likely a configuration option problem. Check *~/services/lib/ ircservices/ircservices.log* to see if it sheds any light on the problem. A common problem is setting an option without loading the required module. If Services doesn't link but appears to start correctly, there may be an error reported in the Services log file, too. You may also get some messages from the IRC server if there is a problem linking.

Now that Services is linked, you must register your nickname with Nick-Serv. You should now have full access to OperServ, allowing you to change settings, add networkwide bans (akills), and exercise various other powers. You can get a list of the various options by typing **/msg OperServ help**.

*—David Leadbeater*

## HACK #97    Set Up Your Own beware ircd Server

If you want a quick and easy IRC server, install and run the beware ircd IRC server on Windows.

*beware* ircd is a small, powerful IRC server for Windows and Linux. It is very easy to set up, yet it is as powerful as the ircds developed by large networks (such as *ircu*, developed by Undernet).

## Downloading beware ircd

Windows and Linux versions can be downloaded from *http://www.bircd.org* or *http://www.xs4all.nl/~beware3/irc*. When you have the ZIP file, decompress it (Windows XP can do this, or you can use a third-party program such as WinZip) to a folder such as *c:\bircd\*. Figure 15-3 shows *bircd* being extracted with WinZip.

Now browse to the directory and open *bircd.ini* in a text editor. This contains settings that enable or disable features of the server (similar to F: linesemployed by other servers). Some common settings you may wish to change are:

ChannelMode
 These modes are automatically set when a user joins a new channel.

ListSecretChannels
 If this is set to 1, IRCops can see secret channels by typing **/list S**.

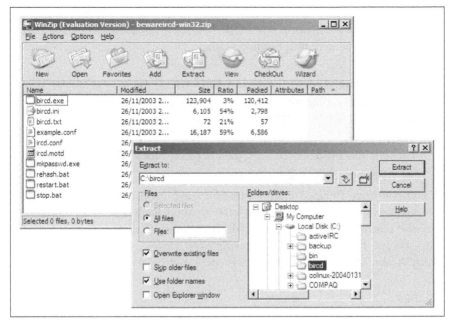

*Figure 15-3. Unzipping bircd*

MaxBans

This is the maximum number of bans that can be set on each channel.

MaxJoins

Users are allowed to join only this many channels.

MaxNick

Any nickname that is longer than this setting will be truncated (i.e., the maximum nickname length is equal to MaxNick).

NetworkName

When a user connects to the server, it will announce this as the name of the IRC network.

NoDie *and* NoRestart

Setting these to 1 disables the die and restart commands, respectively.

GlobalOperFailed

This sends a notice to all IRCops if someone attempts to become an IRCop by using the /oper command and fails.

OperGline

This allows IRCops to set g-lines (server/network bans). If it is set to 1, operators can set local g-lines; if set to 2, they can set global g-lines.

HalfOp

> This enables the half-op (+h) mode. HalfOp gives a user some rights that
> a channel operator has, but not as many.

HeadInSand

> These settings hide information from users, such as server names in
> /whois, g-line reasons, and the /map and /links commands. These
> generally make the network harder to attack.

QnetModes

> This enables modes used on Quakenet that block CTCPs, colors, chan-
> nel notices, and part/quit reasons.

When you have finished editing *bircd.ini*, save it, and open *ircd.conf*. This
file contains a set of *lines*. The first letter denotes each line, and colons separate the parameters. The *ircd.conf* file is the same for most of the available
IRC servers. Because of this, numerous web sites—such as *http://www.irc.
org/tech_docs/ircnet/INSTALL-4.html*—explain how to use it.

## O:Lines

The final settings that need to be changed before you can get your IRC
server fully running are the O:Lines. These control who can use the /oper
command to become an IRC operator. Such users can "kill" other users (disconnect them from the server) and even ban them from reconnecting. If you
have the settings enabled in *bircd.ini,* they could even restart or stop the
server.

The format of an O:Line is as follows:

```
O:Host:Password:Nickname::Class
```

The *Host* parameter specifies which host the user must be using in order to
execute the /oper command successfully. It takes the format of
ident@hostname, and you can use wildcards (*) to match parts of it. Valid
examples are:

```
*@192.168.* - Matches anyone connecting via a LAN
MD87@* - Matches anyone with the ident 'MD87'
MD87@192.168.* - Matches anyone with the ident 'MD87' connecting via a LAN
```

The fewer wildcards used, the better. It is possible to specify *@* for the
host, but this is very insecure—anyone who can guess your ID and password could then use it.

The *Password* parameter tells *beware* ircd the password that must be used
when the authorized user executes the /oper command. This can be plain
text, or it can be encrypted using the mkpasswd program that comes with
*beware* ircd.

The *Nickname* argument tells the ircd what the user's ID will be. This must be sent as the first parameter of the command. If *Nickname* is set to foo and *Password* is set to bar, the user can become an IRC operator by typing:

```
/oper foo bar
```

The *Class* defines which class the new IRC operator will belong to. By default, this is 10, which is the same as the client class, except with a higher *sendQ*. The scndQ determines how much data can be queued for the user before he is kicked from the server. In most circumstances, there is no need to change the class.

A completed O:Line will look something like this:

```
O:MD87@192.168.0.2:foobar:MD87::10
```

This will allow anyone connecting from 192.168.0.2 with the ident "MD87" to execute the /oper command with the ID "MD87" and password "foobar".

Examples for most of the available settings in *ircd.conf* can be found in the *example.conf* file, which is distributed with *beware* ircd.

## Running beware ircd

When you have configured *beware* ircd, you can start it by browsing to the folder you extracted it to and running the *bircd.exe* file. The server should now start running.

To connect to the server from the same computer that *beware* ircd is running on, open your IRC client and connect to 127.0.0.1. To connect to it from a different computer or to allow other users to connect, you need to find out the computer's IP address or hostname. If you aren't sure what this is, web sites such as *http://www.whatismyip.com* will tell you. Note that if you have a firewall or router, you will need to forward port 6667 to the computer that is running the server.

*—Chris Smith*

## HACK #98 Link Two IRC Servers Together

If your IRC server starts getting too busy, the only real solution is to turn it into a network of IRC servers.

Almost all large IRC networks are made up of multiple servers linked together. In order for two servers to link, both need to be configured correctly.

The first step to linking IRC servers into a network is to make sure that both servers can communicate with each other. Different ircds use different protocols. One of the more popular protocols is P10, developed by Undernet and used by *ircu*, *bircd*, and several other ircds. It doesn't really matter which protocol you use, as long as both servers are capable of understanding it. If you are unsure of which protocol your server uses, check the official web site for your ircd. One way to be sure that the servers will be able to communicate is by using the same server software for both of the ircds, although this isn't always possible.

## Configuring the Servers

In order for the network to run smoothly after the servers have been linked, several settings need to be the same for all servers. The settings vary from ircd to ircd, but most will have the following options somewhere (*bircd* uses *bircd.ini*, and *asuka* uses F:lines in *ircd.conf*).

The following settings must be identical:

*Topic length*
> The maximum length of the topic

*Nick length*
> The maximum length for a user's nickname

*Chan length*
> The maximum length for a channel name

If these settings are not identical on all servers, problems will arise. For example, if the channel length is different, channels with longer names would be truncated on some servers, but the truncated channel may already exist.

In addition to these settings, any optional modes should be enabled or disabled across all servers. That is, if the server software supports optional modes, they should be disabled on *all* servers or enabled on *all* servers. If the valid modes differ between servers, a mode change on one server may not be propagated to all users or servers.

## Numerics

Each IRC server on a network is assigned a numeric that uniquely identifies it. No two servers can have the same numeric. In *ircu* and *bircd*, the numeric is set in the M:Line in the *ircd.conf* file. The example given in *example.conf* has a numeric of 1 (the last number on the line):

```
M:London.UK.Eu.UnderNet.org:*:University of London, England:0:1
```

Servers that use the P10 protocol usually have a two-digit numeric that can be made up of numbers, letters (a-z, A-Z), and the [ and ] characters. Other networks use only pure numbers or other combinations. Before linking servers, make sure that they all have a unique numeric. If there is a collision, the servers will cancel the link attempt.

## C:Lines

In order for the servers to link, they need to "know" about each other and to have passwords to use during the link attempt. These are defined in C:Lines in the *ircd.conf* file. The format for these, as shown in *example.conf*, is:

```
C:remote hostname or IP:password:remote server name:port:class
```

The *remote hostname or IP* field can contain wildcards; however, at least one server will need to know the full hostname or IP of the other, so that it can initiate the link attempt. The *password* field specifies the password to be used during the link and should generally be the same for both servers. The *remote server name* field must exactly match that of the other server's M:Line.

The *port* is the port number that the server listens on for connections from other servers (usually set via a P:Line with an S as the penultimate parameter). The *class* field refers to one of the classes defined with Y:Lines. 90 is the default for servers, which gives the connection a low ping frequency and high SendQ and makes automatic connection attempts every 300 seconds.

When you have added C:Lines for both servers and the servers are currently running, you will need to make them reload the config file, usually via the /rehash command or by executing an external program.

## Linking the Servers

Now that the servers are configured properly, it's time to make them link. To do this, make sure both servers are running. One of the servers should attempt to automatically connect to the other within 5 minutes (300 seconds). If this doesn't happen or you're too impatient, you can use the /connect command to force a connection attempt. The syntax for the connect command is:

```
/connect server name
```

The *server name* parameter must be the server name as specified in the C:Line. When the servers link, you should see some server notices (*snotices*) saying that they have linked and when they have finished *bursting*.

## Bursting

When two servers connect, they have to tell each other everything about their users and channels so that the two servers have the same information. For larger networks, this can take several minutes and result in decreased performance for the users. Normally, however, it takes only a few seconds. Sometimes when the servers burst, there will be users with the same nickname or channels with the same name and a different set of channel operators. The servers have to decide what to do with these "collisions."

If two users have the same nickname, the servers will generally *kill* the person who connected to the network last. For example, if Foo connected to server 1 at 2 p.m., and Foo connected to server 2 at 5 p.m. on the same day, Foo on server 2 would be killed when the servers link.

Channel collisions are handled in a similar way. If a channel on server 1 was created before that on server 2, then everyone in server 2 would be de-opped or devoiced, and any modes set on server 1 would override those on server 2. Also, if server 1 had a mode such as +i (invite only) or +k (password required), then some users on server 2 may be kicked because they were not invited or did not join with a password. The particular behavior depends on the type of server you are running.

## Commands

There are several standard commands for managing server links. The /connect command has already been discussed, but it is worth noting that most ircds do not feature a /disconnect command. Instead, the /squit command is used (squit is short for "*server quit*"). This closes the connection with the given server—for example, /squit irc.foo.bar would close any connections to irc.foo.bar. On some ircds, the /squit command can be used to close links only from the local server (i.e., you cannot tell another server to drop one of its connections).

As with most server features, the commands and configuration options vary between different ircds, so it is always a good idea to consult the documentation for information specific to your software.

*—Chris Smith*

### Use MSN/ICQ/Jabber from IRC
You may feel very comfortable with IRC, but some people prefer to stick with other instant messenger networks like ICQ or MSN. Get in touch with these people.

You don't have to install a separate program for chatting with your friends on ICQ, AIM, or MSN any more. A program called BitlBee allows you to talk to all these people through your IRC client. Fortunately, using this program is a lot easier than spelling its name correctly.

BitlBee simulates an IRC server that has just one channel. All of your buddies will join the channel so you can talk to them. You can install BitlBee on your own machine, but if you don't want to or if you just can't, you can also use someone else's BitlBee server.

This hack will tell you how to install and use BitlBee. If you don't want to install your own BitlBee, you can just skip the next section.

> Many people wonder where the name BitlBee came from. BitlBee was just a name derived from "*Little Bee*." Some people also refer to it as "*The Bee*." One important factor was for it to have a unique name, making it easier to find on search engines.

## Installation

BitlBee is available for a number of different platforms. The authors use it on Linux machines, but the program also works on several other Unix platforms. Even AmigaOS and Windows ports are available, though not supported by the authors. Support for some IM protocols may be missing on some ports.

The easiest way to install BitlBee on your machine is probably through the packaging system for your distribution, such as apt-get, emerge, or you can get it from your BSD ports tree. Most packages do all the hard work for you, so after installation you can skip the rest of this section and read more about how to use BitlBee.

If there is no package available for your platform or if you just don't like packages, you can, of course, also install BitlBee from source. First, get the source from the site—*http://www.bitlbee.org*.

Next, you simply unpack the tarball. Then you run the *Configure* script, make (remember to use GNU make on BSD systems!) and make install. This will install all the program files on your machine.

*Configure* might complain about missing dependencies. BitlBee currently needs recent versions of *glib* and GnuTLS to work completely. Of course, later versions of the program may have different dependencies.

BitlBee is not a daemon on its own. It depends on something like *inetd* to talk to your IRC client. Add a line like this to */etc/inetd.conf*:

```
ircd    stream    tcp    nowait    nobody    /usr/local/sbin/bitlbee bitlbee
```

You will have to make *inetd* reload the configuration files. You can do this by sending the HUP signal to the *inetd* process, for example by running the following:

```
% /etc/init.d/inetd reload
```

If you run *xinetd*, which is becoming increasingly common these days, you will have to copy the *doc/bitlbee.xinetd* file from the BitlBee source directory to */etc/xinetd.d/* and send a HUP signal to *xinetd*.

Of course, if you installed BitlBee to a different location, you shouldn't forget to put the correct path in the *inetd* file! Also, if you're already running an IRC server on your machine, you will probably have to change the port number BitlBee listens on. Refer to the *inetd* documentation if you don't know how to do that.

## Using BitlBee

If you installed BitlBee on your own machine, you will now be able to connect to it. In most clients, all you have to do is type **/connect localhost**. If you are running BitlBee on a different machine, specify the name of that machine instead of localhost.

If you decide to use an external BitlBee server instead of installing it yourself, you can get a list of servers from *http://www.bitlbee.org*. Pick a server that is close to you, connect to it with your IRC client, and read on.

When you connect to a BitlBee server, you're force-joined into a channel called #bitlbee. You will receive a welcome message from a bot called *root*. It should look something like Figure 15-4. Some BitlBee packagers rename the root user to something else, but this is usually apparent. The bot will invite you to read the quick start documentation. The quick start may cover some details that are not mentioned in this hack, so it's always a good idea to have a quick look.

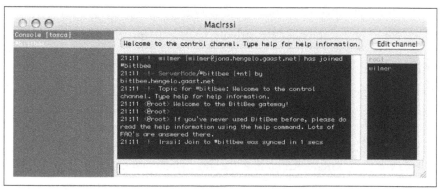

*Figure 15-4. Being welcomed to BitlBee by root*

Now you're ready to start using BitlBee. It's a good idea to register your nickname as soon as possible. This is not to protect your nickname, but simply to make things easier the next time you connect. Because BitlBee is not a real IRC server, you will never notice the other people on the server, as everyone will be in her very own #bitlbee channel. With your nickname registered, BitlBee will remember your settings, your account information, your buddy lists, and everything else. To register your nickname, just say **register *password*** in the #bitlbee channel, where *password* is your password of choice.

When you come back later, say **identify *password***, and BitlBee will restore all your settings and connect to all your accounts. So, let's make a connection right now!

To manage your IM connections, you can send the account command to the #bitlbee channel. First, add all your accounts using the account add command. This command requires at least three arguments: the *protocol*, your username/handle/screenname, and your *password*. For some protocols, you will also have to specify a *servername*. ICQ and AIM, for example, share the same protocol, but use different servers. Here are some examples of accounts being added:

```
account add jabber user@server.com password
account add msn user@domain.com password
account add yahoo nickname password
account add oscar 123456 password login.icq.com
account add oscar aimuser password login.oscar.aol.com
```

After adding all your accounts, say **account on** and see how BitlBee connects to all the services you want. For most protocols, it will also download your buddy lists, and you'll notice some people joining the #bitlbee channel. Only the people who are online will be visible in the channel. As soon as they go offline, you'll see them quitting from the BitlBee server.

Of course, you can also talk to your buddies. Talk to them in the channel as you normally do on IRC or open a query window. The recipient won't notice the difference, so use whichever method you prefer most. Remember that #bitlbee is a virtual channel. When you talk to foo here, only foo will get your message, not everyone in the channel. When you are talking in the channel, you can specify the recipient of your message by prefixing it with his nickname, for example:

```
<wilmer> Paul: Hi!
```

If you don't get a buddy list (or if you just want to add more buddies), you can use the add command. Before you use this command, you should check which connection number to use. BitlBee supports multiple protocols and networks, and it allows you to be connected to more than one network at once. So when you add a buddy, BitlBee needs to know what buddy list you want to edit. You can get a list of all your connections using the account list command.

You will get a list like this:

```
<wilmer> account list
<root>  0. OSCAR, 267762 on login.icq.com (connected)
<root>  1. JABBER, lintux@jabber.com/BitlBee (connected)
<root>  2. MSN, lintux@lintux.cx
<root> End of account list
```

As you can see here, only the first two accounts are connected. If I want to add a buddy to my MSN contact list, I have to enable that account first, using the account on 2 command. Fortunately, I can add people to my other lists now. To add a contact, use the add command. This command requires two arguments: a connection number and a handle. If you want, you can also specify the nickname to be given to the contact in BitlBee. If you omit this, BitlBee will generate a unique nickname from the handle. See the following example:

```
<wilmer> add 0 32899265 Paul
<root> User `32899265' added to your contact list as `Paul'
-!- Paul [32899265@login.icq.com] has joined #bitlbee
-!- mode/#bitlbee [+v paul] by root
```

As you can see above, Paul immediately joins the channel and gets voiced by the bot. This means he's online and not set as away. If you don't see the person joining the channel after being added, he is probably just offline.

## More Than Just Talking

One last command you really have to know about is the set command. This command can be used to customize BitlBee in many ways. To get a list of available settings, enter set without any arguments. To change a setting, provide two arguments. The first argument specifies the setting you want to change, and the second specifies the new value for this setting. BitlBee will respond with a confirmation of your changed setting. If the setting doesn't seem to be changed, there was something wrong with what you were doing.

Also, most essential IRC commands like /away and /whois work with BitlBee. Many more root commands are available too. Just enter **help commands** to get a full list. You can also get more information about specific commands. For example, to get help about the account command, you can enter **help account**.

There's not enough space in this book to explain everything about BitlBee. If you're interested and want more, it's probably a good idea to read the documentation. Reading the quick start guide is probably the best place to begin, as it tries to get the reader started with BitlBee as quickly as possible, but ends up discussing more features than this hack can.

—*Wilmer van der Gaast*

# Combine BitlBee and CtrlProxy

**HACK 100**

We've already covered both BitlBee and CtrlProxy separately, but IRC power users will be delighted to learn how effective the two combined can be.

Some frequently requested BitlBee features don't really have to be implemented in BitlBee, because CtrlProxy can do all of them. Some of these features are:

*SSL support*
> This encrypts all traffic between the IRC client and server. Although this is not quite top security—most Instant Messaging protocols send all conversations unencrypted anyway—it at least makes sure nobody can sniff your passwords.

*Keep-alive connections*
> This means that your session will stay running when you close your IRC client.

*Server-side logs*
> You will be able to keep your IRC logs on the machine that runs Ctrl-Proxy.

As you may have noticed, these points don't really make sense when you run BitlBee and your IRC client on the same machine. But when you regularly connect to your BitlBee server from different (remote) places, they can prove to be very useful.

## Setting Up CtrlProxy and BitlBee

Setting up CtrlProxy and BitlBee is quite easy. First, read the hacks "Set Up an IRC Proxy" **[Hack #93]** and "Use MSN/ICQ/Jabber from IRC" **[Hack #99]**) about the two programs to read how to install them. Reading the parts about getting and compiling them should be enough—you can skip the configuration part. When using CtrlProxy, you can leave out the *bitlbeed/inetd* setup, because CtrlProxy can start BitlBee directly, as demonstrated in the following configuration file:

```
<?xml version="1.0"?>
<ctrlproxy>
    <plugins>
        <plugin autoload="1" file="libsocket">
            <sslcertfile>/home/wilmer/.ctrlproxy/ctrlproxy.pem</sslcertfile>
            <sslkeyfile>/home/wilmer/.ctrlproxy/ctrlproxy.pem</sslkeyfile>
        </plugin>
        <plugin autoload="1" file="librepl_memory"/>
        <plugin autoload="1" file="libadmin"/>
        <plugin autoload="1" file="liblog_irssi">
            <logfile>/home/wilmer/.ctrlproxy/logs/</logfile>
```

```
            </plugin>
            <plugin autoload="1" file="libstrip"/>
            <plugin autoload="1" file="libnickserv"/>
            <plugin autoload="1" file="libantiflood"/>
            <plugin autoload="1" file="libauto-away">
                <message time="300">"I'm currently away, sorry!</message>
            </plugin>
        </plugins>
        <networks>
            <network autoconnect="1" client_pass="secret" name="BEE">
                <listen>
                    <ipv4 port="6668" ssl="1"/>
                </listen>
                <servers>
                    <pipe>
                        <path>/usr/sbin/bitlbee</path>
                        <arg>-d/home/wilmer/.ctrlproxy/bitlbee/</arg>
                    </pipe>
                </servers>
                <nickserv>
                    <nick name="wilmer" password="beedifferent"/>
                </nickserv>
            </network>
        </networks>
    </ctrlproxy>
```

Obviously, you may need to change the file and path names to suit your setup. Don't forget this when copying the configuration file. Save this into a file called *ctrlproxyrc* in the *.ctrlproxy* directory in your home directory. If this directory doesn't exist yet, you must create it. Don't forget to create the log and BitlBee configuration directories you specified in this file as well, since they won't be created automatically. The password specified in the NickServ configuration will be the password you should use as your BitlBee NickServ password. Pick anything you want here, as CtrlProxy will take care of sending this information to BitlBee.

If you want to use SSL, you will need to create an SSL certificate/key. The script called *mksslcert.sh* in the CtrlProxy source directory can do this for you. It creates a file *ctrlproxy.pem* in the current directory. Just run the script and make sure you put the generated file at the place you refer to in the configuration file.

## Starting CtrlProxy

When this is all done, you can finally start CtrlProxy. You can do this like so:

```
% ctrlproxy -D -r ~/.ctrlproxy/ctrlproxyrc
```

When running CtrlProxy for the first time, it may be a good idea to leave out the -D argument, so the program will start in the foreground and send some information to the terminal so you can troubleshoot, if necessary.

When everything is OK, you should see something like this when you start the program:

```
ruby~$ ctrlproxy -r ~/.ctrlproxy/ctrlproxyrc
** Message: Using SSL certificate from /home/wilmer/.ctrlproxy/ctrlproxy.pem
and SSL key from /home/wilmer/.ctrlproxy/ctrlproxy.pem
Added linestack backend 'memory'
Filter 'repl_simple' added
Adding new client hook 'repl_simple'
Filter 'admin' added
Filter 'log_irssi' added
Filter 'strip' added
Adding lose client hook 'nickserv'
Filter 'nickserv' added
Filter 'antiflood' added
Filter 'auto-away' added
socket-Message: Listening on port 6668(socket 3)
Connecting with pipe for server BEE
Joining channel #bitlbee
```

The last line is especially important. If you don't get the "Joining channel #bitlbee", CtrlProxy probably failed to start BitlBee. Also, if the first line says something about a missing SSL certificate/key file, something went wrong while creating the *ctrlproxy.pem* file, which means SSL support will not work. A configuration problem is the most likely cause of this problem, so double-check what you have written in the configuration file.

As you can see, #bitlbee is joined automatically, although that's not specified in the CtrlProxy configuration file. This is normal BitlBee behavior. You don't have to put the channel in the CtrlProxy configuration, as CtrlProxy handles this force-join quite well.

Now, find out whether your IRC client supports SSL connections. Most decent clients know about SSL these days. *irssi* does, for example. SSL support for mIRC seems to be available as a plug-in. If you don't know whether your IRC client supports SSL connections yet, just check the documentation. If SSL is not supported, you can choose to switch to a different IRC client or disable SSL in CtrlProxy. You can do this by changing the 1 into a 0 in the ssl argument to the listener definition.

Finally, you can now try to connect the IRC client to the proxy. A simple /connect or /server with just the server name as an argument won't be enough. You have to tell the IRC client to connect to the correct port, use

SSL, and send the password. If you use *irssi*, you can connect to a server called *ruby* by typing the following:

```
/connect -ssl ruby 6668 secret
```

## Starting the Session

If everything went well, you'll see a regular BitlBee session coming up. You may notice some differences when you look at the server messages, but the control channel should look familiar to you if you have used BitlBee before.

Now, go ahead and set up the Bee **[Hack #99]**. When you register your nickname, don't forget to use the password you chose when you wrote the CtrlProxy configuration file. If the passwords don't match, automatic identification will not work, and you'll have to manually identify yourself to root and NickServ every time you sign in.

When you're done, it might be interesting to kill CtrlProxy. There are two ways to do it. Sending SIGTERM to the CtrlProxy process is one way, but you can also do it using your IRC client. Typing **/CTRLPROXY DIE** should do the job. If that doesn't work, try **/QUOTE CTRLPROXY DIE**. Now start up CtrlProxy again. If everything goes well, it will set up the BitlBee connection and identify you to NickServ automatically. So when you connect your IRC client to CtrlProxy, the session will be up and running already.

Now it's time for some more experimentation. Start up a second IRC client and connect it to the same CtrlProxy. See how you get exactly the same session there, and how you can do whatever you want in both sessions? Close both IRC clients and start one again to connect it to the proxy. You should notice that the whole session is reproduced, and nobody ever noticed you were away (unless you enabled the autoaway module). It should look something like Figure 15-5.

You will also have full logs of all your conversations on the machine where CtrlProxy runs. You can now disable logging in your IRC client, as there is little point in creating two copies. The benefit of using CtrlProxy to make your logs is that wherever you run your IRC client, your logs will always be in the same place.

## Hacking the Hack

Maybe you're not completely comfortable yet? Maybe you want the logs to be formatted a bit differently? Maybe you want to connect to other networks as well? Maybe you don't like some of the BitlBee default settings? Most of these things are explained in the hacks about the two programs (see "Set Up an IRC Proxy" **[Hack #93]** and "Use MSN/ICQ/Jabber from IRC" **[Hack #99]**) or the online

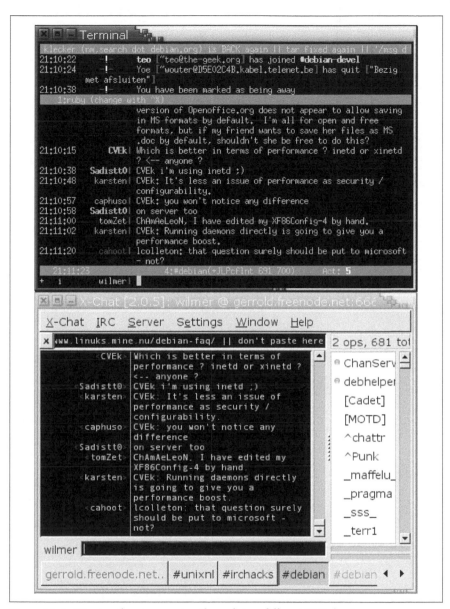

*Figure 15-5. Viewing the same session through two different IRC clients*

manuals. Don't forget to read them, as they cover far more topics than these hacks can. Many features requested by users already exist, but they're just not obvious enough to be discovered without reading some documentation.

*—Wilmer van der Gaast*

# Index

We'd like to hear your suggestions for improving our indexes. Send email to *index@oreilly.com*.

announcement bots (*continued*)
    welcoming visitors
        welcome options, 247
        WelcomeBot class (Java), 247
ANT, build system used by PPF, 174
Apache Axis package for Web
        Services, 204, 206, 210
Apache Axis SOAP
        implementation, 220
Apache web server, 145
apt packaging system, 4
artificial intelligence bot, 237–242
    JMegaHal package, 238, 240
    JMegaHalBot, compiling and
        running, 241
    Markov modeling, 238
ASCII carriage return and linefeed (\r\n),
        ending IRC message lines, 305
asynchronous IRC protocol, 304
attacks
    mounted by war bots, 134
    nick collision attack, 323
        after implementation of TS, 325
auth levels (PPF), 166
authentication
    automatic, using your hostname, 31
    with Q (QuakeNet L channel
        bot), 37
authorization, MatchEd bot, 261
autoconnects, XChat, 5
"auto-join-on-invite" feature of IRC
        clients, 134
auto-op flag (+a), 301
auto-replace strings, setting up on
        XChat, 8
AWAY command, changing Here or
        Gone flag, 54
away messages, setting up with all-server
        commands, 7
Axis (see Apache Axis package for Web
        Services)

# B

+b channel mode, 41
backgrounds, mIRC client, 79
bad words (see profanity, filtering)
banning users from a channel, 23
    +b notation, 41
    irssi blacklist, persistent, 101

mIRC client, script for, 73
    unbanning yourself with
        ChanServ, 35
bash shell, redirections, 141
Bersirc client, 1
beware ircd server, 368–371
    downloading, 368
    editing bircd.ini, 368–370
    editing ircd.conf file, O:Lines, 370
    running, 371
!bflive command (PPF), 171
BFTracks plug-in (PPF), 171
BitchX, nickname-completion
        feature, 65
BitlBee, 374–378
    combining with CtrlProxy, 379–383
        setup, 379
        starting CtrlProxy, 380
        starting the session, 382
    configuring, 375
    installing, 375
    set command, 378
    using, 376–378
blog bot, 145–149
    MySQL database, 146
        creating blog from, 147
    PHP script getting entries from
        database, 147
    Weblog class (Java example), 146
        compiling and running, 148
    WeblogMain class (Java
        example), 148
Bluetooth, Pocket PC connections to
        IRC, 337
bold text
    formatting in mIRC, 75
    formatting with a bot, 76
bot master (PPF auth level), 166
bot owner (PPF auth level), 166
bots, xv
    banning of by IRC servers, 134
    checking your IRC network's policy
        on, 291
    clients vs., 111
    colored messages, sending from, 80
    community (see community bots)
    Eliza, 86
    formatting text with, 76
        PircBot, 77
    infobots (see infobots)

tabs (continued)
  $t referring to tabbed line for
      indented nicknames
      (XChat), 10
tagged data (CTCP), 327
tail -f (shell command), 144
tail log files, 273–277
  TailBot class, 274
  TailBotMain class, 276
  TailThread class, 274
takeovers of channels
  example of, 42
  fixing takeover with CHANFIX
      (example), 42
  nick collision attacks and, 324
  after TS implementation, 325
tar command, 294
tasks, scheduling for later
      execution, 227
TCP socket connection for simple Perl
      IRC client, 115
TellBot class (Java example), 189
  passing on a message, 191
TellBotMain class (Java example), 190
Telnet
  connecting a newsgroup server, 250
  IRC connection over, 112–115
    joining channels and sending
        messages, 114
    keeping connection alive, 113
    running Telnet from command
        prompt, 112
templates, comic strip, 243
terms, abbreviations, and phrases, 24
  acroynms and initialisms, listing
      of, 26–29
  correction syntax, 25
  phonetics and keyboard layouts, 25
text
  colorizing, 77–81
    IRC color codes, listing of, 77
    sending colored text from
        bots, 80
    using colors in mIRC, 78–80
  formatting, 75–77
    in mIRC, 75
    with a bot, 76
  smaller type, made more readable
      with ClearType, 339

text box
  expanding on ChatZilla, 19
  setting up for XChat user interface, 6
text strings, automatic replacement of
      (XChat), 8
third-party access to IRC servers, 97
thread safety, NntpBot class, 252
threads
  launching shell process in its own
      thread, 269
  sending ISON requests, 217
  TailThread class, 274
time of last visit of a given person (on a
      channel), 53
time zone for a user
  comparing Amsterdam time with
      GMT, 47
  CTCP TIME request, 48
  Time Zone Converter, 46
timer (egg timer bot), 227–230
timestamps
  applying to messages for continuity
      bot, 151
  channel, use by CHANFIX, 42
  displaying channel timestamp with
      TS, 326
  mIRC messages, adding to, 65–67
    greater resolution for
        timestamps, 67
    simple timestamps, 66
  showing for messages in
      ChatZilla, 18
  TS protocol, 322–327
+tmrc permission (infobot), 160
tokens, 238
topics
  filtering for a channel, using regular
      expression, 60
  finding with search engine, 45
  protecting channel topic, 284–288
    erasure of topic, 285
    filtering profanity, 285
    formatting and colors, 285
    topic protection mode, 285
    TopicBot class (Java), 286
    TopicBotMain class (Java), 287
toString( ) (Date), 151
translator Web Service, 207–210
  information needed about, 207

# Colophon

Our look is the result of reader comments, our own experimentation, and feedback from distribution channels. Distinctive covers complement our distinctive approach to technical topics, breathing personality and life into potentially dry subjects.

The tool on the cover of *IRC Hacks* is a hacksaw. The hacksaw is a saw specifically designed for cutting short or thin metal building materials as well as PVC pipe. It has an adjustable frame and uses thin, flexible blades that are stretched tightly in the frame. The blades are meant to be disposed of after they become dull from use. The finer the teeth on a hacksaw blade, the thinner the piece of metal that can be cut. A junior hacksaw is used for even finer cutting, and intricate cutwork in metal requires a piercing saw.

In Greek mythology, the saw was invented by Talos, who was the nephew of the preeminent inventor Daedalus. By the time he was twelve, Talos had invented not only the saw, but the potter's wheel and the compass. Daedalus murdered his nephew out of professional jealousy, luring him to the top of the Acropolis and then pushing him off. The Furies—who punished criminals, especially murderers—strongly disapproved of parricide, and manipulated events such that Daedalus' son, Icarus, perished while flying in one of Daedalus' own inventions.

Sarah Sherman was the production editor and Norma Emory was the copyeditor for *IRC Hacks*. Catherine Morris was the proofreader, and Matt Hutchinson and Emily Quill provided quality control. Ellen Troutman wrote the index.

Hanna Dyer designed the cover of this book, based on a series design by Edie Freedman. The cover image is from the DJ Soft Tools V39 CD. Emma Colby produced the cover layout with QuarkXPress 4.1 using Adobe's Helvetica Neue and ITC Garamond fonts.

David Futato designed the interior layout. This book was converted by Julie Hawks to FrameMaker 5.5.6 with a format conversion tool created by Erik Ray, Jason McIntosh, Neil Walls, and Mike Sierra that uses Perl and XML technologies. The text font is Linotype Birka; the heading font is Adobe Helvetica Neue Condensed; and the code font is LucasFont's TheSans Mono Condensed. The illustrations that appear in the book were produced by Robert Romano and Jessamyn Read using Macromedia FreeHand 9 and Adobe Photoshop 6. This colophon was written by Reg Aubry.

# Get even more for your money.

**Join the O'Reilly Community, and register the O'Reilly books you own. It's free, and you'll get:**

- $4.99 ebook upgrade offer
- 40% upgrade offer on O'Reilly print books
- Membership discounts on books and events
- Free lifetime updates to ebooks and videos
- Multiple ebook formats, DRM FREE
- Participation in the O'Reilly community
- Newsletters
- Account management
- 100% Satisfaction Guarantee

**Signing up is easy:**

1. Go to: oreilly.com/go/register
2. Create an O'Reilly login.
3. Provide your address.
4. Register your books.

Note: English-language books only

**To order books online:**
oreilly.com/store

**For questions about products or an order:**
orders@oreilly.com

**To sign up to get topic-specific email announcements and/or news about upcoming books, conferences, special offers, and new technologies:**
elists@oreilly.com

**For technical questions about book content:**
booktech@oreilly.com

**To submit new book proposals to our editors:**
proposals@oreilly.com

**O'Reilly books are available in multiple DRM-free ebook formats. For more information:**
oreilly.com/ebooks

Spreading the knowledge of innovators        oreilly.com

# Have it your way.